Essentials
of
Risk Control

Volume I

Essentials
of
Risk Control

Volume I

Edited by

George L. Head, Ph.D., CPCU, ARM, CSP, CLU

Vice President
Insurance Institute of America

Second Edition • 1989

INSURANCE INSTITUTE OF AMERICA
720 Providence Road, Malvern, Pennsylvania 19355–0770

Second Edition • December 1989

Library of Congress Catalog Number 89-86035
International Standard Book Number 0-89462-047-9

Printed in the United States of America

Foreword

Over the years, the American Institute for Property and Liability Underwriters and the Insurance Institute of America have responded to the educational needs of the property and liability insurance industry by developing courses and administering national examinations specifically for insurance personnel. These independent nonprofit educational organizations are encouraged and supported by the insurance industry in fulfilling these needs.

The American Institute maintains and administers the program leading to the Chartered Property Casualty Underwriter (CPCU®) professional designation.

The Insurance Institute of America offers a wide range of associate designations and certificate programs in the following technical and managerial disciplines:

Accredited Adviser in Insurance (AAI®)
Associate in Claims (AIC)
Associate in Underwriting (AU)
Associate in Risk Management (ARM)
Associate in Loss Control Management (ALCM®)
Associate in Premium Auditing (APA®)
Associate in Management (AIM)
Associate in Research and Planning (ARP®)
Associate in Insurance Accounting and Finance (AIAF)
Associate in Automation Management (AAM®)
Associate in Marine Insurance Management (AMIM®)
Certificate in General Insurance
Certificate in Supervisory Management
Certificate in Introduction to Claims
Certificate in Introduction to Property and Liability Insurance

The Associate in Risk Management program presents a logical

decision-making process for minimizing the adverse effects of accidental losses. The process determines optimum combinations of techniques for preventing or reducing losses and for financing recovery from those losses that cannot be effectively controlled. The process can be used successfully by any private organization or public entity. The ARM program focuses on risk management, whether applied by a risk manager for the benefit of his or her employer, by insurance agents, brokers, or consultants to serve clients, or by an insurer's commercial lines specialist to improve underwriting results. ARM 54 examines the entire decision process. ARM 55 concentrates on risk control techniques that prevent or minimize losses. ARM 56 considers techniques for financing recovery from accidental losses that cannot be prevented.

As with all Institute publications, this text has been extensively reviewed by a group of academic and industry experts, and they are recognized in the preface. Throughout the development of this series of texts, it has been—and will continue to be—necessary to draw on the knowledge and skills of Institute personnel. These individuals will receive no royalties on texts sold; their writing responsibilities are seen as an integral part of their professional duties. We have proceeded in this way to avoid any possibility of conflict of interests.

We invite and welcome any and all criticisms of our publications. It is only with such comments that we can hope to provide high quality study materials. Comments should be directed to the Curriculum Department of the Institutes.

Norman A. Baglini, Ph.D., CPCU, CLU
President and Chief Executive Officer

Preface

Essentials of Risk Control is a two-volume text developed primarily for the Insurance Institute of America's ARM 55 course of the same name. It is the second of three texts for the three courses leading to the Associate in Risk Management (ARM) designation awarded by the Institute. The other texts are *Essentials of the Risk Management Process* (for ARM 54) and *Essentials of Risk Financing* (for ARM 56). Although tailored to the needs of the ARM Program, these texts also should prove useful to persons who perform or are responsible for risk management in any organization—whether as its risk manager, as its insurance agent or broker, as the underwriter of its property-liability insurance, or as a risk management consultant.

This is a book on risk control for risk managers and other executives, not for loss control or safety engineers, for whom many excellent technical texts on reducing loss frequency and severity—and a separate Institute educational program (Associate in Loss Control Management)—already exist. Consequently, this book strives to present primarily a general overview of risk control strategies, combined with enough technical information to enable the risk management professional to work effectively with those more thoroughly trained in the highly technical aspects of property, liability, personnel, and net income protection. This book is designed to enhance the risk management professional's abilities to recognize the need for, to make requests to, and to evaluate the work of, those technical loss control experts to whom the risk management professional presumably has access.

The two volumes of this text present the shared output of the several authors, shown on the following page as contributing authors, all of whose work has been edited by George L. Head of the Institute's staff. Because most of the work has been done collegially, no single chapter or specific portion of any chapter can be meaningfully attributed to any one author. In particular, it would be improper to hold any of the authors accountable for any statement in this book, for, although they each contributed highly meaningful material, the

Institute—rather than any of the individual authors—determined the final content of the text.

This book adapts and reproduces others' copyrighted material; therefore, the Insurance Institute of America acknowledges with gratitude the permission of Harris & Walsh, Management Consultants, Inc., to adapt for publication as Chapter 4 in this text material drawn from several chapters of *Principles of Security Management*, which is copyrighted by Harris & Walsh. Moreover, the Institute is grateful to Industrial Risk Insurers for permission to reprint as an appendix to Chapter 12 a section of IRI's *Overview PEPlan*, to which IRI holds the copyright.

To increase the clarity, accuracy, and relevance of this text, various chapters have been reviewed by a wide range of experts, including Steven M. Barnett, ARM, Supervising Underwriter, General Insurance Company, Florham Park, New Jersey; Arnold J. Goldberg, Ph.D., CPCU, President, AIG Consultants, New York; P. Richard Hackenburg, CPCU, Staff Vice President and Assistant Treasurer, Allegheny International, Inc.; Robert Healy, Risk Manager, Pima County, Arizona; Jane I. Lataille, PE, ARM, Barnhart, Johnson, Francis, and Wilde, Inc., Avon, Connecticut; Al Mangone, Ed.D., ARM, Director—Customer Training, Loss Prevention Department, Liberty Mutual Insurance Companies, Boston, Massachusetts; Kenneth McGreevy, CPCU, Prudential—LMI Commercial Ins. Co., Mansfield, Ohio; Stover Snook, Ph.D., Project Director—Ergonomics, Research Center, Liberty Mutual Insurance Companies, Hopkinton, Massachusetts; Mary Anne Weber-Dubin, Assistant Risk Manager, Bronx-Lebanon Hospital Center, New York City; and Millicent W. Workman, CPCU, Belz Enterprises, Memphis, Tennessee. George Head received the invaluable assistance of the Institutes' Publications Department in editing and integrating the entire text.

Reviewers' comments provide intellectual "loss prevention" or "loss reduction" for the authors, making their errors less frequent or less severe. But, like the accidents that even the best risk management cannot stop completely, errors are bound to occur. Not being "held harmless" against them, the editor stands responsible for whatever errors may remain. On the basis of the insights of students, teachers, and other readers, the editor will work to remove these errors from the next edition.

Dr. George L. Head
Editor

Contributing Authors

The Insurance Institute of America acknowledges, with deep appreciation, the help of the following contributing authors:

Laurie J. Bilik
Associate Professor
College of Insurance

Joseph M. Boslet, CPCU, PE, ARM, ALCM
Manager of Loss Control and Premium Auditing
Pennsylvania National Insurance Company

Suzanne Crager, ARM
Risk Manager
Provident National Bank

Sharon A. Falkenburg, MS, OTR
Health and Ergonomic Consultant
NATLSCO

Susan Fitzpatrick
Managing Partner
Fitzpatrick Enterprises

Alan Friedlander, PE, CSP, ARM
Vice President
Alexander & Alexander

George L. Head, Ph.D., CPCU, CLU, ARM, CSP
Vice President
Insurance Institute of America

Ralph E. Johnson, CSP (Retired)
Division Loss Prevention Manager
Liberty Mutual Insurance Companies

Lynne M. Miller
President
Environmental Strategies Corporation

Richard H. Soper
Richard H. Soper Consulting, Inc.

Thomas P. Vaughan, Ph.D.
Management Consultant

Stanley A. Waldrop
Technical Director/Property
Liberty Mutual Insurance Companies

Timothy J. Walsh, CPP
President
Harris & Walsh
Management Consultants, Inc.

Table of Contents

Letter to the Student 1

Chapter 1—Framework for Risk Control 5

Definition and Importance of Risk Control ~ *Definition of Risk Control; Importance of Risk Control*

Theories of Accident Causation and Control ~ *The Domino Theory; The General Methods of Control Approach; The Energy-Release Theory; Technique of Operations Review (TOR) System; System Safety Approach*

Applications of Risk Control Techniques ~ *Exposure Avoidance; Loss Prevention; Loss Reduction; Segregation of Exposure Units; Contractual Transfer for Risk Control*

Summary

Appendix—Review of Some Quantitative Techniques for Risk Control ~ *Forecasting Accidental Losses; Evaluating Investment Alternatives*

Chapter 2—Controlling Fire Losses 69

Firesafety and Life Safety ~ *Fundamental Considerations; Principles of Firesafety*

Building Construction and Design ~ *Building Construction; Fire Divisions; Exterior Exposures*

Control of Fuels and Ignition Sources ~ *The "Fire Triangle" and the Energy-Release Theory; Classification of Ignition Sources*

Internal and External Fire Protection ~ *Internal Fire Protection; External Fire Protection*

Firesafety for Typical Occupancies ~ *Storage; Spray Painting Activity; Handling Flammable Liquids; Food Preparation Activity; Computer Operations*

Summary

Chapter 3—Controlling Losses from Natural Perils.. 121

Risk Control for Meteorological Perils ~ *Violent Winds; Flood; Winter Weather; Drought and Heat Wave; High Humidity and Corrosion*

Risk Control for Geological Perils ~ *Earthquake; Land Subsidence; Landslide/Mudslide; Avalanche; Erosion; Soil Expansion; Volcanic Action; Collapse*

Emergency Response Plan for Natural Perils ~ *Reasons for Developing an Emergency Response Plan; Major Areas Addressed by an Emergency Response Plan; Procedure for Establishing an Emergency Response Plan*

Analyzing Sequential Risk Control Decisions ~ *Constructing Decision Trees; Analyzing Options*

Summary

Chapter 4—Maintaining Security................................ 165

Nature of Security Exposures ~ *Classification of Security Exposures; Recognition of Security Exposures; The Economics of Security Risk Control*

Essentials of a Security Program ~ *Education; Prevention; Detection*

Computer Security ~ *Computer Center-Related Exposures; Access Controls for Computer Facilities*

Prevention of Embezzlement and Fraud ~ *Types of Losses; Conditions Leading to Embezzlement and Fraud*

Prevention of Violent Crime ~ *Robbery; Burglary; Riot; Vandalism; Arson*

An Integrated Security Risk Control Program ~ *Exposure Avoid*
Loss Control (Prevention and Reduction); Contract
(Noninsurance) Transfers for Risk Control

Summary

Chapter 5—Protecting the Health Potential of Personnel 225

Human Health Potential ~ *Definition of Human Health Potential;*
Factors Affecting Human Health Potential; Risk Management
Responsibilities Related to Human Health Potential

Applying the Risk Management Process to Work-Related Injuries and
Illnesses ~ *Exposure Identification and Analysis; Developing*
Risk Control Alternatives; Selecting the Best Risk Management
Alternative(s); Implementing the Chosen Risk Control Tech-
nique(s); Monitoring the Effectiveness of Risk Controls

Summary

Chapter 6—Workplace Design 271

Workplace Design: Definition and Significance ~ *Benefits of Sound*
Workplace Design; Indicators of Potentially Unsound Work-
place Design; Workplace Design Checklists

Ergonomic Applications ~ *Manual Materials Handling; Controlling*
Cumulative Trauma Disorders; Design of the Workplace;
Design and Location of Machine Displays and Controls;
Reducing Fatigue

Establishing a Workplace Design Program ~ *Obtaining Management*
Commitment; Initiating Training Programs; Encouraging
Employee Participation in the Program

Summary

napter 7—Rehabilitation Management...................... 331

Definition of Rehabilitation Management ~ *Rehabilitation Management; Development of Rehabilitation Management; Opportunities for Rehabilitation Management*

Risk Management's Responsibility in Rehabilitation ~ *Personnel Department; Claims Department; Legal Department; Medical Personnel in the Organization; Labor Unions*

Case Management Strategy ~ *Planning the Initial Response; Administrative Barriers to Rehabilitation*

Financial Evaluation of Rehabilitation Programs ~ *Logic of Evaluation; Illustrative Evaluation*

Summary

Index.. 361

LETTER TO THE STUDENT

It is best to begin the text by renewing the mutual pledge with which the student and the authors began the first book in this series:

Reading a book is somewhat like taking a journey, with the authors as your guide. Before setting out on a journey over several hundred pages, however, you have a right to know where the authors intend to take you and what route they will follow. The authors in turn are duty bound to set forth a clear itinerary, to adhere to it, and to reach all the promised destinations. Beyond these rights and duties, the reader and the authors will be better traveling companions if, at the outset, they agree on the destinations they seek to reach and the route they will take in getting there.

To best benefit from *Essentials of Risk Control*, the student and the authors need to make clear (1) how this book fits into the Insurance Institute of America's trilogy of risk management texts, (2) the assumptions that underlie their study together, and (3) the meaning of "essentials" as this term relates to the study of risk control.

A Trilogy of Texts

Essentials of Risk Control is one of a trilogy of texts that constitute the study material for the Insurance Institute of America's Associate in Risk Management Program leading to the ARM designation. The other two texts are *Essentials of the Risk Management Process* and *Essentials of Risk Financing*. An understanding of the structure of this trilogy is essential to both the student's effective use of *Essentials of Risk Control* and the authors' purpose in writing it. The trilogy reflects the Institute's and the authors' concept of risk management as a structured sequence of steps for making and implementing decisions about how an organization can cost-effectively protect itself against accidental losses. This entire process is set forth in *Essentials of the Risk Management Process*, the text for ARM 54— the logical first book in the trilogy and the best first course for the student seeking the ARM designation.

An understanding of the overall risk management process indicates that any entity—any organization, family or individual—can

1

follow two, and only two, fundamental strategies: either (1) stop accidental losses from happening or (2) finance recovery from those accidental losses that do occur. Speaking very generally, "stopping losses from happening" is the fundamental purpose of risk control; "financing recovery" from accidental losses is the essential purpose of risk financing. Therefore, the trilogy of texts in the ARM Program devotes one text and one course (ARM 55) to risk control and another (ARM 56) to risk financing. Although logically risk control best precedes risk financing, the ARM 55 and ARM 56 texts and courses may be studied in either order. They both, however, should be preceded by study, or other basic understanding, of the overall risk management process as presented in ARM 54.

Assumed Knowledge Base

On the assumption that the student using this text has already studied *Essentials of the Risk Management Process* for ARM 54—or will have learned comparable material elsewhere—the authors will devote very little time to recapitulating what the student presumably already knows. Specifically, the present text is written on the assumption that the risk management professional already knows and can apply substantial knowledge with respect to the first three steps in the risk management decision process, namely, identifying and analyzing loss exposures, examining alternative risk management techniques, and selecting the most appropriate technique or combination of techniques for dealing with any given loss exposure. This text further assumes that the student is able to apply the quantitative techniques set forth in the ARM 54 text—particularly the techniques of probability analysis, time-series analysis, and the regression analysis—throughout these first risk management decision steps. Consequently, the current *Essentials of Risk Control* builds on this knowledge and focuses on the last two steps in risk management decision making as it applies to risk control: first, implementing and, second, monitoring measures for reducing the frequency and severity of accidental losses.

Although it is best to begin with ARM 54 and *Essentials of the Risk Management Process,* some students will not be able to do so. For them, the ARM 55 Course Guide, revised annually by the Institute, suggests some optional reading that can serve as a partial review of the ARM 54 course.

"Essentials"

The technology of risk control, particularly loss prevention, is extensive, and the volumes of technical material that even profession-

als in fire safety, industrial accident prevention, and industrial hygiene must master number literally thousands of pages. This *Essentials* text cannot summarize this technical information. Further, few risk management professionals personally have direct technical responsibility for loss prevention and most other risk control techniques.

Instead, the risk management professional is most commonly responsible for managing the efforts of risk control specialists—outside experts or other professionals in the organization's own staff. Therefore, this text treats as the "essentials of risk control" the kinds of information the risk management professional needs to meet these managerial responsibilities—particularly at the implementing and monitoring stages of the risk management process—to accomplish the following:

- Set objectives for the organization's risk control efforts and monitor compliance with those objectives,
- Describe in largely nontechnical language to other managers throughout the organization the risk control options available to the organization in coping with various exposures to accidental losses, and
- Forecast and evaluate the likely cashflow and other operational effects of various risk control measures available to the organization.

Even within these largely nontechnical "essentials," parts of the study material on risk control for particular exposures to accidental losses such as fire, industrial hygiene hazards, or environmental pollution will appear to some students to be highly specialized. Other students, however, already familiar with some of the technology in these particular risk control specialties, will see correctly that the discussion in this text deals only with the broadest of risk control principles—principles with which the risk management professional needs to be conversant to communicate effectively with and meaningfully manage risk control specialists.

Although risk control and risk financing are equally important families of risk management techniques, risk control (particularly safety engineering) has a much longer history than does risk financing; consequently, there are many more, essentially engineering-oriented, specialties within risk control. Consequently, most risk management professionals will have direct personal involvement in an organization's risk financing decisions, but only managerial responsibilities for much of an organization's risk control efforts. However, to design an effective risk management program that balances risk control with risk financing, a vital "essential" for the risk management professional is to know enough about risk control to be able to manage it as well as he or she manages risk financing. It is toward this last "essential" that this text is primarily directed.

PLAN OF THE TEXT

The opening chapter of this two-volume text defines risk control, explains theories of accident causation and control, and catalogues risk control techniques. The remaining chapters explain how to apply these techniques to particular types of losses.

Chapter 2 focuses on controlling fire losses, Chapter 3 on losses caused by natural perils, and Chapter 4 on crime losses. Chapters 5 through 7 explore various aspects of preventing work-related employee injuries and diseases through protecting the health of an organization's personnel, designing workplaces in which employees can work most safely and productively, and rehabilitating those employees who may become injured or diseased. Chapters 8 through 10 describe, respectively, procedures for reducing the frequency and/or severity of liability losses, losses caused by environmental pollution, and the net income losses an organization may suffer from damage to its property, from liability claims against it, and from loss of the services of key personnel.

The last three chapters of the text examine the various ways in which specific risk control measures can be organized into system safety programs (Chapter 11), crisis management plans (Chapter 12), and appropriate procedures for motivating and monitoring an organization's overall risk control efforts (Chapter 13).

CHAPTER 1

Framework for Risk Control

This chapter defines risk control and then sets forth two sets of general concepts about risk control, which later chapters will apply to the control of property, liability, personnel, and net income losses for various perils. One set of concepts describes various theories of how accidents are caused and how they can be controlled by countering these causes. The second set is related to the various risk control techniques viewed with a general risk management perspective. These two sets of concepts are intended to unify the text. They provide a general framework for integrating each of the following chapters' largely independent discussions of how to control the frequency and the severity of, or to make more predictable, various types of losses.

The very concept of an accident—a sudden, unplanned, often violent event that causes loss—has long been difficult to analyze. While several theories of how or why accidents occur have a substantial following of experts in safety, there is no one theory that has gained general consensus. Therefore, this text presents and applies several such theories about how accidents are caused and (by implication) how they can be prevented by controlling these causes. These theories include the following:

- The domino theory—developed mainly from the study of workplace accidents and injuries, it presumes that accidents are the end result of a chain of falling dominoes, the most crucial of which represents an unsafe act or condition.
- The energy-release theory—views accidents as a result of uncontrolled energy impinging on animate or inanimate structures that cannot withstand that energy and suggests a number of strategies for preventing or reducing the damage that energy, once released, may cause.

5

- General methods of industrial hygiene control—suggested by studies of work injuries and illnesses, it recommends substitution of less hazardous materials, changes in or isolation of hazardous processes, use of personal protective equipment, and other physical and administrative controls to reduce workplace accidents and illnesses.
- Technique of Operations Review (TOR) system—views the root causes of accidents as management failures in planning, assigning responsibility and authority, supervising subordinates, and other management functions that, if correctly performed, would prevent accidental losses or reduce their severity.
- The system safety approach—analyzes every organization, every operation within that organization, and the economy as a whole as a system of interrelated components—all needing to function properly to prevent accidents—and tries to predict where an accident may disrupt the system and, therefore, how that accident may be prevented.

These general approaches to accident causation and control were developed before, or independently of, risk control techniques. These techniques are a family of ways of reducing accident frequency, severity, or unpredictability through exposure avoidance, loss prevention, loss reduction, segregation of exposure units through either separation or duplication, and contractual transfer for risk control. As a foundation for later chapters, the current chapter defines these risk control techniques, illustrates their application, and explains how each one implements the various theories of accident causation and control.

DEFINITION AND IMPORTANCE OF RISK CONTROL

Definition of Risk Control

Risk control may be defined as *any conscious action (or decision not to act) intended to reduce the frequency, severity, or unpredictability of accidental losses.* Although this definition is relatively brief, three important aspects of it require careful attention.

First, risk control focuses on actual harm, not on amounts of money paid to restore, compensate for, or otherwise finance this harm—such financing matters are the concern of risk financing. For instance, the destruction of a particular machine or the death of a particular person brings with it a given loss of resources to an organization, a family, or society as a whole. Risk control strives to reduce the frequency or the severity of this loss of resources. For risk control purposes, the extent of such a loss of resources is not changed just because, for example, price inflation or deflation increases or decreases the monetary valuation of the loss. Similarly, the fact that the owner of the machine or the family of the deceased may receive financial compensation for the loss from insurance, a court verdict, or some other source does not reduce the severity of the loss from a risk control perspective. Thus, no risk financing technique—no form of retention or transfer for risk financing surveyed in ARM 54—is a risk control technique.

Second, the impact of any given risk control technique can be measured only from the perspective of a given entity. For example, with respect to potential automobile accidents, pedestrians are exposed to bodily injury from being struck by automobiles; for the drivers of those automobiles, such accidents pose an exposure to liability. The pedestrians' exposure to injury and the drivers' exposure to liability are two different exposures growing out of the same accidental events.

Therefore, any risk control technique that safeguards pedestrians from being struck by automobiles (for example, an elevated pedestrian walkway over a busy intersection) has different risk control effects for the pedestrians and for the automobile drivers. For the pedestrians, it is a safeguard against bodily injury; for the automobile drivers, it is protection against liability. For one entity, the elevated walkway is risk control for a personnel loss; for the other, it is risk control for a liability loss. For both, and for the economy or society as a whole, the elevated walkway safeguards two resources: (1) the health and personal productivity of pedestrians who might otherwise be injured and (2) the resources that would be expended in the legal system to determine liability for an accident if a pedestrian were injured in that accident. For all three entities (the pedestrian, the driver, and the economy or society), the added safety represented by the elevated pedestrian walkway preserves resources by reducing the frequency of accidental losses.

A third crucial aspect of the definition of risk control is that a given risk control measure—such as installing fire-suppression sprinklers (loss reduction with respect to fire)—is risk control only with respect to one or more specified exposures. For example, fire-fighting sprinklers are risk control with respect to fire damage, but not for, say, loss by embezzlement. In the same vein, a sprinkler system may be effective risk control for most fires, but if the system uses water as an extinguishant, it may be a hazard rather than a safety measure for fires involving grease or any other material whose spread or flammability is increased by water. In short, specifying a risk control measure also requires specifying the exposure being controlled.

Moreover, a particular measure that seeks to control one kind of loss (reducing its frequency and/or severity) may increase the frequency or severity of other losses. For example, an organization concerned about its potential liability for environmental pollution arising out of its present waste transport and off-site disposal activities may decide to incinerate these wastes on its own premises. Such incineration may, however, increase its on-premises fire hazards, especially if the incineration requires storage of substantial amounts of fuel. In a different setting, equipping employees working in oxygen-deficient environments with breathing apparatus using portable oxygen tanks probably will reduce health hazards related to oxygen deficiency, but it will also increase the fire hazards associated with using, storing, and maintaining portable tanks of pressurized oxygen.

As another illustration of the specificity of risk control measures, some have argued that installing a fire-fighting sprinkler system may control fire losses, but it may also increase sprinkler leakage losses from the untimely discharge of the water or other extinguishant in the system. Therefore, these observers contend, introducing the peril of "sprinkler leakage" may be a valid reason for not installing such a system. Others assert that the sprinkler leakage peril strikes less frequently and with less severity than does fire; consequently, the danger of sprinkler leakage is not a major argument against sprinklering a facility.

In any case, an action that is good risk control for one exposure may increase the frequency or the severity of losses from another. Therefore, to contribute to an organization's overall risk management program, any risk control measure should, on balance, reduce aggregate accident frequency and severity—that is, decrease the expected value of the organization's overall accidental losses.

Importance of Risk Control

Risk control preserves resources for individual organizations and for society as a whole. Risk control is concerned with preventing, making less severe, and speeding recovery from various kinds of losses, whether they involve bodily injury or illness, property damage, loss of use of property, or liability claims. The persons, items of property, and organizations protected through effective risk control benefit because they remain unharmed and productive, or are quickly returned to productivity after any mishap. Emphasizing risk control can be expected to make a risk management program more cost-effective by reducing the costs of risk financing by more than is invested in risk control. It is possible, in some rare cases, to overemphasize risk control, to spend more on safety than is justified by the resulting decrease in accident frequency or severity. There are also cases—much more frequent—where an organization has no real choice about risk control because a state or federal statute mandates some specific safety measure, such as protecting employees from disability or safeguarding the environment against pollution.

Recognizing that it is possible to spend more on safety than is justified by the resulting decrease in accidents leads to an important insight about the underlying purpose of risk control. Risk control measures, designed to reduce the frequency or severity of accidental losses, cost money—now or in the future. These costs of risk control measures, like the costs of the losses they aim to control, are cash outlays to an organization, and are part of the "cost of risk" to the organization. The underlying objective of risk control is to minimize the totals of these two kinds of costs; more precisely, to reduce the expected present value of the organization's total cost of risk.

Risk control decisions need to reflect the expected value of these costs to take proper account of the effects that risk control measures have on the probabilities of losses occurring and of their size. These decisions also need to be based on present values of cash outlays to recognize properly the timing of the necessary cash outlays (now or in the future) for losses or for the costs of reducing them. The procedures for computing expected and present values are detailed in the ARM 54 text and will be summarized briefly as needed in this text.

THEORIES OF ACCIDENT CAUSATION AND CONTROL

Although the very concept of "accident"—an event or outcome that is unplanned by those to whom the event causes loss—appears at first to defy predictive analysis, many students of safety (literally dating back to biblical times) have studied accidents to determine their cause(s). Implicitly or explicitly, their reasoning has been that knowing the cause(s) of past accidents will permit preventing future accidents by removing such cause(s). Unquestionably, the resulting safety efforts have removed or controlled many hazards and perils (particularly for fire, injury, and illness losses). However, accidents continue to occur.

No single theory of accident causation, and thus prevention, has achieved consensus. Nonetheless, each of these theories (briefly defined in the beginning of this chapter) has some adherents and can contribute to any organization's risk control efforts. As a foundation for the discussion of risk control for particular types of accidents in later chapters, this section describes the logic of several of the more widely held theories of accident causation and approaches to accident prevention: the *domino* theory, the *general methods of control* approach developed by industrial safety and hygiene specialists, the *energy-release* theory, the *Technique of Operations Review* system and *system safety* approach.

The Domino Theory[1]

The domino theory was developed primarily during the 1920s by H. W. Heinrich, a leading industrial safety engineer. This theory holds that all accidents, in industrial settings and elsewhere, are the result of a chain of five categories of conditions and/or events: (1) ancestry and social environment, (2) the fault of a person, (3) an unsafe act and/or mechanical or physical hazard, (4) the accident itself, and (5) the resulting injury. (These five "accident factors" are portrayed in Exhibit 1-1.) Heinrich described each of these five factors as a "domino," emphasizing that (1) every accident sequence begins with a negative ancestry or social environment for a person and ends with an injury and (2) removal of any of the four dominoes preceding the injury would prevent that injury.

Heinrich emphasized that removing the third domino—eliminating the unsafe act or condition—usually is the best way to break the chain and prevent the resulting injury. He believed that unsafe human acts, such as improper use of a machine, were far more frequent than unsafe conditions (such as a defect in a machine) and that correcting unsafe acts was the most efficient method of preventing injuries. Although others before him also had accepted the domino theory, most of his predecessors in industrial accident prevention had stressed unsafe conditions rather than unsafe acts and had concentrated, therefore, on designing "safe" machines and other surroundings. Heinrich innovated by focusing mainly on human failings as the cause of industrial injuries. His third domino, for example, indicates that both unsafe acts and unsafe conditions result from human faults.

Because of its emphasis on human failings, the domino theory is most applicable to losses growing out of situations where human action, either faulty or safe, plays a major role. The theory was developed to explain on-the-job injuries to employees, a type of accident that centers around a human being whose actions clearly are important to his or her personal safety and the safety of other workers. Extending this theory to other types of losses in which the action of the injured party does not play a key role—natural disasters or crime losses, for example—may well put too much strain on a theory that places such emphasis on human failing. On the other hand, the domino theory seems well suited to accidental losses that directly grow out of human activity—losses directly or indirectly attributable to the same

Exhibit 1-1
Heinrich's Theory of Accident Causation*

Accident Factors	Explanation of Factors
1. Ancestry and social environment.	Recklessness, stubbornness, avariciousness, and other undesirable traits of character may be passed along through inheritance.
	Environment may develop undesirable traits of character or may interfere with education. Both inheritance and environment cause faults of person.
2. Fault of person.	Inherited or acquired faults of person; such as recklessness, violent temper, nervousness, excitability, inconsiderateness, ignorance of safe practice, etc., constitute proximate reasons for committing unsafe acts or for the existence of mechanical or physical hazards.
3. Unsafe act and/or mechanical or physical hazard.	Unsafe performance of persons, such as standing under suspended loads, starting machinery without warning, horse-play, and removal of safeguards; and mechanical or physical hazards, such as unguarded gears, unguarded point of operation, absence of rail guards, and insufficient light, result directly in accidents.
4. Accident.	Events, such as falls of persons, striking of persons by flying objects, etc., typically are accidents that cause injury.
5. Injury.	Fractures, lacerations, etc., are injuries that result directly from accidents.

*Adapted with permission from H.W. Heinrich, Dan Petersen, and Nestor Roos, *Industrial Accident Prevention*, 5th ed. (New York: McGraw-Hill Book Co., 1980), pp. 22-23.

human failings to which the domino theory attributes employee injuries.

The General Methods of Control Approach[2]

Only a few decades after Heinrich's domino theory emphasized unsafe employee actions as the cause of industrial accidents, industrial hygienists and safety engineers formulated a somewhat different theory that stressed that unsafe physical conditions, usually more than unsafe employee acts, resulted in workplace injuries and illnesses. From this theory, these hygienists and engineers deduced eleven general methods to control industrial accidents and illnesses, which generally are listed as follows:

1. Substitution of a less harmful material for one that is more hazardous to health
2. Change or alteration of a process to minimize worker contact
3. Isolation or enclosure of a process or work operation to reduce the number of persons exposed
4. Wet methods to reduce generation of dust in operations such as mining and quarrying
5. Local exhaust at the point of generation and dispersion of contaminants
6. General or dilution ventilation with clean air to provide a more healthful atmosphere
7. Personal protective devices, such as special clothing, eye, and respiratory protection
8. Good housekeeping, including cleanliness of the workplace, waste disposal, adequate washing and eating facilities, healthful drinking water, and control of insects and rodents
9. Special control methods for specific hazards, such as reduction of exposure time, film badges and similar monitoring devices, or continuous sampling with preset alarms
10. Medical programs to detect intake of toxic materials
11. Training and education to supplement engineering controls

These general methods of control naturally suggest the causes of industrial accidents and illnesses: absence of one or more controls causes an industrial accident or illness. These general methods of control also can be visualized, as in Exhibit 1-2, as being applicable at the source of a hazard, along a "path" between the source and the exposed employee, or to the employee directly. Note in Exhibit 1-2 that some of the general methods of control can be applied at more than one of these locations. These general methods emphasize the physical elements of accident causation and focus on the loss prevention and loss reduction measures that industrial hygienists and safety engineers bring to their work. It follows that this approach to analyzing the causes and controls of accidents is best suited to situations in which physical forces and conditions rather than human error appear to cause most accidents.

The Energy-Release Theory[3]

Dr. William Haddon, Jr., an expert in public health and the first president of the Insurance Institute for Highway Safety, pioneered in the 1970s the energy-release theory of accident causation and control. This approach views accidents in terms of energy being released and then impacting objects, including living things, in amounts or at rates that the impacted object cannot tolerate. In describing accidents as "a major class of ecologic phenomena," Haddon states:

> A major class of ecologic phenomena involves the transfer of energy in such ways and amounts, and at such rapid rates, that inanimate or animate structures are damaged. The harmful interactions with people and with property of hurricanes, earthquakes, projectiles, moving vehicles, ionizing radiation, lightning, conflagrations, and constant bruises of daily life illustrate this class.[4]

Thus, for Haddon and those who have followed his thinking, the basic cause of accidents is energy out of control. Quite logically, therefore, the resulting approaches ("strategies") for preventing these accidents or reducing the harm they cause focus on controlling that energy and/or reducing the harm caused by that energy when it is released. The ten basic strategies of the energy-release theory usually are stated as follows:

1. Preventing the marshaling of the energy in the first place, such as by banning development of nuclear weapons (or ordering them dismantled), forbidding the production of particularly high-powered vehicles, or preventing the conception of tigers in order to avoid subsequent human injuries.
2. Reducing the amount of energy marshaled, such as by limiting the size of bombs or firecrackers, the height of diving boards above swimming pools, or the speed of vehicles.
3. Preventing the release of built-up energy, such as keeping elevators from falling, tigers from escaping, reckless drivers from having access to automobiles, using retaining walls to prevent mudslides, or requiring window washers to wear belts when cleaning tall buildings.
4. Modifying the rate or spatial distribution of the release of energy, such as by reducing the slope of ski trails, installing

Exhibit 1-2
Generalized Diagram of Methods of Control*

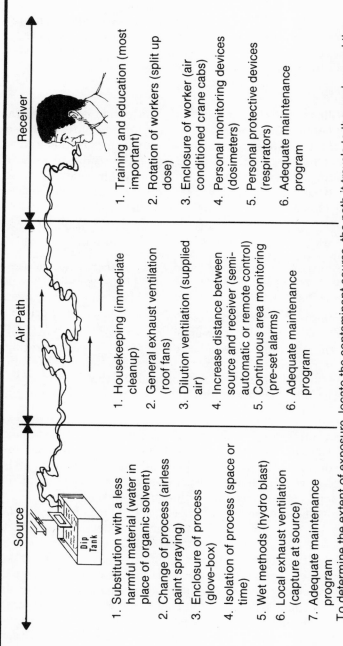

Source

1. Substitution with a less harmful material (water in place of organic solvent)
2. Change of process (airless paint spraying)
3. Enclosure of process (glove-box)
4. Isolation of process (space or time)
5. Wet methods (hydro blast)
6. Local exhaust ventilation (capture at source)
7. Adequate maintenance program

Air Path

1. Housekeeping (immediate cleanup)
2. General exhaust ventilation (roof fans)
3. Dilution ventilation (supplied air)
4. Increase distance between source and receiver (semi-automatic or remote control)
5. Continuous area monitoring (pre-set alarms)
6. Adequate maintenance program

Receiver

1. Training and education (most important)
2. Rotation of workers (split up dose)
3. Enclosure of worker (air conditioned crane cabs)
4. Personal monitoring devices (dosimeters)
5. Personal protective devices (respirators)
6. Adequate maintenance program

To determine the extent of exposure, locate the contaminant source, the path it travels to the worker, and the employee's work pattern and use of protective equipment.

*Reprinted with permission from Julian B. Olishifski, "Methods of Control," *Fundamentals of Industrial Hygiene*, ed. Barbara A. Plog, 3rd ed. (Chicago: National Safety Council, 1988), p. 458.

explosion vents or explosion-relieving walls, and requiring deep sea divers to undergo slow decompression.

5. Separating, in space or in time, the energy being released from a susceptible animate or inanimate structure, such as by building divided highways separated by open space, establishing separate lanes for pedestrian and vehicular traffic, and controlling the time interval between landings and takeoffs at airports.

6. Interposing a physical barrier between the energy and the susceptible structure, such as by requiring firedoors in public buildings, using a sunscreen to filter ultraviolet sunrays, using automobile seat belts, and requiring workers to wear appropriate protective clothing.

7. Modifying the contact surface or basic structure that can be impacted, such as by installing "breakaway" highway light poles, requiring padding on automobile dashboards to cushion occupants' impact, and allowing young children to use only specially dulled scissors.

8. Strengthening the susceptible structure that might be damaged by the energy, such as by requiring special building construction in earthquake zones, fireproofing structural members, giving special training to soldiers or those who work in other hazardous conditions, or requiring vaccination of those potentially exposed to illness.

9. Moving rapidly to detect and evaluate damage and to counter its continuation or spread, such as by giving first-aid, activating fire suppression systems and notifying the fire department, encircling escaped oil polluting the surface of water, protecting property in imminent danger of fire, and recapturing escaped tigers.

10. Taking long-term action (after the emergency period) to reduce further damage, such as the rehabilitation of injured persons or salvage of damaged property.

Some of those who have followed Haddon's work have simplified his strategies. For example, Robert I. Mehr and Bob A. Hedges have identified five "accidental control points":

1. Control the built-up energy.
2. Control the injurious release of built-up energy.
3. Separate the released energy from persons and objects susceptible to injury.
4. Create an environment which minimizes injurious effects of the released energy.
5. Counteract injurious effects of the released energy.[5]

Exhibit 1-3 demonstrates the interrelationships and basic consistency between Haddon's "strategies" and Mehr and Hedges' "accident control points" and also their common consistency with the industrial hygiene general methods of control. (Note, however, that linking training and education, a method of industrial hygiene control, with Mehr and Hedges' fourth control point, creating an environment that minimizes injurious effects, is somewhat arbitrary. Effective training and education of all personnel within an organization may have positive effects on all five of Mehr and Hedges' control points.)

Technique of Operations Review (TOR) System[6]

Several modern students of management focus on one or more management shortcomings as a basic cause of any organization's failure to achieve its objectives—accidents being one class of such failures. Thus, as Dan Petersen, a well-known safety consultant, has said with respect to workplace accidents:

> Root causes often relate to the management system. It may be due to management's policies and procedures, supervision and its effectiveness, training, etc. In our example. . ., some root causes could be a lack of inspection procedures, a lack of management policy, or definition of responsibilities (supervisors did not know they were responsible. . .), and a lack of supervisory or employee training.[7]

This perspective on the root causes of all accidents befalling organizations leads Petersen to five basic principles of risk control:

1. An unsafe act, an unsafe condition, and an accident are all symptoms of something wrong in our management system.
2. Certain sets of circumstances eventually will produce severe injuries. These circumstances can be identified and controlled.
3. Safety should be managed like any other company function, management should direct the safety effort by setting achievable goals and by planning, organizing, leading, and controlling to achieve them.
4. The key to effective line safety performance is management procedures for accountability.
5. The function of safety is to locate and define the operational errors that allow accidents to occur. This function can be carried out in two ways: (1) by asking why accidents happen—searching for their root causes—and (2) by asking whether certain known effective controls are being utilized.

Thus, the cause of all accidents is managerial shortcomings. Although Petersen's discussion focuses particularly on industrial work injuries and illnesses, his approach—and the Technique of Operations

Exhibit 1-3
Three Perspectives on the Energy-Release Theory — Some Lines of Commonality

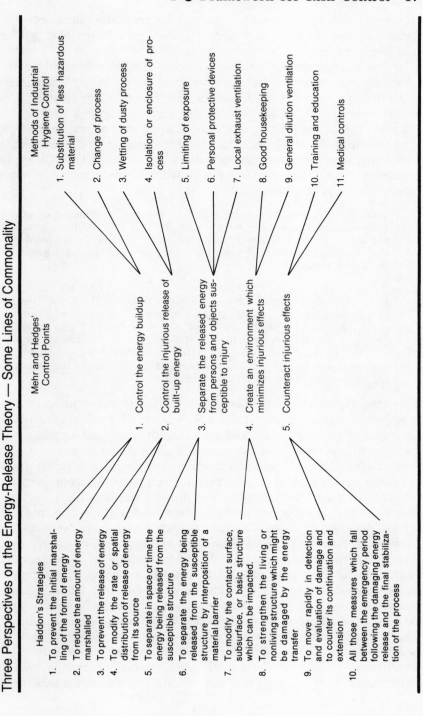

Haddon's Strategies

1. To prevent the initial marshalling of the form of energy
2. To reduce the amount of energy marshalled
3. To prevent the release of energy
4. To modify the rate or spatial distribution of release of energy from its source
5. To separate in space or time the energy being released from the susceptible structure
6. To separate the energy being released from the susceptible structure by interposition of a material barrier
7. To modify the contact surface, subsurface, or basic structure which can be impacted.
8. To strengthen the living or nonliving structure which might be damaged by the energy transfer
9. To move rapidly in detection and evaluation of damage and to counter its continuation and extension
10. All those measures which fall between the emergency period following the damaging energy release and the final stabilization of the process

Mehr and Hedges' Control Points

1. Control the energy buildup
2. Control the injurious release of built-up energy
3. Separate the released energy from persons and objects susceptible to injury
4. Create an environment which minimizes injurious effects
5. Counteract injurious effects

Methods of Industrial Hygiene Control

1. Substitution of less hazardous material
2. Change of process
3. Wetting of dusty process
4. Isolation or enclosure of process
5. Limiting of exposure
6. Personal protective devices
7. Local exhaust ventilation
8. Good housekeeping
9. General dilution ventilation
10. Training and education
11. Medical controls

Review, which that approach generates for preventing accidents—is, in principle, applicable to any accident that gives rise to a property, liability, personnel, or net income loss.

The Technique of Operations Review (TOR), originated by D. A. Weaver and endorsed by Petersen and other safety management consultants, identifies particular shortcomings of an organization's management, grouping them in the eight categories portrayed in Exhibit 1-4. The TOR system calls upon managers to recognize shortcomings in their own (or their colleagues' or subordinates') managing to correct these shortcomings. According to the TOR system, removing these management faults will eliminate most, if not all, accidents. As Weaver has said:

> TOR analysis creates real insights into the real circumstances of a real organization. Reality begins with the fact that TOR analysis is applied to an incident, some untoward event, that really occurred in the organization but that need not occur again if the management fault is corrected.
>
> An accident or an injury is the clearest example of such an incident, but the word "incident" includes all sorts of wasteful and inefficient occurrences...[such as] 500 gallons of product down the drain, a costly delay and frantic search for a special truck shipment, and product defects. Such incidents of greater or lesser significance occur in every business day, often are hardly observed. Someone corrects the symptoms [of the particular incident] but no one seeks the causes, the underlying operating errors of management.[8]

The TOR system can be extended to identify the causes and suggest corrective actions for a wide variety of accidental losses. For example, a product defect and resulting products liability loss might well be attributable to a managerial failure listed in any one of the sections of Exhibit 1-4: from Section A, failure to instruct factory workers on how to assemble product components; from Section B, absence of clear responsibility for product quality; from Section C, mistakes in product design decisions because designers were not aware of problems experienced with competitors' comparable products; from Section D, failure to enforce rules that instruct dealers to prepare the product properly before final delivery to customers; from Section E, poorly maintained and out-of-date records showing where products have been delivered, thus making recalls difficult; from Section F, inadequate staffing of the company's legal department so that claims are not handled properly; from Section G, the uncooperative attitude of the company's chief marketing executive, who is more concerned with sales volumes than the quality of the product when delivered to customers; and from Section H, performance appraisals that are inadequate because they do not evaluate plant managers and/or supervisors in terms of the quality of their output. Correcting these or other managerial errors the TOR system could identify would make products liability or any other accidental losses less likely and/or less severe.

System Safety Approach

System safety begins with the concept that the entire universe (1) is a single system and (2) is made up of a great variety of smaller, interrelated systems (ranging in size and complexity from, say, the parts of an electric switch, the bones and muscles in the human body, the parts of a factory machine or an automobile, the factory or the highway system itself, the economy of an entire nation, to the entire world economy or global transportation network). An accident occurs when a human or a mechanical component of a system fails to function when it should. System safety attempts to forecast how these failures may occur so that appropriate action can be taken either to prevent the failure or to minimize its consequences.

System safety originated in the military and has been elaborated through various aerospace and industrial programs—each made up of numerous components or subsystems—in order to increase the reliability of the entire military, aerospace, or industrial effort. System safety analyzes the entire system, product, or operation through the following:

1. The identification of potential hazards,
2. The timely incorporation of effective safety-related design and operational specifications, provisions, and criteria,
3. The early evaluation of design and procedures for compliance with applicable safety requirements and criteria, and
4. The continued surveillance of all safety aspects of the system throughout its total lifespan, including disposal.[9]

Within this broad perspective, system safety relies on a number of specific techniques for identifying and evaluating hazards and determining how these hazards may lead to system breakdowns and more accidents. These techniques can be used to estimate the probability of particular kinds of breakdowns (based on the probabilities of the events that come together to produce the breakdown) and to suggest cost-effective ways of preventing these system failures.

System safety provides the most comprehensive set of concepts for analyzing how accidents occur and how they may be prevented. The analytical processes of system safety allow room for all of the other theories of accident causation and control, making system safety more valuable as a procedure for considering the various ways in which

Exhibit 1-4
TOR Review — Categories of Management Faults*

A. Inadequate Coaching

Unusual situation, failure to coach (new man, tool, equipment, process, material, etc.)

No instruction. No instruction available for particular situation

Training not formulated or need not foreseen

Correction. Failure to correct or failure to see need to correct

Instruction inadequate. Instruction was attempted but result shows it didn't take

Supervisor failed to tell why

Supervisor failed to listen

B. Failure to Take Responsibility

Duties and tasks not clear

Conflicting goals

Responsibility, not clear or failure to accept

Dual responsibility

Pressure of immediate tasks obscures full scope of responsibilities

Buck passing, responsibility not tied down

Job descriptions inadequate

C. Unclear Authority

Bypassing, conflicting orders, too many bosses

Decision too far above the problem

Authority inadequate to cope with the situation

Decision exceeded authority

Decision evaded, problem dumped on the boss

Orders failed to produce desired result. Not clear, not understood, or not followed

Subordinates fail to exercise their power to decide

D. Inadequate Supervision

Morale. Tension, insecurity, lack of faith in the supervisor and the future of the job

Conduct. Supervisor sets poor example

Unsafe acts. Failure to observe and correct

Rules. Failure to make necessary rules, or to publicize them. Inadequate follow-up and enforcement. Unfair enforcement or weak discipline

Initiative. Failure to see problems and exert an influence on them

Honest error. Failure to act, or action turned out to be wrong

Team spirit. Men are not pulling with the supervisor

Co-operation. Poor co-operation. Failure to plan for co-ordination

E. Workplace Disorder

Work flow. Inefficient or hazardous layout, scheduling, arrangement, stacking, piling, routing, storing, etc.

Conditions. Inefficient or unsafe due to faulty inspection, supervisory action, or maintenance

Property loss. Accidental breakage or damage due to faulty procedure, inspection, supervision, or maintenance

Clutter, Anything unnecessary in the work area. (Excess materials, defective tools and equipment, bins, scrap barrels, janitorial service, etc.)

Voluntary compliance. Work group sees no advantage to themselves

F. Inadequate Planning/Organization

Job procedure. Awkward, unsafe, inefficient, poorly planned

Work load. Pace too fast, too slow, or erratic

New procedure. New or unusual tasks or hazards not yet understood

Short handed. High turnover or absenteeism

Unattractive jobs. Job conditions or rewards are not competitive

Job placement. Hasty or improper job selection and placement

Co-ordination. Departments inadvertently create problems for each other (production, maintenance, purchasing, personnel, sales, etc.)

G. Personal Deficiencies

Physical condition — strength, agility, poor reaction, clumsy, etc.

Health — sick, tired, taking medicine

Impairment — amputee, vision, hearing, heart, diabetic, epileptic, hernia, etc.

Alcohol — (if definite facts are known)

Personality — excitable, lazy, goof-off, unhappy, easily distracted, impulsive, anxious, irritable, complacent, etc.

Adjustment — aggressive, show off, stubborn, insolent, scorns advice and instruction, defies authority, antisocial, argues, timid, etc.

Work habits — sloppy. Confusion and disorder in work area. Careless of tools, equipment and procedure

Work assignment — unsuited for this particular individual

H. Poor Organizational Structure/Planning

Policy. Failure to assert a management will prior to the situation at hand

Goals. Not clear, or not projected as an "action image"

Accountability. Failure to measure or appraise results

Span of attention. Too many irons in the fire. Inadequate delegation. Inadequate development of subordinates

Performance appraisals. Inadequate or dwell excessively on short range performance

Mistakes. Failure to support and encourage subordinates to exercise their power to decide

Staffing. Assign full or part-time responsibility for related functions

*Adapted with permission from Dan Petersen, *Techniques of Safety Management* (New York: McGraw Hill Book Company, 1978), pp. 166-167.

accidents may be caused and the alternatives for preventing them or reducing their severity.

APPLICATIONS OF RISK CONTROL TECHNIQUES

When applied to a variety of property, liability, personnel, and net income losses, theories of accident causation and control generate an almost infinite number of specific risk control measures. To bring order to these possibilities, it is useful to bear in mind the basic risk control techniques. Every risk control measure is a specific application of one or more of the following risk control techniques:

- Exposure avoidance,
- Loss prevention,
- Loss reduction,
- Segregation of loss exposure units through
    - separation of loss exposure units or
    - duplication of loss exposure units, and
- Contractual transfer for risk control.

Exposure Avoidance

Definition Exposure avoidance makes loss from a specified exposure impossible. It reduces the probability of such a loss to zero by either eliminating or deciding not to undertake a specified asset or activity. Properly practiced, exposure avoidance is the only completely self-sufficient risk management technique: a completely avoided exposure requires no further risk control or risk financing measure.

Applications While exposure avoidance is the only complete risk management technique, it has very limited applications. The clearest examples of this technique include avoiding an exposure to products liability by deciding never to manufacture the product or avoiding exposures arising out of the ownership of land by deciding to not acquire that land. Many exposures, however, are automatically created and cannot be avoided. For instance, the mere existence of an organization automatically creates personnel loss exposures. They cannot be avoided because they are a *fact* of the organization's existence. Similarly, the only way to avoid all types of property loss is to possess no property whatsoever. Therefore, against the broad categories of loss exposure, exposure avoidance is not a feasible alternative.

Certain narrower exposures definitely can be avoided. Suppose a manufacturing company, located on an island and concerned about the weakened condition of the one bridge over which trucks carry its output to market, wishes to avoid the exposure of losing a shipment in a bridge collapse. The company can avoid this exposure by transporting its output to the mainland on boats (which do not pass under the bridge, lest they be damaged in a bridge collapse). Using boats avoids the exposure to trucks being lost in a bridge collapse, but this action exposes shipments to boating accidents. Often, avoiding one loss exposure creates another.

If this company's real concern is not with the exposure to bridge collapse as such, but rather the broader exposure to damage of its output while in transit to the mainland, boats may not be better than trucks. The only ways to avoid the exposure to damage to its output in transit over water are to (1) not transport to the mainland at all or (2) move its manufacturing operations to the mainland.

Despite the inherent difficulties of applying exposure avoidance, an organization should consider this risk control alternative whenever the expected value of the losses from engaging in a particular activity outweighs the expected benefits of engaging in that activity and employing any other risk management technique except avoidance. Thus, it may be quite reasonable for a toy manufacturer to decide not to produce a particular toy because the products liability claims from this particular toy are expected to outweigh the revenue from its sale, no matter how cautious the manufacturer may be in producing and marketing the toy or in arranging to finance its products liability losses.

Exposure avoidance often is mistaken for either loss prevention or contractual transfer for risk control. The proper distinctions among these techniques are made in the definitions of loss prevention and contractual transfer for risk control.

Loss Prevention

Definition Loss prevention is any measure that reduces the probability or *frequency* of a particular loss *but does not eliminate completely all possibility of that loss* (as does exposure avoidance). And it does so without necessarily having an effect on the likely severity of loss. Conceptually, loss prevention differs from exposure avoidance because loss prevention does not eliminate all chance of loss.

Loss prevention also is distinct in principle from loss reduction because loss reduction focuses on reducing the *severity* of losses, not their probability or frequency. In practice, a risk management action may combine elements of both loss prevention and loss reduction, as when lowering the legal highway speed limit in the late 1970s cut both the number of automobile accidents (because drivers have more time to react to dangerous situations) and the seriousness of those accidents which do occur (because less kinetic energy is released when slow moving vehicles collide with any other object).

Applications Most loss prevention measures go hand in hand with concepts of how losses are caused. In general, a loss prevention measure is an action taken before a loss occurs in order to break the sequence of circumstances that are thought to lead to the loss. Breaking the sequence is supposed to stop the loss from happening, or at least make it less likely.

Because of the close link between loss causation and loss prevention, developing effective loss prevention measures usually requires a careful study of how particular losses are caused. For example, because of H. W. Heinrich's theory of accident causation, most work injuries traditionally have been thought to result from a chain of events that includes an unsafe act or an unsafe condition. In this tradition, work safety efforts have focused on trying to eliminate specific unsafe acts or unsafe conditions. For instance, fire safety engineers speak of a "fire triangle"—the three elements of fuel, oxygen, and an ignition source that all must be present for fire to occur. Consequently, preventing fire requires removing at least one of the three legs of the fire triangle.[10]

Loss Reduction

Definition Loss reduction measures reduce the severity of those losses that do occur. To analyze loss reduction opportunities, a risk management professional must assume that a loss has occurred and then ask what could have been done, either before or after this loss, to reduce its size or extent.

For any type of loss from any peril, two broad categories of loss reduction measures are (1) pre-loss measures, which are applied before the loss occurs and (2) post-loss measures, which are applied after the loss occurs. Pre-loss efforts to reduce loss severity may reduce loss frequency—driving ambulances at lower speeds in nonemergency situations, for example. Pre-loss measures generally reduce the amount of property, the number of persons, or other things of value that may suffer loss from a single event. Post-loss measures typically focus on emergency procedures, salvage operations, rehabilitation activities, or legal defenses to halt the spread of loss or to counter its effects. For example, erecting firewalls to limit the amount of damage from any one fire is a pre-loss measure; an effective fire detection/suppression system is a post-loss measure.

Applications The many opportunities for loss reduction are suggested by the strategies of the energy-release theory. For example, reducing the amount of energy marshaled, modifying the rate or spatial distribution of the release of that energy, modifying the contact surface or structure that may be impaired, and strengthening the structure that might be damaged all are pre-loss forms of loss reduction. An automatic fire detection/suppression system, as a further example, reduces the damage caused by fires that trigger the system by dissipating the heat or extinguishing a flame from such a fire, modifying the rate at which the fire's energy is released, thereby applying Strategy 4 of the energy-release theory. Similarly, the final two energy-release strategies are post-loss measures for loss reduction. (Refer to the examples of these strategies earlier in this chapter to see how, in each example, the severity of the harm suffered is reduced.) These measures (such as setting a maximum speed limit for automobiles) also may reduce loss frequency, making them also appropriate examples of loss prevention. The dual nature of these measures does not create a difficulty with the distinction between loss prevention and loss reduction; it only illustrates the importance of carefully tracing, and distinguishing among, the various effects which a given safety measure may produce.

Segregation of Exposure Units

Segregation of exposure units encompasses two distinct but closely related risk management techniques—*separation* of exposure units and *duplication* of exposure units. Both strive to reduce an organization's dependence of any single asset, activity, or person, thus tending to make individual losses smaller and more predictable. The basic logic of segregation of exposure units is exemplified in the maxim, "Don't put all your eggs in one basket."

Definitions Separation of exposure units involves dividing an organization's existing single asset or operation into two or more separate units. (Two examples are dividing existing inventory between two warehouses or manufacturing a component part in two plants rather than in only one plant.) Separation is appropriate if an organization can meet its goals with only a portion of these separate units left intact. If total loss is suffered by any one unit, the portion of the assets or operations at the other location(s) is sufficient. All separated units normally are kept in daily use in the organization's operations.

Duplication of exposure units involves complete reproduction of an organization's own "stand-by" asset or facility to be kept in reserve. This duplicate is *not* used unless the primary asset or activity is damaged or destroyed. Duplication is appropriate if an entire asset or activity is so important that the consequence of its loss justifies the expense and time of maintaining the duplicate. Maintaining duplicate accounting records is an example of duplication of exposure units.

Separation and duplication are distinct from one another, and both are distinct from other means of loss reduction. Four points need to be noted. First, unlike other means of loss reduction, neither separation nor duplication of exposure units makes any special attempt to reduce the severity of loss to any one single unit. Each unit may still be subject to total loss, but each unit is less significant to the organization. Second, both separation and duplication reduce the severity of an individual loss, but they may have differing effects on loss frequency. Using two distantly separated warehouses instead of one is likely to increase loss frequency because two units are exposed to loss. Duplication is not likely to increase loss frequency because the duplicated unit is kept in reserve and not used; i.e., is not as exposed to loss as is the primary unit put to daily use. (For example, a duplicate vehicle presumably is garaged and is not as vulnerable to highway accidents as is the primary vehicle.) Third, duplication is likely to reduce the average, or "expect-ed" annual loss from a given exposure because duplication reduces loss severity without increasing loss frequency. Fourth, separation may or may not decrease the average "expected" loss. Much depends on whether the reduction in loss severity from separation is more important than, or is overshadowed by, the increased loss frequency that separation normally entails.

Both separation and duplication tend to be expensive, sometimes impractical, risk management techniques. Separation, in particular, seldom is undertaken for its own sake but, instead, is a by-product of another management decision. For example, few organizations build and use a second warehouse simply to reduce the severity of losses to the former single warehouse. However, if an organization is consider-ing the construction of a second warehouse because of a need to expand production, the risk management implications of this new, separate, exposure unit may well be an additional argument in favor of the expansion.

In contrast, duplication—keeping a spare unit on standby, ready for emergency use—often is primarily prompted by risk management considerations. Senior management recognizes the crucial nature of a particular operation or asset and is willing to invest in duplicating it in order not to be without this essential element of its operations. Duplicate records, spare machinery parts, and cross-training employees to do several jobs within their departments are typical risk manage-ment safeguards and are recognized and justified as such.

Applications For cost reasons, separation of exposure units (keeping all units in daily use) typically has more practical application than does duplication of exposure units (where standby units remain idle except during emergencies). Opportunities for separation include:

- Maintaining several warehouses at different locations in which to store inventory rather than maintaining an entire inventory at one location.
- Operating on a daily basis with only partial loads 5 or 10 percent more trucks or busses than would be absolutely required in order to have some "excess capacity" for when some portion of the fleet is disabled or requires maintenance, during which the remaining portion of the fleet that is operational will work at full capacity.
- For a firm that regularly operates several facilities, equipping each facility to perform a variety of operations so that, if one is temporarily shut down, the others can maintain the firm's overall output.

Opportunities for duplication include:

- Maintaining duplicates of accounting records and other valuable documents in a safe location to be used only if the original documents are damaged or otherwise unavailable.
- Keeping an inventory of spare machinery parts or even spare machines to be used when the primary ones are unusable for any reason.
- Entering into a mutual aid pact with similar organizations for use of one another's facilities—such as computers, printing presses, refrigerated storage, and the like—when one member's normal facilities are damaged or otherwise unavailable.

Contractual Transfer for Risk Control

Definition A contractual transfer for risk control is an agreement under which one party (the transferor) shifts to another (the transferee) the loss exposures associated with an asset or activity. The "shift" is accomplished by requiring the transferee to perform certain activities and, as an element of those activities, to assume certain exposures and to bear any losses that arise out of those exposures. Under a contractual transfer for risk control, the transferor seeks no indemnity or other compensation from the transferee but, rather, expects the transferee to perform certain activities the transferor deems unduly hazardous. (This absence of any expectation of indemnity distinguishes a contractual transfer for risk control from a contractual transfer for risk financing, either through insurance or from a transferee who is not an insurer.)

Contractual transfer for risk control easily can be mistaken for exposure avoidance. Some incorrectly have said that, for example, one way to avoid the physical damage exposures inherent in operating a fireworks factory is to sell the factory to someone else so that the new owner now faces these exposures. The seller, the former owner, is sometimes wrongly said to have avoided these exposures. This analysis fails to recognize that the exposures inherent in operating that factory still exist—they have not been eliminated but rather merely shifted to the new owner through a contract of sale (from the seller's standpoint, a contractual transfer for risk control). True exposure avoidance eliminates the loss exposure for everyone, even for society as a whole, by either abandoning this factory or not constructing it initially.

Application The diversity of modern business contracts offers many opportunities for risk control through contractual transfers of property, liability, personnel, and net income loss exposures. In examining these opportunities, it is important to note that the contractual transfers are for risk control, not for risk financing; the transfer here is of the ownership of an asset or legal responsibility for an activity, not the risk financing transfer created by an indemnity or other compensation agreement.

For property exposures, the most common contractual transfer for risk control is through a lease or other rental arrangement. Under such arrangements, the lessor (landlord/owner) and the lessee (tenant/user) apportion between themselves the loss exposures associated with the ownership and use of the leased or rented property. The lessor normally bears the exposures to property loss, thus allowing the lessee—in exchange for rental payments—use of the property. Should the property be damaged, then—in the absence of contrary lease provisions—the lessor is obligated to replace the property for the lessee's use. Under some lease arrangements, the lessee bears property losses caused by some perils and agrees to restore any property damage caused by them. Thus, by properly tailoring a lease or rental agreement covering real or personal property, the lessor and the lessee can apportion—and transfer where appropriate—property loss exposures from one party to the other.

It is through the subcontracting of specific activities that individuals and organizations can apportion between themselves, and thus transfer as desired, responsibility for performing particular activities and, thus, for bearing the liability, personnel, and net income exposures arising from those activities. For example, an organization particularly concerned about the hazardous nature of one of its operations—say, the assembly of a component of a manufactured product—may subcontract this activity to another firm more skilled (or less cautious) in dealing with these hazards.

In effect, by agreeing to deliver a specified number of these components by a specified date at a specified price, the subcontractor assumes the liability, personnel, and net income loss exposures associated with that work. These exposures might involve liability for workers compensation benefits to employees engaged in this hazardous activity, the resignation of a key technician or executive on whose skill the feasibility of the particularly hazardous subcontracted operation depends, and shutdown of the hazardous assembly operation (perhaps because of a products-related accident).

If the transferor is able to shift to the subcontractor these and other related exposures at a cost lower than the cost to perform the subcontracted activities, this contractual transfer for risk control is cost-effective for the transferor. If the price paid also is reasonable from the transferee/subcontractor's standpoint, this contractual shift of loss exposures benefits both parties and hence, society and the economy in general.

Note, however, if the transferor subcontracts an activity to only one transferee, and if that transferee is shut down for an extended period, both the transferor and the transferee may incur substantial net income losses. Therefore, to forestall this result, the transferor may subcontract with several other organizations, thus practicing some segregation of this net income exposure. Note, further, that subcontracting with several suppliers—each of whom regularly supplies a portion of the manufacturer's/transferor's needs—would be separation of exposure units; relying on only one primary supplier, with others ready to step in as "backups" if the regular supplier were shut down, would be duplication of exposure units from the transferor's perspective. This illustration, combining elements of both contractual transfer for risk control and segregation of exposure units, demonstrates the general principle that it is often both feasible and advisable to apply more than one risk control technique to a given exposure.

Special problems may arise in attempts to control liability exposures and personnel exposures through business contracts. The extent to which an organization can succeed in contractually transferring a liability loss exposure depends on the courts' attitude toward the attempted transfer. Courts generally are somewhat reluctant to allow one organization to escape liability to a third party by subcontracting with another organization. Often the courts will hold both the subcontractor and the transferor responsible for damage to others, frequently on the basis that the subcontractor is the agent of the primary organization. This is particularly the case when the subcontractor is not financially strong and the courts' concern for adequately compensating the claimant leads it to seek other defendants.

Subcontracting crucial operations can be a very effective way for an organization to transfer some significant personnel loss exposures. For example, if an organization finds itself especially dependent on an EDP technician for its computer operations, the organization could subcontract this work. The subcontractor would be obligated to complete its work under this contract, regardless of death, disability, resignation, or retirement of any one particular employee of the subcontractor on whose special talents the subcontractor relied to carry out the contract.

For any organization, however, there are certain key executive functions that cannot be transferred to an outside organization. Examples of such functions often include strategic marketing, finance, product development, legal, or other decisions that typically can be made only by an organization's own senior executives. Transferring the authority and responsibility for these decisions to outsiders would be more an evasion of responsibility than effective use of contractual transfer for risk control.

SUMMARY

This chapter defines risk control and explains its importance, relates risk control to several theories of accident causation and control, and enumerates the general techniques of risk control as part of the risk management process. Risk control may be defined as reducing the frequency, severity, and/or unpredictability of any accidental loss. Applying risk control measures to the property, liability, personnel, and net income losses to which an organization is exposed can reduce that organization's operating costs and thereby increase its profits or operating efficiency.

Beyond these benefits for individual organizations, risk control also has advantages for the entire economy. Appropriate risk control measures preserve existing economic resources and reduce the expenditure of resources that otherwise would be needed for restoring damage and operating the administrative and legal processes for determining financial responsibility for these preventable losses. In most situations, reducing the frequency, severity, or unpredictability of losses is more cost-effective—both for individual organizations and for the economy as a whole—than is paying to finance restoration of property, liability, personnel, or net income losses.

The general techniques of risk control may be defined as follows:

- *Exposure avoidance*—abandoning or never undertaking an activity or an asset, thus reducing to absolute zero the probability of a particular loss arising from that asset or activity;
- *Loss prevention*—reducing (but not completely eliminating) the frequency of a loss from a given exposure;
- *Loss reduction*—reducing the severity or likely size of a loss from a particular exposure;
- *Segregation of exposure units*—increasing the number of independent exposure units upon which an organization relies, thus reducing the likelihood that all units will be impaired by the same accident through:
  - *separation*—dividing one exposure unit into two or more independent units, all for use in the organization's normal operations, or
  - *duplication*—maintaining duplicate or standby assets or activities, with the duplicates being used only when the ones the organization normally employs suffer loss; and
- *Contractual transfer for risk control*—shifting, as through a lease or a subcontract, to another entity the responsibility for a particular asset or activity—thus also shifting both legal and financial responsibility for any accidental losses arising out of that asset or activity.

The choice of specific risk management measures through which to apply these general risk control techniques depends, in part, on particular assumptions about how accidents are caused and, therefore, how they may be prevented or made less severe in the future. Because different sets of assumptions imply different causes of accidents—some primarily human and others primarily mechanical—differing theories of accident causation suggest different ways of removing those causes. Five widely accepted sets of assumptions, or theories, about accident causation and control are as follows:

- *The domino theory*—developed mainly from the study of workplace accidents and injuries, it presumes that accidents are the end result of a chain of falling dominoes, the central and most crucial of which represents an unsafe act or condition.
- *The energy-release theory*—views accidents as a result of uncontrolled energy impinging on animate or inanimate structures that cannot withstand that energy and suggests a number of strategies for preventing or reducing the damage that energy, once released, may cause.
- *General methods of industrial hygiene control*—suggested by studies of work injuries and illnesses, it recommends

substitution of less hazardous materials, changes in or isolation of hazardous processes, use of personal protective equipment, and other physical and administrative controls to reduce workplace accidents and illnesses.

- *Technique of Operations Review system*—views the root causes of accidents as management failures in planning, assigning responsibility and authority, supervising subordinates, and other management functions that, if correctly performed, would prevent accidental losses or reduce their severity.
- *The system safety approach*—analyzes every organization, every operation within that organization, and the economy as a whole as a system of interrelated components—all needing to function properly to prevent accidents—and tries to predict where an accident may disrupt the system and, therefore, how that accident may be prevented.

The chapters in the remainder of this text apply the risk control techniques to various property, liability, personnel, and net income losses; the specific risk control measures through which these basic techniques are applied reflect the most directly applicable theories of accident causation and control.

Chapter Notes

1. The development of the domino theory has been due primarily to the efforts of H. W. Heinrich, whose leading text, *Industrial Accident Prevention*—first published in 1931—is now in its fifth edition. The discussion under this heading draws heavily from H. W. Heinrich, Dan Petersen, and Nestor Roos, *Industrial Accident Prevention—Safety Management Approach*, 5th ed. (New York: McGraw-Hill Book Company, 1980), pp. 20-41.
2. The discussion under this heading draws heavily from Julian B. Olishifski, ed., *Fundamentals of Industrial Hygiene*, 2nd ed. (Chicago: National Safety Council, 1978), pp. 613-636.
3. The discussion under this heading draws heavily from William Haddon, Jr., M.D., "On the Escape of Tigers: An Ecologic Note," *Pathology Review*, May 1970.
4. Haddon.
5. Robert I. Mehr and Bob A. Hedges, *Risk Management: Concepts and Applications* (Homewood, IL: Richard D. Irwin, Inc., 1974), pp. 425-431.
6. The discussion under this heading draws heavily from Dan Petersen, *Techniques of Safety Management*, 2nd ed. (New York: McGraw-Hill Book Company, 1978), pp. 22-30 and 165-171.
7. Petersen, p. 18.
8. As quoted by Petersen, pp. 165-167.
9. Frank E. Bird, Jr. and Robert G. Loftus, *Loss Control Management* (Loganville, GA: International Loss Control Institute, 1976), p. 465.
10. Arthur E. Cote and Jim L. Linville, eds., *Fire Protection Handbook*, 16th ed. (Boston, MA: National Fire Protection Association, 1976), pp. 4-43.

APPENDIX

Review of Some Quantitative Techniques for Risk Control

The techniques of data analysis and decision making employed throughout the ARM curriculum, and therefore essential to the study of risk control in ARM 55, were first presented in ARM 54. This Appendix summarizes these techniques for ARM 55 students who have not taken ARM 54 or who wish to refresh their recollection of these techniques. This Appendix is an integral part of the material assigned in ARM 55—knowledge of the techniques it reviews, or applications of these techniques, may be required on the ARM 55 national examination.

Many risk control decisions—particularly those dealing with where to focus risk control activities or which risk control measures to adopt—first, require forecasts of accidental losses and second, projections of cash flows and rates of return that can be expected from commitments of resources to loss control. Therefore, this Appendix reviews techniques for forecasting losses and for evaluating investment alternatives.

FORECASTING ACCIDENTAL LOSSES

Need for Forecasting

Many business decisions and much executive thought often appear to be based on the false assumption that the future is perfectly predictable and static. Managers frequently make statements like "if we invest in this machine, it will raise our annual output by X units and lower our unit cost of production from $Y to $Z for each of the next ten years." Based on such statements, many managers then compare such

35

a machine with others about which they often make equally confident statements.

If questioned closely and asked to be more precise in their thinking, many of these executives recognize the assumptions underlying such statements. They grant that the statement assumes that (1) the machine will be productive for ten years, no more and no less; (2) all other cost factors will remain unchanged, so that only the changes brought about by this machine need to be considered in deciding whether to purchase it; and (3) customers will continue to want the products related to this machine and will continue to pay the same price for those products, so that the per unit revenue from the machine will remain unchanged. In their defense, these executives may quite correctly claim that assumptions based on a known, unchanging world simplify their investment decisions.

Economists and other analysts of business decisions have labeled such assumptions *ceteris paribus*, Latin for "everything else remains unchanged" and can be predicted with absolute certainty. *Ceteris paribus* is a most useful assumption because it permits the conceptualization, as in Exhibit 1A-1, of an organization's costs and revenues under varying conditions. In Exhibit 1A-1, the downward sloping marginal revenue (MR) line in the upper portion of the diagram depicts the projected amount of *additional*, that is, marginal, revenue that in classical *ceteris paribus* economics is assumed a firm can earn by selling each additional unit of its product or service. The marginal cost (MC) line in this same portion of the exhibit indicates the presumed *additional* cost of producing each unit—again, a cost that in classical economics is generally assumed to be known with certainty. Marginal revenue is presumed to decline because, as consumers' desires for a product or service are more fully satisfied with greater output, they are willing to pay less for each additional, less needed unit. The shape of the MC line is determined by the fact that (1) the cost of the first item produced includes substantial start-up costs, (2) the marginal (additional) cost of each unit declines as efficiency increases until short-term capacity is reached, and (3) for still larger quantities, marginal cost rises in the short run as some existing productive resource (such as land and equipment or managerial skill) becomes overtaxed. This reduces operating efficiency (and raises the cost of each additional unit) as output even further increases.

Profit is the excess of revenue over cost. In this classical analysis, profit is maximized by increasing output until rising marginal cost equals falling marginal revenue. Below the maximum profit point, E in the upper portion of the exhibit, the marginal (additional) revenue generated by producing one more unit still exceeds the additional cost of that unit, indicating that profit can be increased by raising output.

However, for additional output beyond level E, marginal cost exceeds marginal revenue, thus reducing profit. The same result is shown in the lower portion of Exhibit 1A-1, where the total revenue (TR) and total cost (TC) lines cumulate the per unit marginal results in the upper portion of the diagram. The greatest distance between the total revenue and total cost curves in this lower diagram corresponds to the output level for point E in the upper portion of the diagram, where marginal cost equals marginal revenue.

If costs can be known with certainty, and if the world does not change, output level E maximizes profit for a profit-seeking organization. (For a nonprofit organization, the output level E allows the organization to achieve the greatest budget surplus or to generate the greatest output within a given budget.) Therefore, the total profit (TP) line in the lower portion of the exhibit, which shows the distance by which the TR line rises above the TC line, peaks at output level E. (Note that profit is negative at very low output, where total revenue does not yet balance high start-up costs, and in very high outputs where excessive marginal costs swamp declining marginal revenues.)

In reality, however, the world is not static but dynamic. Change makes an organization's revenues and costs much less precisely predictable than the classical analysis suggests. Some changes, as in technology, consumer tastes, the costs of raw materials and other productive inputs, and government regulations, are external to an organization and may affect its revenues or costs favorably or unfavorably. Other internal factors also may have similar effects on revenues and costs. Some of these internal factors are the direct concern of risk management. The more obvious factors are the effects that accidental losses and the costs of recovering from them may have on the organization's revenues and costs. For example, an accident striking the organization or a key supplier may reduce the organization's revenues or increase its costs, thus cutting the organization's profitability. (Conversely, favorable events, which are not typically a concern of risk management, may increase the organization's profits beyond predicted levels by either increasing the organization's revenues or decreasing its costs.)

The economic possibilities that can occur in a changing world are graphed in Exhibit 1A-2, which is an adaptation of the upper portion of Exhibit 1A-1 dealing with marginal revenues and costs projected for various levels of output. In Exhibit 1A-2, the marginal revenue and marginal cost curves of Exhibit 1A-1 are shown as ranges of possible outcomes, not as single-value predictions, for any given output. These ranges, created by uncertainty and change, make decisions less precise and goal achievement less clearly defined.

The original marginal revenue and marginal cost curves from

Exhibit 1A-1
Profit Maximization with No Uncertainty and No Dynamic Change*

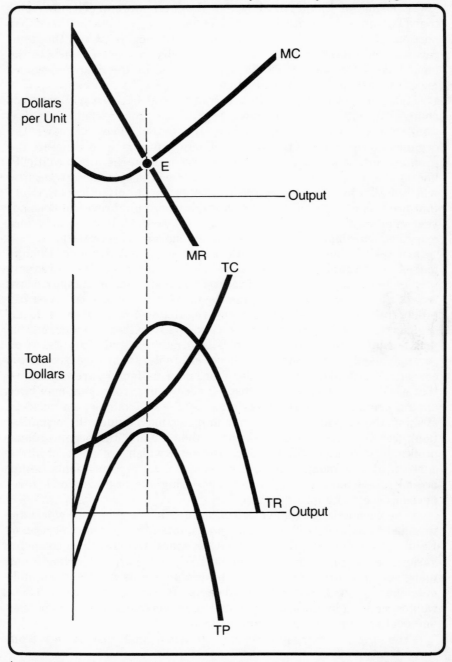

* Adapted with permission from Paul A. Samuelson, *Economics*, 11th ed. (NY: McGraw-Hill Book Co., 1980), p. 469.

Exhibit 1A-1 are shown in Exhibit 1A-2 as the curves, MR_1 and MC_1. Each is bordered by two additional MR or MC curves. Revenue and cost results less favorable than the single-value projections (MR_1 and MC_1) are shown as MR_2 and MC_2—lower revenues and higher costs than originally forecast. Results more favorable than those originally anticipated, higher revenues and lower costs, are portrayed by the MR_3 and MC_3 curves. Exhibit 1A-2 indicates that if favorable revenue results combined with favorable cost results at E_G, the organization can maximize profits by planning an output of O_G. If unfavorable revenues combine with unfavorable costs, then the organization can maximize profits by planning an output of O_B, which is shown on the horizontal output axis as significantly less than O_G, and revenue conditions. Because of changes and the managerial uncertainty they create, an organization's senior executives may not be able to decide in advance to plan for output of O_G or O_B. Not being certain exactly what output to target, the organization's managers may not be able to maximize its actual profits.

The activities of management can be viewed as an attempt to make more precise decisions by reducing uncertainty and adjusting for changes. (Uncertainty in Exhibit 1A-2 is approximately the rectangular area, UE_BLE_G, anywhere within which the ideal profit maximizing output level E may fall.) This rectangle can be reduced by narrowing the range of possible outcomes around the classical MR_1 and MC_1 curves, thus reducing the gap between O_B and O_G. In general, reducing this gap helps management to be more certain and precise about making decisions. The purpose of such decisions is to bring profitability as close as possible to the "ideal" (Point E) shown in Exhibit 1A-1.

As a specialty within the general field of management, risk management deals primarily with the particular set of dynamics and uncertainties associated with situations that scholars refer to as "pure risks." Pure risks derive from those situations that can have only two types of outcomes, status quo or a loss, but no gain. In contrast, situations involving "speculative risks" present three possible outcomes, the status quo, a loss, or a gain. Organizations are said to seek speculative risks for the gains they offer. They must also tolerate or endure pure risks as a cost that inevitably accompanies the attempt to secure the potential benefits of speculative risks. Sound risk management strives to minimize and to make more predictable the costs associated with pure risks and with accidental losses. Risk control pursues this objective by reducing the frequency or severity of accidental losses; risk financing seeks this same goal by providing funds—reliably and at a low cost—for financing recovery from those losses that cannot be wholly prevented.

Reaching this risk control objective must therefore reduce uncer-

Exhibit 1A-2
Profit Maximization with Uncertainty and Dynamics

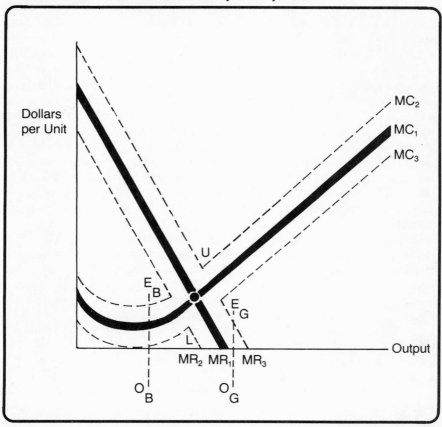

tainties about the occurrence and financing of recovery from accidental losses. This would narrow the ranges around the MR and MC curves in Exhibit 1A-2, bringing them closer to the ideal (Point E) shown in Exhibit 1A-1. Providing cost-effective, dependable risk control requires the best feasible predictions of (1) the frequency and severity of the losses from which the organization will need to finance recovery, and (2) the effects that alternative risk control measures will have on the present value of the organization's expected net cash flows.

Forecasting Techniques

Forecasting accidental losses or any other future event requires detecting past patterns and projecting them into the future. These patterns may be as simple as "no change." Studying the *Farmers'* *Almanac* suggests, more often than not, that tomorrow's weather can safely be presumed to be the same as today's. There also may be much truth in saying that this year's accidental losses for a particular organization will be about the same as last year's.

The pattern for the future may also be one of change. The advance of a cold front may signal more severe weather tomorrow. Plans to increase factory output may foretell a greater number of injuries to employees. Furthermore, if inflation is projected to continue, each of these employee injuries may be more costly next year. Even when the pattern is one of change, there are often important, constant elements: the frequency of work injuries may be predictably related to output levels, and the rate at which inflation increases the financial impact of a given injury may continue past inflationary trends. Thus, forecasting future losses by finding these patterns begins with deciding which of two basic patterns, "no change" or "change in a predictable way," applies. Under "no change" patterns, probability analysis is particularly appropriate for forecasting losses; under "change in a predictable way," regression analysis is the better choice.

Probability analysis is particularly effective when an organization has a substantial volume of data on past losses and fairly stable operations, which seem to suggest that patterns of past losses will continue in the future. In such a basically unchanging environment, past losses may be viewed as a sample of all possible losses that the organization could have suffered in the past and may suffer in the future. The larger this sample and the more stable the environment that has produced it, the more reliable the forecasts of future losses will be.

Like probability analysis, regression (or "trend") analysis looks for patterns in past losses and then projects these patterns into the future. Regression analysis looks for patterns of movement—changes in loss frequency or severity that may tend to move together with changes in some other variable (such as time production or employment) that is easier to forecast accurately than is loss experience.

Probability Analysis For forecasting the frequency and severity of losses, probability analysis is appropriate where the basic forces presumed to cause losses are not expected to change. These forces include the nature of the organization's operations, the technology and personnel it employs, and its physical environment. (Changes in price levels are not relevant here, because price changes alter only the "measuring stick" by which the financial severity of losses, not their physical severity or frequency, is measured.) Probability analysis begins with gathering as large a body of consistent historical loss data as possible. Presumably, data are drawn from a static "constant" probability distribution. These data will be used to estimate the parameters—principally the arithmetic mean and standard deviation—of the probability distribution that is presumed to persist in the future. (In contrast, the regression analysis to be discussed presumes a much more dynamic world with changing causes of losses.)

Probability is the relative frequency with which an event can be expected to occur in the long run in a stable environment. For example, given many tosses, a coin can be expected to come up "heads" as often as it comes up "tails." Given many rolls of one die from a pair of dice, a "4" can be expected to come up one-sixth of the time. According to one standard mortality table, slightly more than 2 percent of men who are sixty-two years old can be expected to die before reaching sixty-three.[1] Finally, of the many automobiles now on the road, insurance company statistics in 1981 indicated that 1 out of every 153 could be expected to be stolen within the year.[2]

Any probability can be expressed as a fraction. The probability of a "head" on a coin toss can be expressed as $\frac{1}{2}$, 50 percent, or 0.50. The probability of a "4" on one roll of one die can be expressed as $\frac{1}{6}$, $16\frac{2}{3}$ percent, or 0.167. Similarly, $\frac{1}{153}$, 0.654 percent, or 0.00654 are each proper ways of indicating the probability that a particular automobile would have been stolen during 1981. The probability of an event that is totally impossible is 0, the probability of an absolutely certain event is 1.0, and the probabilities of all events that are neither totally impossible nor absolutely certain are greater than 0 but less than 1.0.

Probabilities can be developed from theoretical considerations or from historical data. Probabilities associated with coin tosses or dice throws can be developed theoretically and are constant given the unchanging physical properties of devices like coins and dice. Probabilities associated with events such as the occurrence and frequency of car thefts must be developed from historical data, which, when considered together, will create a sample from which similar events may be predicted. While theoretical probabilities are always accurate, probabilities developed from historical data depend for their accuracy on sample size and representativeness. They are also subject to change as the data changes. Therefore, in order to maintain the accuracy of historically determined probabilities, the new data must be fed into the analysis as a "constant."

Characteristics of Probability Distributions. A probability distribution is a representation in a table or in a graph of all possible outcomes of a particular set of circumstances and of the probability of each possible outcome. Because every such distribution includes the probability of every possible outcome, which makes it certain that one and only one of these outcomes will occur, the sum of the probabilities in a complete probability distribution *must* be 1.0.

In addition to these definitional features, probability distributions are also described in terms of two other characteristics, central tendency and dispersion. The *central tendency* of a probability distribution is the single outcome within the distribution which, in some sense, is the "most representative" of all possible outcomes. The central tendency of a distribution may or may not correspond to the value directly beneath the hump of the distribution, depending on which measure of central tendency is used and on whether the distribution is "balanced" or symmetrical. The second characteristic, *dispersion*, describes the extent to which the distribution is spread out, rather than concentrated at a single outcome.

Central Tendency. Most probability distributions cluster around a particular value, which may or may not be in the exact center of the range of the distribution. This value often is used as the most representative outcome and, as stated, is referred to as central tendency. The three most widely accepted ways of identifying or measuring this most representative outcome are the *arithmetic mean,* the *median,* and the *mode.*

The arithmetic mean of a distribution is a more precise name for the common "average," which is the sum of the items in the distribution divided by the number of items. Calculating the arithmetic mean of a probability distribution is only slightly more complex: each outcome is multiplied by its respective probability, and the sum of these products is the mean of the distribution, or its "expected value." This procedure weights each value of the distribution by its probability, and the arithmetic mean (or expected value) of the distribution is this weighted average.

The second measure of central tendency is the median. The median of a series of numbers or of a probability distribution is the "value in the middle," that is, the value for which the number of lower observations or outcomes equals the number of higher observations. (When the number of observations or outcomes is an even number, the median is the arithmetic mean of the middle two.) The median of a probability distribution is the value for which the probability of higher outcomes is equal to the probability of lower outcomes. This value can be found by summing the cumulative probabilities in the distribution to find the outcome for which a cumulative probability of 50 percent is reached.

The third measure of central tendency is the mode. The mode of either a series of numbers or of a probability distribution is the single value that occurs most frequently. When a distribution has a single "hump" (or is unimodal), the mode is the value of the outcome directly beneath the peak of that "hump." For historical statistics on losses, no single precise dollar amount or exact number of annual losses may occur more frequently than any other specific quantity. However, if the losses are grouped, for example, into frequency classes such as 0 to 10, 11 to 20—or into severity classes like under $1,000, $1,001 to $2,000, and so on—then one of these classes will contain the greatest number of losses. This class, then, can properly be called the modal class of the frequency or loss severity distribution.

Dispersion (Variability).   The second important characteristic of a probability distribution is its dispersion. This is the degree of variability around the mean or other essential tendency of the distribution. The less the dispersion of the distribution, the greater the likelihood that actual results will fall within a given range of that central tendency. Thus, less dispersion means less uncertainty in predicting that a result close to that central point will actually occur.

The most widely used measure of dispersion is the standard deviation. The standard deviation of a set of numbers is the square root of the average of the squared deviation of each number from the arithmetic mean of these numbers. It is a special kind of average, an average of deviations (or differences) between individuals, varied values, and the arithmetic mean of those values. The precise method for computing a standard deviation depends on whether the numbers whose standard deviation is sought are individual historical outcomes (such as the amounts of actual losses) or are, instead, values within a probability distribution (like the probability of a loss in the $5,001 to $10,000 class).

The following steps are used to find the standard deviation of a set of individual observations not involving probabilities:

1. Find the arithmetic mean of the observations (the sum of the observations divided by the number of observations).
2. Subtract the mean from each of the observations (with the result being positive for each observation larger than the mean and negative for each observation smaller than the mean).
3. Square each of the resulting differences (the rules of algebra making all resulting squares positive).
4. Find this sum of these squares.
5. Divide this sum by the number of observations minus one. (The theoretical justification for subtracting one is beyond the educational objectives of this course.)
6. Find the square root of the resulting quotient.

The following procedure is used to find the standard deviation for a probability distribution:

1. Find the expected value (arithmetic or mean) of the distribution.
2. Subtract this expected value from each outcome in the distribution.
3. Square each of the resulting differences.
4. Multiply each resulting square by the probability associated with the outcome for which the squared difference was computed in step 3.
5. Sum the resulting products.
6. Find the square root of the resulting sum.

The Normal Distribution—A Special Case. The normal distribution is a particular type of probability distribution that applies to a wide variety of physical phenomena involving variations around some central, average, or expected value. To illustrate, the useful lives of the belts that connect a series of machine tool lathes to their central power source are governed by a normal probability distribution. Each belt has a particular average or expected life before it will break, and the variability from belt to belt around this average is described by a normal probability distribution. Scheduling belt replacements often enough so that the probability of a belt breaking while in use is small requires knowing not only the arithmetic mean but also the standard deviation of the normal distribution of belt life.

In all normal distributions certain percentages of all outcomes fall within a given number of standard deviations above or below the mean of the distribution. As shown in Exhibit 1A-3, 34.13 percent of all outcomes fall within one standard deviation below the mean. By addition and because all normal distributions are symmetrical around this mean, 68.26 percent of all outcomes are within one standard deviation above or below the mean. The portion of a normal distribution that is between one and two standard deviations above the mean contains 13.59 percent of all outcomes, as does the portion between one and two standard deviations below the mean. Therefore, the area between the mean and two standard deviations above the mean contains 47.72 percent (34.13 + 13.59 percent) of all outcomes, and another 47.72 percent are two standard deviations or less below the mean. Consequently, 95.44 percent (twice 47.72 percent) of all outcomes are within two standard deviations above or below the mean.

Similarly, 2.15 percent of all outcomes are between two and three standard deviations above the mean, and another 2.15 percent are between two and three deviations below the mean. Thus, 49.87 percent (34.13 + 13.59 + 2.15 percent) of all outcomes are three standard deviations or less below the mean. The portion of the distribution

Exhibit 1A-3

The Normal Distribution — Percentages of Outcomes Within Specified Standard Deviations of the Mean

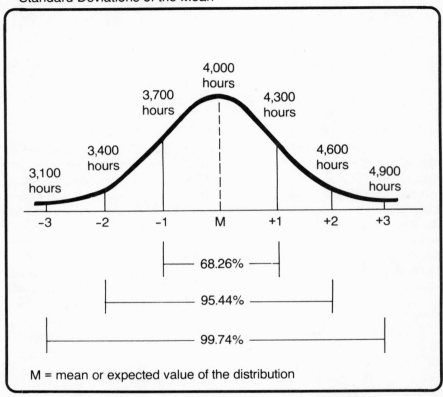

M = mean or expected value of the distribution

between three standard deviations above the mean and three standard deviations below the mean contains 99.74 percent (twice 49.87 percent) of all outcomes. Only 0.26 percent (100 percent − 99.74 percent) of all outcomes lie beyond three standard deviations from the mean, and these are divided equally—0.13 percent above the mean and 0.13 percent below it.

To understand these relationships, recall the machine belts, each of which has an expected arithmetic mean life of 4,000 hours with a standard deviation of 300 hours. If replacement of these belts is scheduled for their "expected life," after 4,000 hours of use, then there is a 50 percent chance that a belt will break before its scheduled replacement. However, if each belt is changed after only 3,700 hours of use (one standard deviation below the mean), then there is only a 15.87 percent (50 percent − 34.13 percent) chance that a belt will break before being changed. If this probability of breakage is still too high, then changing each belt after 3,400 hours of use (two standard deviations below the mean) reduces the probability of breakage to only 2.28 percent, the portion of any normal distribution that is more than two standard deviations below the mean. (This probability can be calculated as 50 percent minus the sum of 34.13 percent and 13.59 percent.) A more cautious practice would be to change belts routinely after only 3,100 hours (three standard deviations below the mean) so that the probability of a belt breaking before replacement would be only 0.13 percent, slightly more than one change in 1,000.

Probability Calculations. Probability calculations usually are expressed in some generally useful symbols. The symbol p() means "probability of" the term in parentheses, so that p(A) means "the probability of A" occurring in a given time period, where A represents any specified event. Similarly, p(A + B) means "the probability of A and B" occurring in a given period. The symbol p(A or B) means the "probability that either A or B, or possibly both" will occur in a given period. This notation is flexible because any event or combination of events can be specified in the parentheses.

The symbol n appears frequently in probability distributions to designate the number of separate units from which a probability is developed or to which it is applied. The symbol m represents the number of these units that experience a particular event that is of interest. In a risk management context, n typically designates the number of exposures from which an empirical probability of loss is derived, and m indicates the number of exposures actually suffering loss. Thus, the general equation for the probability of a loss can be expressed as:

$$p(loss) = m/n$$

By algebraic manipulation, m—the expected number of losses—becomes:

$$m = expected\ loss\ frequency = np$$

The concept of a long-run expected value is so common in working with probabilities that the symbol E() is used to express "the expected number or value" of the event specified in the parentheses. For example, if n exposure units are subject to the probability, p, of loss annually, then the expected number of losses per year, E(L), can be expressed as:

$$E(L) = np$$

which can be read as "the expected annual number of losses equals the number of exposure units times the probability of loss to any one unit."

. An important assumption in computing probabilities is that an event either occurs or does not occur—there are no other possibilities. These two alternatives are mutually exclusive; together they exhaust all possibilities. Therefore, the probability of any event, p(A), occurring and the probability of it not occurring, p(not A), add to one. For example, if the probability of loss to one unit in one year is 0.000950, then the probability that there will be no loss to that unit that year is 0.999050. In general:

$$p(A) + p(\text{not } A) = 1.$$

and, by algebraic manipulation:

$$p(A) = 1 - p(\text{not } A)$$
$$p(\text{not } A) = 1 - p(A)$$

This basic notation is used in all probability analyses. Two applications most useful in risk management are computations of joint probabilities (the probability that two or more events will occur together at a given time) and of alternative probabilities (the probability that any one of two or more events will occur in a given time period). A joint probability is a probability that two or more events will happen within a given time. Before computing a joint probability, it is necessary to determine whether these events are independent. Two events, A and B, are independent if the occurrence or nonoccurrence of one does not affect the probability that the other will or will not occur. If A and B are independent, the probability of A is unchanged by the occurrence or nonoccurrence of B. Similarly, the probability of B is unchanged by the occurrence or nonoccurrence of A. For example, the probabilities that two buildings, widely distant from one another, will burn are independent of each other because a fire at one will not endanger the other. However, if the two buildings are close enough together that fire can spread from one to the other, their probabilities of loss from that fire are not independent. Specifically, each building alone may have a 3 percent chance of fire in a given year. But if the buildings are close together, a fire in one of them will raise the probability of fire in the other.

For independent events, the joint probability that all the events will occur in a given period is the product of their separate probabilities of occurring in that period. That is, if the two buildings just mentioned are distant, then the probability that both will burn in a year, p(2 fires), is equal to the probability of one, p(F1), times the probability of fire in the other, p(F2). Consequently:

$$p(2 \text{ fires}) = p(F1)p(F2)$$
$$p(2 \text{ fires}) = (0.03)(0.03) = 0.0009$$

For probabilities of dependent events—such as fires in both buildings if they are close together—the joint probability that both will burn is determined by multiplying the probability of fire in one building times the probability of fire in the second, given that there already is a fire in the first. This second probability, known as a conditional probability, can be expressed as P(F2 F1). If this conditional probability is 0.25, then, continuing with the same example, the probability of a fire in the first building followed by a fire in the second is determined by:

$$p(F1 \text{ followed by } F2) =$$
$$p(F1)p(F \ F1) =$$
$$(0.03)(0.25) = 0.0075$$

Notice that this calculation is used to find the probability of a particular sequence of events, a fire in the first building followed by a fire in the second. It is not the probability of any other sequence of events, such as a fire in the second building spreading back to a fire in the first, nor does it include any allowance for the independent and simultaneous but not causal occurrence of both events. Thus, in dealing with joint probabilities of dependent events, it is crucial to specify both the nature of the events, their sequence, and whether or not it was causal.

Along with joint probabilities of the combined occurrences of several events, risk management sometimes calls for the calculation of alternative probabilities of at least one (or more) of several events occurring in a given time period. Computing alternative probability requires knowing if the events are mutually exclusive. Two or more events are mutually exclusive if the occurrence of one makes the occurrence of any of the others impossible. For example, the occurrence of a fire loss and theft loss on the same day are not mutually exclusive events—both may happen on the same day. In contrast, the dollar amount an organization might suffer next year will be either (1) less than $5,000 or (2) $5,000 or more. These two categories of loss size are mutually exclusive.

For mutually exclusive events, the probability that either one will occur in a given time is the sum of their respective probabilities for occurring during that time. For example, assuming that a building cannot be destroyed both by fire and by flood in the same year and also that the probability of destruction by fire is 0.01 and by flood is 0.02, then the probability that the building will be destroyed by either flood or fire next year is 0.03. In general, for mutually exclusive events A and B, the alternative probability of one or the other occurring is:

$$p(A \text{ or } B) = p(A) + p(B)$$

When two or more events are not mutually exclusive, when more than one of them can occur in a given time period, care must be taken not to overstate the probability that at least one of them will occur. Such overstatement is common because of the mistaken "double accounting" of the joint probability of two or more of these alternative events. For events that are not mutually exclusive, the probability that at least one of them—and possibly both or all—will occur is the sum of their separate probabilities minus their joint probability.

The following example illustrates this concept. Assume that the probability of pilferage loss to goods in transit is 0.09, and the probability of a flood loss to these goods is 0.06 on a particular trip. It follows that the probability of loss by pilferage, water damage, *or both*, is:

$$
\begin{aligned}
p(\text{pilferage or water damage or both}) &= 0.09 + 0.06 - (0.09)(0.06) \\
&= 0.15 - 0.0054 \\
&= 0.1446
\end{aligned}
$$

To compute the probability of pilferage or water damage, *but not both*, sum the probabilities of the two mutually exclusive ways that this result can occur. These are the probabilities of pilferage but no water damage and water damage but no pilferage. (Recall that the probability of an event not occurring equals one minus the probability of its occurring.) Computing these two probabilities and finding their sum yields:

p(pilferage but no water damage) = (0.09)(1 − 0.06)
= (0.09)(0.94)
= 0.0846

p(water damage but no pilferage) = (0.06) (1 − 0.09)
= (0.06)(0.91)
= 0.0546

Therefore, p(pilferage or water damage but not both) = 0.0846 + 0.0546 = 0.1392. The probability of either kind of damage but not both is smaller than the probability of either kind of damage and possibly both because the first probability excludes the chance of a mutual occurrence.

Summary of Probability Analysis. If the world can be assumed to be stable, and then all past losses are only a sample of all possible losses, and that sample may or may not be representative. However, the greater the number of past losses, the larger the sample, and the more reliable the forecasts of future losses can be. The discussion about the basics of probability analysis has assumed such a stable world in which the causes of loss remain the same. In contrast, the explanation of how to forecast losses by regression assumes a more dynamic world.

Regression Analysis Like probability analysis, regression analysis looks for patterns in past losses or other events and then projects these patterns into the future. Unlike probability analysis, however, regression looks for patterns of movement. For example, changes in loss frequency or severity may tend to move together with changes in some other variable (such as time measured in years or production in volumes of output), which is easier to forecast accurately than is loss experience. Regression analysis is also often called trend analysis, a name that reflects the fact that two or more trends—one more easily predictable than the other—tend to move together. Knowing one trend helps forecast the other.

Common sense trending can be done simply by charting some points on a graph and then connecting them with a straight or curved line that seems to fit. An example of such a trend line appears in

Exhibit 1A-4
Generalized Form of Hand-Drawn Linear Trend Line

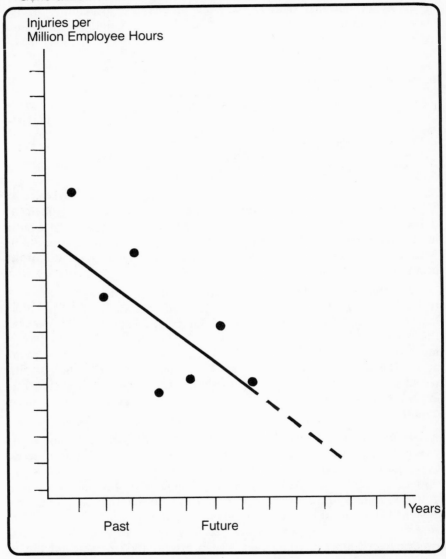

Exhibit 1A-4. It shows the improving loss experience of a firm whose work injury rate has been declining (as shown by the solid portion of the trend line) and presumably will continue declining as suggested by the dashed portion of the line.

Regression analysis (technically, linear regression because only straight lines are calculated) involves computing the two determinants of a straight line which best "fits" the available data. The general equation for any straight line is:

$$Y = a + bX$$

where Y is the dependent variable, graphed vertically and to be predicted (such as loss frequency or severity), and X is the independent variable, graphed horizontally and used as a basis for forecasting the dependent variable. The value for a represents the point at which the straight regression trend line intersects the vertical Y axis; and the value for b represents the slope of the line (the amount by which the line rises and falls for each unit change in the independent variable, X). The letter a or b may be either positive or negative. A positive b value indicates an increasing trend, and a negative b value indicates a decreasing trend. The independent variable, X, can be any factor (time, production, sales, number of trips, or personnel) that is quite readily known or predictable and that has some reasonable relationship with the dependent variable to be forecast.

Regression computations first involve gathering historical data on the joint movements of the independent and dependent variables, such as annual output, X, and annual number of losses, Y, as shown in Columns (1) and (2) in the upper portion of Exhibit 1A-5. Second, the values shown in Columns (3) and (4) in this Exhibit are computed; and third, the totals of these four columns are used to compute values for a and b using the following general equations:

$$a = \frac{(\text{Sum } y)(\text{Sum } x^2) - (\text{Sum } x)(\text{Sum } xy)}{n(\text{Sum } x^2) - (\text{Sum } x)^2}$$

$$b = \frac{n(\text{Sum } xy) - (\text{Sum } x)(\text{Sum } y)}{n(\text{Sum } x^2) - (\text{Sum } x)^2}$$

In these equations, n indicates the number of data points—four in this case—that is, the number of paired X and Y values. For clarity, these formulas also use the symbol, Sum, to mean the sum of the variable following the symbol. For example, Sum Y means the sum of the annual number of losses, nineteen in all. The resulting equation: Y = 2.46 + 0.035X can be interpreted as the annual number of losses, Y can be expected to be 2.46 plus 0.035 times annual output (measured in

Exhibit 1A-5
Computation of Linear Regression Line

(1)	(2)	(3)	(4)
Output (x 100)	Annual Number of Losses		
(x)	(y)	(xy)	(x)²
35	4	140	1,225
60	4	240	3,600
72	5	360	5,184
95	6	570	9,025
262	19	1,310	19,034

$$a = \frac{(19)(19,034) - (262)(1,310)}{4(19,034) - (262)} \qquad b = \frac{4(1,310) - (262)(19)}{4(19,034) - (262)}$$

$$= \frac{361,556 - 343,200}{76,136 - 68,644} \qquad = \frac{5,240 - 4,978}{76,136 - 68,644}$$

$$= \frac{18,426}{7,492} \qquad = \frac{562}{7,492}$$

$$= 2.46 \qquad = 0.035$$

some convenient unit such as hundreds of tons). For example, if the organization's output were 8,500 tons, the number of losses it would be reasonable to forecast would be:

$$Y = 2.46 + 85(0.035)$$
$$= 2.46 + 2.975$$
$$= 5.435 \text{ losses}$$

Fractional losses being impossible (there may be five or six loss occurrences, but nothing in between), a reasonable forecast would be five losses in a year when the firm produced 85 units of output (each unit being 100 tons).

While arithmetically correct, these values may not be valid for very low or very high output. The use of mathematics must therefore be accompanied by common sense, for example, not extending a regression line too far beyond the limits of past occurrences.

EVALUATING INVESTMENT ALTERNATIVES

Cash enables an organization to obtain resources to fulfill its objectives. Cash—or more precisely, purchasing power, including credit—is a *necessary* means to *all* other ends. The net cash flow during any period measures an organization's ability to function effectively during that period and in the future. Therefore, in selecting uses for an organization's resources, senior management should give priority to commitments that promise the greatest net cash flow.

Concept of Present Value of Expected Annual After-Tax Net Cash Flow

An organization's net cash flow during any period is its cash receipts minus its cash disbursements for that period. If cash receipts exceed disbursements, net cash flow is positive; if disbursements exceed receipts, it is negative. Projecting how net cash flows are likely to be generated by alternative assets or activities provides an organization's management with a valid criterion for choosing where to invest to obtain the expected present value of the organization's future net cash flows.

In selecting an asset or activity, an organization must at least initially also take the loss exposures created by that asset or activity. How the organization chooses to cope with these loss exposures through any one or a combination of management techniques affects the cash flows from that asset or activity and thus also influences the net cash flow from the activity or asset. An organization maximizes its operating efficiency—expressed as profits for a profit-seeking organization and as budget surpluses or maximum output within a given budget for a nonprofit organization—by selecting that combination of assets and activities that, when coupled with the most cost effective combination of risk management techniques, maximizes the expected present value of the organization's future net cash flow. Applying this decision rule in selecting risk control techniques requires an understanding of (1) expected net cash flows, (2) present value of net cash flows, (3) annual after-tax net cash flows, and (4) the special tax status of certain organizations.

Expected Net Cash Flows An expected value is the arithmetic mean or average of a series of numbers or of a probability distribution. Several probability distributions are implicit in the projection of the future net cash flows from an organization's business activities. These may include probabilities of consumer demand and resulting revenues, of cash expenses, and of dividend and other distributions to stockholders and/or other owners. The organization's actual net cash flow for a future period is the joint outcome of the events covered by these probability distributions. Risk management introduces comparable probability distributions for the combined effects of (1) accidental losses and (2) the risk management techniques for managing them. Traditional managerial finance largely has ignored risk management concerns.

The best single estimate of the outcome of each of these probability distributions is the arithmetic mean of that distribution; therefore, the net cash flow generated by the arithmetic mean outcomes of the probability distribution is referred to as the "expected net cash flow." There is no assurance that the expected net cash flow actually will materialize in the next accounting period, but this expected value is the single best estimate for any one future period. Therefore, in the long run, the best decisions, the ones which have the greatest chance of being accurate, are based on these expected values.

Present Value of Net Cash Flow Some assets or activities require cash expenditures and generate cash receipts all in a single accounting period. For example, a food processing firm is likely to buy raw materials or merchandise inventory to process and sell much of this inventory in the same accounting period. For such operations, cash inflows and outflows tend to match period for period, and there is little concern for what is known as the "time value of money." However, other assets or activities are likely to entail current cash expenditures (as well as future expenditures) that can be expected to generate cash receipts only in the future. When cash receipts and expenditures are spread over several accounting periods, these cash flows must be "discounted" for their distance into the future. This discounting reduces all future cash inflows and outflows to "present values," thereby reflecting the "time value of money." A dollar presently available, or "in hand," has a greater time value than does a dollar to be received in the future because the dollar in hand can be invested to start earning money now. In contrast, a dollar to be received in the future cannot be invested to generate earnings until that future date. The greater the rate of return a dollar in hand can earn, the greater is its value relative to a future dollar, and the lesser is the value of the future dollar relative to the present dollar. Conversely, the longer it will be until a future dollar is received, the less is its present value when compared with the value of a dollar in hand. It follows that the present value of a dollar varies inversely with the interest rate the dollar could earn if currently in hand and when in the future the dollar is to be received.

To properly evaluate a business proposal, as for an investment, in terms of the present value of the cash inflows and outflows that can be expected from that proposal, it is important to know how to compute the present value of (1) a present payment, (2) a single future payment, (3) a series of equal future payments, and (4) a series of unequal future payments.

The present value of a *present payment* (the value of a current receipt or disbursement) is the face amount of that payment; no discounting is required. The present value of a *single future payment* can be found by referring to a "present value table" as shown in Exhibit 1A-6. This type of table indicates the amount that must be invested today at a given interest rate for a given number of years to generate $1 as a single payment at the end of that number of years. Similarly, a table such as Exhibit 1A-7 accumulates the individual present values from Exhibit 1A-6 to give the present value of a series of *equal future payments*. This present value is the sum that must be invested today at a given annual interest rate to generate $1 at the end of each of the next specified number of years, when the initial investment and the interest earned will have been exhausted. The present value of a series of *unequal future payments* can be found by multiplying the face amount of each future payment by the appropriate present value factor from Exhibit 1A-6 and then summing the present values of these individual payments to find the present value of the entire stream.

Annual After-Tax Net Cash Flow In and of itself, the net cash flow from an investment made in any year or other given period is equal

Exhibit 1A-6
Present Value of $1 Received at the End of Period

Years Hence	1%	2%	4%	6%	8%	10%	12%	14%	15%	16%
1	0.990	0.980	0.962	0.943	0.926	0.909	0.893	0.877	0.870	0.862
2	0.980	0.961	0.925	0.890	0.857	0.826	0.797	0.769	0.756	0.743
3	0.971	0.942	0.889	0.840	0.794	0.751	0.712	0.675	0.658	0.641
4	0.961	0.924	0.855	0.792	0.735	0.683	0.636	0.592	0.572	0.552
5	0.951	0.906	0.822	0.747	0.681	0.621	0.567	0.519	0.497	0.476
6	0.942	0.888	0.790	0.705	0.630	0.564	0.507	0.456	0.432	0.410
7	0.933	0.871	0.760	0.665	0.583	0.513	0.452	0.400	0.376	0.354
8	0.923	0.853	0.731	0.627	0.540	0.467	0.404	0.351	0.327	0.305
9	0.914	0.837	0.703	0.592	0.500	0.424	0.361	0.308	0.284	0.263
10	0.905	0.820	0.676	0.558	0.463	0.386	0.322	0.270	0.247	0.227
11	0.896	0.804	0.650	0.527	0.429	0.350	0.287	0.237	0.215	0.195
12	0.887	0.788	0.625	0.497	0.397	0.319	0.257	0.208	0.187	0.168
13	0.879	0.773	0.601	0.469	0.368	0.290	0.229	0.182	0.163	0.145
14	0.870	0.758	0.577	0.442	0.340	0.263	0.205	0.160	0.141	0.125
15	0.861	0.743	0.555	0.417	0.315	0.239	0.183	0.140	0.123	0.108
16	0.853	0.728	0.534	0.394	0.292	0.218	0.163	0.123	0.107	0.093
17	0.844	0.714	0.513	0.371	0.270	0.198	0.146	0.108	0.093	0.080
18	0.836	0.700	0.494	0.350	0.250	0.180	0.130	0.095	0.081	0.069
19	0.828	0.686	0.475	0.331	0.232	0.164	0.116	0.083	0.070	0.060
20	0.820	0.673	0.456	0.312	0.215	0.149	0.104	0.073	0.061	0.051
21	0.811	0.660	0.439	0.294	0.199	0.135	0.093	0.064	0.053	0.044
22	0.803	0.647	0.422	0.278	0.184	0.123	0.083	0.056	0.046	0.038
23	0.795	0.634	0.406	0.262	0.170	0.112	0.074	0.049	0.040	0.033
24	0.788	0.622	0.390	0.247	0.158	0.102	0.066	0.043	0.035	0.028
25	0.780	0.610	0.375	0.233	0.146	0.092	0.059	0.038	0.030	0.024
26	0.772	0.598	0.361	0.220	0.135	0.084	0.053	0.033	0.026	0.021
27	0.764	0.586	0.347	0.207	0.125	0.076	0.047	0.029	0.023	0.018
28	0.757	0.574	0.333	0.196	0.116	0.069	0.042	0.026	0.020	0.016
29	0.749	0.563	0.321	0.185	0.107	0.063	0.037	0.022	0.017	0.014
30	0.742	0.552	0.308	0.174	0.099	0.057	0.033	0.020	0.015	0.012
40	0.672	0.453	0.208	0.097	0.046	0.022	0.011	0.005	0.004	0.003
50	0.608	0.372	0.141	0.054	0.021	0.009	0.003	0.001	0.001	0.001

18%	20%	22%	24%	25%	26%	28%	30%	35%	40%	45%	50%
0.847	0.833	0.820	0.806	0.800	0.794	0.781	0.769	0.741	0.714	0.690	0.667
0.718	0.694	0.672	0.650	0.640	0.630	0.610	0.592	0.549	0.510	0.476	0.444
0.609	0.579	0.551	0.524	0.512	0.500	0.477	0.455	0.406	0.364	0.328	0.296
0.516	0.482	0.451	0.423	0.410	0.397	0.373	0.350	0.301	0.260	0.226	0.198
0.437	0.402	0.370	0.341	0.328	0.315	0.291	0.269	0.223	0.186	0.156	0.132
0.370	0.335	0.303	0.275	0.262	0.250	0.227	0.207	0.165	0.133	0.108	0.088
0.314	0.279	0.249	0.222	0.210	0.198	0.178	0.159	0.122	0.095	0.074	0.059
0.266	0.233	0.204	0.179	0.168	0.157	0.139	0.123	0.091	0.068	0.051	0.039
0.225	0.194	0.167	0.144	0.134	0.125	0.108	0.094	0.067	0.048	0.035	0.026
0.191	0.162	0.137	0.116	0.107	0.099	0.085	0.073	0.050	0.035	0.024	0.017
0.162	0.135	0.112	0.094	0.086	0.079	0.066	0.056	0.037	0.025	0.017	0.012
0.137	0.112	0.092	0.076	0.069	0.062	0.052	0.043	0.027	0.018	0.012	0.008
0.116	0.093	0.075	0.061	0.055	0.050	0.040	0.033	0.020	0.013	0.008	0.005
0.099	0.078	0.062	0.049	0.044	0.039	0.032	0.025	0.015	0.009	0.006	0.003
0.084	0.065	0.051	0.040	0.035	0.031	0.025	0.020	0.011	0.006	0.004	0.002
0.071	0.054	0.042	0.032	0.028	0.025	0.019	0.015	0.008	0.005	0.003	0.002
0.060	0.045	0.034	0.026	0.023	0.020	0.015	0.012	0.006	0.003	0.002	0.001
0.051	0.038	0.028	0.021	0.018	0.016	0.012	0.009	0.005	0.002	0.001	0.001
0.043	0.031	0.023	0.017	0.014	0.012	0.009	0.007	0.003	0.002	0.001	
0.037	0.026	0.019	0.014	0.012	0.010	0.007	0.005	0.002	0.001	0.001	
0.031	0.022	0.015	0.011	0.009	0.008	0.006	0.004	0.002	0.001		
0.026	0.018	0.013	0.009	0.007	0.006	0.004	0.003	0.001	0.001		
0.022	0.015	0.010	0.007	0.006	0.005	0.003	0.002	0.001			
0.019	0.013	0.008	0.006	0.005	0.004	0.003	0.002	0.001			
0.016	0.010	0.007	0.005	0.004	0.003	0.002	0.001	0.001			
0.014	0.009	0.006	0.004	0.003	0.002	0.002	0.001				
0.011	0.007	0.005	0.003	0.002	0.002	0.001	0.001				
0.010	0.006	0.004	0.002	0.002	0.002	0.001	0.001				
0.008	0.005	0.003	0.002	0.002	0.001	0.001	0.001				
0.007	0.004	0.003	0.002	0.001	0.001	0.001					
0.001	0.001										

Exhibit 1A-7
Present Value of $1 Received Annually at the End of Each Period for N Periods

Years (N)	1%	2%	4%	6%	8%	10%	12%	14%	15%	16%
1	0.990	0.980	0.962	0.943	0.926	0.909	0.893	0.877	0.870	0.862
2	1.970	1.942	1.886	1.833	1.783	1.736	1.690	1.647	1.626	1.605
3	2.941	2.884	2.775	2.673	2.577	2.487	2.402	2.322	2.283	2.246
4	3.902	3.808	3.630	3.465	3.312	3.170	3.037	2.914	2.855	2.798
5	4.853	4.713	4.452	4.212	3.993	3.791	3.605	3.433	3.352	3.274
6	5.795	5.601	5.242	4.917	4.623	4.355	4.111	3.889	3.784	3.685
7	6.728	6.472	6.002	5.582	5.206	4.868	4.564	4.288	4.160	4.039
8	7.652	7.325	6.733	6.210	5.747	5.335	4.968	4.639	4.487	4.344
9	8.566	8.162	7.435	6.802	6.247	5.759	5.328	4.946	4.772	4.607
10	9.471	8.983	8.111	7.360	6.710	6.145	5.650	5.216	5.019	4.833
11	10.368	9.787	8.760	7.887	7.139	6.495	5.988	5.453	5.234	5.029
12	11.255	10.575	9.385	8.384	7.536	6.814	6.194	5.660	5.421	5.197
13	12.134	11.343	9.986	8.853	7.904	7.103	6.424	5.842	5.583	5.342
14	13.004	12.106	10.563	9.295	8.244	7.367	6.628	6.002	5.724	5.468
15	13.865	12.849	11.118	9.712	8.559	7.606	6.811	6.142	5.847	5.575
16	14.718	13.578	11.652	10.106	8.851	7.824	6.974	6.265	5.954	5.669
17	15.562	14.292	12.166	10.477	9.122	8.022	7.120	6.373	6.047	5.749
18	16.398	14.992	12.659	10.828	9.372	8.201	7.250	6.467	6.128	5.818
19	17.226	15.678	13.134	11.158	9.604	8.365	7.366	6.550	6.198	5.877
20	18.046	16.351	13.590	11.470	9.818	8.514	7.469	6.623	6.259	5.929
21	18.857	17.011	14.029	11.764	10.017	8.649	7.562	6.687	6.312	5.973
22	19.660	17.658	14.451	12.042	10.201	8.772	7.645	6.743	6.359	6.011
23	20.456	18.292	14.857	12.303	10.371	8.883	7.718	6.792	6.390	6.044
24	21.243	18.914	15.247	12.550	10.529	8.985	7.784	6.835	6.434	6.073
25	22.023	19.523	15.622	12.783	10.675	9.077	7.843	6.873	6.464	6.097
26	22.795	20.121	15.983	13.003	10.810	9.161	7.896	6.906	6.491	6.118
27	23.560	20.707	16.330	13.211	10.935	9.237	7.943	6.935	6.514	6.136
28	24.316	21.281	16.663	13.406	11.051	9.307	7.984	6.961	6.534	6.152
29	25.066	21.844	16.984	13.591	11.158	9.370	8.022	6.983	6.551	6.166
30	25.808	22.396	17.292	13.765	11.258	9.427	8.055	7.003	6.566	6.177
40	32.835	27.355	19.793	15.046	11.925	9.779	8.244	7.105	6.642	6.234
50	39.196	31.424	21.482	15.762	12.234	9.915	8.304	7.133	6.661	6.246

18%	20%	22%	24%	25%	26%	28%	30%	35%	40%	45%	50%
0.847	0.833	0.820	0.806	0.800	0.794	0.781	0.769	0.741	0.714	0.690	0.667
1.566	1.528	1.492	1.457	1.440	1.424	1.392	1.361	1.289	1.224	1.165	1.111
2.174	2.106	2.042	1.981	1.952	1.923	1.868	1.816	1.696	1.589	1.493	1.407
2.690	2.589	2.494	2.404	2.362	2.320	2.241	2.166	1.997	1.849	1.720	1.605
3.127	2.991	2.864	2.745	2.689	2.635	2.532	2.436	2.220	2.035	1.876	1.737
3.498	3.326	3.167	3.020	2.951	2.885	2.759	2.643	2.385	2.168	1.983	1.824
3.812	3.605	3.416	3.242	3.161	3.083	2.937	2.802	2.508	2.263	2.057	1.883
4.078	3.837	3.619	3.421	3.329	3.241	3.076	2.925	2.598	2.331	2.108	1.922
4.303	4.031	3.786	3.566	3.463	3.366	3.184	3.019	2.665	2.379	2.144	1.948
4.494	4.192	3.923	3.682	3.571	3.465	3.269	3.092	2.715	2.414	2.168	1.965
4.656	4.327	4.035	3.776	3.656	3.544	3.335	3.147	2.752	2.438	2.185	1.977
4.793	4.439	4.127	3.851	3.725	3.606	3.387	3.190	2.779	2.456	2.196	1.985
4.910	4.533	4.203	3.912	3.780	3.656	3.427	3.223	2.799	2.468	2.204	1.990
5.008	4.611	4.265	3.962	3.824	3.695	3.459	3.249	2.814	2.477	2.210	1.993
5.092	4.675	4.315	4.001	3.859	3.726	3.483	3.268	2.825	2.484	2.214	1.995
5.162	4.730	4.357	4.003	3.887	3.751	3.503	3.283	2.834	2.489	2.216	1.997
5.222	4.775	4.391	4.059	3.910	3.771	3.518	3.295	2.840	2.492	2.218	1.998
5.273	4.812	4.419	4.080	3.928	3.786	3.529	3.304	2.844	2.494	2.219	1.999
5.316	4.844	4.442	4.097	3.942	3.799	3.539	3.311	2.848	2.496	2.220	1.999
5.353	4.870	4.460	4.110	3.954	3.808	3.546	3.316	2.850	2.497	2.221	1.999
5.384	4.891	4.476	4.121	3.963	3.816	3.551	3.320	2.852	2.498	2.221	2.000
5.410	4.909	4.488	4.130	3.970	3.822	3.556	3.323	2.853	2.498	2.222	2.000
5.432	4.925	4.499	4.137	3.976	3.827	3.559	3.325	2.854	2.499	2.222	2.000
5.451	4.937	4.507	4.143	3.981	3.831	3.562	3.327	2.855	2.499	2.222	2.000
5.467	4.948	4.514	4.147	3.985	3.834	3.564	3.329	2.856	2.499	2.222	2.000
5.480	4.956	4.520	4.151	3.988	3.837	3.566	3.330	2.856	2.500	2.222	2.000
5.492	4.964	4.524	4.154	3.990	3.839	3.567	3.331	2.856	2.500	2.222	2.000
5.502	4.970	4.528	4.157	3.992	3.840	3.568	3.331	2.857	2.500	2.222	2.000
5.510	4.975	4.531	4.159	3.994	3.841	3.569	3.332	2.857	2.500	2.222	2.000
5.517	4.979	4.534	4.160	3.995	3.842	3.569	3.332	2.857	2.500	2.222	2.000
5.548	4.997	4.544	4.166	3.999	3.846	3.571	3.333	2.857	2.500	2.222	2.000
5.554	4.999	4.545	4.167	4.000	3.846	3.571	3.333	2.857	2.500	2.222	2.000

to the cash inflows or revenues it produces minus the cash outflows or expenses it requires during that period.

However, net cash flow is subject to one complication, income taxes. Like other cash outlays, income taxes must be deducted from cash revenues in computing net cash flows. The peculiarity of income taxes arises from the fact that they are computed as a percentage of *taxable income*, not as a percentage of net cash inflows. Therefore, in computing the cash outflow for income taxes, noncash revenue and expense items must be considered to arrive at taxable income. For risk management purposes, noncash revenues such as an increase in accounts receivable are not germane. However, an important noncash expense, the accrual of depreciation on assets whose useful life extends beyond one annual accounting period, is most pertinent.

In this text and the ARM Program, straight-line depreciation is used to compute this noncash depreciation expense unless otherwise specified. Salvage value is assumed to be zero unless otherwise specified. Thus, for example, if the initial investment in an asset with a seven-year useful life is $35,000, the annual depreciation expense is $5,000. While not a cash outflow, depreciation should be added to other expenses when computing taxable income. Also in this text and the ARM program, income taxes are assumed (for ease of calculation) to be 50 percent of taxable income unless otherwise specified.

Exhibit 1A-8 illustrates the general procedure for calculating annual after-tax net cash flows—actually, the *differential*, or changed, net cash flows. In this case, an organization buys the $35,000 machine with the seven-year expected useful life as mentioned. Assume that purchasing this machine is expected to add $12,000 a year to the organization's revenue, $500 to its annual maintenance expenses, and $100 to its insurance costs. Under these assumptions, the differential after-tax net cash flow (NCF) as a result of investing in the machine can be expected to be $8,200 as shown at the bottom of the exhibit.

A simple case of how risk management decisions can affect net cash flows is the possibility that improved maintenance for this machine, costing an additional $25 per year, would qualify the machine for a reduced insurance rate, cutting annual insurance expenses by $40. Such an additional maintenance expenditure would raise the before-tax NCF on the machine by $15 to $11,415, and the after-tax NCF accordingly.

Evaluation of Net Cash Flows

When funds invested in one accounting period generate cash revenues in one or more future periods, four factors are involved in evaluating the net cash flows from that investment:

Exhibit 1A-8
Calculation of Differential Annual After-Tax Net Cash Flow

			$12,000
Differential cash revenues			
Less: Differential cash expenses (except income taxes):			
Maintenance expense	$ 500		
Insurance expense	100	600	
Before-tax NCF:		$11,400	
Less: Differential income taxes:			
Before-tax NCF	$11,400		
Less differential depreciation expense ($35,000/7 years)	5,000		
Taxable income	$ 6,400		
Income taxes (50%)		3,200	
After-tax NCF:		$ 8,200	

Evaluation of Differential Annual NCF

Factors:
Initial investment — $35,000
Useful life — 7 years
Differential annual after-tax NCF — $8,200
Minimum acceptable rate of return —14% annually.

Evaluation by the Net Present Value Method:

Present value of differential NCF	
($8,200 x 4.288)	$35,161.60
Less: Present value of initial investment	35,000.00
Net present value	$ 161.60

Evaluation by the Time-Adjusted Rate of Return Method:

$$\frac{\text{Initial investment}}{\text{Differential NCF}} = \frac{\$35,000}{\$ 8,200} = 4.268 = \text{present value factor}$$

Interpolation to Find the Exact Time-Adjusted Rate of Return (r):

Rate of Return	Present Value Factors	Present Value Factors
15%	4.288	4.288
r		4.268
15%	4.160	
Differences: 1%	0.128	0.020

r = 14% + ([0.020/0.128] x 1%)
  = 14% + 0.16%
  = 14.16%

- The amount of the initial investment,
- The annual rate of return, expressed as a percentage of the initial investment,
- The estimated useful life of the proposal, the number of years (or other periods) for which it will produce cash flows, and
- The differential annual after-tax net cash flows associated with the proposal.

Any projected set of net cash flows can be evaluated by either of two methods, the net present value method of the time-adjusted rate of return method. The lower portion of Exhibit 1A-8 demonstrates both methods for evaluating a proposal that involves a $35,000 acquisition. The estimated useful life of the investment is seven years, and it is expected to generate additional annual after-tax net cash inflows of $8,200.

Net Present Value Method The net present value method can be used only when there is a predetermined minimum acceptable rate of return, here presumed to be 14 percent after taxes. Typically, this minimum rate will be given to, not established by, a risk management professional. This person will use the rate to evaluate the cash inflows and outflows from any proposed investment, including a proposed risk financing technique.

Any proposed investment whose projected cash inflows have a present value greater than the present value of the required outflows is acceptable by this criterion. In Exhibit 1A-8, for instance, the additional annual net cash inflows are a constant $8,200 each year, and the only required cash outflow is the $35,000 initial cost of the investment. The first step in using the net present value method is to calculate the net present value of the additional annual after-tax net cash flows.

Exhibit 1A-7 indicates that the present value of $1 received annually at the end of each year for the next seven years at 14 percent interest compounded annually corresponds to a value of 4.288. Multiplying this present value factor by $8,200 yields the present value of the differential net cash inflows, $35,161.60. In other words, $35,161.60 is the amount that would have to be invested today at 14 percent interest compounded annually to receive $8,200 at the end of each year for the next seven years. The last $8,200 would leave the fund with the zero balance. The net present value of the proposed investment is the present value of the differential net cash inflows minus the present value of the investment, $35,000. Therefore, the net present value of this proposed investment is $161.60, which is derived by subtracting the required $35,000 initial investment from the $35,161.60 present value of the investment's future cash inflows. This positive result shows that the proposed investment will generate at least the minimum acceptable 14 percent rate of return.

Time-Adjusted Rate of Return Method Exhibit 1A-8 also illustrates the same result using the time-adjusted rate of return method. The cost of the investment is $35,000; it is expected to generate after-tax net cash flows of $8,200 a year for seven years. Therefore, $35,000 can be considered the present value of $8,200 to be received annually at the end of each of the next seven years at some yet unknown time-adjusted rate of return. To find this rate, divide $35,000 by $8,200, yielding a present value factor of 4.268 for the investment. Therefore, $4,268 is the present value of $1 to be received annually at the end of each of the next seven years at the yet undetermined time-adjusted rate of return. To determine this rate, look in the seven-year row in Exhibit 1A-7 for the present value factor that comes closest to 4.268. The factor of 4.268 lies between 4.288 for a 14 percent rate of return and 4.160 for a 15 percent return over a seven-year period. Therefore, the time-adjusted rate of return for this investment is between 14 and 15 percent compounded annually.

Finding a more precise time-adjusted rate of return for this investment requires an interpolation process as is illustrated at the bottom of Exhibit 1A-8. The total difference between the present value factors for 14 percent and 15 percent returns is 0.128 (4.288 − 4.160). The difference between the present value factor for a 14 percent return and the present value factor for this asset is 0.020 (4.288 − 4.268). Since lower present value factors are associated with higher rates of return for any given number of years, the asset has a time-adjusted rate of return that is higher than 14 percent. It is higher by an amount equal to 0.020/0.128 of 1 percent. (The 1 percentage point is the difference between the rates of return for the two columns in Exhibit 1A-7 used for this interpolation.) Because 0.020/0.128 of 1 percent is approximately 0.16 percent, the time-adjusted rate of return on this asset is approximately 14.16 percent (14 percent + 0.16 percent), which is less than the minimum acceptable rate of return of 14 percent. Therefore, again the asset should be made.

Tax Considerations After-tax, not before-tax, net cash flows determine an organization's command over productive resources. Because an organization cannot use for its own purpose the cash it must pay as taxes, taxes reduce usable cash inflows. Therefore, for organizations subject to taxes of any kind, cash outflows to pay taxes reduce net cash flows available to purchase productive resources for the present and the future.

One of the reasons risk financing decisions for public entities may differ from those of private profit-seeking organizations is that public organizations generally are not subject to federal or state income or excise taxes. Therefore, computations of expected after-tax net cash flows tend to be simpler for these public organizations than for profit-seeking private enterprises. Furthermore, such organizations do not distinguish between before-tax and after-tax net cash flows, making depreciation an irrelevant expense for any tax purposes. For a public organization that does not pay taxes, the after-tax net cash flow is equal to the before-tax (and the before-depreciation) net cash flow. For example, in Exhibit 1A-8, the after-tax NCF for a taxable organization is $8,200; for a tax-exempt organization, the equivalent figure is the before-tax NCF of $11,400 shown near the top of the exibit.

Summary of Cash Flow Analysis

To enhance its operating efficiency, every profit-seeking and nonprofit public or private organization needs to make the best possible use of its cash, the resource through which it purchases all of its other productive resources. Using cash most effectively requires maximizing the expected present value of the organization's future annual after-tax net cash flows. The choice by an organization of a particular risk management alternative affects its net cash flows. Therefore, to the extent feasible, an organization should select those risk management, particularly risk financing, alternatives that contribute most to the expected present value of its annual after-tax net cash flows. However, organizations often have other objectives besides maximizing operating efficiency; moreover, legal requirements, owners' and senior management's tolerance for uncertainty, and simple shortages of resources may keep an organization from achieving an ideal level of operating efficiency. Nonetheless, the accurate evaluation of expected present values and net cash flows will move an organization to a better level of operating efficiency, thus improving its means of achieving its fundamental mission.

Appendix Notes

1. Gathering historical data involves not only data on the frequency and severity of losses but also on the circumstances (physical conditions, levels of output, or state of the economy, for example) that logically may be related to the frequency or severity of these losses. This requires compiling data that is complete, consistently expressed, relevant to risk management (especially with respect to valuation of losses), and organized to facilitate the analysis.
2. Federal Bureau of Investigation and Federal Highway Administration data reported in *MVMA Motor Vehicle Facts and Figures* (Detroit, MI: Motor Vehicle Manufacturers Association, 1982), p. 93.

CHAPTER 2

Controlling Fire Losses

Fire is both a friend and a foe to human beings. As a friend, it adds to the value of human life by heating the spaces in which people live and work; it powers, directly or indirectly, much of the machinery and appliances of factories and homes; and generally contributes to the standard of living throughout most of the world. In contrast, fire also causes much harm. For risk management purposes, a fire becomes "hostile" when its flame, sparks, ashes, smoke, or heat escapes its intended receptacle, such as a furnace or boiler, or when it is used purposefully to destroy, as with arson. Out of control, fire does the following:

- Kills people who cannot escape its smoke, gases, and heat,
- Destroys buildings, their contents, and other tangible property,
- Brings temporary or permanent closure, loss of income, and perhaps bankruptcy to business organizations and to those who derive their incomes from working for, owning, lending money to, or levying taxes on those organizations,
- Destroys irreplaceable reminders of human heritage, and
- Destroys vegetation, forests, and wildlife.

Therefore, the challenge fire poses to every risk management professional centers on how best to enable an organization to enjoy the benefits of fire without suffering the harm it can cause. To enjoy fire's benefits, an organization must make use of fire as a direct or an indirect source of energy and yet be safeguarded from potential loss of the property, personnel, and resulting income caused by fire. In addition, negligently allowing fire to become ignited or to spread to others' property can expose an organization to liability for that spreading fire—"fire legal liability."

The material in this chapter can help the risk management

professional to work alone and with others to achieve this delicate balance. Specifically, this chapter is designed to better enable the risk management professional to do the following:

- Explain principles for protecting people from fire-related injury or death.
- Describe how the features of a building's construction and design can improve the safety of the property and the persons that building houses.
- Recognize and control potential sources of ignition for hostile fire, thus reducing the frequency of fire losses.
- Specify the general characteristics of appropriate fire detection/suppression systems, thus reducing the severity of physical damage caused by hostile fire.
- Recognize and control the fire hazards associated with particular operations that are common sources of hostile fire in organizations.
- Describe how an organization's fire risk control program can be analyzed and strengthened through application of
  - the domino theory of accident causation/control,
  - the energy-release theory of accident causation/control, and
  - the TOR (Technique of Operations Review) approach to accident causation/control.

This chapter focuses primarily on protecting lives and property from fire; the control of liability and net income losses attributable to fire are dealt with in Chapters 8 and 10, respectively.

FIRESAFETY AND LIFE SAFETY

Historically, fire protection engineering emerged as a physical science, a branch of engineering concerned with protecting property and people from being damaged, injured, or killed by hostile fire. Safeguarding people from such fire has grown in relative importance throughout the twentieth century because of the increasingly humanitarian emphasis of Congress and other legislative bodies and because of the ever-growing liability claims being won by or on behalf of those injured or killed by others' negligence in allowing fires to start or to spread or in not properly extinguishing them. Fire legal liability, especially for bodily injury and death, has become a very prominent liability exposure. Therefore, today's business executives, including risk management professionals, need to be especially concerned about how their fire risk control programs protect not only property but people as well.

This increasing emphasis on protecting people from injury or death in fires has led to a distinction between "firesafety" and "life safety." Firesafety refers to all measures to prevent and/or minimize damage to property and harm to persons because of hostile fire. In the context of the present chapter, life safety refers to a portion of firesafety—the portion focusing on protecting persons occupying a burning building from injury or death. (Life safety also refers to harm from perils other than fire.) Life safety focuses on how various major categories of buildings need to be designed and equipped to reasonably assure the occupants of safe exit from the burning portion of the building into either the open air or a portion of the building free from fire or smoke. Every organization's fire risk control program should strive to provide the same assurance for its employees, customers, and other members of the public who may be on its premises when a hostile fire occurs.

Fundamental Considerations

Effective life safety measures must take into account the characteristics of the persons who can be expected to occupy various kinds of buildings and the design features of these buildings that will reasonably ensure safe exit (or "egress") when fire strikes.

Characteristics of Persons Life safety engineers have identified six general characteristics of individuals and of groups of people that affect their susceptibility to injury or death caused by fire in any building they occupy. For specific individuals, these factors are age, mobility, awareness of the fire, and knowledge of the building. For entire groups of people, two additional factors are density (or crowding) and the extent to which the occupants can be controlled, guided, or trained in their response to the fire. Exhibit 2-1 elaborates on these factors.

Types of Buildings (Occupancies) The firesafety for a given set of individuals also is determined by the use being made of the buildings they occupy—i.e., the occupancy of the building. Life safety engineers have categorized all types of occupancy into nine classes: assembly, educational, healthcare, detention and correctional, residential, mercantile, business, industrial, and storage. The characteristics of these types of occupancies are indicated in Exhibit 2-2. This classification is relevant to life safety because each of these occupancies tends to be characterized by certain features that affect occupants' safe egress. Thus, the specific life safety requirements for a given

Exhibit 2-1
Factors Affecting Building Occupants' Susceptibility to Fire*

Age	Age is the most easily identified characteristic of an occupant exposed to fire: the very young and very old have a significantly higher fire fatality rate. In addition, many other important characteristics — such as mobility, awareness of the fire, knowledge of fire, and controllability — may be a direct function of age.
Mobility	Mobility is largely a function of age — the very young and the very old are less mobile. Others with impaired mobility, for whom special life safety measures should be carefully considered, include those with any kind of physical or mental handicap, those who are hospitalized or otherwise institutionalized, and the incarcerated.
Awareness of the Fire	A major factor is whether the occupant is awake and alert (as in workplaces or in mercantile occupancies) or whether they may be asleep (as in any of the various residential occupancies). In addition, limited awareness may be found among those affected by drugs or alcohol or by diversions such as motion pictures and sporting events. Most occupancies can be expected to contain individuals with a range of decision-making capabilities.
Knowledge of the Environment	"Knowledge" here embraces factual knowledge of the particular situation, competence in self-preservation, and even blind instinct for emergency response. Training in fire drills may increase the level of self-preservation knowledge of occupants and their ability to react spontaneously or assist others. Regular occupants of a particular building are likely to have a better knowledge of its exits than are transient visitors.

Density (Crowding)	The number of people in a given enclosed area increases both the potential loss of life, the time needed for the occupants to leave the area, and, hence, the needed exit capacity — number and size of exits — from the area.
Control of Occupants	People subject to disciplinary control and training — as in schools, some types of institutions, and some places of employment — will respond rapidly and in an orderly way to clear instructions in a fire emergency. This control reduces the likelihood of panic and increases the occupants' ability to deal with a fire emergency.

*Adapted with permission from John M. Watts, Jr., "Assessing Life Safety in Buildings," in *Fire Protection Handbook*, 16th ed. (Quincy, MA: National Fire Protection Association, 1986), pp. 9-3 to 9-4.

building are determined jointly by the characteristics of the people in it (the occupants) and the use to which the building is put (the occupancy).

Principles of Firesafety

Joint consideration of the general characteristics of building occupants and occupancy has led life safety engineers to extensive sets of specific firesafety standards for particular kinds of buildings. These standards have been codified in the *Life Safety Code* published by the National Fire Protection Association and incorporated explicitly or by reference into the statutes and ordinances of most localities in the United States. Therefore, compliance with the applicable sections of the *Life Safety Code* usually is a legal requirement; failure to comply is not only a breach of an ordinance (bringing fines and other penalties) but also can be substantial evidence of negligence in failing to adequately safeguard others from injury or damage by fire. Consequently, not complying with the *Code* increases the likelihood not only of property and personnel losses, but also of liability losses.

Therefore, an important function of every organization's risk management department is to determine, and comply with, the provisions of the *Life Safety Code* (or local ordinances), which govern the life safety features of the building(s) the organization owns or

Exhibit 2-2
Characteristics of Classes of Occupancies*

Class	Characteristics
Assembly	Places of assembly include, but are not limited to, all buildings or portions of buildings used for gathering together 50 or more persons for such purposes as deliberation, worship, entertainment, amusement, or awaiting transportation. Assembly occupancies include:

Theaters
Motion picture
  theaters
Assembly halls
Auditoriums
Exhibition halls
Museums
Libraries
Skating rinks
Gymnasiums
Bowling lanes
Pool rooms
Armories
Restaurants
Churches

Dance halls
Club rooms
Passenger stations and
  terminals of air, surface,
  underground, and
  marine public transpor-
  tation facilities
Recreation piers
Courtrooms
Conference rooms
Drinking
  establishments
Mortuary chapels
College and university
  classrooms, 50
  persons and over

Occupancy of any room or space for assembly purposes by less than 50 persons in a building of other occupancy and incidental to such other occupancy shall be classed as part of the other occupancy and subject to the provisions applicable thereto.

Educational   Educational occupancies include all buildings or portions of buildings used for educational purposes through the twelfth grade by six or more persons for 4 or more hours per day or more than 12 hours per week. Educational occupancies include:

Schools
Colleges
Academies

Nursery schools
Kindergartens
Day care facilities with
  significant occupant load

Other occupancies associated with educational institutions shall be in accordance with the appropriate parts of this *Code.*

Health Care Health care occupancies are those used for purposes such as medical or other treatment or care of persons suffering from physical or mental illness, disease or infirmity, and for the care of infants, convalescents, or infirm aged persons. Health care occupancies provide sleeping facilities for four or more of the occupants and are occupied by persons who are mostly incapable of self-preservation because of age, physical or mental disability, or because of security measures not under the occupants' control.

Health care occupancies include:
(a) Hospitals
(b) Nursing homes
(c) Limited care facilities

Health care occupancies also include ambulatory health care centers, and other facilities providing care to those with special physical, mental, or social needs.

Detention and Correctional Detention and correctional occupancies (also known as Residential-Restrained Care Institutions) are those used to house occupants under some degree of restraint or security. Detention and correctional occupancies are occupied by persons who are mostly incapable of self-preservation because of security measures not under the occupants' control.

Detention and correctional occupancies include:
Houses of correction
Residential-restrained care
Penal institutions
Reformatories
Jails
Detention centers
Correctional centers
Pre-release centers

Residential Residential occupancies are those occupancies in which sleeping accommodations are provided for normal residential purposes and include all buildings designed to provide sleeping accommodations.

Residential occupancies are treated separately in this Code in the following groups:

    (a) Hotels
        Motels
    (b) Apartments
        Apartments for the elderly
        Condominiums and cooperatives
    (c) Dormitories
        Orphanages for age 6 years and older
    (d) Lodging or rooming houses
    (e) One- and two-family dwellings
    (f) Board and care facilities

Mercantile

Mercantile occupancies include stores, markets, and other rooms, buildings, or structures for the display and sale of merchandise. Included in this occupancy group are:

Supermarkets	Shopping centers
Department stores	Drug stores
	Auction rooms

Minor merchandising operations in buildings predominantly of other occupancies, such as a newsstand in an office building, shall be subject to the exit requirements of the predominant occupancy.

Business

Business occupancies are those used for the transaction of business (other than that covered under Mercantile), for the keeping of accounts and records, providing a service, and similar purposes. Included in this occupancy group are:

Doctors' offices	Outpatient clinics, ambulatory
Dentists' offices	
City halls	College and university instructional buildings, classrooms under 50 persons, and instructional laboratories
General offices	
Town halls	
Court houses	
Laboratories for basic or applied research not including hazardous chemicals	

Minor office occupancy incidental to operations in another occupancy shall be considered as a part of the predominating occupancy and shall be subject to the provisions of this *Code* applying to the predominating occupancy.

Industrial

Industrial occupancies include factories making products of all kinds and properties devoted to operations such as processing, assembling, mixing, packaging, finishing or decorating, and repairing. Industrial occupancies include:

Factories of all kinds	Smokehouses
Laboratories involving hazardous chemicals	Laundries
	Creameries
Dry cleaning plants	Gas plants
Power plants	Refineries
Pumping stations	Sawmills

Storage

Storage includes all buildings or structures utilized primarily for the storage or sheltering of goods, merchandise, products, vehicles, or animals. Included in this occupancy group are:

Warehouses	Parking garages
Cold storage	Hangars
Freight terminals	Grain elevators
Truck and marine terminals	Barns
Bulk oil storage	Stables

Minor storage incidental to another occupancy shall be treated as part of the other occupancy.

*Reprinted with permission from James K. Lathrop (ed.) *Life Safety Code Handbook*, 4th ed. (Quincy, MA: National Fire Protection Association, 1988), pp. 30-34.

occupies. Although these provisions are quite detailed and vary significantly among types of occupancy and types of structure, the fundamental requirements of the *Code*, as set forth in Exhibit 2-3, should be familiar to every risk management professional.

BUILDING CONSTRUCTION AND DESIGN

The first consideration in evaluating and controlling the threat posed by hostile fire to persons and property in a particular building is that building's construction, design, and location. Effective risk management calls for specific attention to the type of building construction, the presence of separate "fire divisions" within the building, and the extent to which the building is exposed to fire from outside sources, such as neighboring buildings. (A fire division is a building, or a portion of a building, separated from every other building or portion of a building such that no fire originating outside the division can be expected to spread into the division.)

Building Construction[1]

To call upon the skills of, and to cooperate with, experts in fire risk control, the risk management professional needs to be familiar with the seven classes of building construction into which firesafety experts group most buildings: frame, joisted masonry, noncombustible, masonry noncombustible, modified fire resistive, fire resistive, and mixed construction.

Frame In wood frame construction, the exterior walls, floors and roof surfaces, and their supports are constructed of wood or other combustible material. This type of construction differs from ordinary construction only with respect to the exterior wall surfaces. These are combustible in frame and noncombustible in ordinary construction. An example of frame construction is shown in Exhibit 2-4.

While most building codes make no distinction between protected and unprotected frame buildings, they may require certain *fire-stop* devices. A fire-stop is an element of construction inserted in a concealed space, either a wall or roof area, that will prevent the passage of flame from one point to another. By containing the fire within the area of origin, the fire-stop will aid early detection and possible extinguishment.

While frame construction is certainly less desirable than fire resistive or masonry noncombustible, certain occupancies may be acceptable within this construction type, such as occupancies of a low combustible nature or ones bearing a high level of protection. The basic

Exhibit 2-3
Fundamental Requirements of Life Safety Code*

Every building or structure, new or old, designed for human occupancy shall be provided with exits sufficient to permit the prompt escape of occupants in case of fire or other emergency. The design of exits and other safeguards shall be such that reliance for safety to life in case of fire or other emergency will not depend solely on any single safeguard; additional safeguards shall be provided for life safety in case any single safeguard is ineffective due to some human or mechanical failure.

Every building or structure shall be so constructed, arranged, equipped, maintained and operated as to avoid undue danger to the lives and safety of its occupants from fire, smoke, fumes, or resulting panic during the period of time reasonably necessary for escape from the building or structure in case of fire or other emergency.

Every building or structure shall be provided with exits of kinds, numbers, location, and capacity appropriate to the individual building or structure, with due regard to the character of the occupancy, the number of persons exposed, the fire protection available, and the height and type of construction of the building or structure, to afford all occupants convenient facilities for escape.

In every building or structure, exits shall be so arranged and maintained as to provide free and unobstructed egress from all parts of the building or structure at all times when it is occupied. No lock or fastening shall be installed to prevent free escape from the inside of any building.

Every exit shall be clearly visible or the route to reach it shall be conspicuously indicated in such a manner that every occupant of every building or structure who is physically and mentally capable will readily know the direction of escape from any point. Each means of egress, in its entirety, shall be so arranged or marked that the way to a place of safety is indicated in a clear manner. Any doorway or passageway that is not an exit or a way to reach an exit, but is capable of being confused with an exit shall be so arranged or marked to prevent occupant confusion with acceptable exits. Every effort shall be taken to avoid occupants mistakenly traveling into dead end spaces in a fire emergency.

When artificial illumination is required in a building or structure, exit facilities will be included in the lighting design in an adequate and reliable manner.

In every building or structure of size, arrangement, or occupancy that a fire itself may not provide adequate occupant warning, fire alarm faciliites shall be provided where necessary to warn occupants of the existence of fire. Fire alarms will alert occupants to initiate escape. Fire alarms facilitate the orderly conduct of fire exit drills.

Two means of egress, as a minimum, shall be provided in every building or structure, section, or area where the size, occupancy, and arrangement endangers occupants attempting to use a single means of egress which is blocked by fire or smoke. The two means of egress shall be arranged to minimize the possibility that both may be impassable by the same fire or emergency condition.

Every vertical way of exit and other vertical opening between floors of a building shall be suitably enclosed or protected, as necessary, to afford reasonable safety to occupants while using exits and to prevent spread of fire, smoke, or fumes through vertical openings from floor to floor before occupants have entered exits.

Compliance with this *Code* shall not be construed as eliminating or reducing the necessity for other provisions for safety of persons using a structure under normal occupancy conditions. Also no provision of the *Code* shall be construed as requiring or permitting any condition that may be hazardous under normal occupancy conditions.

*Reprinted with permission from James K. Lathrop (ed.) *Life Safety Code Handbook*, 4th ed. (Quincy, MA: National Fire Protection Association, 1988), pp. 15-17.

frame members can be protected against both the vertical and horizontal spread of fire. In addition, the inherent problem of external surfaces being of a combustible nature and thus subject to fires from the outside can also be alleviated by such things as an external sprinkler system.

When discussing frame construction, it should be remembered that materials other than wood may be used in the building without changing the construction classification. Various composition boards may be used in place of wood, and many other exterior wall covering materials may be used. The following are some examples:

1. Brick or stone veneer, consisting of a single thickness of brick or stone (two or six inches thick) over a wood-framed structure, and dependent upon bonding to the wood structure for stability. This gives a building the appearance of standard brick or stone construction, but is not in any way equivalent. It does provide

Exhibit 2-4
Example of Wood Frame Platform Construction*

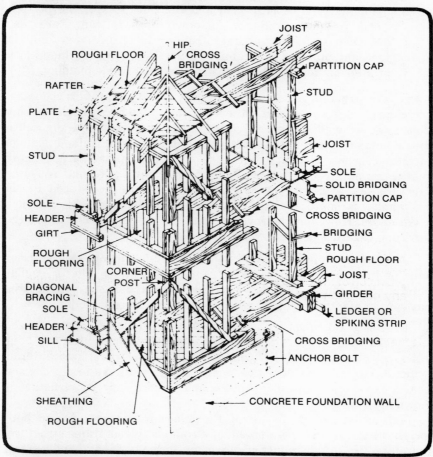

*Reprinted with permission from *Fire Protection Handbook,* 16th ed.
(Quincy, MA: National Fire Protection Association, 1986), p. 7-63.

some degree of protection against external exposure to fire such as grass or brush fires.

2. Metal-clad construction consists of a sheet metal (steel or aluminum) covering fastened to the wooden structure or cement asbestos shingles or corrugated cement asbestos sheets over wood siding. While the covering may prevent the wood from being ignited by small flames, it has relatively little value in protection against fires from the outside. This type of construction is most commonly used in diners.

3. Stucco, consisting of cement plaster on lath over wood frame construction, has a slight degree of fire resistance depending upon the type of lath used and the thickness of the plaster.

4. Concrete block walls of unknown fire resistance are also classified as frame buildings from an insurance viewpoint. In fact, any building that cannot be classified properly due to lack of information must be tentatively called a frame building.

Frame construction is found generally throughout this country, particularly in areas where other building materials, such as clay bricks, are unavailable or expensive. The northwest and the south central areas of the country contain a number of large frame buildings for these reasons. In addition, because of the earthquake hazard, many smaller frame structures are found throughout California. A frame structure that will give or bend with the tremors produced by an earthquake is more resistive to this peril than one of masonry construction. However, the reverse is true in the Southeast, where the hurricane hazard is of great concern.

Joisted Masonry   Joisted masonry construction has exterior walls of brick, adobe, concrete, gypsum block, stone, tile, or similar materials with combustible floors and roofs. Joisted masonry structures may consist of either ordinary construction or mill construction.

Ordinary Construction.   Ordinary construction is characterized by exterior bearing walls that can withstand fire for at least one hour without collapsing and by combustible floors, roofs, and interior surfaces. Ordinary construction is also referred to as "brick," "wood joisted," or "brick joisted." An example of ordinary construction is shown in Exhibit 2-5.

This construction has all of the inherent hazards, due to both horizontal and vertical fire spread, of a combustible or frame structure. Therefore, fire-stops are just as important in the horizontal and vertical areas in ordinary construction as in frame.

Ordinary constructed buildings are found most in the major metropolitan areas in the northern states. They are infrequently over three stories high, since by definition the exterior walls must be bearing walls. The great majority of these were built prior to World War II. While an ordinary building is less desirable in an area subject to earthquakes, it has proven to be adequate in areas subject to hurricane-force winds.

Mill Construction.   This type of construction is sometimes referred to as "slow-burning construction." This additional classification exists where (1) there is a minimum of two-hour fire resistance rating on the bearing walls; (2) the wood columns are not less than eight

Exhibit 2-5
Ordinary Construction*

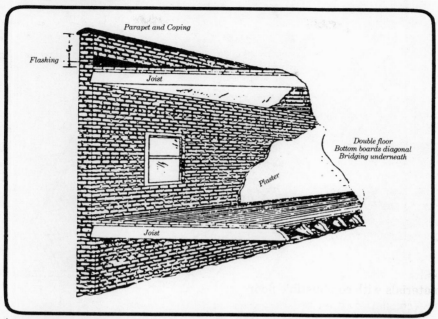

*Reprinted with permission from Charles C. Dominge and Walter O. Lincoln, *Building Construction as Applied to Fire Insurance*, 4th ed. (Philadelphia: Chilton Co., 1949), p. 32.

inches thick in any direction; (3) the wood beams, supports, and ties are not less than six inches in width or ten inches in depth; and (4) the floors are of "tongue and groove planks" not less than three inches thick with a one-inch overlay and the roof decks on heavy timbers with at least a two-inch thickness.

While heavy timber or mill construction is a subclass within the broader joisted masonry class, this may lead to some confusion. A major characteristic of the mill constructed building is the *absence* of floor joists and their attendant air spaces and voids. Mill construction is shown in Exhibit 2-6.

Mill construction has two important characteristics:

1. The heavy floors, built without concealed spaces, constitute a fire-stop retarding the spread of flames.
2. The heavy timbers of the beams and columns give the building great structural strength, reducing the likelihood of collapse.

A structure of this type would be very expensive to build today, though it nonetheless would stand a severe fire test. These mill buildings are

Exhibit 2-6
Heavy Timber Mill Construction*

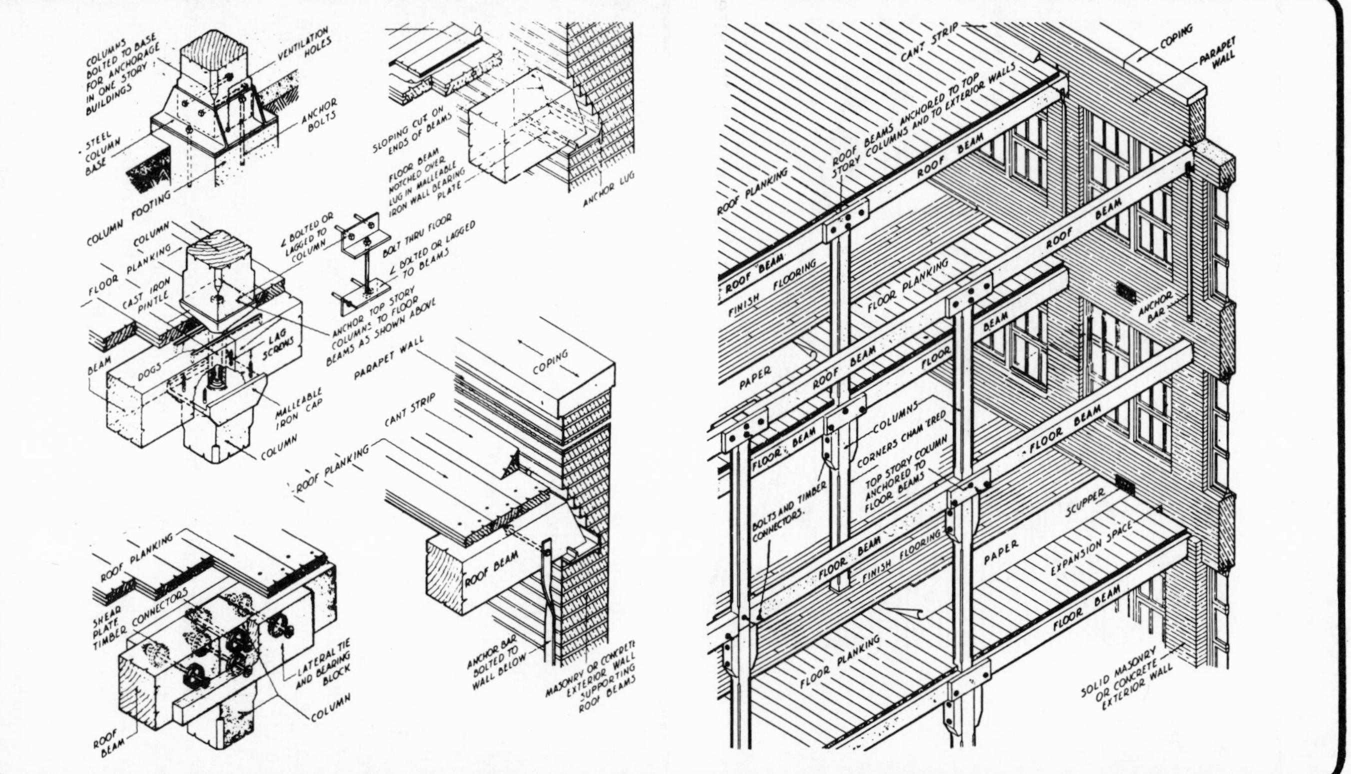

* Reprinted with permission from *Fire Protection Handbook*, 15th ed. (Quincy, MA: National Fire Protection Association, 1981), pp. 5-25, 5-26.

often found in the northeast. Many of them were constructed
and immediately after the Civil War.

On occasion, a mill-type building with laminated beams will be
found in the western states. A structure of this type is usually a
relatively new building, and if truly of mill construction, it is highly
acceptable for most occupancies, such as a shopping center, church, or
winery. However, many times these buildings will be unusual, with
unique architectural design and configuration. As a result, repair and
replacement cost coverage may present problems in reconstruction.

Noncombustible This class includes buildings with exterior
walls, floors, and roof of noncombustible materials supported by
noncombustible supports such as metal and gypsum. These buildings
are usually made of metal, which is unprotected and hence, not fire
resistive.

Masonry Noncombustible This class includes buildings with
exterior walls of masonry with noncombustible or slow-burning floors
and roof. A *slow-burning floor or roof* is defined as having a flame
spread rating of twenty-five or less. The main benefit of noncombustible
construction, as opposed to either joisted masonry or frame construction, is that it will not aid in the spread of fire. On occasion, the integrity
of a noncombustible structure will be violated through the use of
materials such as asphalt or felt vapor barriers on noncombustible roof
deckings. A large loss in 1953 in Livonia, Michigan, of a noncombustible
building was attributed to this problem. The heat of the fire began to
melt the asphalt roof surface, causing a near distillation process.
During the fire, combustibles were generated, which in turn were
consumed by the spreading fire, causing a chain effect that ultimately
totally destroyed the building.

The typical noncombustible building has a masonry nonbearing
wall surface, a cement floor, some type of metal deck roof, and
unprotected steel webbing supported by unprotected columns and roof
members. Buildings of this type have withstood major windstorms and
earthquakes with little or no damage. Low initial cost and low
maintenance coupled with the ability to withstand these perils have
made this type of construction extremely popular.

Most structures of this type are not provided with interior fire-
stops in the form of fire walls. Thus, the horizontal spread of fire may
present an additional hazard.

Modified Fire Resistive This class includes buildings with
exterior walls, floors, and roof constructed of masonry or fire resistive
materials that can burn for between one and two hours without
collapsing.

Fire Resistive This class includes buildings constructed of any combination of the following materials:

1. Exterior walls or exterior structural frame
   - Solid masonry, including reinforced concrete
   - Hollow masonry not less than twelve inches in thickness
   - Hollow masonry less than twelve inches, but not less than eight inches in thickness, that can withstand a fire for at least two hours
   - Assemblies that can withstand a fire for at least two hours
2. Floors and roof
   - Monolithic floors and roof of reinforced concrete with slabs not less than four inches in thickness
   - Construction known as "joist systems" with slabs supported by concrete joists spaced not more than thirty-six inches on centers with a slab thickness of not less than two and three-quarters inches
   - Floor and roof assemblies with a fire resistance rating of not less than two hours
3. Structural metal supports—horizontal and vertical load-bearing protected metal supports (including horizontal pre-stressed or post-tensioned concrete units) with a fire resistance rating of not less than two hours.[2]

From a firesafety standpoint, this is the best construction. These buildings have walls, floors, columns, and roofs constructed of a noncombustible material. The materials either can withstand fire for at least two hours, or they are protected through the use of a noncombustible covering such as plaster or gypsum to obtain such a rating. "Fire resistive construction" is a general term that encompasses buildings that can withstand fires without collapsing for two to four hours. In terms of structural integrity, this is a wide range.

Virtually all types of occupancy classes may be found in fire resistive buildings. Most high-rise office and apartment buildings are constructed to these standards. Other important fire resistive occupancies include warehouses with high fuel loads and heavy manufacturing plants where large structural supports for machinery are required.

Mixed Construction Many buildings do not fit exactly into any single construction type. The architectural design may have been an attempt at mixing building types or additions, and changes may have been made by owners over the years. Depending upon the existence of proper fire divisions, the decisions dealing with possible and probable losses can be made separately for each division. In the absence of proper divisions, such decisions must weigh the relative values of the different types to arrive at a single decision for the entire structure.

Fire Divisions

Many buildings that are not as firesafe as those of noncombustible or fire resistive construction do contain one feature of fire resistant construction: internal firewalls. A firewall is a floor-to-roof wall made of noncombustible materials and having no open doors, windows, or other spaces through which fire can pass. Doors in such walls, known as "fire doors," are designed to remain closed when not actually in use and have a "fire-resistance" rating expressed as a length of time during which the door will not allow fire to pass.

An area enclosed by firewalls or surrounded by empty space sufficient to retard the spread is a fire division. A fire igniting within a fire division should not spread beyond the division; conversely, a fire outside a fire division should not penetrate or damage property within such a division. Thus, creating and maintaining a fire division is one technique of loss reduction, controlling the severity of fire losses by both (1) keeping any fire contained within the fire division where it starts and (2) protecting from external fire the property within a fire division. Use of firewalls, fire doors, automatic devices to close off ventilation, and elevator shafts also can be viewed as illustrations of Strategy 5 of the energy-release theory: creating physical or spatial barriers between fire energy and the persons or property it may harm.

Establishing—and, more importantly, maintaining—the integrity of firewalls and fire divisions is crucial to limiting the severity of fire losses. If a poorly designed building, or even a series of adjoining buildings, has no fire divisions, then the entire building or series of buildings is vulnerable to any one fire. Therefore, careful attention to fire divisions and firewalls, and to the fire doors that safeguard them is an important risk management responsibility. Preferably, every firewall should be freestanding—it should not be used as support for any structural beams or columns. If the structure on one side of the firewall should become fully involved in a fire, resulting in a collapse, the firewall should stand as a barrier for the other building side.

To create a true fire division, the division wall must go through the roof and extend above the roof, creating a parapet. Such a parapet is essential to prevent fire spread along the underside of the floor from one side of the wall to the other. Also, since steel conducts heat, the heating of the steel by the fire on one side can transmit or conduct heat to the other side of the wall, possibly igniting combustibles on the side away from the fire. Without the parapet, the wall is not the "stop" that is essential for good fire protection.

For structures with combustible walls, the division wall has to be taken a step further to minimize fire spread. "Fender walls," side extensions of the existing division wall that protrude through the sides of the frame building from ground level to the parapet in order to prevent fire spread around the sides of the wooden walls as well as over the top, are also needed.

Another concern related to firewalls is an unguarded opening in the wall. Any door opening (for pedestrians or for moving materials) must be equipped with a self-closing, Underwriters Laboratories-listed fire door rated to provide fire protection at least equal to that of the surrounding walls. These doors are made self-closing by using springs or gravity to close the door when a *fusible link* releases the door. A fusible link is a thin piece of metal that normally holds the door open, but melts when the fire raises the ambient temperature.

There may be cases when there is a need for the door to close faster than it would if it depended on the heat of a fire to melt a fusible link. This might be true if the building is a high bay-type building on both sides of a fire wall, which would require a heavy fire buildup before link release. The fuel loading on one side could result in rapid fire spread, as in the presence of aerosols or flammable liquids; or the contents may be very damageable by smoke, as are hanging garments. This could result in extensive damage and in fire traveling through the door opening before the link released the door.

Conditions such as these may require the installation on both sides of the wall of heat and/or smoke detectors electrically connected to a fire door release. This device immediately releases the fire door in the event of a fire, thus minimizing the opportunity for fire or smoke to spread through the door openings. In addition, electrically connecting the door to a fire suppression system, such as sprinklers, will close the door when the system is activated.

For larger openings, the fire door can be a horizontal sliding door or an overhead door, but it still must be rated to provide the same fire protection as the surrounding walls. In many instances, one door will be sufficient. However, if the fire loading—the aggregate amount of readily combustible material within a division—is heavy and can create a very serious fire (such as with rolled paper storage), two doors, one on each side of the division wall opening, may be required. If piping passes through the wall, any opening around the piping should be sealed tightly with material that will enable the wall to maintain a three-hour rating.

When fire doors are installed, they cannot be forgotten. Like any other feature of fire protection, they must be inspected and tested at least annually to make sure that they are free from forklift or other damage, operate freely, fit tightly when closed, and are never blocked open. If the doors are not inspected and tested, and the walls are breached, reliance upon this fire protection "barrier" may well be worthless.

Exterior Exposures

One structure may be ignited by a fire spreading from another structure. To guard effectively against this fire exposure—known as an *exterior exposure*—an organization's fire risk control program should call for evaluating exterior exposures and reducing unacceptable ones.

Evaluating Exposures The extent to which a particular structure is threatened by fire spreading from another building is influenced by characteristics of both the exposing building (from which the fire may spread) and the exposed building (which the fire may damage).

Exposing Buildings. The features of the exposing building that affect the fire hazard it imposes on other structures include the following:

- Building Construction. As explained above, the construction features of the exposing building—for example, whether it is frame or fire-resistive—influence the frequency and severity of the fires that may start there.
- Occupancy. As explained later in this chapter, the occupancy of a building and the types of activities conducted there can affect fire frequency and severity. For example, a woodworking shop or a petroleum storage facility usually involves a more hazardous occupancy than does a department store. A particularly significant "occupancy" in an exposing building may be that building's vacancy. A vacant building receives less care, its stairwells and elevator shafts may provide "chimneys" through which fire may spread, any automatic fire detection/suppression system could be inoperative, and vacant buildings are frequent shelters for vagrants and are targets of arsonists.
- Ground Floor Area and Building Height. The larger the exposing building, the greater the hazard. For buildings that are *vertically* large, the hazard is greater because (1) taller buildings allow more intense fires to develop, (2) windblown fire brands travel farther from taller buildings, and (3) fire fighters have greater difficulty reaching the upper floors. For buildings that are *horizontally* large, the hazard is greater because fire fighters have difficulty reaching fires that cover large ground floors. Another concern associated with large buildings is that the square foot area of a facing wall affects the amount of heat

radiated from that wall to an exposed building, a larger wall posing a greater hazard.

- Wall Openings. Preferably, the facing wall of the exposing building will have no openings. This blank wall can act as a firewall by forcing the heat and flames up through the roof. In this manner, the wall acts as a barrier to diminish the amount of heat that can be radiated from a fire in that building.

- Sprinkler Protection. If the exposing building is fitted with an operational automatic fire detection/suppression (sprinkler) system, any fire that occurs in an exposing building should be contained. This lessens the impact of a fire from an exposing building. To the extent that the wall contains openings, its effectiveness as a barrier is reduced.

Exposed Buildings. The features of an exposed building that affect its vulnerability to an external fire include the following:

- Type of Construction. Certain types of construction that are particularly vulnerable to fire create greater exposure of hazards for other structures. Whether frame, noncombustible or fire resistive, the structure provides varying degrees of ignitability and damageability from an exposure fire.

- Wall Openings in the Exterior Walls Facing the Exposure. The greater the number and size of the openings of this wall of the exposed building, the greater the chance that flame or radiated heat will pass through these openings, igniting the walls or the contents of the building.

- Sprinkler Protection. To safeguard the exposed building, an automatic fire detection/suppression system should respond to heat or the rate of temperature rise to ensure that the system would be activated as soon as, or even before, the external fire reaches the building.

- Distance from the Exposing Building. Depending on the size and occupancy of the exposing building, the greater the distance between it and the exposed building, the better the chance for minimal or no damage from an exposing fire.

Controlling Exposures The appropriate corrective actions for the risk management professional to recommend counter the hazardous conditions described above for exposing and exposed buildings. Generally valid recommendations include the following:

- Reducing the Extent of Wall Openings Facing the Exposure. This can be done by closing off the wall openings with masonry material, reducing the size of the openings, installing glass blocks for the openings, replacing the existing windows with wired glass windows in noncombustible frames, installing fire shutters for the windows, or installing window sprinkler protection.

- Removing Combustible Material from the Building Facing the Exposure. This may involve replacing combustible window frames, overhangs, and siding that could be ignited. If the entire wall is combustible, then a new masonry wall may have to be constructed to lessen the ignition potential.
- Clearing the Area Between the Buildings. If this area is obstructed by a wall or a fence, it is difficult for fire-fighters to position hose lines so that the discharge of water can be on the building surface to reduce the heat intensity from the exposing fire. If the area is covered with brush, junk storage of a combustible nature, or stacks of pallets of waste paper, for example, there is a ready fuel source that can create an avenue for the rapid spread of fire. Removing this material will hinder and/or retard firespread.
- Constructing a Free-Standing Barrier Wall Between the Buildings. If the exposure to fire spread is severe, and there is little that can be done to minimize that exposure, then constructing a barrier wall may be necessary to act as a shield to absorb the heat from the exposing fire.
- Installing a Water Spray System. A water spray system has open, directional spray nozzles to soak an exposed building. When used for exposure protection, water spray systems are usually activated manually.

In conclusion, it is clear that building construction design features affect, both positively and negatively, the frequency and severity of fire losses.

CONTROL OF FUELS AND IGNITION SOURCES

In addition to building construction, major considerations for fire control are the potential fuels for fire and the possible sources of ignition.

The "Fire Triangle" and the Energy-Release Theory

A traditional and very useful analytical tool for firesafety engineering is the "fire triangle," whose three sides are (1) fuel, (2) an ignition source, and (3) oxygen to support combustion. Most firesafety measures either relate to controlling or eliminating one or more of these three factors in order to prevent or extinguish a fire. For example, this chapter's previous discussion of types of building construction and design, as well as the subsequent discussion of the hazards of particular operations, deal with the "fuel" element of this triangle. The techniques for extinguishing fire—discussed below in terms of either internal or external fire protection—remove at least one of these three elements, thus halting a hostile fire.

The current discussion of ignition sources focuses on removing sources of heat sufficient to ignite fuel. Minimizing the amount of combustible material in a given area, thus controlling the "fuel" side of the fire triangle, tends to reduce the severity of any fire. Fire extinguishing techniques that remove oxygen from a flame by "smothering" it either mechanically or chemically effectively extinguish a fire; removing the oxygen from a hazardous enclosed area by filling it with an "inert" gas prevents any fire from starting. Finally, some chemical fire extinguishants, such as Halon, put out fires by interfering with the process by which oxygen reaches an established flame.

Each of these measures for preventing or extinguishing a fire applies at least one of the "strategies" in the energy-release theory of accident causation and control. Minimizing fuel is an application of Strategy 2, reducing the amount of potential energy "stored" in combustibles. Controlling sources of ignition, not allowing this potential energy to be released, illustrates Strategy 3. From a different perspective, keeping potential sources of ignition away from combustible materials also applies Strategy 6: separating sources of energy in time or space from structures which that energy may damage. Removing oxygen from a potentially combustible environment also prevents the release of energy through fire, another application of Strategy 3.

Classification of Ignition Sources

Firesafety engineers generally classify all sources of ignition into four classes: chemical heat energy (oxidation), electrical heat energy, mechanical heat energy, and nuclear heat energy. Oxidation always generates heat, and if the oxidation is sufficiently rapid, this heat also generates flames. The heat from electrical energy also may ignite a flame, or electricity also can cause fires through leaking or arcing electrical current and through accumulation of static electricity in, for example, the rubbing together of two kinds of material or the flow of fuel through a pipe. Natural lightning also releases electrical energy that might ignite fire. Mechanical energy generates heat and ignites fire through friction sparks (such as between gears or pulleys) and through compression of a gas in an enclosed space, such as in an engine, warehouse, or silo. Nuclear energy, which generates heat through collision of atomic particles, is a significant ignition source only where substantial amounts of nuclear fuel are used (as in nuclear power generating stations and nuclear weapons manufacture).

Excluding nuclear heat sources, which require special cooling and other controls, Exhibit 2-7 presents some examples and appropriate controls for each of these ignition sources. Cigarette smoking is chosen as the example of chemical heat sources because careless smoking remains the single greatest cause of unintended ignition of fire in workplace settings.

In controlling the ignition of hostile fires, special attention must be given to arson—the intentional destruction of property by fire. Here, the "source of ignition" is man. Although the owners or managers of an organization may intentionally set fire to property to collect insurance or to mask some other crime, most of the appropriate loss prevention measures to stop arson from occurring can be developed by presuming that the arsonist is not a member of the organization. Some of these controls include increasing the physical security provided by fences, alarms, lighting, or dogs at the perimeter of the property or in the immediate areas of specific items of property that are particularly valuable or vulnerable to arson.

INTERNAL AND EXTERNAL FIRE PROTECTION

For fires that cannot be prevented, the best risk control technique is loss reduction, reducing the harm these fires cause. Some loss reduction measures, such as confining fire within firewalls and reducing the amount of combustible material exposed to fire, have been discussed. The major remaining loss reduction option is to extinguish any hostile fires as soon as possible.

Firesafety engineers categorize the facilities for extinguishing hostile fire into two large groups—internal and external fire protection. Corresponding to what traditionally has been called "private" fire protection, internal fire protection consists of measures an organization can take to extinguish fires striking its own property. Corresponding to what traditionally has been called "public" fire protection, external fire protection consists of fire departments and other public facilities that the community makes available to safeguard the general public from the spread of hostile fire. (In some communities, "private" fire departments provide fire protection only to members of, or subscribers to, the department; for present purposes, these departments constitute external fire protection because, like public resources, they are external to an organization's fire protection resources.)

Exhibit 2-7
Representative Ignition Sources and Controls

Ignition Sources	Control
Chemical (smoking)	Prohibiting smoking within the entire plant when operations deal with explosive atmospheres and highly combustible materials
	Designation of "No Smoking" areas in the plant and provide for safe smoking areas.
	Developing and publishing regulations governing smoking within the plant
	Good housekeeping
	Education and supporting supervisors
	Monitoring all non-smoking areas
Electrical (overheating of electrical equipment, escape of electricity)	Proper maintenance of electrical equipment
	Electrical preventive maintenance program
	Proper training of personnel operating electrical equipment
	Adequate wiring to support electrical load
Mechanical (sparks from cutting and welding operations)	Use of a physically separate area for cutting and welding, free of unnecessary combustible materials
	Establishment of a "hot work" permit system to monitor cutting and welding activities for maintenance and repair work
	Performance of a fire safety check by a supervisor of the work area for potential problems
	Removal or protection of all combustible materials in the work area, with provision for a fire watch (including extinguishing equipment) during "hot work" operations
	Inspection of "hot work" areas after work is completed to verify that fire has not begun to smolder or ignite combustible materials
	Provision for permanent or portable shields for fixed welding and cutting stations to deflect and contain sparks during operations

Static Electricity	Evaluation of the process, materials involved in the process, and the work atmosphere
	Implementation of risk control measures to include:
	• grounding and bonding techniques being used
	• increasing humidity levels
	• increasing conductivity of surrounding air to bleed off static charges

Internal Fire Protection

To extinguish fires on the premises they occupy, most organizations rely on (1) automatic fire detection/suppression (sprinkler) systems, (2) portable fire extinguishers, and/or (3) standpipe systems.

Automatic Fire Detection/Suppression Systems Automatic fire detection/suppression systems may use water, dry or wet chemicals, carbon dioxide, foam, or Halon as extinguishants. These automatic systems rely on fire detection devices to sense the presence of a hostile fire and on signaling devices to alert personnel on or off the premises to the danger. Many organizations supplement these systems for detecting and suppressing fire with human resources in the form of guard services and fire brigades.

Every automatic sprinkler system consists of piping with discharging nozzles or heads, control valves for directing extinguishants within the system, gauges for monitoring pressure within the system, and alarm devices to signal when the system becomes operative. (Some systems also have other "monitoring" alarms that call attention to any malfunction or disabling of the system so that it can be repaired.) These automatic systems are classified by the types of extinguishants they use.

Water Systems. Systems that rely on water are supplied from such sources as public water, gravity tanks, or—supported by an appropriate pump—in-ground tanks or natural bodies of water. The water is discharged from one or more sprinkler heads. This occurs when a fire creates a sufficient level of heat to melt the sprinkler head operating mechanism allowing the water to discharge. The water discharges either upward (through an upright sprinkler head) or downward (through a pendant sprinkler head), striking a deflector that is designed to break up the waterstream into water droplets. This spray pattern provides for a greater surface area to absorb the heat of the fire, cools the surrounding material and area, and confines, controls, and leads to extinguishment of the fire. To conserve water in the system and to avoid water damage to property not endangered by fire, only the sprinkler heads that are directly affected by the heat of the fire open; the entire system does not "go off."

The two basic types of water-based sprinkler systems are "wet" and "dry" systems. In a wet system, the piping is full of water and will immediately discharge that water when the sprinkler head begins to operate. Since the piping is filled with water at all times, the system responds faster than a dry system. However, also because of the water in the piping, a building with this type of system must be continuously heated to prevent the water from freezing.

In a dry system, the piping is filled with air under pressure. This air holds back a greater amount of water pressure through the use of an air clapper. The advantage of this type of system is that it can be installed in unheated buildings. The only area where heat is needed is around the dry-pipe valve, and this can be provided by enclosing the dry-pipe valve(s) in a noncombustible enclosure and heating the area(s) around the valve(s) with electric space heaters.

However, there are limitations to the dry-pipe system. Because air is in its piping, any sprinkler head operations triggered by fire require the air to be released first. This action creates a delay that results in more heads operating than would be in operation with a wet system under similar conditions. Also, the dry-pipe system cannot protect as large a building area as can a wet-pipe system. If that situation is identified, then additional systems will be needed to be installed to provide the needed protection.

The sprinkler system must be properly designed to provide protection equal to the fire exposure. A system installed on a light hazard occupancy (such as an office) will not be adequate to provide the level of protection required, say, for a tire warehouse. The fact that a sprinkler system is present does not automatically guarantee that the system is adequate; it is essential to verify whether or not the protection available is acceptable for the exposure.

Although water-based sprinkler systems usually function effectively, there are a number of recognized reasons for some notable failures. The following are the most prevalent:

- Closed or inoperable valves, either the main control valve or a sub-control valve,
- Sprinkler protection for only a portion of a building,

- Inadequate maintenance and testing of the system,
- Painted and obstructed sprinkler heads,
- Inadequate water supply and pressure, and
- Hazards of occupancy exceeding the system's design capabilities.

A sound fire risk control program will include specific steps to eliminate all these reasons that water-based sprinkler systems sometimes fail.

In addition to basic wet and dry sprinkler systems, there are other types of water systems. One of them, the *deluge system*, is a sprinkler system in which all the heads remain permanently open; water is allowed into the system by a deluge valve, which in turn, is activated by a separate detection system. Deluge systems are used to protect against fires that could spread faster than conventional sprinkler heads can open, as in spills of flammable liquids.

Another type of water-based system is a *preaction system*. This is the same as a deluge system except that the sprinkler heads normally are closed. Therefore, both the sprinkler heads and the detection components of a preaction system must operate before any water is released. Preaction systems are especially appropriate for occupancies that are unusually susceptible to water damage, such as computer rooms or small libraries.

A third alternative, *water spray systems*, can have either open or closed nozzles. Instead of conventional sprinkler heads, these systems have directional nozzles specifically designed for the configuration of the space being protected and the hazards in that space. For example, water spray systems are used to safeguard aircraft in hangars, combustible cooling towers, and chemical plant reactors.

Dry Chemical Systems. This type of extinguishing system contains finely divided powders stored in a cylinder. The cylinder is connected by pipes to nozzles positioned to allow for full distribution over the fire exposure area. Activation of the system can be by a heat detector, fusible link, or manual release.

The dry chemical extinguishing system is listed by Underwriters Laboratories for use on Class B (flammable liquid) and Class C (energized electrical) fires. Thus, it has applications for exposures involving dip tanks, cooking operations, flammable liquid storage, spray painting, and oil-filled transformer rooms. When discharged, however, the dry chemicals leave a residue and would not be suitable protection for areas housing computer operations or sensitive electronic testing equipment. Care must be exercised if a dry chemical system protects an area within the vicinity of computer or electronic equipment—the discharge of the system and air movement in the building may cause some of the dry chemical to settle on the equipment, thus interfering with its functions.

Carbon Dioxide Systems. In a carbon dioxide system, this gas is stored as a liquid under pressure and discharged as a gas through the pipes of the system to the site of the fire. The system is activated by a heat or smoke detector, fusible link, or manual operation.

The carbon dioxide system is suited to the same types of Class B and Class C fires as is a dry chemical system. However, since the extinguishant changes into a gas when discharged, there has to be enough of the agent to extinguish the fire since the agent dissipates as it is released. For a total flooding system, such as for a flammable liquid storage room, all doors and vent openings to the area must be interconnected with the system so that when the system is activated, the openings will be closed off to contain the carbon dioxide concentration within the protected area.

Carbon dioxide controls fire by oxygen displacement. This becomes particularly important when the system is protecting a vault or other area that may be occupied by employees at one time or another. To protect personnel in such an area, a pre-alarm signal is necessary before the system's activation to allow time for personnel to evacuate the area. Signs should be posted at the entrance and in the protected area advising of the type of protection and the necessity to leave the area immediately if an alarm sounds.

Halon Systems. The general term "Halon" refers to a series of ionized hydrocarbon gases and liquids that have the ability to halt chemical reactions and thus extinguish fires particularly rapidly. Halogenated hydrocarbon extinguishants are effective on flammable liquids, electrical equipment, and surface fires in paper, wood, or other ordinary combustibles. These extinguishants put out fires very quickly, without water damage, and without contaminating the area as do other chemical extinguishants. Halon is frequently used in computer rooms, telephone equipment installations, and other electrical control rooms. Unlike carbon dioxide, which extinguishes fire by smothering, Halon extinguishes fire by breaking the combustion chain reaction. Therefore, much lower concentrations of Halon than of carbon dioxide may be used. Fires can be extinguished with as little as a 5 percent concentration of Halon in air; it does not have harmful effects on humans until a 7 percent concentration is reached, and it does not have long-lasting adverse affects on people until a 10 percent concentration is reached. Its primary disadvantages are cost and environmental concerns (such as ozone depletion).

In areas with moderate or high concentrations of combustibles, most authorities agree that Halon should not be considered as a substitute for more traditional, water-based sprinkler protection; rather, Halon should be considered a supplement to such protection. If a fire were to become sufficiently intense to open the sprinkler in a traditional wet-pipe or dry-pipe system, Halon probably could not extinguish such a blaze. Nonetheless, rooms with minimal combustibles can be protected by Halon alone.

Halon can be effective as an extinguishant only if it is released into an area engineered to prevent it from leaking—or to prevent leaking of air through doors, air ducts, pipes, windows, ceilings, drains, porous masonry, or other openings. Such a closed environment is critical for the proper use of Halon not only so that it can reach its required concentration to be effective, but also to maintain this concentration for at least ten minutes. Therefore, Halon should be installed only in areas that have been designed by knowledgeable engineers for its use.

Detection and Signaling Systems Any extinguishant in an automatic suppression system is released only when that system is activated. Furthermore, these automatic systems usually need to be supplemented by human intervention from a public fire department or private fire brigade. Thus, two integral parts of every suppression system are (1) detectors to activate the system and (2) signals to alert an outside fire department or internal brigade.

Detection Devices. To be effective, detectors must be properly located; must respond to hostile fire, but not to extraneous, nonhazardous conditions; and must be designed for the structure in which they operate. The following are some areas where, and purposes for which, detectors are particularly crucial:

- Hallways and rooms of hotels and motels,
- Hallways of apartment buildings, nursing homes, and hospitals,
- Air handling systems for the purpose of shutting down the system in event of smoke conditions,
- Computer rooms to provide for early alert of a fire,
- To release magnetic door closures to zone off areas,
- To activate an extinguishing system protecting specific hazards, and
- To protect property in remote geographic areas where this may be the only type of fire protection that is feasible.

To respond when danger truly exists while giving a minimum number of "false alarms," detectors may respond to heat, rate of temperature increase, smoke, flame, or to a combination of these circumstances. Thus, firesafety engineers distinguish among the following types of detectors:

- Fixed temperature heat detectors—which can respond to a predetermined temperature level;
- Rate of rise heat detectors—which respond to a present speed of temperature rise;
- Fixed temperature-rate-of-rise detectors (also called rate-of-rise compensated)—designed to respond to a fixed temperature determination or to an increase in that temperature that exceeds a predetermined level;
- Smoke detectors—which can respond to visible as well as invisible products of combustion;
- Flame detectors—designed to respond to the presence of flame in its very early stages; and
- Combustible gas/vapor detectors—which detect the presence of flammables or combustibles in the surrounding area.

For the detection system to be effective, it must cover all building areas. If only partial protection is installed, then a gamble is being made that fire will start in the protected area(s) only or will occur in close proximity to a detector, which will respond and transmit the alarm.

Prompt, reliable response by any type of detector requires suitable maintenance of the detector system. For this purpose, the system should be inspected regularly to answer such questions as the following:

- Are the detectors and the wiring adequately supported?
- Are the detectors clean of dirt and grime?
- Are the detectors damaged in any way that would affect proper functioning?
- Are the detectors obstructed by shelving, partitions, or stock?
- Have the detectors been accidentally painted (which would hinder their efficiency)?
- Is the system tested at least on an annual basis to verify that all alarms function and are audible?
- Is the electrical or other power source that activates the system operational and reliable under all reasonably foreseeable circumstances?

Designing a detection system for the structure it protects requires not only careful attention to covering every part of the structure that may burn, but also being alert to the following factors:

- Ceiling/roof shape,
- Number of detectors required for the room volume,
- Any building areas that are subdivided into separate fire areas,
- Room air movement that can create a lag in detector operation,

- Normal versus abnormal room temperatures that, in a given area, could trigger "false alarms," and
- Nature of fire expected.

Signaling Systems. Except in very unusual circumstances (for example, when a fire occurs in a totally unpopulated area or facility), an adequate firesafety program requires that human beings also act to extinguish the fire or protect exposed property from damage by fire. Therefore, one of the basic functions of virtually every automatic system is to automatically emit a signal to alert people to take appropriate actions. For such signaling, there are five basic categories of alarms, classified in terms of where the alarm signal is received. As shown in Exhibit 2-8, these alarms are local alarms, auxiliary alarms, remote alarms (sounding at either a police department or a fire department), proprietary alarms, and central station alarms.

Supervisory Signals. Well-designed fire extinguishing systems monitor their own readiness and signal any lapse in that readiness. Such signals should be distinct from alarm signals that are transmitted when fire is detected. The supervisory signals should also indicate the nature and possibly the location of the lapse in the system. For example, the signals should indicate any abnormally high or low water level, low water temperature, high or low air pressure, loss of electric power, fire pump driver trouble, fire pump running, and system control valve tamper. The supervisory signals thus generated help those who supervise the system to detect and correct any system flaw. Ultimately, of course, the supervisory signaling system itself requires supervision—and here, human intelligence and ingenuity again are indispensable. Supervisory signaling system circuits are often monitored for shorts, grounds, and loss of supervising current. The signals received under these conditions are called trouble signals.

Fire Extinguishers Fire extinguishers are "first aid" devices to be used to control fire in its early stages. To be available for use, each extinguisher should be readily accessible, visible, properly inspected, and the proper extinguisher for the hazard. In many instances, the extinguisher may be used by an unskilled operator. Thus, education is an important element in the proper use of extinguishers. Education includes teaching personnel about the location of the extinguisher, its discharge range, its capabilities and limitations, the method of putting it into operation, and for some highly hazardous operations, the chance for "hands on" use of the extinguisher on training fires.

Beyond equipping and training personnel to use fire extinguishers, an important responsibility of a risk management department is to select the type of extinguisher(s) appropriate for the fire(s) likely to occur. As shown in Exhibit 2-9, there are four classes of extinguishers.

Exhibit 2-8
Basic Types of Fire Alarm Systems

Type of Alarm	Where Signal Sounds
Local Alarm	Rings only at the premises to notify occupants. If the alarm rings outside during hours when the building may not be occupied, action is required by a passing police officer or a "good Samaritan" to notify the fire department.
Auxiliary Alarm	is connected to an existing municipal alarm system on the same circuits that carry signals from the street fire alarm boxes. Any activation of this system causes the box alarm signal to be transmitted to the fire alarm dispatch. Responding fire units first verify that the box has not been pulled at the street, then go to the protected property to investigate.
Remote Alarm	is transmitted over leased phone lines from protected property to a fire department or a police department. Separate concerns apply to each: • police department: is this a dedicated responsibility of the department, or performed only as a convenience? In the event of a fire alarm, it is vital that the fire department be initially dispatched, rather than a police dispatch for investigative purposes. • fire department used away from larger cities where the alarm transmission can be to the fire station in the area. There may be on-duty personnel with volunteer response. Upon receipt of a fire alarm, the station would be emptied and a void would exist between the time of the initial equipment response and volunteer personnel arriving at the station to cover other alarms. During that interim, any additional alarm will not be noted until the personnel have arrived at the station. In addition, the qualifications and capabilities of personnel responding to cover the station must be considered. Will they know what action to take in the event of another alarm signal from a protected property?

Proprietary Alarm	Rings to alert occupants (or "proprietors") on protected property or on another facility of the same organization and staffed with its personnel trained to handle alarms. This is a good arrangement for a large plant or one that has several buildings. Any alarm signal received permits the duty personnel to investigate and to take the necessary action, whether restoring the system for a needless alarm or initiating immediate notification of the fire department.
Central Station Alarm	Rings on the premises of a company that is in the business of handling alarms. The central station staff is trained in handling fire alarms and in notifying the proper fire department as well as notifying the individuals on the customer's call list. The central station company also has personnel who go to the protected property to verify that each alarm transmission device is functional and the central station alarm center receives each signal from each device being tested.

Another crucial risk management responsibility, with fire extinguishers as with automatic extinguishing systems and all components of an organization's firesafety program, is thorough, periodic inspection and maintenance. The maintenance requirements vary in their specifics and intervals with the type of extinguishant, and different extinguishers even in the same class require different inspection procedures. Here, the general responsibilities of the risk management professional are to (1) determine the maintenance and inspection requirements for each extinguisher, (2) be certain that an employee of the organization or a qualified outside specialist performs this inspection and maintenance, and (3) maintain extinguisher inspection and maintenance records.

Standpipe Systems Combining elements of both automatic sprinkler systems and portable fire extinguishers are standpipe systems, which can be used by an organization's specially trained firefighting personnel and/or a public fire department. A standpipe system is a series of pipes running throughout a building through which water can be supplied to hoses that, in the event of an

Exhibit 2-9
Types of Fire Extinguishers

Type	Extinguishant	For Fires Involving:
Class A	pressurized water and multi-purpose dry chemical	ordinary combustible materials, such as paper and wood
Class B	ordinary dry chemical, multi-purpose dry chemical, foam, carbon dioxide, and Halon 1211	flammable liquids and gases, such as gasoline, acetone, and propane
Class C	the same as for Class B, with the important criterion that the extinguishant be a nonconductor of electricity	energized electrical equipment
Class D	dry powder agent specifically listed for use on the particular combustible metal that is on fire	combustible metals, such as magnesium, sodium, and lithium

emergency, can be attached to valves in the standpipes. Standpipe systems are classified according to (1) the diameter of the hoses (2.5 to 1.5 inches) that can be attached to the standpipes and (2) the nature of the water supply to the system (ranging from being filled with water at all times to having no independent water supply except that provided by public fire department vehicles or fire hoses). Regardless of how a standpipe system is classified, it increases the efficiency with which a human-operated system can distribute water. Standpipe protection plays an especially important role in getting hose lines into service on upper floors that are too distant to be reached by street level. Thus, installation and maintenance of a standpipe system is essential for fire protection in high-rise structures.

Guard Services   Guard services are another means of providing internal fire protection. Guard services may be provided either through a contract service or by employees of the facility. The watch personnel tour the property and preferably use a portable clock to verify that the guard has visited each station. The intent is for the guard to follow designated routes so that each area of the facility is checked on a definite frequency, building areas are secured, fire hazards are identified and reported, continuous production processes are monitored, fire protection equipment is checked, and the proper authorities can be notified if fire is discovered. Follow-up procedures by management or supervisory personnel should be used to verify that the clock stations are being visited at prescribed times and that the guards are performing their functions.

Fire Brigades   Every facility should have a fire emergency plan that includes some form of fire brigade activity. (A fire brigade is one element of "crisis management," the subject of Chapter 12 in this text, where emergency planning is discussed more fully.) The brigade can range from three individuals responsible for notifying the fire department, initiating evacuation, securing areas, and removing important files that may be in the danger area, to an organization that has a fire chief with assistants and a crew capable of initiating and maintaining an effective attack on a fire.

To determine the size of a fire brigade appropriate for a specific facility, it is important to evaluate the potential for fire, existing on-site protection, the extent of critical operations, the potential magnitude of a fire, and the available public fire protection. Once determined, the risk management professional can design a plan in cooperation with plant personnel and management to include the number of people on the team, designated crew leaders, and guidelines for the functions and duties of the crew. The plan should also outline the training required to make the brigade an effective part of the overall fire protection program.

Status as a "Highly Protected Risk"   Recognizing that outstanding internal fire protection programs should lower fire losses and merit a lower fire insurance rate, some commercial property insurers specialize in providing coverage to "highly protected risks," or "HPRs." These insurers, noted for the quality of their own risk control services available to their insureds, require that a property meet certain underwriting standards to qualify as an HPR. These standards call for the following:

● Automatic sprinklers where needed, with adequate water supplies to feed them, and

- Sprinkler supervision by a central station or, as a substitute for the central station, watchmen with clock rounds,
- Proper protection for special hazards,
- Loss-conscious management,
- Buildings of good construction,
- Satisfactory outside protection,
- Large amount of property to be insured, and
- Absence of severe fire exposure from adjoining or neighboring structures.

Many large, sprinklered manufacturing and other facilities—especially those of noncombustible and fire-resistive construction—qualify as highly protected risks. The HPR insurer supplements the insured's own firesafety program with expert and extensive fire risk control inspections, advice, and other services.

External Fire Protection

External fire protection—the "fire department"—offers meaningful protection to a facility only when (1) adequate public fire hydrants are reasonably accessible and supplied with adequate water and pressure, and (2) fire department personnel are capable of responding to a fire at the facility.

For a facility to be "protected," hydrants are necessary. They must be available to the premises and must be within 500 to 1,000 feet road distance to the premises (not "as the crow flies"). Besides the hydrant locations, consideration also must be given to the underground water mains and the available water supply. Problems exist in older communities where a buildup of scale and sediment has developed in the water mains. This condition can significantly reduce the size of the water main's internal diameter and thus have a major impact on its waterflow capabilities. The facility also could be on a dead-end line, which will allow for waterflow in one direction only. In addition, any nearby development of properties with high water usage may result in a declining water supply.

For these reasons, it is important that water supplies be tested to verify the actual available supply and pressure before beginning new construction or making changes in existing operations. Such changes could increase the fire hazard potential, which might, in turn, have higher water supply and pressure requirements. Proper fact-finding procedures will identify whether or not the water supply is stable, beginning to decline, or has deteriorated to the point that the present level may be inadequate. If inadequacies are discovered, then supplemental supplies must be developed for adequate protection. It is better to identify problems before finalizing construction plans than to discover deficiencies after plans have been completed.

When there is no public fire protection, there must be a greater commitment to strong on-site private protection. This can be in the form of a gravity water tank, standpipe water tank, or ground water tank with fire pump and the installation of a yard system incorporating underground water mains and private hydrants fed by one or more water supply sources. In the event of fire, the system draws upon the use of hose streams supplied by the private hydrants.

To evaluate and improve the capabilities of public fire department personnel to respond to a fire, the risk management professional should be responsible for seeing that appropriate personnel within the risk management department and the entire organization recognize the following:

- The distance the closest public fire department must travel to reach the organization's property.
- The terrain and obstructions that might interfere with fire department response. For example, there may be hilly roads, railroad tracks on the fire department's route to the organization's property, or road areas that may be subject to flooding or other natural perils.
- The need to invite the nearest fire department to the property to review the facility's layout, hazardous operations and storage areas, and fire protection levels.
- The need to develop a "data packet" to be retained on the premises at a designated command post location. This data should include a plot plan of the property and should describe the facility's construction, contents and production operations, fire protection levels, utility shut-off valves, and any other data vital to the fire department personnel in controlling any fire emergency.
- The need to designate a liaison between the fire department and the organization to enhance coordination and communication prior to and during a fire emergency.

By determining the adequacy and accessibility of water supplies and the response capabilities of the public fire department, the risk management professional now identifies the internal and external levels of protection in relationship to the levels of hazard and potential loss severity and begins to formulate the policies and philosophies of the firesafety program for the organization.

FIRESAFETY FOR TYPICAL OCCUPANCIES

A risk management professional must be prepared to apply the firesafety devices and procedures described thus far to a great variety of structures housing a myriad of activities. As suggested earlier, the overall fire hazard in any facility is influenced by the nature of the activity and use (occupancy) existing there. To illustrate how the particular occupancy influences the fire hazard and the appropriate fire protection measures, the material under this heading deals with five activities that raise special firesafety needs: storage, spray painting, handling of flammable liquids, food preparation, and computer operations.

Storage

Storage of goods is a major firesafety concern because of the heavy concentration of inventory values in one place and the manner in which they are stored. For storage in general, firesafety evaluation should include what the fire potential of the commodities might be, how the commodities are arranged, the ease of ignition of the stored materials, the potential rate of firespread, and the rate of heat release.

Among the materials stored indoors that can create a fire hazard, the National Fire Protection Association recognizes four classes of ordinary commodities and three groups of plastics. As shown in Exhibit 2-10, the classifications are based on the combustibility and the heat-generating potential of the stored materials and their packaging.

It is also useful to distinguish among the several ways in which these materials may be stored: on pallets, in racks, in solid piles, on shelves, or in bin boxes. The palletized method, probably the most frequently used, allows for stacking the commodity, ease of material handling, and flexibility for moving the material around the warehouse or storage area. With palletized storage, whether solid pile or in racks, the following are some points to be considered from a firesafety standpoint:

- Height of Storage. Depending on the commodity class and packaging arrangement, storage height can reach levels of thirty or more feet. This height can allow for significant fire development and intensity, making it extremely difficult to control fires.
- Pallet Construction. With the commodity on wood pallets and potentially stacked to thirty or more feet, the resulting air

Exhibit 2-10
Classifications of Indoor Storage*

Classification	Description
Class I	These commodities are essentially non-combustible products arranged on combustible pallets, in ordinary corrugated cartons with or without single thickness dividers, or in ordinary paper wrappings with or without pallets.
Class II	These commodities are Class I products placed in slatted wooden crates, solid wooden boxes, multiple thickness paperboard cartons, or equivalent combustible packaging material with or without pallets.
Class III	These commodities are wood, paper, natural fiber cloth or Group C Plastics with or without pallets. Wood dressers with plastic drawer glides, handles, and trim are examples of a commodity with a limited amount of plastic.
Class IV	These commodities are Class I, II, or III products containing an appreciable amount of Group A Plastics in corrugated cartons and Class I, II, and III products in ordinary corrugated cartons, with Group A plastic packing with or without pallets.
Group A Plastics	Plastics with the highest rate of heat release when burning, such as polyethylene, polyvinyl chloride, and polystyrene. (Less flammable plastics are placed in Class III or Class IV above.)

*Reprinted with permission from Martin M. Brown, "Indoor Rack Storage," *Fire Protection Handbook*, 16th ed. (Quincy, MA: National Fire Protection Association, 1986), pp. 11-2 to 11-3.

spaces within the stacks can facilitate firespread and obstruct the water supply reaching the seat of the fire.
● Aisle Spaces. These should be eight feet in width to provide for some space between storage areas. Any closer arrangement

will allow the fire to spread faster from stack to stack, thus intensifying and extending the range of fire damage.

- Commodity and Packaging Material. As identified in the storage classifications in Exhibit 2-10, the higher the class, the greater the hazard. With a higher level of plastic within the container as part of the commodity or packaging material, there is a greater potential for a more severe fire with a greater heat release.

Another popular method of storage is placing commodities on shelves (or "racks"). With land values becoming increasingly expensive, it becomes more cost-effective for a building manager to go up rather than to spread out materials storage. This makes greater use of the rack storage concept. With the advent of computerized picker equipment, certain storage applications can be mechanized, which allows for storage racks to be constructed first and then wall panels added to the exterior sides of the racks creating the building walls and storage area.

Rack storage poses special firesafety problems. The racks can be single-row, double-row, or multiple-row (classified as aisles narrower than three and one-half feet). With the increased height and type of aisles, vertical and horizontal flue spaces have been created within the racks and around the commodity. These are called multiple chimneys. A fire starting in the lower area of such a chimney will preheat the material above it, bringing the material to ignition and rapidly spreading upward. When the fire reaches the vertical rack flue spaces in its upward path, heat intensity is greatly increased. Moreover, rack storage problems are compounded by the plastic sheeting used to encase the commodity loads for ease of shipment and handling. This wrapping primarily prevents the wetting and cooling of commodities during sprinkler operation, which necessitates increased levels of protection.

Protecting storage areas against such fire hazards as smoking, electric current, power sources for forklift trucks, cutting and welding operations, and arson requires the risk management professional to obtain or exercise engineering expertise to implement the following firesafety measures:

- Sprinkler protection is critical. Preferably, the system should be a wet sprinkler system, and depending on the type, height, and rack arrangement of the storage, one or more additional levels of sprinkler protection may be required within the racks (*in-rack sprinklers*) at specified levels.

- The system should have a waterflow alarm transmitted to an alarm center to immediately notify the appropriate people in the event of sprinkler waterflow.
- Ignition sources must be controlled. The risk management professional must work with plant and senior management to accomplish the following:

  - Designate smoking areas or declare storage areas as "no smoking." The areas should be frequently monitored by supervisory personnel.
  - Develop good maintenance procedures for electrical systems and do not use temporary wiring. All electrical work should be installed according to appropriate electrical codes.
  - Develop a good maintenance program for forklift trucks and designate a service area separated from storage areas by firewalls. In addition, store fuels and perform refueling operations in an appropriate area.
  - Develop a cutting and welding program that includes safety procedures, permits, fire watches, relocation of material, and monitoring after work is completed.
  - Institute good housekeeping procedures that remove all combustible waste materials from the building and keep them away from the building.
  - Install security for the warehouse areas with alarms on all doors, motion detectors for interior areas, and an alarm system to transmit alarm signals to an alarm company.
  - Employ guards to control access to the property and the interior of the warehouse.
- To further enhance both internal and external fire protection, include fire hose streams for interior use, a good water supply with private hydrants (depending on the available public hydrants and the size of the warehouse area), smoke or heat detectors to initiate faster alarms for critical storage areas, fire extinguishers, and a training program so that personnel will know their responsibilities in the event of fire within the storage area.

Spray Painting Activity

Spray applications of paints and powders create potential fire protection problems because many solvents and paints are flammable and combustible. A spray application is also particularly hazardous because it creates fine droplets of the fluid, making it more ignitable than when it is applied with a brush.

An effective risk control strategy is to subcontract spray painting operations to another company—contractually transferring the exposure. However, cost factors and production requirements do not always permit this approach. Where subcontracting is not feasible, the risk management professional should work with those performing or responsible for spray painting activities to reduce the frequency and/or severity of resulting fire losses in the following ways:

- Confine spraying to a noncombustible booth, whether enclosed or "open face," or to a designated spraying room. Within the spraying enclosure, there should be adequate ventilation to help remove the vapors from the painting area and for good airflow to the area. There should also be overspray collectors, such as baffles, dry filters, or a water-wash arrangement to collect the paint residue.
- Install fire protection, such as automatic sprinklers, dry chemical, or carbon dioxide systems. This should include not only the spraying area but, depending on the operation, the drying area and all ducts and plenums as well.
- Minimize electrical hazards (potential ignition sources). The electrical wiring and appliances within the spray area and its proximity should be designed specifically for spray paint and powder operations.
- Follow good housekeeping. Any overspray should be wiped clean, excess paper should be removed from the spray area, and metal trash cans with tight fitting lids should be provided for rags and trash. Sprinkler heads subject to paint buildup should be covered with plastic bags that the water in the system will break once the sprinkler head is open. These bags should be frequently changed.
- Store only the required amount(s) of flammable liquid for a shift use at the spraying area. Solvents should be in flammable liquid "safety cans," and the paint maintained in tight fitting containers. (Safety cans are of substantial metal construction and have pouring spouts with tightly fitting—usually spring-closed—caps or valves and pressure-relief vents to prevent explosion. A suitable safety can should contain no more liquid than is required for use during one work shift.) Any bulk storage should be in a separate storage facility or outside the plant.
- Remove all open flames or spark-producing devices from the vicinity of the spray painting operations.

- Portable fire extinguishers should be accessible for immediate use.
- Use safety interlocks for compressors, fans, air flow through filters, and conveyors.

Handling Flammable Liquids

Flammable liquids—cleaning solvents, fuels, and/or paints—are found in some quantity on the premises of almost every organization. The larger the amount stored and used, the greater the potential for improper handling and/or spillage. The right concentration of vapors and an ignition source can create devastating results. When evaluating this exposure and its potential, it is important to be cognizant of the type of flammable liquid in use, the amount used in different operations, how these liquids are stored, the different locations within the facility where such liquids are stored and/or used, and the characteristics of each of the particular liquids.

With flammable liquids, the principal concern is to minimize the chance of igniting the vapors from improper handling and storage. Appropriate loss prevention and loss reduction measures related to this concern fall into three broad groups: (1) using a less hazardous liquid, other material, or process; but, if this is not possible, (2) using the flammable liquid appropriately, and (3) storing it appropriately. Specific measures for each of these three alternatives, respectively, include the following:

1. Substituting a less hazardous liquid or, preferably, changing the process so that no flammable liquids are involved.
2. Using appropriate precautions in handling flammable liquids by
   a. Relying on Underwriters Laboratories (UL)-listed flammable liquid safety cans for dispensing small quantities, and storing smaller quantities in UL-listed safety cabinets.
   b. Identifying the valves and piping according to the contents, and having emergency shut-off valves away from the area to quickly shut down the flow if a fire or leak occurs when flammable liquids are delivered from a bulk supply.
   c. Utilizing grounding and bonding techniques to minimize the chance for static electricity.
   d. Providing exhaust systems at all areas where flammable liquids are transferred or exposed to the atmosphere within the facility.

    e. Controlling ignition sources, as by providing "explosion-proof" or other suitable electrical equipment, in areas where flammable liquids are handled and stored.

    f. Installing extinguishing system protection or automatic sprinklers to protect areas where flammable liquids are handled and/or stored.

3. For storing larger quantities of flammable liquids, restricting such storage to a specially designed area of the facility—preferably physically separated from other operations—which:

    a. Is constructed of fire-resistive materials,

    b. Is equipped with UL Class I, Div. 2 electrical service, or other electrical service suitable for hazardous locations,

    c. Provides floor ventilation to remove any vapors,

    d. Is protected with an extinguishing system,

    e. Is protected with labeled self-closing fire doors,

    f. Has a floor drain to carry away any spill or discharge of the sprinkler system,

    g. Has grounding and bonding connections to eliminate the potential for static electricity as an ignition source by drawing off harmlessly static charges directly to the earth,

    h. Has, at the entrance to the room, a floor sill or drainage trench to prevent any flammable liquids from entering the facility, and

    i. Has explosion-relieving outside walls.

Food Preparation Activity

Food preparation activity (found in many large operations from offices to industrial plants) is a potential source of fire primarily when grease is allowed to accumulate in the hood and duct areas of stoves, ovens, and related equipment. Such accumulation provides a source of fuel that is readily liquefied to spread flame throughout cooking appliances and cooking areas.

To place this exposure into the "controlled" category, the risk management professional or others responsible for the cooking operations should do the following:

- Provide a ventilation system over the cooking operations with a noncombustible hood equipped with filters and connected to a duct system vented to the outside.
- Install a hood and duct system so that there is a minimum of eighteen inches' clearance from unprotected combustible material. If unprotected material is within eighteen inches of the hood and duct system, the material should be covered with

noncombustible material in a manner that will prevent ignition in the event of fire in the duct system.

- Install an extinguishing system for surface and duct protection of the cooking operations. Such protection can be dry chemical, carbon dioxide, or waterspray sprinklers. Whatever form of protection is installed, it should shut off the fuel supply to the cooking operations upon system activation.
- Maintain the efficiency of the extinguishing system by having it serviced every six months.
- Minimize the amount of grease buildup in the duct work by having the hood and duct cleaned every six months.
- Provide all-purpose fire extinguishers for immediate use against small fires.
- Interlock all equipment for excess temperature and fryers for high and low liquid levels.

Computer Operations

In this age of "information," very few organizations can function effectively without some form of computer operations. Thus, normal operations end up being structured around one, or even several, high-valued computers and their varied functions, turning computer facilities into the "Achilles' heel" of the organization's success. This creates the potential that, if computer operations are damaged or destroyed, the organization will have a very difficult time trying to survive. A fire loss involving this equipment thus has a two-fold impact: (1) a high dollar value loss in physical property and (2) severe consequences for the daily operations of the organization. Knowing the disaster potential that a loss in computer operations can create, the risk management professional needs to direct attention to controls that can prevent or reduce this potential for loss. To effectively protect the organization's computer capabilities from loss by fire—and ignoring here any security or vandalism exposures—the risk management professional must focus attention on both the computer operations area and the data storage area.

The computer room, if located within a larger building, should be of noncombustible or fire-resistive construction, located away from any hazardous operations or large storage areas. The room should be separated from the rest of the building by construction having a minimum fire rating of one hour.

Computer wiring channels and air conditioning duct work may be located in the area under the floor or above the dropped ceiling. With the underfloor area being more susceptible, this area should be free from accumulations of waste material. Special care should be exercised when work is being performed in the underflooring area by outside contractors. After their work is completed, this area should be checked thoroughly for trash accumulation before placing the floor tiles back into position.

A fire detection/suppression system should be installed within the computer room, including the underfloor area, extending protection to outside the computer room. If these adjoining areas are not protected, and an undetected fire occurred in them, the computer room protection would be of little value.

An appropriate automatic extinguishing or suppression system, often one using a halogenated hydrocarbon as an extinguishant, should be coordinated with the fire detection/suppression system for the remainder of the building. This special system should encompass all areas of the computer room and be equipped with audible and visual signals indicating system activation.

To minimize the quantity of combustible material, the interior finish of the computer room should be noncombustible, the furnishings should be noncombustible or of limited combustibility, and the amount of paper in the area should be kept to a level necessary for daily operations.

Any waste material should be removed from the computer room on a daily basis, the objective being to minimize the fuel load within the area so that, should fire occur, flame spread would be limited.

There should be a secure area to give from one to four hours' fire protection to the media (paper, discs, or tape, for example) with either an insulated record container listed by Underwriters Laboratories or a storage vault. Factors influencing the required length of protection are the existing levels of fire protection within the building, the type of building construction (i.e., frame or fire-resistive), and the construction of the data storage area.

The stored data should be protected not only from an external fire but also from a fire originating in the storage area itself and from the discharge of fire hose streams used by the fire department or fire brigade.

Administrative controls should be established to deal with employee education and training regarding the different protection levels and the actions required in the event of fire in the computer room and possible extinguishing system operations. Emergency plans for resuming operations after loss of hardware, software, or data should also be established.

SUMMARY

Every organization needs a firesafety program to protect property and lives from hostile fires. Protecting property preserves both property values and the ability of an organization to generate an income when providing a vital public service using that property. Safeguarding lives from fire both maintains an organization's workforce and prevents fatalities and injuries for which the organization would face liability claims growing out of workers compensation, wrongful death statutes, or the common law of negligence.

This chapter suggests a number of basic approaches to firesafety, including the following:

- Selecting a type of building construction that can withstand the fire hazards likely to arise out of the activities conducted in that structure.
- Creating an adequate number of clear fire divisions beyond which fire will not spread.
- Minimizing exposures from nearby buildings or other structures that might themselves catch fire, allowing fire to spread to the organization's property.
- Controlling sources of ignition, particularly through safeguards in the use of flammable liquids, electricity, and machinery, as well as controlling human activities (such as smoking) that pose substantial fire hazards.
- Designing appropriate internal (or "private") fire detection/suppression/signaling systems to be used in conjunction with fire extinguishers, standpipe systems, patrolling guard, and fire brigades to recognize and respond to hostile fires.
- Establishing appropriate firesafety conditions, procedures, and rules for such activities as storage, spray painting, handling of flammable liquids, food preparation, and computer operations.

The content of this chapter can be summarized and easily recalled in terms of the traditional "fire triangle"—the elements of fuel, an ignition source, and oxygen that are both necessary and sufficient to support fire. Effective fire risk control involves minimizing or eliminating one or more of these three essentials to reduce either the frequency or the severity of any hostile fire.

With respect to fuels, this chapter has discussed how the careful selection of building materials and control of the activities (or "occupancies") within a given building can control fire losses both to the buildings themselves and to the machinery, equipment, and personal property these buildings contain. Where combustibles must be used, minimizing their quantities within any given fire division also helps to reduce the severity of any hostile fire.

With respect to ignition sources, the chapter has described how hazards characteristic of particular occupancies and such general hazards as electricity, flammable liquids, and lightning can be controlled to reduce the frequency of hostile fires.

The third element of the "fire triangle," oxygen, is needed both for a fire to start and for it to sustain itself. Depriving a fire of oxygen is one of the most basic techniques of extinguishing any fire, as is the cooling of the heat of combustion. This chapter has discussed the various internal and external (private and public) means of extinguishing hostile fire through automatic or human systems that not only suppress the flames, but also detect the presence of a hostile fire and send signals to appropriate authorities, both within and outside the organization, to take prompt action to quell the fire.

Chapter Notes

---

1. The material under this heading is from E.P. Hollingsworth and J.J. Launie, *Commercial Property and Multiple-Lines Underwriting* (Malvern, PA: Insurance Institute of America, 1984), pp. 135–143.
2. Francis L. Brannigan, *Building Construction for the Fire Service* (Boston: National Fire Protection Association, 1971), p. 192.

CHAPTER 3

Controlling Losses from Natural Perils

This chapter focuses on natural perils—the largest of the three families of perils introduced in ARM 54, and shown here in Exhibit 3-1. Natural perils are causes of loss that strike without human intervention—no human being causes a flood, an earthquake, or a volcanic eruption. Furthermore, for the most part, no human being can stop these perils from striking. (Human perils, in contrast, are the direct consequences of specific individuals' inadvertent or intentional acts involving, for example, negligence, burglary, riot, or terrorism. Losses stemming from human perils usually can be averted by preventing or correcting human behavior that is in some way deficient. The third family of perils, economic perils, generates losses because of general changes in economic or social conditions that typically cannot be attributed to, or prevented by, any specific group or individual.)

Exhibit 3-1 is far from complete. Rather than attempting to consider every natural peril, this chapter highlights the natural perils that illustrate the general principles of risk control. These natural perils are divided into (1) meteorological (weather-related) causes of loss and (2) geological causes of loss (perils related to the movement of the earth and the gravitational forces that cause such movement).

This chapter also presents mainly risk control measures that, tailored to particular perils, achieve primarily loss prevention (reduced loss frequency) or loss reduction (reduced loss severity). This emphasis on loss prevention and reduction does not mean that other risk control measures—such as exposure avoidance, segregation of exposure units, or contractual transfer for risk control—are completely inapplicable to natural perils. Exposure avoidance, however, is difficult to apply to these perils. Most meteorological perils strike most parts of the earth, and geological forces are at work throughout the world. Therefore, true exposure avoidance for any natural peril is largely unfeasible.

The remaining risk control techniques (segregation of exposure units and contractual transfer for risk control) can be applied to natural perils as they can for any other group of perils. Thus, segregating exposures by using several widely dispersed warehouses instead of one is sound separation of exposures, whether the peril is fire or earthquake (assuming the warehouses are not located in the same earthquake zone). Moreover, if an organization relying on contractual transfer for risk control chooses to occupy a building as a tenant under a lease, that tenant leaves the exposures related to the building ownership with the landlord, regardless of whether the exposure is fire or earthquake. In short, the appropriate uses of exposure avoidance, segregation of exposures, and contractual transfer are much the same regardless of the peril—but, as explained throughout this chapter, appropriate measures for loss prevention and loss reduction need to be tailored specifically to each peril.

Cost effectively minimizing exposures to and losses from natural perils often requires an organization to make a sequence of risk control decisions. Some decisions should be made well before any natural peril strikes, when there is no emergency requiring immediate action. Such decisions may focus on questions like where to locate a new facility, what structural features to incorporate in a building at any given location, and, given a particular structure in a specific location, whether and to what extent to train employees in emergency response procedures appropriate for various natural perils. Because these decisions require careful consideration of interrelated alternatives, a decision-making tool known as a "decision tree"—explained near the end of this chapter—is especially useful.

Other decisions regarding emergencies created by natural perils need to be made as quickly as possible when, or shortly before, such a peril strikes. These decisions determine whether the organization's response to a particular emergency will be appropriate for the specific circumstances. To respond appropriately in a specific case, however, an organization should have developed in advance a number of alternatives from which to choose when an emergency is at hand. These alternatives, and the specific steps for implementing them, should be set forth in a general "emergency response plan" for natural perils. One such plan is presented at the end of this chapter.

Many pre-event and post-event loss prevention and loss reduction measures apply, by implication, both the energy-release theory of accident causation/control and the Technique of Operations Review (TOR) approach to risk control. In the context of the energy-release theory, many risk control measures implement such strategies as separating vulnerable structures in both time and space from the natural forces that may damage them, strengthening the framework or

Exhibit 3-1
General Classifications of Perils

Natural Perils

Cave-in
Changes of
   temperature
Corrosion
Drought
Earthquake
Evaporation
Erosion
Expansive soil
Fire of natural origin
Flood/
   surface water
Fungi
Hail
Humidity extremes
Ice

Landslide/mudslide
Lightning
Meteors
Mildew
Mold
Perils of the air
   (icing, clear air
   turbulence)
Perils of the sea
   (icebergs,
   waves, sand-
   bars, reefs)
Rot
Rust

Static electricity
Subsidence (sinkholes)
Temperature extremes
Tides
Tidal wave
Uncontrollable
   vegetation
Vermin
Volcanic eruption
Water
Weeds
Wind (tornado,
   hurricane, typhoon,
   tempest)

Human Perils

Aircraft
Arson
Building collapse
Chemical leakage
Contamination
Discoloration
Discrimination
Dust
Electrical overload
Embezzlement
Excessive odor
Explosion

Extortion
Fire and smoke
Human error
Molten material
Pollution (smoke,
   smog, water,
   noise)
Radioactive
   contamination
Riot
Sabotage
Shrinkage

Sonic boom
Strikes
Terrorism
Theft, forgery, fraud
Toppling of high-piled
   objects
Vandalism, malicious
   mischief
Vibration
War
Water hammer

Economic Perils

Change in
   consumer tastes
Currency
   fluctuations
Depreciation

Expropriation,
   confiscation
Inflation
Obsolescence

Depression/recession
Stock market declines
Technological
   advances

surface of a building these forces may impact, and reducing the amount of energy marshaled (by locating in low-hazard areas). In terms of TOR analysis, safety from meteorological and geological perils requires (1) careful management planning of facilities and operations to minimize hazards and (2) proper supervision of all employees to make sure they take adequate precautions to safeguard themselves and the organization. Thus, in the TOR framework, deficient managerial planning or supervision is likely to be a common "root cause" of many of the losses dealt with in this chapter.

RISK CONTROL FOR METEOROLOGICAL PERILS

The meteorological perils on which this chapter focuses are violent winds, flood, winter weather, drought/heat wave, and high humidity and corrosion.

Violent Winds

Violent winds may consist of general windstorms, thunderstorms, hailstorms, hurricanes (known as typhoons in some parts of the world), and tornadoes.

General Windstorm Windstorm is a storm with high winds or violent gusts with little or no rain. All areas of the continental United States are subject to significantly violent winds, although local conditions can influence the severity of the exposure. Windstorms commonly occur during "change of seasons" periods, but they can occur anytime when there is unequal heating of two or more surfaces, resulting in convective air movement. However, the areas most likely to incur severe violent wind damage include the Gulf of Mexico, the Atlantic coastal zones, and the central plains, as shown in Exhibit 3-2.

The greater the difference in temperatures and pressure gradient, the stronger the wind currents flow. As illustrated in Exhibit 3-3, most well-built structures generally will not incur damage from winds below approximately forty-seven m.p.h. Higher gusts or higher sustained wind velocity are relatively common. Building roofs are the most susceptible to wind damage, but other features can be exposed to windblown debris, unfastened materials, and inadequate support of outside construction such as conveying systems, guy-supported towers, and in-progress structures.

Pre-Event Actions. The greatest threat from windstorm is building damage and collapsed roofs and outside structures. Property damage may be minimized by following these guidelines for pre-event control:

Exhibit 3-2
Potential Wind Velocities Throughout the United States*

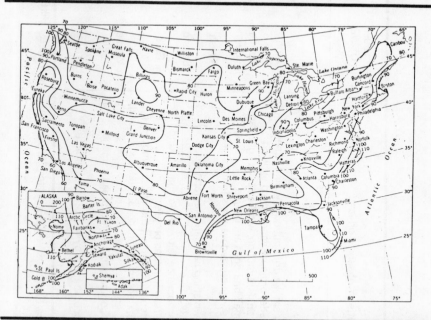

*Reprinted with permission from White, Gergely, Sexsmith, *Structural Engineering* (New York: John Wiley & Sons, 1972), vol. I, p. 69.

- Design buildings and outside structures to withstand anticipated wind loads—design should reflect location conditions where wind velocities may be in excess of general historical trends.
- Provide storm shutters and blinds for windows and other openings not rated to handle higher wind loads.
- Maintain roof and wall systems—including roof tie-downs—in good repair, and provide adequate supports for outside structures.
- Secure materials and equipment in yards around the facility.

Post-Event Actions. Spare construction materials such as plywood panels, tarpaulins, and plastic sheets should be used to repair damage to buildings to reduce further exposure of building construction and equipment to the elements.

Thunderstorm A thunderstorm is a severe electrical storm accompanied by moderately heavy rainfall. A complex generator of locally intense meteorological conditions, a thunderstorm can cause

Exhibit 3-3
Beaufort Scale of Wind Force*

Beaufort number	Miles per hour	Knots	Wind effects observed on land	Terms used in USWB forecasts
0	Less than 1	Less than 1	Calm; smoke rises vertically	
1	1-3	1-3	Direction of wind shown by smoke drift; but not by wind vanes	Light
2	4-7	4-6	Wind felt on face; leaves rustle; ordinary vane moved by wind	
3	8-12	7-10	Leaves and small twigs in constant motion; wind extends light flag	Gentle
4	13-18	11-16	Raises dust, loose paper; small branches are moved	Moderate
5	19-24	17-21	Small trees in leaf begin to sway; crested wavelets form on inland waters	Fresh
6	25-31	22-27	Large branches in motion; whistling heard in telegraph wires; umbrellas used with difficulty	Strong
7	32-38	28-33	Whole trees in motion; inconvenience felt walking against wind	
8	39-46	34-40	Breaks twigs off trees; generally impedes progress	Gale
9	47-54	41-47	Slight structural damage occurs; (chimney pots, slates removed)	
10	55-63	48-55	Seldom experienced inland; trees uprooted; considerable structural damage occurs	
11	64-72	56-63	Very rarely experienced; accompanied by widespread damage	Whole gale
12 or more	73 or more	64 or more	Very rarely experienced; accompanied by widespread damage	Hurricane

*Adapted with permission from *Standard Handbook for Mechanical Engineers*, ed. Baumeister, 7th ed. (New York: McGraw-Hill Book Company).

lightning and tornadoes, produce enough rain to flood low-lying areas, unleash a hailstorm, and develop sufficient wind velocity to uproot small trees and damage buildings. Most of the continental United States is subject to thunderstorm activity from late spring through early fall, but thunderstorms occur most frequently in the Midwest and Southeast.

Even though localized conditions can exceed normally expected historical trends, most storm activity is developed from the heated air rising off the earth's surface, which forms strong convective currents in the atmosphere. Such storms may be intensified by the movement of large cold fronts over these warmer land areas, especially during the summer months. The convective air movements can develop surface wind velocities in the range of thirty-nine to seventy-two m.p.h. (and higher, depending on topographic characteristics) and clouds with differing electrical potentials that discharge themselves as lightning.

Pre-Event Actions. Before any thunderstorm strikes, practices to reduce the severity of property losses include the following:

- Structural design should be adequate to withstand high winds.
- Proper maintenance of building roofs, guying supports for outside structures, and tiedowns for structures of inferior construction should be provided.
- Yard stocks should be moved inside a substantial structure or protected in some other way against high winds.
- A lightning protection system for the building structure and services and secondary service protection from lightning and voltage surge should be provided. (Exposure characteristics such as building construction, occupancy, site prominence, and topography in the vicinity should be evaluated on a case-by-case basis.)

Post-Event Actions. Post-event activities include the following:

- Temporary repairs should be made to damaged portions of the building to prevent further damage.
- Spare construction materials such as plywood panels, tarpaulins, and plastic sheets should be used to reduce further exposure to the elements.
- Personnel should be trained and assigned to handle emergency operations according to an established plan.

Hailstorm Hail is precipitation in the form of irregular ice pellets. It should not be confused with sleet (partially frozen raindrops or a mixture of rain and snow or hail) or freezing rain, although there are some inherent similarities. Most of the continental United States is subject to hailstorm, generally from late spring through early fall. The potential for occurrence is greatest in the Midwest, where dry cold air masses meet with moist warm air masses, and in those regions near the Rockies and Appalachians, where storm system updrafts are intensified by large or isolated mountain ranges.

Although major hailstorms appear to occur at six- to ten-year intervals, frequency and severity are largely unpredictable. Thunderstorms are a precondition for hailstorms. Of every ten thunderstorms, one usually will be a hailstorm or thunderstorm accompanied by hail. The most severe hailstorm to hit the United States in modern history struck parts of Texas and Oklahoma in May 1981, causing over $200 million in damage. Hailstorms generally are localized, with most tracks not more than a few miles in length and fronts of less than a half-mile in width. They last, on the average, from ten to twenty minutes.

Pre-Event Actions. Most hailstorm damage results from hailstone impact on buildings or on materials of low structural integrity. Where hail has weakened or penetrated a building, the accompanying wind and rain may themselves cause further damage. Pre-event risk control practices should include the following:

- Structural design should be adequate to withstand hailstorm; concrete block, concrete, and some heavy gauge steel are acceptable. Roof structures are very susceptible—metal, concrete tile, and certain types of built-up styles seem to withstand the effects better than slate, tiles, and asphalt shingles.
- Anti-hail blinds, shutters, or covers for exposed building features such as windows, skylights, and other features susceptible to damage should be provided.
- Yard stocks and equipment should be protected or moved inside a substantial structure.

Post-Event Actions. Post-event activities should include the following:

- Spare materials such as plywood panels, plastic sheets, and tarpaulins to cover openings or equipment, bracing materials, and other building supplies should be used to make temporary repairs to building structures.
- Personnel should be available to handle emergency operations such as clearing roof drains, removing hailstone accumulation on the roof (because this is a prime cause of collapse losses), and salvage/cleanup. At no time should individuals be exposed to falling hail.

Hurricane/Typhoon A hurricane (typhoon in Pacific regions) is a severe, tropical, spiral-shaped storm with winds in excess of 73 m.p.h. It originates in the tropical regions, traveling north, northwest, or northeast from its point of origin, and usually includes heavy rains and tidal surges. Areas in the continental United States subject to hurricanes include coastal zones from Brownsville, Texas, around the Gulf of Mexico, and extending along the Atlantic seaboard to just north of Portland, Maine. Most hurricanes occur between June and November, although freak storms have been known to develop at other times.

Hurricanes can dominate weather systems over thousands of square miles and last for several weeks. Although wind velocities may approach 200 m.p.h., 80 to 120 m.p.h. is more common. Most damage results from high winds, flooding from heavy rains (winds can reach far inland along the storm track), and tidal surges along the coastlines where elevation above mean sea level is less than ten feet. The storm track is largely unpredictable, although the National Hurricane Center in Miami, Florida issues frequent advisories for potentially exposed areas. This "early warning system" has improved the opportunities to protect property and, most critically, has allowed persons to be evacuated from threatened areas, thus reducing the number of injuries and loss of lives.

Pre-Event Actions. If taken before a hurricane strikes, measures that will minimize possible damage to physical property include the following:

- Adequate structural design to withstand high winds, and carefully selecting building sites that are above the flood zones and tidal surges.
- Proper maintenance of building roofs, supports for outside structures, and tie-downs for structures of inferior construction, approved materials and methods for securing building roofs to wall and support structures (i.e., "hurricane anchorage").
- Yard stocks should be moved inside a substantial structure or protected in some way against high winds and localized flooding.
- Boarding and taping of door, window, and other openings.
- Emergency power equipment should be available to provide utility services, operate pumps, and maintain protection systems.

Post-Event Actions. Post-event procedures should include the following, although a number of these procedures should also be incorporated in pre-event planning:

- Materials such as plywood panels, plastic sheets, and tarpaulins should be on hand to cover building openings such as windows and skylights and to make emergency repairs. Sandbags and flood shields should be available and designed, if possible, to protect buildings and equipment from high water.

- Personnel should be trained and assigned to handle emergency operations, such as knowing the location of gas, electric, and other utility service shutoffs, providing watchman service during emergency periods, operating emergency equipment, and making temporary repairs. Also, personnel should be able to assist with salvage and cleanup and be qualified to restore protection systems and resume normal operations.
- Activities should be coordinated with the local fire and police units.

Tornado A tornado, also known as a cyclone or twister, is a rotating column of air that takes the shape of a funnel-shaped vortex extending downward from a cumulonimbus cloud and that whirls at speeds of up to 300 m.p.h. As Exhibit 3-4 illustrates, tornadoes affect most the continental United States east of the Rocky Mountains in varying degrees of frequency and severity. However, higher frequency areas include the central plains, east central Arkansas, northern Mississippi and Alabama, and central Indiana. According to National Oceanographic and Atmospheric Administration (NOAA) data and other data repositories, central Oklahoma has the highest frequency of tornado activity in the world. Over half of all tornadoes occur between April and June. Nonetheless, tornadoes have been known to happen at just about any time throughout the year. They can cause extensive property damage from extremely high wind velocities and large pressure differentials.

Although strong tornado systems have been tracked for hundreds of miles and lasted a number of hours, most tornadoes are localized. They generally occur between 3 P.M. and 7 P.M., move from southwest to northeast, travel about four miles along a 300-400 yard front at 25-40 m.p.h., have wind velocities of 200-300 m.p.h., and last about six to ten minutes. Although the conditions under which tornadoes occur are known, the exact location and time of occurrence cannot be known in advance; furthermore, the path of a tornado in progress is erratic. Doppler radar has been applied to detect tornado activity to offer early warning for personal safety, but it has not been fully perfected.

Pre-Event Actions. Nothing can be done to prevent losses from *direct* tornado contact except to take shelter. Most construction is not designed to withstand the violent winds generated by a tornado. There have been some particular designs of reinforced concrete construction that have withstood tornado-force winds, but it is neither practical nor economical to build all structures in such a manner. The National Severe Storms Forecast Center in Kansas City, Missouri issues severe

Exhibit 3-4
Tornado Zones of the United States*

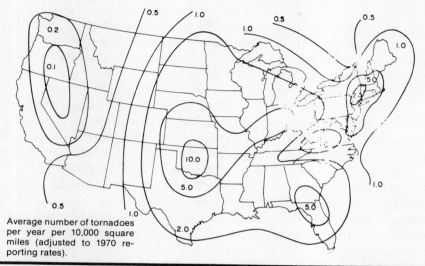

Average number of tornadoes per year per 10,000 square miles (adjusted to 1970 reporting rates).

* Reprinted with permission from Factory Mutual, p. 15.

storm advisories/warnings, including tornado advisories, for the continental United States. The service is currently involved in a research study that should be able to predict with some level of certainty tornado incidence and, from that work, be able to reduce the damaging effects to people and property.

Post-Event Actions. The severity of the tornado damage may or may not leave any meaningful post-event options beyond preserving life and clearing rubble. If the devastation is not total, the appropriate post-tornado actions parallel those appropriate after a hurricane, described previously.

Flood

Inland and coastal areas are subject to flooding from heavy rainfall and melting snow, as well as tidal surges, which may result in extensive damage. Efforts to reduce or eliminate flood exposures have been moderately successful, but since the forces of nature are unpredictable, these efforts at times only serve to create a false sense of security. Vigilance and planning can help alleviate the dangers presented by these hazardous conditions.

Inland flooding occurs when soil and vegetation can no longer absorb falling rain or melting snow, and when water runs off the land in such amounts that it cannot be carried in normal stream channels or contained in natural lakes, ponds, man-made reservoirs, and flood control projects. Flash floods can occur in smaller streams, generally near the headwaters of river basins, and may reach heights of ten to twenty feet, depending on the stream characteristics and local climate conditions. This phenomenon is most prevalent in more arid regions where dry stream beds can be filled with tumbling brown water in a relatively short period even though rain is falling some distance away.

River forecast centers (in most major cities along significant rivers) issue flood forecasts and warnings when the rainfall in watershed areas is enough to cause small tributaries and rivers to overflow their banks or when melting snow in the spring (which may be combined with rainfall) will produce similar effects. Forecast centers can issue warnings in advance of flood conditions by a few hours or days. This is generally enough time to permit evacuation and to implement selected property risk control measures.

Coastal areas, although subject to inland flooding conditions, also are prone to tidal flooding from either storms over the water or seismic activity in deep water or along seaboard fault zones. When combined with high tides, tidal surges from storms may cause the water to rise to heights of ten or more feet above normal, including the effect of high velocity winds that can raise that level. Most seawalls and barriers are designed for normally expected conditions and can help reduce the damage, even though their main purpose is to control coastal erosion. Seismic activity in the ocean can cause a very dramatic event called a *tsunami* or *tidal wave*, which can travel at up to 600 m.p.h. in deep water. As a tidal wave enters the coastal shoals, its velocity is greatly reduced but its wave height increases; some can crest at over 100 feet.

Tidal waves occur most frequently in the Pacific Ocean basin— Alaska and Hawaii being the affected areas in the United States. The Pacific Tsunami Warning System, headquartered in Honolulu, Hawaii, monitors seismic activity and issues warnings to exposed coastal areas. Generally, these advisories suggest that people move to higher ground, and there may be sufficient notice to protect selected property, but only by removing it from exposed areas. The approach of a tsunami usually is signaled by an unusual rise or fall in coastal waters, but such changes are not always obvious to the general public, who may not be aware of the impending danger. Also, a tsunami is not necessarily one gigantic wave, but a series of waves that most coastal regions cannot withstand. Severe losses in Alaska in the mid-sixties attest to that fact.

Pre-Event Actions Even though damage from all types of flooding is quite extensive, procedures can be implemented to reduce property loss exposures. Pre-event activities may include the following:

- Building sites should be carefully evaluated for flood potential.
- Existing structures in flood zones should be analyzed for their ability to withstand normally expected events.
- Flood shields or barriers, use of temporary diking (or landscaping that incorporates diking features), shutters for building openings, and sandbagging (plan sandbagging layout before flood situations) should be provided.
- Emergency supplies should be kept on hand, portable power equipment to maintain vital utility services should be available, and main electrical service equipment should be placed on upper floors of the building away from historical flood stage heights.

Many floods indirectly cause fires that originate in electrical shorts, flammable liquids floating on top of the water, and flammable gas escaping from broken piping. Practices to minimize such exposures include the following:

- No open flames or lights should be allowed near or in a flood-exposed structure.
- All flammable gas piping (whether utility or process services) where exposed to mechanical damage should be protected, and shutoffs or disconnects should be installed above normally expected flood stage heights and should be accessible.
- Flood water should be prevented from entering buildings either by having no openings at lower levels or by covering those openings against water entry.

Post-Event Actions Post-event risk control procedures include the following:

- Personnel should be assigned to implement emergency action plans, such as installing barriers and operating pumps, repairing damage, and disconnecting utility services.
- Salvage should be begun as soon as possible, and facility protection systems (i.e., sprinkler, fire, and burglar alarm) and building systems should be restored.

Winter Weather

Winter weather can cause major property losses from not only storm activity but also the impairment of normal public services and other necessary operations. The best risk control practice to follow is to be prepared for any eventuality that may arise from a snowstorm, ice storm, or severely cold weather.

Snowstorm Snowstorms are characterized by heavy snowfall and are often accompanied by high winds. Severe snowstorms often are termed blizzards when accompanied by high winds and intense cold. Most areas of the continental United States are subject, usually between late fall and early spring, except for the southern tier of the country where snowfall is highly unusual but not unknown. Traditional areas include the Northeast, upper Midwest, and regions along the Rockies, other western mountain ranges, and the Appalachians. Areas along the eastern Great Lakes can be subject to unusually heavy snowfall from what is termed the "lake" effect, where moisture is drawn from the Great Lakes and immediately falls as snow on adjacent land areas. Buffalo, New York, is one such area frequently subject to this phenomenon.

Generally, snowstorms are localized, but severe weather has been known to affect regional areas with durations from several hours to three or four days. Snowfall can accumulate to several feet or more in a twenty-four-hour period, especially at higher elevations. Where high winds accompany snowstorms, drifting can be a problem not only for highway travel but also for building access. Drifting can also adversely affect structural integrity if the snow is permitted to accumulate on roofs or against sidewalls. Intensely cold weather can compound the hazards associated with a snowstorm, such as the ability to maintain building services, heating systems, and fire protection.

Pre-Event Actions. Although extreme weather can cause enough problems in itself, snow loads on roofs generally pose the greatest risk—that of structural collapse from the abnormal static loading. Property damage may be minimized by following these guidelines:

- All buildings and structures should be designed to withstand normally anticipated snow loads, but also loads that could very well exceed general historical levels. A careful evaluation of local conditions is necessary before completing any design or building activities.
- Emergency power equipment should be available to provide backup utility services, operate pumps, and maintain fire protection systems; portable heating devices can be used to keep waterlines from freezing and to maintain space heating needs in critical plant areas.
- Materials such as posts, lumber, plywood panels, plastic sheets, and tarpaulins should be available to make temporary structural bracing and emergency repairs.

Post-Event Actions. Post-event procedures should include the following:

- Roofs should be kept free of any snow accumulation, especially flat or built-up roofs; all drains, gutters, downspouts (or rain water conductors), and roof scuppers should be kept clean and clear.
- Site and building access should be maintained at all times for emergency services, and areas around fire protection and utility services on site should be kept clear.
- All activities should be coordinated with appropriate public officials, particularly the fire and police departments.

Ice Storm An ice storm is a winter storm in which a substantial glaze accumulates from freezing rain or drizzle falling on a surface that has a temperature below 32°F. The freezing rain or drizzle frequently occurs for a short time as a transitory condition between the occurrence of rain or drizzle and snow, and therefore, it usually is more prevalent at temperatures slightly below freezing. Ice storms will occur most often between late December and early March, although freak events can develop outside this period. Ice storms most often occur along a broad belt extending from the central and southern Midwest eastward through and around the Appalachian region to the Atlantic Seaboard and north to the Middle Atlantic and New England states.

Ice storms generally are localized events of short duration, although one storm in the early 1950s hit three southern states and lasted for seven days, causing $67 million in damage. Normal accumulations are less than an inch, but deposits of eight inches or more on utility lines are not unusual due to those particular characteristics of their exposure. According to the National Weather Service, an eight- to nine-inch buildup on roofs of commercial poultry houses was not unusual during a recent ice storm in northern Alabama. This resulted in a major catastrophe from the collapse of these structures, which were not designed to handle the static loading. During a severe ice storm, the average evergreen tree (i.e., fifty feet high by a nominal width of twenty feet) might be coated with as much as five *tons* of ice.

Pre-Event Actions. The most destructive conditions in the continental United States probably will occur in the southern states because most buildings are not designed to withstand unusually severe winter conditions. The major loss exposure is from the collapse of buildings of inferior construction—construction in which design safety margins do not exceed anticipated values. Property damage may be minimized by following these guidelines:

- Structural design should be adequate to withstand normally anticipated ice loading.
- Proper maintenance of building roofs and structural support members and adequate support for outside structures such as towers and conveying systems should be present.
- Materials should be available for temporary structural bracing and to make emergency repairs.
- Tree branches that overhang power lines should be trimmed.
- Emergency power equipment should be available to provide utility services and maintain protection systems. Portable fuel-fired heaters should be used to meet space heating requirements and to help minimize ice accumulations on building surfaces.
- Personnel should be trained and assigned to handle emergency operations including the placement of temporary structural supports, removing ice accumulations, operating emergency equipment, and so on.

Post-Event Actions. Post-event risk control should include the following:

- Emergency repairs should be effected as soon as possible to limit further damage. Damaged openings should be covered with plywood sheets and tarpaulins, and plastic covers should be used to protect equipment and stocks from weather and moisture.
- Salvage and clean-up operations should be started, and building protection should be restored to full and proper operation.

Severely Cold Weather A cold wave brings a rapid drop in air temperature within a short period of time, which requires special procedures and protection for all kinds of operations. A cold wave can produce freezing temperatures (at or below 32°F), but this is not always the case in areas with more moderate climates such as the southern tier of the continental United States. Cold wave situations depend on the relative temperature drops and minimum temperatures, and this can vary with the changing seasons and geographic location. To illustrate, 30°F weather in Pennsylvania during January might not be considered unusual, but the same conditions in central Florida would be disastrous—not only to the citrus crop but to the general populace as well—because many facilities and residential occupancies are not designed to cope effectively with that temperature extreme.

Wind speed, relative humidity, and solar radiation can exert an influence on temperature, providing an equivalent temperature that could be somewhat higher or lower than normal outside air temperature. The cooling effect of wind speed in colder weather can reduce drastically the nominal temperature. This relative temperature is called the "windchill" index, shown in Exhibit 3-5. A twenty m.p.h. wind on a day when the outside air temperature is 30°F can make it "feel" like 4°F. The effects of that lowered temperature may be more pronounced than the nominal temperature without the windchill factor.

Because "seasonably" cold weather can be easily anticipated, it normally poses no major threat; the real danger comes from extended periods of abnormally low temperatures. These "cold snaps" are caused by a change in the upper atmosphere movements, which are the opposite of those patterns that result in droughts or heat waves. In this case, either the continental polar air mass will extend deeper into the United States heartland, or the jet streams will shift and pull colder air in from central Canada. Sustained cold weather is not unusual in many areas of the United States, and most people in these regions are prepared for it.

Pre-Event Actions. Precautions to reduce the adverse effects of cold weather include the following:

- Building insulation should be adequate for the cold weather climate, not only reducing heat loss but also providing a barrier against cooler outside air temperatures. Heating systems should be properly designed and of an adequate size.
- Buildings should be positioned to take advantage of natural terrain features to modify severe weather influences and should be designed with minimum openings on the prevailing "weather" side.
- Emergency supplies such as plywood panels, insulating curtains, and plastic sheets to cover exposed openings should be maintained.
- Temporary heating devices to maintain space temperatures should be provided, exposed systems should be shut off, and protection systems should be kept in service.
- Plant facilities and buildings should be kept in a high state of repair. Energy conservation measures should be practiced.
- Heating fuel supplies should be checked.
- Fire protection equipment should be designed and readied for subfreezing temperatures.

Post-Event Actions. Post-event activities should include the following:

- Damaged areas should be isolated and temporary repairs completed. Cover any building opening caused by the storm event to minimize further damage from weather.

Exhibit 3-5
Windchill Index*

ACTUAL THERMOMETER READING (F)

Wind speed in mph	50	40	30	20	10	0	-10	-20	-30	-40
	EQUIVALENT TEMPERATURE (F)									
calm	50	40	30	20	10	0	-10	-20	-30	-40
5	48	37	27	16	6	-5	-15	-26	-36	-47
10	40	28	16	4	-9	-21	-33	-46	-58	-70
15	36	22	9	-5	-18	-36	-45	-58	-72	-85
20	32	18	4	-10	-25	-39	-53	-67	-82	-96
25	30	16	0	-15	-29	-44	-59	-74	-88	-104
30	28	13	-2	-18	-33	-48	-63	-79	-94	-109
35	27	11	-4	-20	-35	-49	-67	-82	-98	-113
40	26	10	-6	-21	-37	-53	-69	-85	-100	-116
Over 40 mph (little added effect)	LITTLE DANGER (for properly clothed person)				INCREASING DANGER (Danger from freezing of exposed flesh)				GREAT DANGER	

The human body senses "cold" as a result of both the air temperature and the wind velocity. Cooling of exposed flesh increases rapidly as the wind velocity goes up. Frostbite can occur at relatively mild temperatures if wind penetrates the body insulation. For example, when the actual air temperature of the wind is 40 F (4.4C) and its velocity is 30 mph (48 km/h), the exposed skin would perceive this situation as an equivalent still air temperature of 13 F (-11 C).

*Reprinted with permission from *Fundamentals of Industrial Hygiene*, ed. Barbara A. Plog, 3rd ed. (Chicago: National Safety Council, 1988), p. 262.

- Salvage operations and permanent repairs should be started as soon as practicable, and protection systems should be restored.

Drought and Heat Wave

Droughts are long periods without rain or when the average rainfall is more than 15 percent below normal ranges. Concurrent heat waves may produce extremely high temperatures and severe dryness of the soil to a point where hot, dry winds may blow it away. One of the worst examples of these phenomena produced the "dust bowl" in the central United States during the 1930s. It has not been unusual for temperatures to exceed 100°F and extend over several weeks or reach maximums in the 120°F range due to drought or heat wave conditions.

Weather forecasters are not able to predict with any certainty the occurrence of droughts or heat waves, which may be localized or regionalized. In addition, drier-than-normal periods alternate with wetter periods on an irregular cycle. These conditions are caused by an interruption in the normal airflow patterns in the middle to upper atmosphere, which in turn causes the prevailing winds from the southwestern deserts in the continental United States to sweep farther north than usual, blanketing a large region with hot air at ground level, resulting in a drying effect. In addition, heat from the hot, dry ground feeds back into the atmosphere, tending to perpetuate the hot air mass. This situation interrupts the semiregular alterations of instability and equilibrium, hot and cool, moist and dry in the atmosphere, which combine to form the general climate patterns in the United States from June to September.

Because localized areas periodically are subject to drought and heat waves, procedures should be implemented to reduce losses developing from several predominant exposures: lack of adequate water supplies, over-burdened utility systems and services, high temperatures causing plant equipment to malfunction, and the impact on personnel performance, safety, and health. Also, there may be other external exposures, such as brush and grass fires, which could damage or destroy property.

Some of the preparations and precautions that can reduce the severity of property and other losses from drought and heat wave conditions include the following:

- Restrict or forbid nonessential uses of water.
- Provide the capability to temporarily store water during the emergency period for fire protection or critical plant processes that cannot be interrupted.

- Prepare to reduce or shut down operations that may be particularly vulnerable to utility service cutbacks or equipment failures, and provide standby power generators either for emergency use or to maintain critical plant processes.
- Maintain plant facilities, including adequate and proper ventilation, and keep grasses and weeds trimmed around all plant structures and facilities to reduce firespread from brush fires.
- Properly store and isolate combustible and flammable materials. If there is not a high water table, below-ground storage vaults can be effective at maintaining constant temperatures.
- Make temporary arrangements to maintain fire protection systems with either emergency water supplies or more frequent watchman tours of all plant areas.
- Minimize over-exertion and over-exposure of plant staff during the emergency period.

For losses occurring as a result of drought and heat wave conditions, procedures would not differ significantly from those proposed for other emergency situations. It is very important that the plant managers remain in regular contact with public agencies, not only fire and police departments, but also health and civil emergency preparedness authorities.

High Humidity and Corrosion

Excess humidity is a peril in itself; moreover, the high moisture content of the air increases chances of loss by corrosion (or rust). Humidity, the degree of moisture in the atmosphere, affects the durability of indoor equipment and buildings.

High Humidity High humidity promotes corrosion, rot, and other deterioration. Computers and other electronic equipment are especially sensitive to humidity (and temperature) variations, and most industrial equipment is designed to operate efficiently only within somewhat broader, but still limited, ranges of atmospheric conditions.

Maintaining the proper humidity and other atmospheric conditions for computers and other machinery and equipment is made doubly important by (1) cost of equipment repair and (2) the value of lost output during any machinery-related downtime. Generally, problems in operating equipment arise when those systems required to maintain space conditioning, whether it is mechanical ventilation or artificial cooling, fail or slip from pre-set ranges.

Pre-Event Action. The most effective pre-event risk control method for indoor equipment is to install a thermometer and relative humidity gauge where machinery and/or operating equipment is kept.

Readings should be monitored on a regular basis, especially during times of extreme variances. For operations that depend on computer hardware or software that is sensitive to humidity, alternative temporary equipment should be located and tested, while crucial computer software and data files are duplicated and stored elsewhere. Know the safe operating ranges of plant equipment, and follow the manufacturer's recommendations for proper use.

Post-Event Actions.   If there is an equipment failure, post-event procedures would include the following:

- Shutting down operating equipment susceptible to damage from temperature/humidity extremes;
- Providing temporary devices such as portable heaters, fans, or air conditioning units to maintain space temperatures within acceptable ranges; and
- Proving humidistats for low-humidity areas and dehumidifiers for high-humidity areas.

Corrosion (Rust)   Corrosion is the action of wearing away, especially by chemical action. It can be caused by exposures to harmful chemical compounds, gases or vapors, salt, acid rain, or other weather-related influences. Rust is one form of corrosion resulting from the oxidation of metal over time. It can impair the operation of machinery and mechanical apparatus and can weaken the structural support members made from iron or steel, resulting in collapse.

The best way to avoid potential problems, of course, is not to expose those susceptible materials to chemical compounds, gases or vapors, or factors of weather. If that is not possible or practicable, the materials should be treated with rust preventatives or inhibitors. Regular inspection of plant/building components, operating equipment, and mechanical apparatus should provide an opportunity to detect any discoloration or pitting from corrosion.

RISK CONTROL FOR GEOLOGICAL PERILS

The surface of the earth is always moving. Some large movements (such as volcanic eruptions and the shifting of the mass plates that make up the earth's land surface) are caused by the great heat at the earth's core; and other movements (such as landslides, erosion, and collapse) result from gravity, wind, water, and other forces at work on the earth's surface. Many of these geological forces work slowly, building up energy or causing gradual wear, which results in a seemingly sudden shifting upheaval, or collapse of the landscape or the structures upon it. This discussion deals with these geological forces and the losses they cause through earthquake, land subsidence, landslide/mudslide, avalanche erosion, soil expansion, volcanic action, and collapse.

Earthquake[1]

Despite its seeming solidity, the surface of the earth is always in motion, although usually on a scale that can be detected by only the most sensitive seismographs. An earthquake is a sudden movement of a portion of this surface that is large enough to attract people's attention and, often, to cause property damage, injury, and death. Earthquakes result from volcanic action or the sudden release of geophysical forces that have accumulated along the edges of tectonic plates that make up the earth's crust. Volcanic or tectonic action may occur either above or below sea level. Earthquakes at sea often cause massive tidal waves that are highly damaging to coastal areas. Earthquakes that rupture underground gas mains also may cause large fires, which can be especially difficult to extinguish if the earthquake has also broken water mains. As indicated in Exhibit 3-6, all but a few areas of the United States are prone to earthquake activity, especially the regions west of the Rocky Mountains, the Piedmont, upper New York State, and New England.

The extent of the harm caused by a particular earthquake depends on (1) the geologic energy released by the quake at its origin (the epicenter of the quake), (2) the distance between the epicenter and the persons or property exposed to damage, and (3) the ability of those persons or that property to withstand the force of the quake. The energy released by an earthquake at its epicenter is measured by the Richter Scale, which gauges the extent of earth movement at the epicenter and converts this movement to "units of magnitude," typically ranging from 1 to 8, but theoretically unlimited. A one-unit increase on the Richter Scale represents approximately a thirty-fold increase in the energy released by an earthquake at its epicenter. In contrast to the Richter measurement, the Modified Mercalli Intensity Scale (presented in Exhibit 3-7) is a twelve-level set of descriptions of an earthquake's effects at any specified location, near or far from that quake's epicenter. The intensity of the energy released by an earthquake diminishes with the square of the distance from the quake's epicenter (much as the brightness of a light or the loudness of a sound decreases with the square of the distance from its source). Therefore, an earthquake of a given Richter magnitude will have different levels of Modified Mercalli Intensity at different distances from the quake's epicenter.

Exhibit 3-6
Seismic Risk Map of the United States*

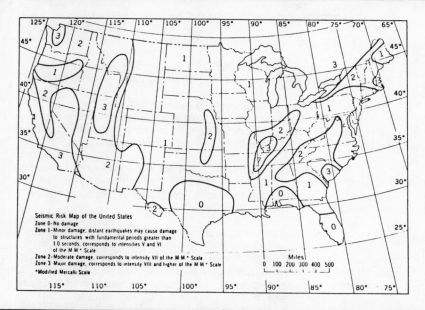

Seismic Risk Map of the United States
Zone 0-No damage
Zone 1-Minor damage, distant earthquakes may cause damage
to structures with fundamental periods greater than
1 0 seconds, corresponds to intensities V and VI
of the M M * Scale
Zone 2-Moderate damage, corresponds to intensity VII of the M M * Scale
Zone 3 Major damage, corresponds to intensity VIII and higher of the M M * Scale
*Modified Mercalli Scale

Miles
0 100 200 300 400 500

*Reprinted with permission from White, Gergely, Sexsmith, *Structural Engineering* (New York: John Wiley & Sons, 1972), vol. I, p. 69.

Pre-Event Actions   It follows that location is—in two senses—a key factor in controlling earthquake damage and injuries. First, persons and property located farther away from volcanic areas and major geological faults (along which earthquakes tend to concentrate) are less likely to experience any detectable earthquakes than those located nearer to such areas. In addition, those quakes that do occur farther away from volcanoes or faults generally will be less intense than those felt nearer to these areas. Second, at any given distance from an epicenter, persons and structures situated on stable earth that can absorb most earthquake shock waves tend to suffer less harm than those located on less stable ground. Consequently, for loss prevention, both the selection of an appropriate geographic region and the choice of a specific site within that region are crucial to earthquake loss control. Evaluation of the quake hazard at any specific site normally requires a detailed geologic analysis beyond the scope of this discussion.

The design of a building or other structure is the second major pre-loss risk control concern for protecting property and people from earthquake harm. A building in an earthquake zone should be

Exhibit 3-7
Modified Mercalli Intensity Scale, 1986 Version*

I. Not felt. Marginal and long-period effects of large earthquakes.

II. Felt by persons at rest on upper floors or favorably placed.

III. Felt indoors. Hanging objects swing. Vibration like passing of light trucks. Duration estimated. May not be recognized as an earthquake.

IV. Hanging objects swing. Vibration like passing of heavy trucks, or sensation of a jolt like a heavy ball striking the walls. Standing motor cars rock. Windows, dishes, doors rattle. Glasses clink. Crockery clashes in the upper range of IV. Wooden walls and frames crack.

V. Felt outdoors, direction estimated. Sleepers wakened. Liquid disturbed, some spilled. Small unstable objects displaced or upset. Doors swing, close, open. Shutters, pictures move. Pendulum clocks stop, start, change rate.

VI. Felt by all. Many frightened and run outdoors. Persons walk unsteadily. Windows, dishes, glassware broken. Knick-knacks, books etc. off shelves. Pictures off walls. Furniture moved or overturned. Weak plaster and masonry D (weak materials such as adobe, poor mortar; low standards of workmanship, weak horizontally) cracked. Small bells ring (church, school). Trees, bushes shaken (visibly, or heard to rustle).

VII. Difficult to stand. Noticed by drivers of motor cars. Hanging objects quiver. Furniture broken. Damage to masonry D, including cracks. Weak chimneys broken at roof line. Fall of plaster, loose bricks, stones, tiles, cornices (also unbraced parapets and architectural ornaments). Some cracks in masonry C (ordinary workmanship and mortar; no extreme weaknesses like failing to tie in at corners, but neither reinforced nor designed against horizontal forces). Waves on ponds, water turbid with mud. Small slides and caving in along sand or gravel banks. Large bells ring. Concrete irrigation ditches damaged.

VIII. Steering of motor cars affected. Damage to masonry C, partial collapse. Some damage to masonry B (good workmanship and mortar, reinforced, but not designed in detail to resist lateral forces), none to masonry A (good workmanship, mortar, and design, reinforced especially laterally and bound together by using steel, concrete, etc., designed to resist lateral forces). Fall of stucco and some masonry walls. Twisting, fall of chimneys, factory stacks, monuments, towers, elevated tanks. Frame houses moved on foundations if not bolted down, loose panel walls thrown out. Decayed piling broken off. Branches broken from trees. Changes in flow or temperature of springs and wells. Cracks in wet ground and on steep slopes.

IX. General panic. Masonry D destroyed, masonry C heavily damaged, sometimes with complete collapse; masonry B seriously damaged. (General damage to foundation.) Frame structures, if not bolted, shifted off foundations. Frames racked. Serious damage to reservoirs. Underground pipes broken. Conspicuous cracks in ground in alluviated areas, sand and mud ejected, earthquake fountains, sand craters.

X. Most masonry and frame structures destroyed with their foundations. Some well-built wooden structures and bridges destroyed. Serious damage to dams, dikes, embankments. Large landslides. Water thrown on banks of canals, rivers, lakes, etc. Sand and mud shifted horizontally on beaches and faultland. Rails bent slightly.

XI. Rails bent greatly. Underground pipelines completely out of service.

XII. Damage nearly total. Large rock masses displaced. Lines of sight and level distorted. Objects thrown into the air.

*Reprinted with permission from "Earthquake Data Sheet" in *Loss Prevention Data* (Hopkinton, MA: Factory Mutual Engineering Corporation, supplemented and revised periodically), Section 1-2, p. 7, Feb. 1987.

constructed so that it can "ride" without damage atop the ground on which it is sitting in case an earthquake strikes. The two major types of earthquake-resistant construction incorporate either *box action design* or *frame action design*. Box action, used in buildings less than three stories tall, integrates roof and floor "diaphragms" that can flex to transmit and distribute the forces an earthquake exerts on a structure, shifting this energy to its exterior walls or to diagonal braces between these walls. Box action buildings are quite "stiff" and able to withstand considerable ground motion, although their foundations or other anchors to the ground may be severed by a severe earthquake. Frame action design relies on the resilience of steel or specially designed reinforced concrete. Selected types of steel or concrete can absorb energy while undergoing considerable distortion, and yet return to their original shapes. Many buildings in quake-prone areas incorporate both box and frame action features.

Post-Event Actions During the perhaps one minute an earthquake is in progress, as well as immediately after the ground motion stops, post-event actions should focus on caring for those who have been injured, protecting uninjured persons, and safeguarding endangered property. A distinctive feature of the earthquake peril is that a major earthquake typically is followed, within the next seventy-two hours, by a series of lesser "aftershocks." Therefore, immediate post-earthquake actions should first focus on protecting lives, and second, on preventing further "aftershock" losses. Weakened buildings or underground piping or other utilities should be reinforced to the extent feasible without endangering persons doing this work. Any buildings that are not designed to withstand earthquake forces should be left temporarily unoccupied, and people should stay clear of areas on which additional debris may fall. Apart from preventing any imminent additional injury or damage, post-loss restoration efforts should wait until the danger of further earthquake action has passed.

Land Subsidence

Land subsidence is the sinking of a land surface, usually over a small area, commonly caused by blasting, mining, ground water (which causes sinkholes to develop), and soil deterioration. Each form of land subsidence creates serious property exposures both to the ground itself and to any structures that may be weakened or collapsed by the affected soil.

Blasting Blasting involves the use of explosive charges to alter the position of the land or to remove materials. For the most part, in the United States, blasting is regulated and specific procedures are to be followed in the use of explosive charges. However, regulation is limited by enforcement, and procedures are only as good as the individuals who interpret and follow them.

Even properly managed blasting can cause unexpected losses. The material subject may not act exactly as anticipated, and buildings can be damaged by flying debris. Also, shock waves can travel some distance within the earth's crust resulting in faults or shifts that can disturb groundwater characteristics—an important exposure for those operations depending on deep wells or even artesian wells for their water supply. The greatest damage, largely from structural collapse, strikes buildings that are resting on unstable ground.

Pre-Event Actions. Pre-event risk control procedures for those exposed to or using blasting agents should include the following:

- Core borings to determine subsurface structure should be completed, and available geological data on the local area should be reviewed with competent, licensed geological or mining engineers.
- The use of many light charges in lieu of one major blast should be considered, and the proper type and size of explosive for the job at hand should be selected.
- Plans should be cleared with local authorities and utilities before blasting, and proper procedures should be reviewed with

the blasting team. Activities and the surrounding area/neighborhood should be monitored for potential blast exposures.

Post-Event Actions. Post-event activities include the following:

- The local area should be inspected for any possible changes in surface conditions not present prior to blasting, such as cracking walls, unusual settling, or changes in small streams or ponds.
- Utilities should be contacted to ensure that services, especially oil and gas pipelines, are intact and fully functional.
- All charges placed should be accounted for, and complete ignition should be verified.

Mining Mining activities involve digging, excavating, or tunneling on or beneath the earth's surface for various minerals and natural ores used in industrial operations. Although surface mining does not present significant hazards to adjacent properties unless blasting is involved, other exposures from these activities present problems such as landslide/mudslide, erosion, and pollution. These will be covered in more detail further on. However, subsurface mining does present some unique exposures to properties from subsidence and from deep mine fires when they break out onto the surface.

Modern mining technology employs methodology developed over a long period and normally does not cause subsidence problems. The planning involved in developing deep mine layouts and the structural support systems prevent subsidence problems. In fact, the deeper the mine, the less likely that subsidence or settling will occur due to the natural geological formations offering support. When problems from subsidence do occur, they usually happen in older mines or independent mining operations. In these instances, mine safety laws were not in effect or were ignored; or mines were dug in the most economical manner, without proper precautions. Over a period of time, due to normal damage and increasing stress on the formation, these mine galleries will cave in. If they are close enough to the surface, the top layer of soil also will drop. Any structures at risk could incur structural damage or, in severe cases, they could totally collapse.

Another significant hazard is a fire deep in a mine, where the remaining coal ignites and can burn for years. Due to the burning fire, formations in the mine and structural supports ultimately will weaken and collapse, causing subsidence, the venting of the fires onto the surface, and the escape of toxic gases released from the combustion process.

Pre-event risk control practices involve means to reduce or eliminate hazardous exposures from subsidence due to mining. After the fact, the only recourse is to leave the area of subsidence since salvage or reconstructive efforts have little value at that point. Before purchasing or siting a plant, an organization should investigate the existence of any deep mines on or adjacent to the site in question by reviewing the site with local and state officials and private mining consulting firms, or by using a physical survey. Necessary core borings should be completed to verify subsurface structure in order to provide evidence should legal recourse be sought.

Sinkholes Sinkholes result from a gradual dissolution of subsurface geological structure (usually limestone) to a point where the cavity caves in, often resulting in a depression on the earth's surface. This dissolution is generally caused by water either percolating through the soil above or contained in subsurface artesian formations. In the continental United States, Florida is particularly susceptible as are many of the valleys within the Appalachian Mountain chain. The geological term for this natural occurrence is *karst topography*, which occurs in various regions. Although many portions of this country have received thorough geologic analysis, the number of sinkholes is surprisingly high. Many of the great caverns that are now public attractions are fine examples of where the limestone strata have been dissolved over a period of years.

The best pre-event risk control practice is to investigate thoroughly the subsurface conditions before purchasing or siting a plant. A qualified geologist or licensed mining engineer can perform a detailed study to determine the acceptability of a particular area. No post-event procedures can adequately provide for salvage or reconstructive efforts.

Soil Deterioration Soil instability or structural deterioration of the soil can be a unique problem to contend with, usually after structures or facilities are placed in the immediate area. Soil is the end product of chemical and physical weathering of rocks. Depending on location and these forces, soil is found in the form of sand. Sometimes, this deterioration can be accelerated by human efforts (such as mining or landscaping), combined with environmental events, to cause a weakening of the soil bearing or support capacity. This condition can lead to instability below building foundations and other supports, collapsing the construction placed on it.

Pre-Event Actions. The best pre-event actions for this exposure include the following:

- Thoroughly investigate surface and subsurface conditions; take borings and samples for analysis.
- Have a qualified geologist or licensed mining engineer perform a detailed study to determine soil integrity acceptability.

- Do not contaminate soil on the property, especially around building foundations, with chemicals or other compounds that break down the soil.
- Protect the soil by following proper land management practices as suggested by the local extension office.
- Inspect building foundations and support pads on a regular basis for any evidence of settling or soil instability; be alert for changes.

Post-Event Actions. Post-event procedures would not be as demanding as those for sinkholes because the hazard associated with recovering materials from structures on unstable ground is less imminent than that associated with sinkholes. The following are some post-event actions:

- Shoring up structures, using wider footings, and/or bracing the structural load on a more stable formation (for example, pilings where shafts are sunk to more stable underground structures).
- Removing and filling areas with more stable material such as concrete, rock, and so on.

Some cases of soil deterioration may require as a loss prevention measure complete demolition and removal of structures even though those structures may currently be undamaged.

Landslide/Mudslide

A landslide is the dislodging and fall (or slide) of a mass of earth and rock. A mudslide combines landslide with water and usually occurs after substantial rainfall.

These phenomena usually develop as a result of building in areas unsuited to supporting structures. Unqualified individuals or determined developers often are responsible for attempting to place buildings in areas where good soil stabilization practices are ignored, exposing the area to potential damage from unusually heavy rainfall. Most structures, once damaged in this way, are difficult to salvage and will be declared a constructive total loss. Unfortunately, a surprising number of people rebuild on exactly the same spot after suffering such a loss.

Pre-Event Actions A proposed site or facility in or near an area known to be susceptible to landslide or mudslide should be surveyed by a competent professional—a geologist, a civil engineer, or a landscape architect. Soil samples and core borings should be taken to determine surface and subsurface characteristics. For a building already erected on a site that might present a landslide or mudslide problem, the following actions may help reduce the exposure:

- The site should be surveyed by a professional, as mentioned above.
- The slope or configuration of the area should be altered to reduce the exposure.
- Natural features should be installed to deflect the slide, such as rock barriers or rip-raps, earth dikes, swales, or trenches. The surface of the slide area should be stabilized with deep-rooted plants or rainfall-deflecting ground cover.
- Structural supports for exposed buildings should be increased to withstand the impact and dynamic/static loading.
- The structure should be moved to a geologically more stable location.

Post-Event Actions The area of a landslide should be secured against unauthorized entry, and utility lines should be checked for breaks or ruptures. A dangerous combination could exist if electric lines are arcing in an area where a natural gas line has been ruptured. In this instance, the area should be evacuated immediately and the utility companies informed. Other post-event activities include the following:

- Temporary supports should be provided for stressed building members exposed to landslide or mudslide material.
- Any facility in a landslide area should be inspected for damage and protected against further harm.
- Salvage and cleanup should be started as soon as possible, and components and equipment exposed to damage should be inspected prior to use. High moisture levels could damage motor windings even though the outward appearance would give no indication of this.
- All activities should be coordinated with public authorities.

Avalanche

An avalanche is a sudden fall or slide of a large mass of rock, earth, or other material down a mountainside or over a precipice. Avalanches during the winter can involve massive collapses of snow-banks. Most avalanches occur in isolated mountain areas generally well away from population centers. However, certain kinds of operations are exposed to avalanches by their very nature, such as winter resorts, mining and lumbering communities, and lines of communication and transportation.

Ski patrols in winter resort areas, federal government and management, state disaster management teams, and some private organizations such as railroad and civil engineering groups will practice avalanche risk control procedures in those areas where exposures can subject their facilities or personnel to damage. Some of their procedures include the following:

- Breaking up dangerous avalanche masses, before the natural forces reach the falling point, by forcing smaller avalanches which cause little or no damage. This is done by firing artillery rounds into the mass or setting off demolition charges to break it loose.
- Covering exposed transportation arteries with substantial structures such as tunnels or covered passages.
- Modifying the local terrain to channel the release or create natural barriers to block the path of movement.

Even though avalanche-prone areas are monitored on a regular basis where the exposure is great to both buildings and personnel, the best risk control practice is to remain entirely away from those areas. The natural forces and the exposures they present cannot always be mollified by man's efforts.

The devastation caused by an avalanche resembles, in its totality, that of a tornado. Therefore, the post-event risk control actions— focusing on the preservation of life and the salvage of any remaining property—are comparable to those appropriate following a tornado.

Erosion

Unlike landslide or mudslide, erosion is a gradual wearing or carrying away of the soil by abrasion or dissolution (disintegration or decomposition). Erosion is commonly associated with the effects of water or wind, and the most common causes are runoff or rainfall drainage. The "dust bowl" in the thirties, however, resulted from wind erosion that caused a catastrophic soil loss and extensive property damage.

Pre-Event Actions Special attention should be focused on rainfall drainage/runoff erosion, which can undermine structures, stressing building components to a point of collapse. Also, the materials contained in the runoff may accumulate against some structure, resulting in a situation similar to the effect of a mudslide. Pre-event procedures include the following:

- Suitable ground cover should be maintained in all areas. Where areas are excavated and left barren, they should be covered with suitable material such as burlap cloth or polysheets to stabilize the soil.
- Proper site drainage should be provided and reviewed by a licensed civil engineer or landscape architect to create gradual runoff slopes in lieu of waterfalls or cascades. Areas around all buildings should be graded away from the foundation, and drainage routes should not pass adjacent to any structure.

Post-Event Actions Post-event procedures are not very complex unless heavy earthmoving equipment is required to backfill the eroded area or an affected structure is in danger of collapse. The following actions may be required:

- Temporarily stabilize an eroding landscape with heavy timbers, rocks, sandbags, or similar material that would not wash away and would hold back some of the soil. Divert the rainfall or runoff stream to some other area.
- Provide temporary supports for stressed building members where foundations or walls have been uncovered by erosion, and protect building openings against the entry of water and foreign material.
- Begin salvage and cleanup as soon as possible.
- Permanently repair eroded area and protect until groundcover has taken root.

Soil Expansion

Soil expansion results when moisture in the soil freezes as the outside air temperature reaches or falls below the freezing point. Depending on the climatic zone, freezing temperatures can penetrate the soil to depths of five feet or more in the continental United States. Water, when frozen, expands—one of the few material elements to do so—and this expansion will deform the soil profile. A heaving-frost is another term for this kind of soil expansion.

A major problem resulting from soil expansion is structural instability of the soil. The mechanical and hydraulic force that can be exerted by soil expansion can raise small structures, crack foundations on larger buildings, and rupture underground piping. Most potential hazards exist because of poor planning or shoddy workmanship.

These loss exposures can be reduced substantially by observing the following construction guidelines:

- Bury subsurface structures such as footings or pilings below the frost line. This can be verified with most contractors, civil engineers, or architects in the immediate area.
- Where construction must extend through the frost line zone, appropriate expansion fittings should be used.

For losses from soil expansion, the following may be applicable to reduce or limit the extent of damage:

- For utility piping, immediately shut off and isolate the damaged area. Repairs should be completed as soon as possible to limit disruptions.
- For foundations, provide temporary bracing with heavy timbers or quick installation jack posts and steel columns, excavate the affected area, and restore soil base integrity with concrete or similar material. An area may be thermally isolated if it is not possible to dig below the frost line by using sheets of rigid plastic insulating board. This material will not rot, deteriorate, or dissolve like some materials.

Volcanic Action

Volcanic eruptions are spectacular events in the continuing change in the earth's form. A volcano is a vent in the earth's crust from which molten or hot rock and steam issue forth. This vent is, essentially, a weak point on the surface of the planet. The superheated material (technically, magma) will start to move upward toward the surface and, from high temperatures and pressures, will soon find the point of least resistance and burst out onto the surface.

Although volcanoes have been observed for many years, only recently have scientists understood some of the basic facts about this phenomenon. They are complex events influenced by many variables, and some of the observed characteristics are so subtle that only slight changes occur over many years. While scientific equipment is becoming more sophisticated, and high-speed computers can make general assessments, it remains very difficult to predict the frequency or severity of volcanic action.

The United States is affected by a string of volcanoes in the western Pacific that touches upon Alaska, Hawaii, Oregon, and Washington. This region is known as the "Ring of Fire." These are the only areas in this country that are significantly exposed to volcanic action. The eruption of Mount Saint Helens in 1979 demonstrated the damage that can result from mudflows, fly ash, and dust thrown into the atmosphere. In fact, the ash, heat, lava flows, and rocks are but a few of the hazards presented by a volcano. Volcanoes can cause tsunamis (tidal waves), inundation, "glowing cloud" (incandescent fly ash that can, from extremely high heat, ignite just about any material), steam (superheated, of course), and noxious/toxic gases including carbon monoxide and hydrogen sulfide. Also, sulfuric acid and hydrochloric acid are formed from chemical changes during an eruption. In fact, an acid rain condition may develop from volcano-induced rainfall when some of the acids combine with condensed particles in the atmosphere.

Nothing can be done to mitigate a volcanic eruption—a force equal to several hundred megaton thermonuclear explosive devices. The best course of action is to thoroughly investigate the site for any potential exposure to eruption. Minor earthquakes often occur prior to and during eruption. In other areas of the world where land use and construction is carefully planned, some building is permitted in proximity to volcanoes, but no site is truly safe. Well downstream from some volcanoes, exposures to lava flows can be reduced by erecting material barriers and channels, cooling the lava front with sea water, and even bombing the lava front to divert the flow. But these are not always successful because such natural events do not often behave in a predictable fashion. The best course of action is to locate far from volcanoes.

Collapse

Collapse is the sudden falling of a structure, natural or artificial, in response to the force of gravity (i.e., "under its own weight"). In buildings, collapse often is caused by improper design, installation, or maintenance of building structural components. Collapse may also be caused by overloading a structure beyond its original design capacity. Most often, the failure involves columns, roof supports, and reinforcing bracing. Extensive damage may result from a local structural failure overstressing adjacent components and causing them to fail as well. A good design, however, will tolerate a local failure. This is why construction should be completed by a licensed structural engineer—an important factor in minimizing future problems. Installation of the structural components must be completed according to the design drawings and specifications and field-checked to verify conformance to proper work practices and correctness of the construction. This follow-up is very important to ensure that all requirements have been satisfied.

Adequate maintenance is necessary to reduce the effects of deteriorating influences such as rust and chemical corrosion and to check for physical damage that could weaken the structural integrity. Physical damage may be caused by industrial trucks colliding with columns, crane loads swinging into side or knee bracing, or deformation of structural members by exposure to high temperatures. Even though a structural support system appears stable, the system may be under considerable stress. Therefore, components should be routinely inspected. Workers should be encouraged to report any unusual conditions without hesitation so that repairs might be made before the structure is further weakened.

Pre-Event Actions Pre-event procedures for reducing or eliminating potential exposures include the following:

- Maintaining adequate clearances between storages and mobile equipment to support members, and using barriers as required around bottoms and corners of upright columns.
- Treating surfaces of structural elements with rust/corrosion/rot inhibitors (paints, plasticizers, and similar coatings).
- Adhering to recommended roof and floor loads.
- Keeping roof drains clear.
- Promptly removing accumulations of ice and snow.

Post-Event Actions The following post-event procedures should reduce or eliminate the extent of loss:

- The area should be cleared of unnecessary personnel and equipment, including storage materials.
- Temporary bracing should be provided with wood or steel elements to relieve as much stress as possible on the damaged member.
- A competent contractor or licensed structural engineer should inspect the damage and begin repairs immediately.

EMERGENCY RESPONSE PLAN FOR NATURAL PERILS[2]

The value of an ongoing risk control program for natural perils is to reduce the potential losses that an organization may suffer when any natural peril strikes. However, even with the most comprehensive and sophisticated program, an organization is subject to certain exposures beyond its control or capacity to respond. Therefore, the risk management professional, in conjunction with senior management and other managerial personnel, should develop an emergency response plan (ERP). An ERP defines needs, assigns responsibilities, organizes resources for effective and efficient response, and describes the courses of action for handling emergency conditions. It is a written statement that will provide sufficient information, direction, and predetermined courses of action to ensure the appropriate response to emergency conditions brought on by natural perils. Emergency response plans for natural perils are special cases of crisis management plans, which are discussed more fully in Chapter 12.

Reasons for Developing an Emergency Response Plan

When an emergency arises, it is too late to plan and implement an adequate response in the wake of confusion, emotional distraction, muddled coordination, and other factors common to catastrophic disasters. The safety of personnel and the viability of future operations may well depend on the effectiveness of the emergency response plan. An ERP can provide the following:

- Adequate time to prepare an effective response before a natural peril strikes,
- An opportunity to investigate and select alternative responses to different possible combinations of natural perils,
- Organization and training of personnel for emergency situations, and
- Advance planning of coordinated efforts with outside agencies.

Major Areas Addressed by an Emergency Response Plan

An effective ERP should address four key concerns: (1) loss prevention measures, (2) loss reduction measures, (3) coordination of emergency responses, and (4) post-emergency recovery actions.

Loss Prevention Measures The likelihood that a building and its contents may be damaged by windstorm, flood, or other natural perils is greatly influenced by the condition of that building and its contents. Good housekeeping and proper storage practices; smoking restrictions; maintenance of building structures and supporting elements; proper installation, operation, and maintenance of production and processing equipment; sound electrical system installation, operation, and maintenance according to National Electrical Code requirements; proper installation, operation, and maintenance of space and process heating equipment; accepted procedures for welding and cutting operations, proper storage and handling of flammable materials and liquids; and adherence to safe work procedures all can make both real and personal property less vulnerable to damage from many natural perils.

Loss Reduction Measures The amount of damage a natural peril brings to a structure and to the property and persons within it can be reduced by such protection/control systems as separations between different occupancies within a single building; properly installed and maintained automatic fire suppression systems; functioning alarm systems; and any other emergency apparatus, equipment, or devices appropriate for the diking of floods, removal of snow, repelling harmful insects, or dealing with other natural perils peculiar to specific environments.

Coordination of Emergency Response A coordinator—ideally, an individual trained and experienced in responding to emergency conditions—should be appointed to work with others within and outside the organization in anticipating potential emergency conditions and planning specific response actions; reviewing plans with public fire protection and emergency services agencies; and working with trade organizations to review program development and to share results.

Post-Emergency Recovery Actions After the storm has passed and as the flood waters recede, an organization needs to be able to clean up, protect, and restore damaged equipment and facilities as soon as possible; contact raw materials suppliers, as well as customers, to reschedule shipments; and to establish a general timetable for resuming normal operations.

Procedure for Establishing an Emergency Response Plan

Due to the diversity of organizations' facilities and operations, an ERP should be tailored to each particular situation. No standard plan can properly address all needs. To develop an effective response to emergency situations arising from natural perils, the organization should identify and evaluate factors that might contribute to major losses and establish procedures for controlling these losses:

1. Management should take an active role in program development and implementation, and continue to emphasize the importance of emergency preparedness. The ERP should be part of the organization's rules and procedures; it should be written, with copies prepared and regularly updated. One copy should be kept at each facility, one copy with the ERP coordinator, and others with local public officials.
2. Detailed drawings should be completed for each facility to show access roads, buildings, ancillary facilities (such as railroad sidings, tank farms, and storage areas), exposing structures and facilities, local topography (elevation, rivers, streams, lakes, hills, and the like), and utility service lines and control valves.

3. Emergency procedures should be designed to evacuate personnel from each building by, at least, two separate routes. Diagrams showing these routes should be posted at each floor or major area in each building, including designated assembly and first-aid points.
4. Procedures should be developed for shutting down potentially hazardous operations so that they do not contribute to the emergency and can be protected from further damage. Specific directions should be posted for each operation and piece of equipment, with definite personnel assignments.
5. A definitive procedure should be established for reporting plant emergencies to public agencies. Emergency telephone numbers usually include fire, police, and rescue departments, insurance companies, utility companies, contractors and salvage companies, and other specialized or emergency services. The ERP coordinator should be the designated spokesperson to handle the news media, and all employees should be instructed to refer news media personnel to this individual.
6. A complete, up-to-date roster of all plant employees should be prepared for roll call purposes and for family contacts in the event of an emergency. This roster should include the employee's name, job position, address, phone number, dates of birth and employment, and persons to contact (address and phone).
7. The ERP should be reviewed with new employees as part of their orientation and training, with all employees whenever the plan is changed, and at least annually in all cases. In addition, practice drills should be conducted in cooperation with outside agencies that normally would respond to emergencies.

ANALYZING SEQUENTIAL RISK CONTROL DECISIONS[3]

In designing a risk control program for natural or other perils, an organization may face a sequence of related choices, where the choice of one option early in the sequence affects the availability or the merits of another option later in the same sequence. For example, in seeking to protect a new factory (or other new facility) from loss due to weather or geological perils, an organization may seek to determine the best combination of location and construction and protection features. Its initial choice of location may, however, affect the later selection of the best construction and protection features. Because choosing the best construction and protection features requires a prior choice of location, the decision tool known as a "decision tree" offers an efficient way of analyzing, in their proper order, all the possible alternatives.

Constructing Decision Trees

Making sound choices among such options—as various locations and construction and protection features—requires that decisions are made in the proper sequence and that each choice is carefully considered in light of all previous choices. The general management tool known as a "decision tree" is most appropriate for analyzing such complex situations.

As a simplified illustration, assume that Gamma Manufacturing Company has the choice of locating a new plant in Quaketon (an area of great seismic activity) or in Steadyville (where detectable earthquakes have never occurred in recorded history). Land on which to build is cheaper in Quaketon than in Steadyville, but if Gamma opts for the Quaketon site, it may decide to erect an earthquake-resistive structure rather than to use the less expensive ordinary construction that would be adequate for the Steadyville site.

These options can be depicted and analyzed through a decision tree like that presented in Exhibit 3-8. Any decision tree consists of a number of "branches" located at points where either (1) an organization must make a choice, or (2) a chance event may create different "states of nature" that affect the financial consequences ("payoffs") resulting from the organization's decisions. By convention, decision trees progress from left to right, decision points are shown as solid squares, and chance events that create different "states of nature" are shown as small solid circles. Thus, in Exhibit 3-8, the first decision point portrays Gamma's choice between locating its facility in Quaketon or Steadyville. If it chooses Quaketon, the organization then faces a second decision: the choice between using ordinary construction or earthquake-resistive construction in Quaketon; however, if it chooses Steadyville, ordinary construction is the only reasonable building style.

Which option Gamma should choose at each decision point depends heavily on its estimates of (1) the frequency and severity of earthquakes in these two locations and (2) the rates of return on its investment Gamma can expect from the new facility under various earthquake conditions. Assume that the seismologists with whom Gamma's risk management professional has conferred concur in estimating that, in any given year in Quaketon, there is a 63 percent chance of no significant earthquake, a 30 percent chance of a moderate quake, and a 7 percent chance of a severe one. In Steadyville, these experts believe there is essentially no chance of any quake, making the probability of "no quake" in any given year essentially 1.0. These

Exhibit 3-8
Illustrative Decision Tree: Earthquake Risk Control

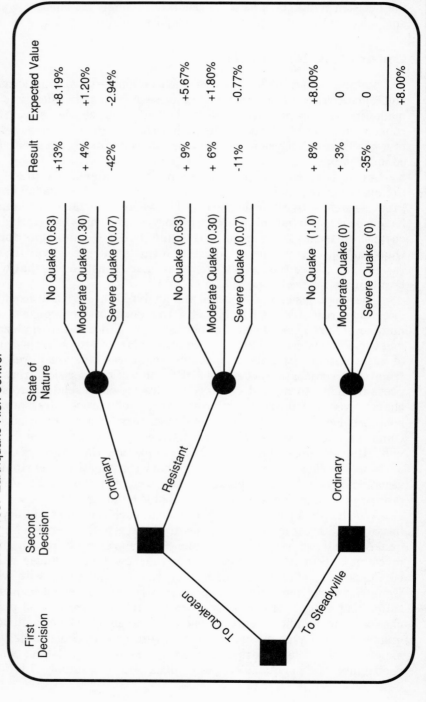

probabilities are shown at the ends of each of nine "branches" near the right side of the decision tree in the exhibit.

Analyzing Options

Based on the interplay between land costs that are lower in Quaketon than in Steadyville and on the costs of earthquake-resistive construction that are higher than those of ordinary construction, Gamma's risk management professional and financial executives have developed the estimated rates of return on the projected new facility for each of the nine possible branches of the tree. These estimated rates of return are shown in the "Result" column near the right side of Exhibit 3-8. For example, the most optimistic possible outcome of Gamma's two decisions and of chance seismic events—using ordinary construction in Quaketon during a year when no quakes occur—probably would generate a 13 percent rate of return for Gamma; moderate quake activity in any given year would yield a 4 percent rate of return; and a severe quake, heavily damaging the new facility and rendering it inoperative for at least two years, would result in a 42 percent negative rate of return for this period. However, if Gamma were to choose to move to Quaketon and erect an earthquake-resistive building, the higher construction cost would lead to a rate of return of only 9 percent in years when no quakes occurred. In a moderate quake, the more resilient structure would yield an estimated rate of return of 6 percent, somewhat higher than the 4 percent rate of return for a building of ordinary construction. In a severe quake, the resistive construction would reduce Gamma's loss on this facility to only 11 percent in that year, in contrast to the negative 42 percent expected from ordinary construction in a year of severe earthquake activity at the Quaketon site.

If Gamma were to locate in Steadyville and use ordinary construction, the higher cost of land would lower its estimated rates of return to somewhat below those the company could expect from using ordinary construction in Quaketon when there is no quake activity. For example, Gamma would realize an 8 percent rate of return in the "No Quake" state of nature in Steadyville in contrast to the 13 percent return under the same state of nature in Quaketon.

This decision tree demonstrates that Gamma has three choices: to use ordinary construction in Quaketon, to use quake-resistant construction in Quaketon, and to use ordinary construction in Steadyville. Determining the expected value of each of these three choices involves two steps. The first is to compute the expected value of each of the nine potential outcomes generated by Gamma's three possible choices in each of the three possible states of nature. The expected value of each outcome can be determined by multiplying each estimated rate of return by the probability of that rate of return being realized. For example, the probability of the +13 percent rate of return is 0.63 percent, giving this result an expected value of an 8.19 percent rate of return, computed as +13% × 0.63. The expected value of the other eight possible results is shown in the "Expected Value" column of the exhibit.

The second step is to find the sum of the expected values of the three possible results for each choice. That is, the expected value of erecting a building of ordinary construction in Quaketon is a +6.45 percent rate of return; that of a quake-resistive structure in Quaketon is +6.7 percent; and that of an ordinary structure in Steadyville is +8 percent.

This illustration of a decision tree, while highly simplified, should demonstrate the value of this technique in structuring and analyzing potentially confusing sets of interrelated decisions. The portrayal of all available options in a single diagram can forestall many questions from managers who may begin their inquiries with "Yes, but..." or "I understand that, but now what if...." Presenting a risk control decision, or any other risk management decision, in a decision tree format can also help a risk management professional be confident that he or she has considered and evaluated all possible alternatives.

SUMMARY

This chapter deals with two major groups of natural perils—meteorological and geological forces. The chapter emphasizes loss reduction measures to reduce the severity of unavoidable losses through appropriate actions before and after these natural, potentially harmful events. It also emphasizes loss prevention through pre-event actions to reduce the likelihood that these natural perils will cause any loss.

Some common threads unify this chapter. One is loss prevention through careful choice of areas in which an organization locates its operations. Such meteorological perils as windstorm, hailstorm, thunderstorm, flood, drought, extreme heat, and severe winter weather are each more likely to occur in some geographic areas than in others. The same is true (although on a more localized basis) for such geological perils as earthquake, land subsidence, landslide, soil erosion, soil expansion, and volcanic action. Therefore, while no location is totally safe from all natural perils discussed in this chapter, some are more secure than others from any specific peril.

All the perils examined in this chapter illustrate a second unifying theme: the critical importance of pre-event planning. Most natural disasters strike so quickly and are so soon past that a response that effectively controls losses cannot be innovated at the moment these perils strike. For such natural disasters, an emergency response plan needs to be devised and in place. It should involve all managers within an organization in planning and practicing loss prevention and loss reduction measures. It should also coordinate in advance the actions an organization's personnel—in addition to police, fire, and other officials—should take to prevent or minimize losses when a natural peril strikes.

Chapter Notes

1. The material under this heading is reproduced by permission of the Factory Mutual Engineering Corporation, *Loss Prevention Data Sheet*, "Earthquake," section 1-2, pp. 6-7 (revised February 1987).
2. The material under this heading is reproduced by permission of Millers Mutual Insurance Company, Harrisburg, PA.
3. The material under this heading draws on E. Frank Harrison, *The Managerial Decision-Making Process*, 3rd ed. (Boston: Houghton Mifflin Company, 1987), pp. 372-381.

CHAPTER 4

Maintaining Security

No organization, profit or nonprofit, private or public, can operate or achieve its objectives without assets. Most broadly defined, an asset is anything of value, whether tangible or intangible, that is owned by some person or organization.[1]

"Security," again in its broadest sense, denotes the protection of assets from all types of harm. Much of this text deals with security in this broad context—protection of an organization's physical, financial, and human assets from damage, destruction, or injury by natural, human, and economic perils. In the narrower context of the current chapter, however, "security" refers to protection of assets, typically tangible but occasionally intangible (such as information or ideas), from crime. This chapter focuses primarily on preventing or minimizing losses from crime. There are some references to other types of losses or disasters that some organizations consider as concerns to be dealt with through their security program.

This chapter begins with a survey of loss exposures associated with violent or surreptitious actions and then describes the essential elements of a security program through which any organization may deal with these exposures. Based on this analysis, the remaining portions of the chapter describe appropriate security measures for a computer center, suitable measures for preventing loss from dishonesty involving an organization's employees (embezzlement and fraud), and effective countermeasures for other forms of violence such as robbery, burglary, riot, and vandalism. The chapter also describes safeguards in terms of the general risk control techniques—exposure avoidance, loss prevention, loss reduction, and the contractual transfers for risk control—to which the safeguards apply.

165

NATURE OF SECURITY EXPOSURES

The proper beginning for a security risk control program is an analysis or classification of an event that may fall within the boundaries of the program. Not every loss is a security loss. For example, the loss of sales due to effective, but legal, competition is not a security loss. The loss of key manpower to another employer who offers a better inducement is not a security loss. Complete loss of a market because a legitimate competitor introduces a product sooner is not a security loss. These losses are not security losses because they do not stem from illegal, violent, or otherwise wrongful human conduct—the conduct that does characterize the security losses on which this chapter focuses.

Classification of Security Exposures

Exhibit 4-1 is a summary of exposures that are common to many organizations. The exhibit does not show all security exposures, but it does include all the primary ones found throughout industry. The first three major categories of security exposures—war, natural catastrophe, and industrial disaster—are security exposures in the broadest sense. The remaining categories—sabotage and malicious destruction, theft, and various other forms of undesirable human conduct—can all generate losses that result directly from the misconduct of individuals. In the restrictive sense of the term "security" adopted for the present discussion, only those losses categorized as resulting from sabotage, malicious destruction, and theft of assets will be treated in detail in this chapter.

The arrangement of the selected exposures in Exhibit 4-1 reflects their "criticality." As detailed below, criticality is a measure of the potential impact of a security loss. How much will it "really hurt" if the loss occurs? Some exposures high on the criticality scale (nearer the top in the exhibit) are showing a marked uptrend in the United States and elsewhere in the world. Incendiary fires and bombings, in particular, have increased in recent years, and the public statement by various militant groups suggests that terrorist techniques involving these perils are an important part of their tactical planning.

Less dramatic, more "routine" crimes are also an increasing menace. Crime in the United States rose 176 percent during the 1960s, another 55 percent during the 1970s, and is rising again after a brief decline in 1982 and 1983. The FBI Uniform Crime Reports (UCR)—the source of crime frequency data—are criticized by some as being misleading or artificial because they are affected by such factors as improvements in the reporting of crime. Yet aside from artificial

Exhibit 4-1
Major Security Exposures

War or Nuclear Attack

Natural Catastrophe

Tornado	Hurricane
Earthquake	Flood

Industrial Disasters

Explosion	Fire
Structural collapse	Radiation incident
Major accident	Toxic substance release

Sabotage and Malicious Destruction

Incendiary fire	Bombs and bomb threats
Labor violence	Civil disturbance
Vandalism	Terrorism

Theft of Assets

Pilferage	Embezzlement
Fraud	Industrial espionage
Records manipulation	Shoplifting
Forgery	Robbery and hijacking
Car thefts	Kidnapping

Conflict of Interests

Employees with their own businesses	Employees working for competitors
	Kickback situations

Personnel Problems

Gambling	Absenteeism
Loan-sharking	Misrepresentation
Disaffection	Substance abuse
Disturbed persons	Antisocial behavior

Miscellaneous Risks

Traffic accidents	National security problems

fluctuations caused by changes in reporting techniques, crime itself is significantly increasing. In the 1967 report by the President's Commission on Law Enforcement and the Administration of Justice, survey data about crime frequency were first presented independently of the Uniform Crime Reports and have continued to be so presented in the annual National Crime Survey. The surveys showed the actual amount of crime in the United States to be several times that reported in the UCR.

Aggravating these commercial exposures is the persistent growth in the size and aggregate value of assets exposed to single-incident losses. The dependence of almost all organizations on their own or others' daily output of computers and electronic data processing facilities has made such equipment a prime security concern. Loss of computer capabilities may have staggering cost consequences because of delay or termination of functions that depend upon these computers.

Recognition of Security Exposures

Recognition of a specific security exposure often requires a special skill; it is not entirely a common sense activity that can be reliably done by typical managers alone. For example, access to an industrial plant or business office is not necessarily limited to entry through doors and windows. Access can be gained through openings such as utility service entrances, ventilators, and roof hatches, or even by the forcible penetration of building walls and/or roofs. An awareness of these unusual opportunities for access is essential to a workable security plan. It should also be recognized that a supply of cash or of items of intrinsically high value will attract a thief irrespective of whether the thief must enter through a door, an air conditioning duct, or a hole in the wall. If all options are available, the thief will most probably select the one that requires the least effort and involves the lowest likelihood of detection. However, securing one or two points of access and ignoring a third may not deter a thief; it will only reduce the options for entry. If the option is safe and easy enough, the thief will take it. Therefore, eliminating some security exposures while ignoring others may be more expensive than having ignored all exposures because the loss may still occur. It will have to be borne in addition to the cost of implementing the incomplete, thus ineffective, security precautions. The point is that the ability to recognize real exposures is primary in the assessment of loss potential.

Each type of criminal or violent loss has its own complex of circumstances and conditions that make it possible. It is not usual for a business manager or owner to be personally familiar with all the factors involved in each exposure within an organization. However, an organization's risk management professional—usually acting with a security or safety specialist within the organization or an outside expert—has a primary responsibility for identifying and designing controls for the organization's security exposures.

A security exposure analysis performed by persons not expert in this field will almost certainly lead to improper controls. Furthermore, as circumstances and conditions change, exposures must be reappraised. This assessment is not a task done once; it is a continuing effort.

Matrix Techniques for Recognizing Exposures In analyzing the extent of particular security exposures, the use of grids or matrixes will increase the likelihood that all relevant factors will be considered. These tools also contribute to assessment of the chance of loss. Exhibit 4-2 is a typical matrix used for analyzing a retailer's exposures of cash to theft. The left side of the exhibit shows where cash is maintained on the premises and, for each place, lists the major factors that affect this exposure. The physical situation, accounting records, alarm protection, cash storage facilities, control and surveillance of admittance, and the presence of bait money are important among such factors. Also important is the known history of cash losses from each location. Because most organizations do not operate on a twenty-four-hour basis, it is necessary—for both exposure analysis and appropriate control measures—to distinguish between crime losses that occur during working hours and those that happen during nonworking hours.

The illustrative matrix in Exhibit 4-2 could have been extended to include many other relevant but somewhat more remote factors, such as whether the cash is kept primarily in coin or paper. Large quantities of coins are not nearly as attractive a theft target as smaller physical volumes, but larger values, in paper money. The selection of precisely which factors are to be included in the matrix is a judgment that requires specialized skills.

An appropriate matrix should be developed for each security exposure identified at each particular location. Each matrix serves as a summary and as a trend marker. In one place and in an integrated fashion, the relevant factors for a particular exposure can be arranged so that they may be rapidly reviewed. Noting whether the same factor appears in several places highlights general security weaknesses. Thus, if it appeared that exposure to theft or unauthorized admittance was frequently increased by the absence of locking devices, this particular security weakness would be manifest.

Probabilities of Security Losses One of the most important functions of a security exposure matrix is to guide estimates of probabilities of loss. A security exposure becomes a greater problem as

Exhibit 4-2
Cash Theft Exposure Matrix

Exposure Factors / Building Location	Amount on Hand, Dollars (NBH)	Amount on Hand, Dollars (OT)	Accountability Records (NBH)	Accountability Records (OT)	Area Has Physical Bounds (NBH)	Area Has Physical Bounds (OT)	Area Locked (NBH)	Area Locked (OT)	Positive Controls on Admittance (NBH)	Positive Controls on Admittance (OT)	Alarm Protection (NBH)	Alarm Protection (OT)	Surveillance Devices (NBH)	Surveillance Devices (OT)	Cash in Storage Container (NBH)	Cash in Storage Container (OT)	Bail Money Kept (NBH)	Bail Money Kept (OT)	History of Cash Loss (NBH)	History of Cash Loss (OT)
Cashier's office	20,000	5,000	Y	Y	Y	Y	N	Y	N	N	Y	Y	N	N	Y	Y	Y	Y	N	N
Manager's secretary	300	300	Y	Y	N	N	N	Y	Y	N	N	N	N	N	Y	Y	N	N	Y	Y
Cafeteria	1,000	0	N	N	Y	Y	N	N	N	N	N	N	N	N	N	—	N	—	Y	N
Employee's store	500	0	Y	N	Y	Y	Y	Y	N	N	N	N	N	N	Y	—	N	—	N	N
Reception	100	0	N	N	N	N	N	N	N	N	N	N	N	N	N	—	N	—	N	N

NBH = normal business hours;   OT = other times;   Y = yes;   N = no the probability of loss increases. A fundamental step in designing security countermeasures is the quantification, to the maximum extent possible, of the probabilities of various losses.

The impact of technical developments on exposures to industrial espionage and theft is of primary importance. To the manager who does not appreciate the difference between a latch, a dead bolt, and a deadlocking latch bolt, the device that secures his plant after hours may be only a passing interest. However, to the potential intruder, the difference may determine whether or not he even makes an attempt at entry. As each security device or procedure is introduced, it is merely a matter of time before a tool or technique is found to defeat or circumvent it. Knowing the array of the most current tools and techniques is a necessary part of assessing an organization's vulnerability.

If two security exposures of approximately equal severity exist, the one with the higher probability of loss deserves greater attention. While this is clear, it is also an oversimplification; in virtually no organization would there be only two exposures that compete for attention. In even the most modest enterprise, there will be dozens, and in the major industrial installations there will be thousands. If prioritizing is indicated when only two vulnerabilities exist, prioritizing is even more necessary when dozens or thousands of security exposures must be considered. Without a systematic theoretical basis on which to proceed, time and money, always limited, may be expended on exposures of lesser importance, while serious problems go unheeded.

Few organizations have sufficient reliable data on which to base the assignment of specific probabilities to particular security exposures. An alternative approach involves a rough grading technique in which the following five broad levels of probability are assigned to various classes of events, based substantially on subjective evaluations: (1) the event is virtually certain to occur; (2) the event is highly probable; (3) the event is moderately probable, that is, equally likely to occur or not to occur; (4) the event is improbable; or (5) the probability of occurrence is unknown.

The risk management professional or a security consultant should be able to use data within a particular organization or to use industry-wide statistics to assign one of the first four levels of probability to any specific security exposure. If there is any doubt about which level of probability is applicable, conservatism calls for assigning the higher level of probability to that event in order not to underestimate any significant security exposures. When the probability of loss for a given exposure is not known, or more precisely where there is no reliable data upon which to base an estimated probability, every risk management professional should consider the "probability unknown" rating as only provisional and should seek additional data on chances of loss. In time, this provisional rating should be replaced by a more definite evaluation of loss probabilities.

A meaningful determination or estimate of security loss probabilities requires that exposures arising from an organization's every operation and at an organization's every location be scrutinized. In all instances, the search should be for *hazards*. These are factors that make more likely or more severe the occurrence of a loss. These hazards fall into one of the following classes: (1) *physical environment*, including location, composition, and spatial relationships, (2) *procedural aspects*, (3) *history*, particularly history of past losses, and (4) *criminal state of the art*.

The fourth class requires special note. To know whether a security exposure involves high or low probability sometimes demands a technical awareness of the range and capability of tools available to a thief or other aggressor. Safes and vaults, for example, provided an entirely different level of physical security against forced entry before the development of the thermal lance than they have since. As another illustration, microminiature radio transceivers featuring integrated circuits can be concealed in places once too small to be feasible, and they can operate longer on low-output power sources.

Costs and Criticality of Security Losses Assigning probability to an event or events, important though it is, is not the only basis for developing corresponding countermeasures (or risk control measures). A loss may be highly probable, even certain to occur, but may be of such small financial consequence as not to deserve attention, or at least it will not be a priority. The second characteristic to be evaluated for each exposure is its criticality.

Most simply defined, the *criticality* of a security loss is the potential financial impact of that loss. Dollars matter because dollars (more precisely, cash flows) determine any organization's ability to command resources to meet that organization's objectives. Security specialists sometimes say that they find management unresponsive to security problems. In most of those cases, further study reveals that the management has not been given a proper basis for response. If an executive with profit-and-loss responsibility is to determine whether to devote available dollars to a security program, he or she must be able to discount those dollars in alternative cash flow patterns. An organization should spend money to prevent security losses only when the long-term dollar benefits of such expenditures exceed the present value of the needed outlays.

It is in this area that serious oversights are committed. Although a risk manager or consulting adviser can identify the types of security exposures and even assess the probability of their occurrence without direct help from the organization, it is improbable that either will be able to determine the criticality of a loss without assistance. The reason is that more information is needed on costs of alternative controls to prevent or minimize security losses.

Costs. Criticality can involve four types of costs: permanent replacement costs, temporary replacement costs, consequential costs, and opportunity costs.

Permanent Replacement Costs. If an asset is lost or destroyed (whether by theft, violence, or other peril), it may be necessary to replace it to continue operations. This would be true, for example, for a stolen machine tool, a burned out electric transformer, or a damaged computer main frame. Permanent replacement cost—depending upon whether the replacement asset is purchased or made by the organization—may include (1) purchase price, (2) freight and installation, (3) labor, (4) materials costs, and (5) other costs. One example of other costs would be travel or communications expenses to locate a source from which to procure the permanent replacement asset.

Temporary Replacement Costs. Not every asset that is lost or destroyed will require a temporary replacement, but many assets will. If sabotage destroys a piece of manufacturing equipment, delivery and contract commitments may require that, pending permanent replacement or repair, some other equipment be used. The other equipment also may be fully committed, requiring extra expenses or special efforts to extend its use to accommodate the production normally generated by the damaged equipment. Furthermore, it may be necessary to subcontract the interim work and pay the subcontractor's extra costs. The cost of such a temporary substitute should be attributed to the security loss that made the original equipment unavailable.

Consequential Costs. Consequential costs are typified by idle time or waiting time expense. For example, following a civil disturbance in which incendiary devices are hurled through plant windows severely damaging some equipment, processing must stop until the equipment is restored to service. The cost of the stoppage is part of the security loss because it is a consequence of the peril that breached security and damaged the equipment.

Opportunity Costs. Opportunity costs are the result of giving up something (or some amount of something) in order to have something else. It is a measure of the benefits associated with one choice that are *foregone* when another choice is made. For example, a society may have to choose between military goods and civilian goods, perhaps between tanks and passenger cars. Since similar resources such as rubber, steel, glass, and workers are required to produce both the tank and the car, and since these resources are limited, choices must be made between the two commodities. The cost of manufacturing a tank may be expressed as so many thousands of dollars, but from an economic point of view, the cost of manufacturing a tank should be measured in terms of the number of passenger cars sacrificed. Forgoing the opportunity of producing cars makes possible the production of tanks, or vice versa. The concept of opportunity costs shows that pursuing any one option means forgoing some other option.[2]

It follows that cash used to meet permanent and temporary replacement costs as well as the consequential costs deprives the organization of cash that it normally could have put to more productive uses. The earnings that would have been generated from these normal uses are the opportunity costs of a security loss.

Criticality. Estimating all the costs attributable to a given security exposure leads to the criticality level for that exposure. Just as estimated probabilities can be divided into five groups, so it is best to use five general levels of criticality, defined qualitatively rather than in precise dollar terms.

These five classes of criticality as shown in Exhibit 4-3 are (A) *fatal* to the business if the cost is so high that the business is terminated, (B) *very serious* if the impact, although not enough to destroy the organization, is enough to require a major adjustment in investment policy, (C) *moderately serious* if the impact on earnings and return on investment is sufficient to require some comment to the equity owners, (D) *relatively unimportant* if the cost can be absorbed within existing contingency reserves or if overall profitability is affected only slightly, (E) *seriousness unknown* when all the cost factors have not yet been identified or quantified. Like "probability unknown," "seriousness unknown" is a provisional assignment and will be replaced by a definite criticality judgment after necessary research is complete.

After each exposure has been assessed for both its probability and criticality, each can be rated, or prioritized, by a combined rating reflecting both probability, and criticality. Exhibit 4-3 summarizes these ratings—a number reflects probability, and a capital letter indicates criticality or potential severity. For example, if a given exposure were rated 1-A, the loss would be almost certain to occur and probably would be fatal to the organization. Such an exposure—one best avoided entirely—would lead the list of priorities. Other exposures might be rated 3-D or 4-C and would receive significantly lower priority.

The risk management professionals and senior management of some organizations tend to prioritize exposures primarily on the basis of criticality (ranked by the letters), while others place more emphasis

Exhibit 4-3
Degrees of Probability and Criticality for Security Losses

Degree of Probability	Degree of Criticality
1. Virtually certain	A. Fatal to the business
2. Highly probable	B. Very serious
3. Moderately probable	C. Moderately serious
4. Improbable	D. Relatively unimportant
5. Probability unknown	E. Seriousness unknown

on probability (ranked by the numbers). For example, organizations that set priorities primarily on the basis of probability will give greater attention to an exposure rated 3-D than to one rated 4-C. Conversely, an organization that stresses criticality will consider a 4-C exposure more important than a 3-D exposure. While there can be no general guidelines as to which dimension of a loss is always more important, it is crucial that an organization's risk management professional and its senior management agree on the relative significance of these dimensions. Furthermore, these ratings should be reviewed periodically to ensure that they reflect both the organization's current exposures and management's attitude toward these potential losses.

Most organizations are likely to conclude that it is best to give greater weight to criticality than to probability of losses. As a result, those in charge of developing risk control measures would first consider all losses of very serious criticality with moderate or higher probability. Secondary consideration would be given to losses involving moderate criticality even though they may have a very high probability.

System Approach to Recognizing and Analyzing Security Exposures As Chapter 11 will explain in detail, a system is any set of interrelated parts that perform a particular task. In the context of maintaining an organization's security, for example, a system can be the entire organization (ideally, functioning smoothly without loss), a particular device (such as a burglar alarm system or a lock) for safeguarding a particular activity or asset, or the entire set of physical or procedural safeguards for maintaining the security of the organization as a whole. As also explained in Chapter 11, system safety encompasses a variety of techniques for predicting how a system may fail and for preventing such failures or minimizing the resulting harm.

The following paragraphs give a preview of *fault tree analysis*, one system safety technique to be discussed in Chapter 11.

After determining and prioritizing security exposures, an organization can develop measures to address these exposures. Because it costs money to institute such measures, it is in the organization's best interest to choose those measures that achieve the most favorable cost-benefit outcome. That is, the best security measures should provide either (1) adequate safeguards and an acceptable level of confidence in their reliability for the least cost or (2) the greatest attainable degree of security and reliability for a given cost. Excessive emphasis on, or exclusive concern with, cost will cripple or frustrate a security program. Cost effectiveness, not absolute lowest cost, should be the standard. It is with security exposures arising out of an interconnected series of deficiencies, rather than separate flaws, that the system safety technique known as fault tree analysis is especially helpful in evaluating cost effectiveness. This analysis is especially useful in identifying and controlling points at which deficiencies, or "faults," that contribute to security losses are located. Because these points of fault are known, it is more likely that the organization will choose adequate rather than arbitrary security measures.

For an example of how a fault tree works, consider an organization's exposure to undetected after-hours entry into one of its buildings—burglary. If burglary is conceived in terms of the activities that precede it, it can be analyzed as a fault tree, as shown in Exhibit 4-4. The event (burglary) is shown as Level 1 at the top of the fault tree. The activities and conditions that lead to this event (Levels 2, 3, and 4) are called "faults" or breakdowns in security. Finding the means to prevent the loss depends both on the relationship of these activities and conditions to one another and to the loss itself. For instance, the conditions that take place at Level 2 make it clear that a burglary can occur if some entryway is left unlocked *and* the actual entry remains undetected. The activities that take place at Level 3A make it clear that an entryway can be unlocked if someone has left the door open at the end of a shift *or* if the burglar has been able to open the lock. The conditions that are present at Level 3B make it clear that an undetected entry depends on (1) no witness to entry, (2) no record of entry, *and* (3) no alarm at the time of entry.

The "or" relationship between the activities at level 3A means that *either one* of these activities can compromise security. Given that fact, both must be prevented in order to keep the entry locked and stop the burglary. Chapter 11 describes this type of relationship and its consequences as an "or gate." The "and" relationship between the conditions at Level 2 and Level 3B means that *all* the conditions must be present to compromise security. Given this fact, only one condition

Exhibit 4-4
Fault Tree for Undetected, After-Hours Entry

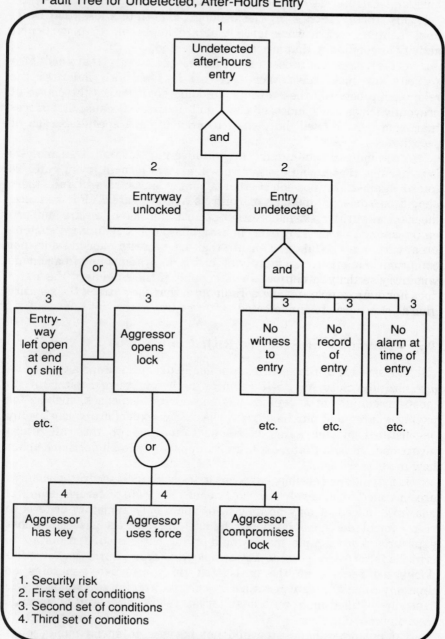

1. Security risk
2. First set of conditions
3. Second set of conditions
4. Third set of conditions

at each level must be prevented in order to detect the entry and stop the burglary. Chapter 11 describes this relationship as an "and gate." By "closing" these "gates" anywhere along the path to a loss (that is, by implementing security measures that are applicable to a particular activity or condition), that loss can be prevented.

A fault tree analysis thus identifies the events that lead to a security (or most any other type of) loss. It also indicates the relationship between these events. In doing so, it makes the choice of preventive measures more efficient and accurate because it ensures that each measure will be geared to preventing a specific breach of security.

A common and potentially fatal disadvantage of fault tree analysis is to assume that a single measure will always block a given gate. To guard against the possibility that a single measure will fail, there should be some redundancy of controls at the "gates." For instance, mechanical burglar alarms or other security alarms often are supported by canine guards. However, in designing such a redundant system, great care must be taken to ensure that one security measure does not compromise another. Again, relying on alarm systems and guard dogs will increase the reliability of a system only if the ringing of the alarm does not distract or upset the dogs enough that they attack the security guards.

The Economics of Security Risk Control

The essence of the security function is to conserve the assets of an organization. Security itself requires both long-term capital investments in equipment as well as ongoing current expenses, such as for paying guards and purchasing supplies. Such expenditures can ideally be justified by the same cost-benefit analysis or rate of return investment criteria that most organizations apply to all decisions about how to allocate cash.

It may not be possible, however, to insist that all security measures are justified exclusively by cost-benefit or rate-of-return financial analysis. Indeed, it may be unwise to apply only monetary criteria to risk control decisions involving human life and its associated loss exposures. For example, many would argue that it is not appropriate to criticize efforts to protect key employees from harm in terrorist-dominated regions on the basis that this protection generates no precisely calculable rate of return. Such safeguarding of human lives is typically justified more on humanitarian, religious, or ethical grounds than on economic ones.

On the other hand, it would not be wise to spend money on a security program that produced no tangible benefits. Therefore, a risk management professional or other responsible executive often will gather data documenting how an organization has benefited from security through (1) reductions in retained theft losses and other expenses made necessary by human violence, (2) reduced premiums for insurance covering security exposures, and (3) improved organization morale and productivity. These benefits, plus the psychological value of knowing that people and property are more safe from criminal acts, should suffice to justify most well-designed security programs.

ESSENTIALS OF A SECURITY PROGRAM

Three essential elements should be included in a security program: employee education, loss prevention, and detection of losses caused by deficiencies in security. The first two are the most important because, together, they reduce losses that result from breaches in security. The following are consequences of good employee education and loss prevention:

- Individuals who would be tempted to act against the organization are discouraged by the great likelihood that they will be discovered.
- Lax security that might cause serious losses is discovered at an early stage.
- The cost of insurance is kept at a minimum.
- Information used in making managerial decisions can be expected to be more reliable. For example, falsification of vital information to conceal thefts or fraud will be less likely and, as a result, senior management will be less likely to base important decisions on erroneous information.

The detection of losses that are caused by deficiencies in security, the third element, is important because the sooner management becomes aware of a weakness in its security program, the more rapidly it can move to prevent any future losses. These three elements are described below.

Education

An employee education program should include three groups within the organization: senior officers, supervisors at all levels, and other employees.

Any effective security program must be completely accepted by senior officers. They should also understand the broad outline (not necessarily the technical details) of the security measures and should appreciate the loss exposures the organization would face if it had no security program. Moreover, top managers should convey to all personnel their full support of the security program.

Supervisory personnel should also become part of the overall security effort if it is to succeed. The key to their participation is their understanding of, and respect for, the security program's purpose and importance. Experience has shown that virtually all individuals who understand the reasons for a security program will accept it. If, however, they do not believe in the program or do not want it to be effective, the program cannot be enforced. Security personnel alone cannot enforce the program. To rely merely on an organization's security personnel, without the active participation of supervisory management, is much like depending only on the police of a city, and not on its citizens, to uphold the law.

All other employees must be motivated to support a security program as well. Therefore, education is the cornerstone of an effective security program. All employees should become part of the program, participating in its enforcement—not grudgingly accepting it as a necessary evil while giving it "lip service" or, worse, fighting it.

The security education of employees may be formal or informal, depending on the size of the organization and the criticality of its security exposures. Regardless of how it is conducted, education should give each employee a full explanation of the purposes and extent of the security program. However, much of the data on the technical aspects of the security operation should not be included in the education because it could allow an employee to subvert any security measure. In addition, all employees should be assigned, and evaluated on their performance of, specific responsibilities for the protection of the organization's assets. These responsibilities may include protecting the assets with which each employee works or the actions each employee should take during a security emergency. These responsibilities are detailed more fully in Chapter 12 on crisis management.

Educational efforts must not be limited to a lecture on security for each new employee. Instead, an effective program should use the employee newspaper, bulletin boards, and participatory meetings. All policies and procedures should be defined in writing. For example, if the organization prohibits employees from accepting bribes, this policy should be published and distributed throughout the organization. Also, employees should be clearly informed in writing that theft, regardless of the amount, will not be condoned. The effect that dishonest actions can be expected to have on the organization, how those actions reduce financial results, and in turn, how they impact employees' employment and personal physical security in the organization should be highlighted. Employees should also be informed of the corrective or disciplinary actions they can expect if they violate security policies and procedures.

An organization's security personnel should be responsible only for *assisting* management in such corrective actions. The primary responsibility lies with line management. And even the procedures that they follow should include a plan for supervisors who are reluctant to act when a problem is referred to them. The system will often provide a plan that recommends referral to higher management.

The importance of this type of employee education in security cannot be overstressed. When an employer or supervisor properly explains how a security system works and why it is needed—and emphasizes that the system is designed to protect the physical safety and reputations of honest employees from violent crime and dishonest employees—then most employees will accept the security system as a normal control.

Prevention

Preventing breaches of security from employee dishonesty or other criminal acts requires screening applicants for employment, installing physical security controls, regular transfers of personnel who are in sensitive positions, and developing emergency plans.

Applicant Screening Applicant screening is one preventive measure that should precede the hiring and training of employees. If a mistake has occurred in selecting employees, even the best educational and supervisory programs will not prevent employees from causing serious losses.

The primary objective of a screening program should be to hire and retain a reasonably suitable, trustworthy, and competent work force. This objective can be met by checking personal and professional references given by prospective employees on their job applications. The organization can also verify previous places of employment, education, and other personal data given by the applicant. Because various state and federal laws that recognize employees' rights to continued employment may complicate efforts to discipline or dismiss an employee, applicant screening often provides the best opportunity to eliminate threats by employees to security. The importance of applicant screening is also discussed at the end of this chapter as part of the discussion on developing an integrated security risk control program.

Physical Security Controls Physical security controls protect access to an organization. Controls include gates and fences; human or canine guards; locks on doors to buildings, rooms, or cabinets; alarm systems; lights to reveal intruders; and safes, vaults, and other specially secured spaces.

Physical controls have been described as impediments designed to deter the undetermined and to delay the determined, the former is a psychological deterrent. They should make trespassing appear to be unprofitable in terms of the likely gain relative to the danger involved for the trespasser.

Transfer of Personnel Transferring personnel within an organization or periodically rotating them is an effective device for preventing breaches of security. If employees are aware that their job assignments may be shifted, they will be less likely to perform acts that might be discovered after they are transferred. Transfer is not always possible, but consideration should be given to rotating employees in sensitive positions from one job to another. For example, branch managers can be shifted from time to time to different offices just as the routes of truck drivers can be changed. Foremen and supervisors may be rotated within a factory, and clerks and supervisors who handle the financial affairs of an organization may be periodically shifted. A programmer who was responsible for a sensitive activity should be shifted from that program to another.

Some managers may object that their, or their subordinates', transfers disrupt effective working relationships within departments, create unnecessary staffing and training needs, and complicate career planning. To minimize these objections, rotations should be included in the job descriptions, the transfers should occur in a reasonably predictable fashion, and they should be only as frequent and as long as is necessary to ensure security. Employees should expect that they will normally be transferred in this way so that they recognize such shifts as routine and a necessary part of the overall security system that protects *them* as well as the organization. Above all, it should be clear to all concerned that a security-oriented transfer does not imply any discipline, suspicion, or criticism of personnel being transferred.

Emergency Planning/Crisis Management Many criminal acts, especially those accompanied by violence, create emergencies that Chapter 12 describes as situations that must be dealt with immediately to prevent or minimize serious future losses. Planning for emergencies does not aim to prevent the crisis, but instead, seeks to set forth actions that will save lives and property when an emergency does arise. Thus, emergency planning in a security context is but a special case of the more general types of crisis management described in Chapter 12.

That chapter will emphasize that a crisis management plan should be suited to the needs of the organization and tailored to the characteristics of the peril creating the crisis. For example, many crimes are characterized by violence, the destruction or theft of property, and the escape of the criminal. Therefore, the general plan to manage this type of emergency usually should focus first on protecting anyone at the scene of the crime from violence; second, on minimizing harm to property; and third, on gathering information that will help to identify and apprehend the criminal. The plan should also account for the time it takes to implement emergency procedures. Nevertheless, the characteristics of specific crimes may call for different emergency procedures. For instance, an armed robber should probably be allowed to promptly leave the premises to minimize danger to employees and/or the public at the scene. In the case of embezzlement, the planned response would most likely focus on detecting the crime and identifying the criminal through auditing procedures.

Despite the differences in emergency response actions, they should all emphasize preserving the organization's productive capabilities and returning to normal operations as soon as possible. This recovery from any breach of security typically calls for the regular practice of emergency procedures for replacing or restoring any lost funds or property; rehabilitating and/or replacing any injured personnel; and reassuring customers, creditors, and suppliers of the immediate continuity and long-term viability of the organization.

"Practice" is a most appropriate word in the context of any emergency, and it applies to procedures implemented during and after an emergency. Practice means that the personnel most likely to implement emergency procedures be periodically rehearsed in those procedures. Just as many organizations have fire drills or simulated severe weather or civil defense emergencies, so should organizations practice dealing with security emergencies: a simulated robbery, or embezzlement, or a test of the security system that protects the data in an organization's computer. These "security drills" can educate personnel in the appropriate responses to emergencies. They also ensure that the procedures set forth in the emergency plan remain appropriate for any changes in underlying conditions or exposures.

Detection

Detection of losses that are caused by failures in security is the third essential element in an effective security program. This element is important because the sooner deficiencies are uncovered, the sooner they can be corrected, thus minimizing future losses. Inspections and security tests are two ways to detect the failures in a security system.

Inspections and Spot Checks   Guards as well as other security personnel should make frequent, unannounced inspections and spot checks of all the operations in each facility. In addition, supervisors should inspect their own areas to uncover potential breaches of security. If deficiencies or breaches in security are found, they should be immediately reported to appropriate personnel.

Each inspection should be designed to determine if security procedures are being followed and if the intended preventive measures are operating effectively. All elements of the security program should be reviewed not only to ensure that all its aspects are functioning properly, but also because protection requirements change. Inspections may reveal gaps in the security program, or they may reveal that security controls are no longer needed in some areas because of changed operations.

Testing the System   To test the components of the physical security system and employees' responses to them, incidents that challenge the system should be planned. If the alarms do not ring, if incidents are not reported, or if employees do not follow any other security procedures, security personnel should conduct an immediate, thorough investigation to determine the corrective action. To illustrate, a supplier might be asked to ship more of an item than was ordered— with some of these items being defective—to determine if personnel in the receiving area are detecting and reporting discrepancies in quantities and quality of goods received.

COMPUTER SECURITY

American organizations of all kinds utilize and heavily depend upon computers. However, in many organizations, little serious thought has been given to the protection of computers and the information they process. Despite its great advantages, a computer may actually cause serious losses if proper security is not in place. This section discusses typical computer-related exposures and describes the controls that can be implemented to ensure adequate, cost-effective security.

Computer Center-Related Exposures

The first step in designing any computer security program is to analyze computer-related exposures. The principal exposures that affect computers can be divided into two classes: (1) those that threaten the physical integrity of the computer facilities and equipment and (2) those that threaten data. These exposures are described below. Also explained are various ways to manage them, including control of access to computer facilities.

Facilities and Equipment Exposures   There are five principal perils facing the entire computer installation: (1) fire, (2) acts of sabotage, (3) industrial accident, (4) natural disaster, and (5) mechanical or electrical malfunction of the system. (The perils of fire and natural disaster were treated more generally in Chapters 2 and 3; the following discussion of these perils relates specifically to computers.)

Fire.   The most serious and most common physical danger to computer installations is fire. Because the most significant computer equipment—including the mainframe and principal peripheral items like disk drives, tape drives, multiplexers, and various input-output devices—is electrically energized, there is the constant possibility of circuit failure, electrical overcurrent conditions, insulation fires, and related combustion problems. Moreover, expensive damage can be caused by prolonged heat and combustion byproducts such as smoke, particulate matter, and acids. Despite the development of computer fire protection concepts and the availability of a variety of automatic detection and extinguishment systems, many large computer installations are relatively unprotected against fire loss.

The National Fire Protection Association (NFPA) publishes, among its National Fire Codes, Standard 75 for the protection of electronic computer/data processing equipment. It should be the basic guide to fire prevention and extinguishment for all computer installations. Standard 75 is technically oriented, but easily understood, and should be read by any manager responsible for any computer facility. In barest outline, this standard requires that computers be separated from other activities by fire-resistive barriers; that adequate extinguishment equipment, preferably automatic, be provided; that all assigned personnel be trained in the use of the equipment and in emergency response actions in the event of fire; that building and computer room design features should minimize the spread of any fire that may start in the computer area; and that certain housekeeping and administrative practices be instituted to reduce the causes of such fires. These requirements may be considered as pre-event risk control actions. Any actions to restore the facility or operations after a fire are post-event risk control actions.

Sabotage.   Sabotage is the deliberate destruction of property or disruption of productive processes by hostile persons. It can be as obvious as a bomb or as surreptitious as the application of a large magnet to a computer's magnetic storage media. Blows with a hammer or other heavy instrument to computer components, spillage of caustic solutions on circuit boards and wires, or the introduction of foreign matter into a computer's or printer's moving parts are acts of sabotage.

The basic hazard underlying sabotage is unauthorized access to the computer installation. Effective access control, in which positive personnel identification, coupled with "need to know" and tight supervision of computer operations and equipment, reduces the probability of loss through exposure. Another important risk control measure is adequate personnel selection and screening to ensure a high level of trustworthiness in those who have regular access to the computer.

Industrial Accident. Aside from fire, other major industrial accidents may adversely affect computer facilities. Selecting a computer location that is not too near a high-hazard area is therefore an important risk control consideration. Perils that have extensively damaged computer facilities include building collapse, explosion, leakage from plumbing and fire suppression systems, and interruption in such utility services as electric power and air conditioning. Even momentary electrical surges (swings above or below the rated current) can do serious damage to equipment and software because they require constant power, so the surges can change the internal behavior of computer circuits.

Loss of air conditioning is another industrial accident that affects computers. The distortion temperature of magnetic media is around 140°F. At that temperature, random changes in magnetic characters can produce changes in computerized information. Sustained temperatures above 140°F can also cause random malfunctions of internal parts of a computer's central processing unit and peripheral equipment. The continued operation of computers without controlled air exchange will rapidly increase temperatures until they are at or beyond this critical temperature.

The principal risk control measure against power failure is an independent emergency generator that can provide the minimum power needed to maintain essential operations. In determining such standby power needs, careful consideration should be given to the maximum time an organization can be without power and to the availability of competent technical personnel to troubleshoot problems during such a period. If there is no need for constant power, the tolerable downtime may be anywhere from a few moments to a few hours. If competent technical personnel are immediately available to diagnose problems, it may be preferable to rely on manual, rather than automatic, transfer to standby power. This will prevent the unnecessary switching for readily correctable difficulties. If there is any question of the availability of technical personnel, or if the downtime limit is very short, automatic switching may be required. Some immediate, automatic standby power supply may be required just to permit an orderly shutdown even if secondary power is not provided to continue operations.

Natural Disasters. Floods and earthquakes are among the perils most likely to have serious effects on computer installations. The availability of real estate and its cost are not the only factors to consider in locating computer facilities; considering the whole environment is an important risk control action. To the greatest extent possible, installations should be in areas without histories of, or predispositions to, natural perils to which computers are particularly vulnerable. For example, lowland along regularly flooding rivers would be a poor choice, as would property within hurricane or tornado belts.

Other selection factors should include accessibility by public transportation, availability of public utilities, favorable labor markets, and the availability of "make-ready" or development funds or tax incentives from local governments—many of the standard site selection criteria for any activity. However, an organization's decision to provide its own electric power for a major computer installation on a purely proprietary basis, although more expensive than purchasing electricity from a public utility, may be justified by the greater reliability of this power source. Geographic remoteness, particularly from major metropolitan areas, population concentrations, may be highly desirable as a form of access control. Extreme remoteness—putting the facility out of the response range of police and fire departments—can, however, be an even more serious threat to security than being located in too densely populated an area. The adequacy and availability of emergency services also must be evaluated in site selection. An organization's own installation of automatic fire and disaster control resources and of integrated security systems can do much to lessen dependence upon municipal emergency service facilities.

Mechanical/Electrical Incompatibility or Malfunction. Perhaps the most serious problem associated with a disaster at a computer center is finding temporary alternate equipment and software. There is a popular belief that knowing of, and reaching agreement in principle with, another facility with the same basic computer hardware justifies relying on that facility in an emergency. This attitude is likely to be unwise for at least five reasons:

1. The machine configuration at the alternate site may not entirely correspond to the original equipment. For example, if the memory core is smaller at the other location, or if there are fewer printers there, data processing operations probably will have to be modified before any program can be run.
2. There may not be any available time at the backup facility when required. An objective of having high-cost computers is to use

them as much as possible to maintain their productivity. Therefore, it is reasonable to expect that there will be progressively less "open" time on any given computer that has been operating a few years.

3. There may be software incompatibilities that prevent running programs on the alternative computer. For example, the operating systems of the two computers may be quite different.

4. The information flow to an organization's regular computer may depend upon telecommunication resources that are not available at the alternate site or that are tailored to the needs of the alternate site proprietors.

5. If the loss of an organization's regular computer has resulted from a widespread problem such as failure of the public utility or a natural disaster, the alternative facility may be equally disabled. As is true of alternative storage sites for recorded data, sites for emergency computer backups should be beyond the radius of any common disaster. For some perils such as earthquake, this can be a substantial distance.

To avoid these problems, the following risk control procedures may be used to address mechanical/electrical incompatibility or malfunction. A matrix should be developed of all the computer programs and projects being run or planned. The matrix should rank these activities in descending order of criticality and should show the hardware and software configuration, the scheduled machine time, the processing routines, and any special factors that make each activity difficult or impossible to duplicate with another internal computer or on alternative outside equipment. The matrix should also indicate the locations of all potential backup resources, the most recent date on which the backup was contacted to confirm its availability, the switchover time required to run programs on the alternative hardware, and any mechanical or legal limitations on the use of the alternative facility. Such a matrix should be updated regularly.

It is possible that the matrix may only establish that no practical emergency alternative computer facilities are available, thereby emphasizing the need for thorough on-site security planning. If backup arrangements are made for alternative facilities, then actual runs should be done at these facilities to ensure that all operational difficulties have been overcome. This should be done periodically. Whether or not backup facilities are an option, matrix planning should give management the required decision options.

In addition to safeguarding against potential mechanical and electrical malfunctions, risk control efforts for computer security must consider human faults. Operator error, for example, may erase vital data that cannot readily be reconstructed.

Data-Related Exposures In addition to the perils that threaten the actual physical computer and its facilities, computer operations are exposed to loss through perils associated with data. These perils include the following:

- Fraud, embezzlement, and sabotage, which occur as a result of the surreptitious manipulation of data;
- Time-sharing arrangements that result in unauthorized, but overt, access to information;
- Theft of data through surreptitious listening gear or the covert removal of tapes;
- Theft of computer time; and
- Espionage.

Fraud, Embezzlement, and Sabotage. An employee may manipulate data in many ways to defraud his or her employer. For instance, a single change in a computer program can convert abnormally high inventory shortages to apparent breakage. Material reported as "broken" can then be removed without the theft being noted; the evidence can be destroyed by simply reversing the computerized accounting entry. Alternatively, a data processing employee in a financial institution might grow rich by rounding off fractions of cents in interest calculations and transferring the accumulated resulting amounts to his or her personal account. A computer payroll system also is a vehicle for fraud. For example, fictitious paychecks can be printed, or extra wages and overtime can be programmed to be paid to designated individuals.

A typical example of embezzlement is a $1 million concealed inventory shortage suffered by a pharmaceutical manufacturer at the hands of a computer manager at one of its manufacturing plants. Another example is the case of a back office investment house employee who embezzled more than $250,000 over seven years, becoming a vice president before his actions were discovered. Because losses from embezzlement and fraud are the most common and serious, these two perils are treated more extensively in a separate section entitled, "Prevention of Embezzlement and Fraud."

Just as subtle and dangerous to an organization is sabotage. This deliberate manipulation of data can render an entire computer program unreliable because of the introduction of random errors. The results are dangerous and long-lasting for two reasons: (1) the crime is extremely difficult to detect and (2) the information generated by a computer is used to make short-term and long-term decisions and as a basis for ongoing activities in the organization. The fact that these activities and decisions can be based on erroneous information makes sabotage extremely detrimental to the organization.

Time-Sharing Arrangements That Result in Unauthorized but Overt Access to Data. Time-sharing systems can present some of the greatest dangers to computer operations. There are three basic security objectives associated with time-sharing: (1) ensuring that only authorized persons have access to a program, (2) preventing a system malfunction from accidentally disclosing data, and (3) preventing authorized access that would result from the unauthorized change or manipulation of data.

Time-sharing is an arrangement in which several users have access to a single computer in which one or more programs are processed. Access may be through a local area network (LAN) within a single organization, as when various departments use the same central computer; or it may be through a service bureau or central facility that employs a large computer to process several programs for different, unrelated customers. The ultimate time-sharing arrangement is the now common multiprogram, multiprocess operation in which many unrelated users have access to a single mainframe for simultaneously processing many unrelated programs.

The most common way to limit computer access to authorized persons only is to use a code or password. To gain access, each person using the computer must first give a personal code word or symbol. This can be as elaborate as required; it can also be known only to the person who will use it. Furthermore, this code word or symbol may be valid only if given together with some other item of personal identification, such as name or payroll number. The computer will check these two items against a stored memory table to confirm that they are the two required matching items. Making the password or symbol truly random, not related in any way to the personal identification data, achieves a high level of access control.

This security may be defeated, however, if the authorized person deliberately or negligently discloses his or her password, or if some other person within the computer center to whom the code is known further discloses the codes. Another breach of security could occur if the computer is not programmed to suppress passwords and not to repeat or print them out elsewhere in the network.

A more elaborate check on unauthorized access requires both a physical identifier and a password. For example, a card may be coded with personalized information in a magnetic format. The authorized individual would insert the card into a card reader that controls the computer's electrical supply or activates an intrusion alarm. The individual's card must be used along with a code word to energize the terminal and/or to prevent an alarm from sounding if the terminal is used. The authorized individual's fingerprints, voiceprint, or retina scan may also serve as the physical identifier.

Finally, access from remote terminals can be made more secure by restricting each individual to preassigned terminals or programs. Each of their personal passwords may authorize access to only certain terminals or programs. A supervisory program within the central mainframe itself should signal any attempt to gain access to a program not authorized for that user, stop all data output to that terminal, and print a description of the attempted unauthorized transaction.

Each additional measure in this chain of security adds to overall security cost, mostly as software cost because of the additional programming required. The extent to which these measures are implemented should be determined by the criticality/cost trade-offs and the availability of alternative countermeasures.

Theft of Data Through Surreptitious Listening Gear or Covert Removal of Tapes. The theft of data can be motivated by the desire to learn trade secrets to anticipate a competitor's marketing or financial strategy, or for any "conventional" industrial espionage purpose. The difference between stealing information through a computer and by other means is that most computerized operations have *all* their business information on a computer. Given access to this data, the thief is ensured of success. If a thief does not have the advantage of being part of a time-sharing arrangement, he or she may steal data by using surreptitious listening gear or by covertly removing hard copy or tapes from the computer facility.

Surreptitious Listening Gear. Because vast amounts of data are in transit between computers within a facility, or between computers in different facilities, one way to steal electromagnetic data is to capture it through the analysis of signals for data retrieval. This is simply a form of intercepting ongoing communications by tapping into a line or electronic signal used to move data either from unit to unit within a computer center or to other locations. It is accomplished by an interceptor who gets close enough to the computer center or to the communications link; has suitable equipment for monitoring the spectrum of signals and identifying the frequency used to transmit the information; and has some way to convert the electronic signal into readable messages. The thief need not do everything from the original access point; it is enough to record the transmission, carry the recording away, and later reduce the recorded information to a readable message whenever convenient.

Three security measures to reduce or prevent the occurrence of this type of theft are to (1) physically encase the computer facility in protective electronic shielding that will suppress the transmission of signals, (2) "harden" the link itself, which involves using shielded cables for hard-wire connections and random frequency changes for microwave or radio signals, and (3) process the data itself to make it difficult to capture and/or read. The third option involves two techniques: (a) simultaneous transmissions and (b) encoding.

Simultaneous transmission is the simpler and less expensive alternative. It means that multiple communications are simultaneously transmitted over the same link. They may be nonsense signals or mixed legitimate messages. To recover any specific communication, the receiver or interceptor must be able to recognize and filter out all the other signals to isolate the targeted one. For anyone except the intended receiver, this may be so difficult or expensive as to preclude any serious effort at theft by anyone outside the computer center.

Encoding is the more complex and expensive option. It involves encrypting and decrypting data, which increases the chance of mistakes because of frequent changes in codes or because of human error.

Because encasing and encoding are expensive, they are usually reserved for computers running highly sensitive information. However, when proprietary information is critical enough, these options should be considered, particularly as part of plans for new computer centers.

Another consideration in developing security measures for the theft of data is the position of the interceptor. The closer the interceptor is to the initiating or receiving terminal, the easier is his or her task. Sound risk control would thus call for providing more protection at the points of origin and receipt of computer data than at other locations. If the data is transmitted by telephone lines, the multiple transmission technique just described automatically becomes a protective feature when the computer signal joins others on the common carrier telephone lines. Protection is also essentially "automatically" provided by the telephone company—that is, the choice of specific sets of wires for the transmission of particular signals over telephone networks is dependent on load. Automatic telephone company switchgear selects the optimum transmission path at the moment the message is sent. Consequently, the thief has no way of knowing in advance what path that will be. He or she is thus faced with the dual problem of multiple signals and an unknown wire path.

A final consideration in developing security for this type of theft is the attacker who can gain access to the wires *inside* the transmitting or the receiving terminal. Accessing and retrieving data in this way is like any other telephone tap. It involves either physical or inductive electronic connections between the targeted terminal and the surreptitious listening gear. Such a connection is possible from any point at which the target is accessible and identifiable. The leads from the computer center to the various telephone terminal boards and from the terminal boards into cables leaving the facility are all vulnerable. Adequate physical security also must be maintained over the link from the junction points outside the facility back to the computer on one end, and to the input/output terminal on the other. Achieving security means locking terminal and mainframe rooms, enforcing strict controls on people who have access to areas that contain communications equipment, and maintaining cooperative arrangements with the telephone company in providing acceptable protection for junction points on the perimeter of the premises. This protection probably will be some combination of lock controls, live surveillance, and intrusion alarms.

Covert Removal of Tapes.   When there are no effective security controls, a thief with access to the computer center can quickly and easily remove or copy records or tapes. These materials can be used by the thief or sold. They often include secret customer lists, invaluable product formulations, or crucial operating procedures.

Theft of Computer Time.   The unauthorized use by employees of computer work-time for personal purposes is a significant kind of theft. It can occur when the use of a computer is not supervised or audited. Risk control efforts to reduce the possibility of loss from this peril include a continuous record of each person who has had access to computer hardware or software, along with the dates and times of their use. An "exceptions logbook" should also be used to maintain a record of program running times. Anyone can look back at the log to make certain that the programs that should have been run were, and that unscheduled programs were not run. There have been cases in which computer personnel have maintained entire sets of records for an outside business run by themselves or others. (The unauthorized use of computer time for personal reasons also increases the probability of loss from the surreptitious manipulation of data.)

Espionage.   Because computer systems now store most of the information critical to the operation of an organization, espionage is a primary peril; this crime can be committed most easily from within the facility housing the computer. Copies of disks, tapes, or computer-generated reports may contain concentrations of data that otherwise would take a thief months or years to accumulate. In organizations centered around proprietary processes, data may be available from process control programs or from computer-generated management reports.

A "spy" can acquire information either as "hard copy" (printed material) or in a computer-readable format, as on a magnetic tape or disk. Unsupervised access to this information is usually enough for a skilled thief with a good memory. When information has been stolen but there is no evidence of its theft, the loss is doubly expensive because the victimized organization continues to operate on the assumption that the data is safe. If the compromise in security had been known, additional losses and related expenses might have been avoided even if the data could not have been retrieved.

Access Controls for Computer Facilities

Most of the perils, other than natural perils, that threaten a computer facility occur because access to the building and/or to the computer itself is weakly controlled or not controlled at all. As described in the preceding section, computer security can be at stake particularly because of perils that threaten data. In response to this situation, risk control efforts to maintain computer security include controlling access to (1) the entire computer facility, (2) designated portions of the facility that house especially sensitive activities, and (3) particular computer programs. Controls for these areas and programs are discussed below.

Building/Facility Access A physical control system should prohibit unauthorized personnel and visitors from entering any part of the computer facility. Some organizations, however, view their computer installations as showplaces. They encourage visitors and often fail to provide minimum security precautions because they have not adequately considered the potentially serious losses that might result from such open access.

Controls for the overall computer center should deal separately with two periods: (1) when the center is not in use and (2) when it is in use. When the center is not in use, the entrance and all other openings should be securely locked. Also, the walls, ceilings, doors, and floors should be so constructed that surreptitious entry is very difficult, and that any break-in is obvious and immediately signaled to an appropriate security center. A proper security system also should be installed, including alarms that signal either surreptitious or forced entry as well as periodic, but randomly timed, inspections by human or canine guards.

When the computer center is being used, it is possible to control entry in a variety of ways. It is good practice to secure the entrance with a lock and to designate someone to monitor and keep a log of those entering and leaving. If the center is occupied by only a few employees, a supervisor on site may be given responsibility for access control. A telephone or other audio connection might be installed immediately outside the center for those seeking admittance, or they may use a doorbell to alert someone inside. More elaborate security controls could include closed-circuit television with a camera outside and a monitor inside the center or at a central security station. If the computer area is too large or the traffic through the entrance too heavy to be controlled from inside the center, a specified person may be placed at a desk outside the entrance to control entry.

Regardless of overall control, an accurate, current list of those authorized to enter is essential. This list should either be held by the employee controlling access or should be incorporated into automated access controls.

Area Access Within Buildings Not all individuals working in a computer facility need free access to all its areas. Programmers, for example, usually will not require access to the main computer controls. Similarly, most operators do not need access to areas where files are maintained. It follows that the overall computer center should be so designed that access to areas within the center is properly controlled. The controls may be structured to give access to the entire facility only to those relatively few people whose responsibilities require it.

Because software and data files are critical to computer systems, a storage library should be established, and access controls should be implemented to protect this storage area. Only authorized personnel should have access to any part of the library; most persons will need access to only specified parts of the library. Files should be removed from the library only when they are needed for specific tasks. Records of file use should be kept, and a file should be checked in and out of the library area in the name of the person actually taking the file.

Only one person or operating group should be responsible for any operation at any one time. This requires sharp distinctions between employees who authorize a computer transaction, those who produce the input, those who process the data, and those who use the output for reports or other management purposes. The same separations of authority and responsibility should govern scheduling, manual and machine operations, maintenance of programs, and related functions. Programmers should not have access to the entire library of programs. Nor should they operate the hardware to complete a project without special permission. If these programming and project duties are properly separated, the probability of loss to hardware or software is minimized. The technique of separating duties is discussed again at the end of the chapter as part of the discussion on developing an integrated security risk control program.

Access to Computer Software and Output Despite efforts to physically protect the computer center and areas within the buildings, data can still be innocently or intentionally damaged. The potential harm from both can be sharply reduced by controls built directly into software programs that signal most types of errors or unauthorized procedures. Developing these controls is a programming task, but ensuring that the controls are used is a management responsibility with the following requirements:

- *Require changes to master files* be made by different personnel than those who handle day-to-day operations to reduce opportunities for fraud. If the person who handles the daily operations cannot change the master file, and the person who changes the file does not have regular access to the operating programs, there is less chance that either one alone can make an improper change in the data. If the programs themselves automatically update master files, then copies of such files (made prior to updating) should be retained long enough to confirm that the updates were correct.
- *Document master data changes* by requiring authorized signatures, limited access to serially numbered forms, and retention of the authorization document until the updating is verified.
- *Require limits to be stated on the face of checks* issued by the organization to ensure that a large disbursement cannot be made without executive approval. For example, a check might carry the message "Not Valid For More Than $100.00" or "No Paycheck Exceeds $2,500.00."
- *Establish individual users' "territories"* within the computer memory so that only authorized personnel have access to especially sensitive information and programs.
- *Test new programs* before allowing them to process actual data. Tests should not be run "on line" or on production files in order to guard against the possibility that testing a faulty program may disrupt operations or destroy important data.
- *Use batch and "hash" (or cross-check) totals* to ensure that all required transactions have been performed, but unauthorized transactions have not. These totals utilize input data to verify operating processes. For example, if a given number of consecutively numbered sales orders have to be processed, the serial numbers of the individual orders can be totaled: comparing this serial number total with a predetermined reference total would indicate any omitted or inserted order(s).
- *Maintain time and error logs* to record the time it takes to perform computer activities. Program standards, mentioned earlier, should indicate how much time is required for various "normal" computer runs. The time logs will then indicate how much time was actually used for various operations. If the

actual time exceeds the "normal" time by a significant margin, then the accompanying error log should contain an explanation of the additional time used to correct an error. If no error is indicated, there should be some other explanation of the extra computer running time. If no explanation is found, supervisors and management should investigate the possibility of unauthorized computer use.

PREVENTION OF EMBEZZLEMENT AND FRAUD

Organizations worldwide suffer much larger and more frequent crime losses at the hands of their own employees than through those of robbers, burglars, rioters, vandals, arsonists, or other violent criminals. Nonviolent theft by employees (with or without cooperation from outsiders) is called embezzlement. This typically totals several times an organization's losses from violent crimes. This section treats the control of embezzlement and fraud (a general term for other nonviolent crime). The control of robbery, burglary, riot, vandalism, and arson is discussed in the next major section.

Types of Losses

Embezzlement and fraud losses can deprive an organization of money, other property, future sales and markets, personnel, reputation, and goodwill. In some situations, a single theft can involve losses of all these assets.

The most common losses are of money and other property. Other losses can include the loss of a market through the effects of successful industrial espionage. These can have even greater long-term adverse effects. The losses of reputation and goodwill often are consequences of an organization's inability to deliver goods or render timely performance to customers. For example, certain international air carriers, because of repeated theft losses of high-fashion merchandise, have found that their regular clients often shift their business to other carriers.

Even the theft of the most commonplace items of property can generate substantial losses. Among such thefts that have actually occurred are $15,000 in brooms over a six-month period, $50,000 in cardboard boxes over three years, and $50,000 in non-narcotic pills from a pharmaceutical house. Frequently, the mere opportunity to steal property will result in theft even though the thief has no plan to use or to sell the property.

Conditions Leading to Embezzlement and Fraud

The most common and controllable conditions leading to embezzlement and fraud are negligence, naivete, and lack of appropriate controls. Negligence is the result of management's failure to examine theft exposures critically or to take preventive action when indicated; naivete is the result of some common but incorrect assumptions about people's honesty; and lack of controls is the result of the incorrect presumption that controls are unnecessary.

Negligence Negligence is often the most important condition leading to embezzlement and fraud losses. Negligence can include such minor oversights as leaving a drawer or door unlocked at the end of the work day and the failure to check entry passes to verify that the picture on the pass is, in fact, of the holder of the pass. It can even involve more extreme cases of impersonation, in which an industrial spy posing as a building inspector goes unnoticed. Cases of negligence such as these and others that lead to embezzlement and fraud often originate in senior management indifference to controls. A phrase used so often in management circles—"expect and inspect"—has special relevance to eliminating negligence as a means of theft control.

Some negligence stems from simple ignorance or misunderstanding. For example, some managers believe that they and their organizations will face civil or criminal penalties if suspected thieves are arrested or prosecuted but not convicted. Such beliefs lead to policies of not arresting, or not prosecuting, persons who are almost certainly criminals. In reality, these managers' potential liability to the organization for losses from continued embezzlement or fraud is far greater than their exposure to personal liability for the wrongful arrest of innocent but suspicious employees. Some knowledge of basic law, together with awareness of proper procedures, will minimize any manager's liability for wrongful arrest.

Managerial Naivete Many managers often wrongfully assume that production or hourly workers are more likely than upper level employees to steal. In fact, more serious cases of embezzlement and fraud are attributable to managers and other executives. Studies show that, in at least embezzlement from banks, presidents, vice-presidents, managers, and head cashiers are most frequently the culprits.

Most embezzlement and fraud is committed by persons in authority and in positions of trust. This is true for several reasons. First, such persons are familiar with security routines; they know what wrongdoing is likely to be discovered and what is not. Second, they have access to money and other valuable property and the opportunity to take it. Unlike hourly workers, who often may be questioned when they are away from an assigned work area or are involved in any task but an assigned one, upper level employees frequently have authority to work in many places and to be involved in many activities. Third, the opportunities to get into difficult personal financial positions often are greater for more senior executives than for others. A corporate officer usually can borrow more than can subordinates, even though this executive may not be in any better position to repay a loan when it falls due. Fourth, managers frequently believe, with good reason, that their organizations will attempt to conceal rather than expose a theft by a senior employee. Thus, for many executives, fear of punishment is often not really a deterrent. For these reasons, it is crucial for an organization to be highly aware of the behavior of its upper level employees.

Lack of Controls The lack of sound procedural controls for maintaining security is another factor responsible for embezzlement and fraud. This condition is typified by the release of drawings or product specifications to vendors who have not been screened and without a warning against disclosure of the material to third persons. (The warning should really be attached regardless of whether or not the vendor has been screened.) Although the vendor may disregard this warning, at least the wording can alert vendors to their resulting exposure to liability for doing so.

Other areas that should be governed by policies and procedures, but often are not, include (1) entering the premises, (2) removing property from the premises, (3) screening and selection of employees, (4) salvaging or scrapping of materials, and (5) separating among several persons functions that involve cash. Developing controls for these areas should begin with management who sets broad guidelines and objectives for the overall security program. These guidelines should then be implemented through procedural controls, which, in turn, are followed by physical controls. However, in too many cases, the physical controls are often considered first, and as a result, often are not properly related to overall security planning.

PREVENTION OF VIOLENT CRIME

An organization is exposed to violent as well as nonviolent crime. Five important violent crimes that result in loss are robbery, burglary, riot, vandalism, and arson.

Robbery

Robbery is the taking of property from a person through the use of threat of force. It is robbery to take money or other property from someone at gunpoint, to state or imply that the victim's family or associates will be harmed unless the robber's request for money or other property is granted, or to offer to rescue the victim from danger the robber has created only if the victim will give the robber money or other property. Risk control efforts to reduce the frequency or size of robberies should focus on pre-robbery safeguards, the victim's conduct during a robbery, and the identification and capture of the robber(s) after the crime has been committed.

Risk control efforts strive to make robbery appear unattractive or impossible. The following are some actions that may accomplish this objective:

- Minimizing the quantity of cash (or of other high-value, portable property such as office equipment or works of art) on the organization's premises,
- Posting prominent signs indicating that cash register operators and other employees cannot open registers or safes,
- Transferring large amounts of cash or other valuable property as privately and unobtrusively as possible, and according to highly unpredictable schedules and routes so that potential robbers cannot accurately anticipate the transfer.
- Training and regularly drilling employees in (1) identifying any suspicious conduct of persons, such as "casing" the premises and (2) remaining calm and observant during a robbery.

When a robbery is in progress, it is ironic that both robber and victim share two objectives: (1) to act calmly and (2) for the robber to leave the scene as soon as possible. For a robber, these objectives help increase the amount of property stolen and promote a safe getaway. For the victim, staying calm but not excessively friendly to the robber reduces the chance of being physically harmed and increases the opportunity to make observations about the robber that may assist the police and criminal courts. Therefore, while a robbery is under way, a victim's conduct should be as follows:

- Follow a robber's instructions—neither challenge nor attempt to outwit the robber—so that the robber does not feel he or she is losing control of the situation, motivating him or her to resort to violence to reestablish dominance.
- Trigger any "silent" alarms on the premises to alert police without making any sound or giving other signals that the premises is being robbed.
- Focus intently on any characteristics of each robber—physical characteristics, patterns of speech or movement, any names of

persons or places that may be mentioned—that may help to later apprehend and prosecute the robber.

- Give the robber any property that may have been prepared as a "trap" to provide evidence of theft. This may be a packet of paper money containing consecutively numbered bills or special, commercially produced packets of "money" that give off tear gas or red dye after a delay that should allow the robber to leave the premises.
- Refrain from pursuing the robber in order to avoid further endangering the victim as well as any bystanders, but observe the robber's route in order to provide any further identifying information.

After a robber leaves, the first priority is to give medical attention to anyone who may have been injured when the crime was committed. Next, each victim should attempt to gather his or her recollections about the robbery, writing down any crucial facts that will help them to remember the crime and to inform the police. Although victims may wish to discuss the event among themselves to reinforce their memories, it is best that each victim first reconstruct and record his or her own version of the events without any influence from others', perhaps incorrect, memories.

Burglary

Burglary is the unauthorized removal of property from a building into which the burglar has broken when the building (a business or residence) is not open. (Breaking out after having stolen something is also part of the burglary.) Burglary is distinct from robbery in that it does not involve the taking of property directly *from persons* by violence or threat of violence. Burglary also is distinct from the more general term, "theft," which encompasses all forms of stealing of property including not only robbery and burglary, but also sneak thievery and fraud.

To succeed, a burglar needs (1) information about the premises, (2) an opportunity for concealment, (3) time, and (4) ease of access and egress. Pre-event risk control procedures should address those four items in order to reduce or avoid the burglary exposures. Actual or attempted burglary may result in considerable physical damage from burglars breaking in, or trying to enlarge egresses to remove property. The following are some effective ways to reduce the likelihood of burglary:

- Deny information—caution employees about divulging specific data to strangers concerning valuable shipments, payrolls, hard currency and securities, watchmen rounds, burglar alarm systems, or any other knowledge that pertains to the internal operations of the company.

- Eliminate possible concealment—vegetation or other screens to points of building access should be eliminated, and blind spots should be well-lighted; watch areas of trash containers, which can block inspection (and watch what is going out in the trash—you might be surprised); locate storage areas away from buildings, and, in the case of flammable materials, they should be separately enclosed; and park vehicles away from the building in a well-lighted area.
- Extend the time the intruder needs on site—the longer he or she must spend neutralizing physical barriers, the greater the chance of detection.
- Protect means of access and egress—systems and barriers may be designed in such a way to permit, with some difficulty, access, but will effectively limit egress (i.e., the cookie jar syndrome—you can get your hand in, but to remove it with cookies poses some restrictions). Generally, this kind of protection involves the use of fencing, moats, watchmen, detection and alarm systems, closed circuit television (CCTV), secured storage, and off-site facilities. Any intrusion prevention system should be established with appropriate redundancy and proper verification methods.

Post-event methods to prevent subsequent thefts include securing the site to investigate the crime and collect evidence, taking inventory to determine what has been taken and to verify the condition of other areas of the plant, analyzing how the burglar gained access to the building, and remaining vigilant for the possibility of repeat occurrence.

Riot

A riot is public violence, tumult, or disorder by (under the statutes of most states) three or more persons assembled together and acting with a common intent. A civil commotion or civil disorder is very similar and can include any display of public discontent ranging from a disgruntled mass to a full-blown uprising. A *strike* is a work stoppage by a body of workers aimed at forcing the employer to comply with workers' demands. A strike can be a peaceful protest or it can erupt into a riot-like disruption. Certain areas (disadvantaged neighborhoods in the inner city) and certain kinds of businesses (steel, coal mining, and railroads) are more prone to riot. This exposure can be difficult to predict in some cases, and it is best to assume the worse-case condition and prepare the facility, as part of an emergency action plan, to meet it.

Because riot often results in property damage, the following measures to minimize property losses are also applicable to the peril of riot:

- Secure the site, and take actions to protect the plant facilities and employees. Additional manpower may be needed temporarily for the security force.
- Keep fire protection systems in service, and protect control valves and main switching points for all utility services.

The following additional procedures should also be implemented to handle a riot during and after the disturbance:

- Immediately call public authorities.
- Maintain communications around the site between inspection and surveillance teams. Use CB or hand-powered radios because other types of communications may be disrupted.
- Photograph the crowd to help identify perpetrators/leaders and to verify the action for civil authorities.

If rioters penetrate the organization's premises, it may be advisable to use water spray or some other nonlethal and nonhazardous agent to discourage them. Under no circumstances should anyone except police use firearms or noxious gases to quell a riot. Above all, the organization should strive to maintain a favorable image in the eyes of the public and to deal firmly but fairly with those causing the disturbance. It should be remembered that there are effective, nonviolent ways to handle civil commotion without complicating or aggravating the situation.

Vandalism

Vandalism is the willful, malicious destruction or defacement of property, often as an indirect attack on its owners whom the vandals are reluctant to or unable to reach directly. Property that is unguarded, poorly lit, or unoccupied for extended periods is particularly attractive to vandals. Therefore, the most effective strategies for preventing vandalism include protecting valuable properties with good fencing (including locked gates) and other perimeter protection, and providing human or canine guards as well as ample nighttime lighting. It is also wise to design facilities so that features attractive to vandals are not visible to passers-by.

Arson

Arson is the intentional burning of property. It is generally motivated by one or more of the following: fraud (for insurance proceeds), to hide another crime, jealousy, revenge, thrill (pyromania, juvenile, sexual), need to terminate lease, some reason to relocate the business, or an unprofitable contract. Most arson fires occur in storage areas (estimates range from 60 percent to 75 percent), but other areas are as susceptible if the conditions are favorable. Often, if the first attempt is unsuccessful, a repeated attempt will be made within two weeks (a 33 percent chance).

Several key arson control practices: (1) maintain the sprinkler system in full operating condition and lock all control valves in the open position—limit access to valve rooms, (2) survey areas, especially storage, on a frequent but random basis, and (3) control access to all areas, especially flammable liquid storage.

After arson has occurred, the first step in handling is to retain a qualified investigator who specializes in arson work—the scene should not be disturbed until it can be properly surveyed. The focus of arson investigation is to pinpoint anything at the scene that does not belong and to note the absence of anything that does. Investigators question anything unusual. If it is determined that arson is the cause of the fire, the organization should make legal arrangements to handle the crime. Many arsonists are repeat offenders—and they should be prevented from committing further crimes. As for post-event actions the standard procedure for restoring losses should be followed: (1) make temporary repairs, (2) begin clean-up, (3) effect salvage, and (4) make permanent repairs and restore operations.

AN INTEGRATED SECURITY RISK CONTROL PROGRAM

The specific controls for security exposures should be brought together into a coordinated risk control program. The program is likely to be structured primarily in terms of the risk control techniques applicable to any peril that threatens security. These techniques include exposure avoidance, loss control (loss prevention and loss reduction), and contractual (noninsurance) transfer to risk control.[3]

Exposure Avoidance

Some crime exposures can be avoided, thus eliminating any possibility of loss. For example, if no furs are carried in inventory by a clothier, there is no exposure to burglary of fur garments—that particular exposure has been avoided.

However, when one exposure is avoided, it is important to recognize that others still exist and may even become more serious, and that new exposures may also be created. For example, just because money is removed from the premises overnight, the exposure to theft during the day is not avoided. Moreover, this measure requires that a messenger will take money to a bank or residence every night—a practice that may increase the possibility of robbery while the messenger is in transit or when the money is deposited. Another example is the use of *independent contractors* instead of employees. Perhaps it is technically possible to avoid the employee dishonesty exposure—but the practical effect will usually be to increase the probability of theft by nonemployees. For exposure avoidance to be a viable part of a security program, management must realize that it cannot be the only risk control technique.

Loss Control (Prevention and Reduction)

Crime loss control measures may be roughly divided into five groups:

1. Physical protection for premises in order to delay access by the criminal;
2. Installation of alarm systems and other devices or the use of guards or security patrols that will indicate when access to the premises has been gained by an outsider;
3. Use of automatic cameras or closed circuit television systems to help identify criminals in order to facilitate their arrest and conviction;
4. Various protective *procedures*, including procedures for handling money and securities that will reduce the likelihood of theft or reduce the amount of property accessible to a thief; and
5. Management and personnel measures directed specifically toward the employee dishonesty exposure, e.g., the use of polygraph tests.

Physical Protection A businessowner can install passive restraints to entry. The type of lock used on doorways can make a difference of several minutes in the entry time needed by a thief. The ordinary snap lock can be manipulated in a matter of seconds. A deadbolt lock cannot be manipulated in the same way as a snap lock, but usually requires the picking of the tumblers or the use of force. Lockpicking requires tools and skills that many ordinary burglars do not possess.

The rear doors in a store or office can be barred from the inside so that access is difficult. Bars, grates, or other coverings can be put across windows or doorways. An "unbreakable" glazing material can be used for doors or windows where the proprietor wishes to maintain a clearly visible window display. (It is worth noting that any measure that impedes entry or exit by burglars may also impede entry by firefighters or exit by members of the public during an emergency.)

Many burglaries are committed by breaking a show window and grabbing valuable items. Ordinary plate glass is easily broken. Varieties of breakage-resistant glass and plastic materials often improve protection, particularly for smaller windows. In jewelry display windows, another device effectively impedes the access of a burglar. This is a sheet of breakage-resistant glass suspended behind the show window glass. This second sheet is hung on chains from the top of the show window so that it swings backward when struck. The show window can be broken, but this second sheet of glass is difficult to break—because of its composition and, particularly, because it swings. It is difficult for a thief to reach around such a glass when it is properly installed.

The installation of good locks, grates, bars, breakage-resistant glass, and similar devices may provide satisfactory protection for mercantile stocks of low value. This may be particularly true if the premises are under frequent surveillance by police and in a low crime area. However, such passive restraints merely delay the entrance of a burglar and do not guarantee that a burglary will not occur. The adequacy of such measures also must be considered in light of the values involved and whether small volume and weight plus high value would make the merchandise attractive to a burglar.

Safes are another type of physical protective device. Safes vary in their vulnerability to burglary. Many safes are basically fire protection devices, referred to as *record safes*, and offer little resistance to the burglar. Designed to protect money and valuable records from fire damage, *fire resistive safes* generally have square doors and are mounted on wheels.

Money safes are designed to be burglar resistive. They generally have round doors and are not mounted on wheels. (However, some modern money safes have been designed with square doors to facilitate their use with cash register trays.) As shown in Exhibit 4-5, there are different categories of safes, each including a variety of models with different degrees of resistance to fire and/or burglary. The exhibit also shows the classifications used in rating some crime policies and gives some idea of the different degrees of protection afforded by the different types of safes. Like other physical protection devices, safes do not eliminate the possibility of a loss. However, they do reduce the likelihood of loss relative to the quality of the safe and the skill of the thief.

Alarm Systems Unlike some physical protection devices, alarm systems do not prevent the entry of a burglar. Except to the extent that they serve as a deterrent, the function of an alarm system is to indicate when an intruder has entered the premises.

Some alarm systems use simple electrical circuits that sound an alarm when an electrical connection is made or broken. Other systems use more sophisticated electronic devices. These may give alarms when a foreign body, such as a burglar, is within the premises. Some use invisible light rays that, when broken, give an alarm signal. The principal varieties of these devices are described below.

A simple alarm system consists of electrical contacts or metal tapes on each door, window, or other opening into the building. Usually, the system is wired so that an electrical current is passing through the system constantly. Opening a door or window interrupts the electrical current, which activates an alarm system. This is a *perimeter system;* the intent is to give an alarm whenever the building is entered through a door, a window, or other opening that is protected by the system.

A perimeter system protecting all doors, windows, and other openings still gives no protection against entry through a roof or a wall. A more complete system also signals entry through a roof or wall. This may require the installation of wires or other devices that protect the areas of wall or roof accessible from neighboring buildings. Various sensing devices are illustrated in Exhibit 4-6. Sensing devices usually are connected to either local or central station alarms.

Alarms are not limited to preventing burglary. They may also be used to reduce the robbery exposure. Holdup buttons or foot pedals may be situated so they can be triggered by a bank teller or store clerk, sending a "silent" alarm to a central station company or to the police. (The "silent" alarm is silent at the location being robbed.) If rapid response is possible, the police may arrive while a robber is still on the premises.

Local Alarms. Many simple alarm systems are connected to an interior gong or alarm and also to a gong on the outside of the premises. An interior alarm system may be effective in a store with security personnel on duty at all times—the alarm system would alert such security personnel to entry by a burglar. However, the outside alarm may be almost completely useless in an industrial or mercantile district where few people are present during the night. Such local alarms often ring for hours before anyone pays any attention to them. Sometimes neighbors call the police only because the noise eventually

Exhibit 4-5
Safe and Vault Classification*

Safe, Chest, Cabinet or Vault Classification	CONSTRUCTION		
	Doors	WALLS	
		Safe, Chest or Cabinet	Vault
B (Fire-resistive)	Steel less than 1" thick, or iron	Body of steel less than ½" thick, or iron	Brick, concrete, stone, tile, iron or steel
	Any iron or steel safe or chest having a slot through which money can be deposited		Not Applicable
C (Burglar-resistive)	Steel at least 1" thick	Body of steel at least ½" thick	Steel at least ½" thick; or reinforced concrete or stone at least 9" thick, or non-reinforced concrete or stone at least 12" thick
	Safe or chest bearing following label: "Underwriters' Laboratories, Inc. Inspected Keylocked Safe KL Burglary"		Not Applicable
E (Burglar-resistive)	Steel at least 1½" thick	Body of steel at least 1" thick	Same as for C
ER (Burglar-resistive)	Safe or chest bearing the following label: "Underwriters' Laboratories, Inc., Inspected Tool Resisting Safe TL-15 Burglary"	Underwriters' Laboratories, Inc. Inspected Tool Resisting Safe TL-15	Not Applicable
F (Burglar-resistive)	Safe or chest bearing one of the following labels: 1. "Underwriters' Laboratories, Inc. Inspected Tool Resisting Safe TL-30 Burglary" 2. "Underwriters' Laboratories, Inc. Inspected Torch Resisting Safe TR-30 Burglary" 3. "Underwriters' Laboratories, Inc. Inspected Explosive Resisting Safe with Relocking Device X-60 Burglary"	Underwriters' Laboratories, Inc. Inspected Tool Resisting Safe TL-30	Not Applicable

G (Burglar-resistive)	One or more steel doors (one in front of the other) each at least 1½″ thick and aggregating at least 3″ thickness	Not Applicable	Steel at least ½″ thick; or reinforced concrete or stone at least 12″ thick; or non-reinforced concrete or stone at least 18″ thick
H (Burglar-resistive)		Safe or chest bearing one of the following labels: 1. "Underwriters' Laboratories, Inc. Inspected Torch and Explosive Resisting Safe TX-60 Burglary" 2. "Underwriters' Laboratories, Inc. Inspected Torch Resisting Safe TR-60 Burglary" 3. "Underwriters' Laboratories, Inc. Inspected Torch and Tool Resisting Safe TRTL-30 Burglary"	Not Applicable
I (Burglar-resistive)		Safe or chest bearing one of the following labels: 1. "Underwriters' Laboratories, Inc. Inspected Torch and Tool Resisting Safe TRTL-60 Burglary" 2. "Underwriters' Laboratories, Inc. Inspected Torch, Explosive and Tool Resisting Safe TXTL-60 Burglary"	Not Applicable
J (Burglar-resistive)		Safe or chest bearing the following label: "Underwriters' Laboratories, Inc. Inspected Torch and Tool Resisting Safe TRTL-30×6 Burglary"	Not Applicable
K (Burglar-resistive)		Safe or chest bearing one of the following labels: 1. "Underwriters' Laboratories, Inc. Inspected Torch and Tool Resisting Safe TRTL-60 Burglary" 2. "Underwriters' Laboratories, Inc. Inspected Torch Explosive and Tool Resisting Safe TXTL-60 Burglary"	
Vaults meeting these specifications or better.	Steel at least 3½″ thick		Steel at least 1″ thick or 18″ of reinforced concrete or 36″ of non-reinforced concrete

* Reprinted with permission from *Commercial Lines Manual*, p. CR-SV-2, copyright Insurance Services Office, Inc., 1985.

Exhibit 4-6
Burglar Alarm System Design*

Door Switches (Contacts) These devices are usually magnet-operated switches. They are affixed to a door or window in such a way that opening the door or window removes the magnetic field. This, in turn, activates the switch causing an alarm.

These devices may be surface-mounted or recessed, exposed or concealed. A variety of switches exists for every kind of door or window and for all levels of security.

Metallic Foil (Window Tape) Metallic foil is the traditional means for detecting glass-breakage. Strips of thin foil are affixed to a glass surface. Breaking glass ruptures the foil and interrupts the detection circuit to signal an alarm.

Thin foil, however, is easily damaged by people or objects accidentally touching the glass surface. Also, bonds at the corners and between multiple-foil strips deteriorate with time. Metallic foil, therefore, requires frequent maintenance, especially on glass doors.

Wooden Screens Openings such as air-duct passages and skylights can provide paths for an intruder. These can be secured by a cage-like frame of wooden rods. An intruder breaks the wire embedded within the frame which triggers an alarm.

Wood screens are custom-built for each application. They can be mounted permanently or removed when the alarm system is turned

Continued on next page

off. Wooden screens require little maintenance. They are suitable for protecting openings where aesthetics are not important.

Lacing (Paneling) Lacing can protect walls, doors and safes against penetration. Lacing is a closely woven pattern of metallic foil or fine brittle wire on the surface of the protected area. An intruder can enter only by breaking the foil or wire. This activates the alarm. A panel over the lacing protects it from accidental damage.

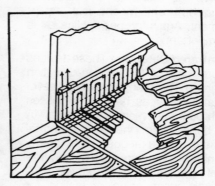

Photoelectric (Eyes, Beams) Photoelectric devices transmit a beam across a protected area. When an intruder interrupts this beam, the photoelectric circuit is disrupted. This starts an alarm.

Modern photoelectric devices are a great improvement over their predecessors. Today's photoelectric devices use diodes that emit infrared light. These make the beam invisible to the naked eye. The beam usually pulses rapidly to prevent compromise by substitution.

Photoelectric devices are effective and reliable. Some have ranges of more than 1,000 feet for large buildings and hallways. These devices provide excellent protection for relatively low-risk areas.

Ultrasonic Detectors These devices also sense movement. Ultrasonic means "above the range of hearing." An intruder disrupting the ultrasonic wave pattern initiates the alarm.

Ultrasonic devices can be mounted on the ceiling or wall. They protect three-dimensional areas with an invisible pattern. However, they are

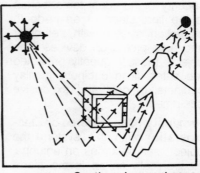

Continued on next page

prone to false alarms, due to excessive air currents or ultrasonic noises from mechanical equipment. Again, proper application is important.

Infrared Detectors These devices are part of the motion-detection group. They sense the body heat of an intruder as he or she passes through the protected area. A change from the area's normal heat profile triggers an alarm. Infrared detectors are relatively free of false alarms. They provide relatively inexpensive protection for confined areas.

Microwave Detectors This kind of motion detector uses high-frequency radio waves, or microwaves, to detect movement. Microwave devices have greater range than ultrasonic. Since microwave devices do not use sound, or air, they are not prone to false alarms from air currents. However, they can cause false alarms, because they penetrate materials such as glass, and metal objects reflect them. This means microwaves can detect motion outside the protected area if the detectors are not properly installed.

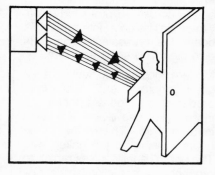

Object Protection

Object protection provides direct security for individual items. It often is the final stage of an in-depth protection system with perimeter and area-protection devices. The objects most frequently protected are safes, filing cabinets, display cabinets, models and expensive equipment.

Proximity (Capacitance or Electrostatic) With this system, the object itself becomes an antenna, electronically linked to the alarm

Continued on next page

control. When a person approaches or touches the object, its electrostatic field becomes unbalanced. This initiates the alarm. Only metal objects isolated from the ground can be protected this way.

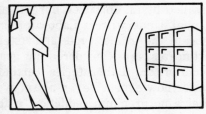

Vibration Detectors (Seismic)
These sensing devices use a highly sensitive piezoelectric crystal or microphone to detect the sound pattern that a hammer-like impact on a rigid surface would generate. These devices are attached directly to safes and filing cabinets or walls and floors.

The devices instantly detect a vibration an intruder makes. Some vibration detectors are adjustable. They can be adjusted to detect a sledge-hammer attack on concrete or the delicate penetration of a glass surface.

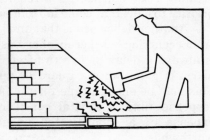

This kind of protection generally is for securing the perimeter surfaces of a vault. The correct number, spacing and location of these sensors is important for suitable detection.

---

*Reprinted with permission from *Alarm Handbook for the Security Manager,* Honeywell, Inc. 1984, pp. 8-11.

interferes with their sleep. In the meantime, the burglars have left with the stolen goods.

Central Station Alarms. A more effective type of alarm system is connected directly to a central station of an alarm company. The central station of an alarm company is monitored at all hours. Electrical or electronic monitoring of all circuits is performed from the central station. When an alarm is received at the central station, a guard is sent to the site from which the alarm was transmitted. The police are also notified that an alarm was received from those premises.

Selection of Alarm Systems. Alarm systems vary as to their quality and extent of protection. Insurance rate manuals generally give credits only for *approved alarm systems.* An approved system is one installed by an approved burglar alarm company named in the rating manual. Underwriters Laboratories, Inc., issues alarm certificates that indicate the grade, type, and extent of the alarm system, and these certificates are considered in granting insurance rate credits. An Underwriters Laboratories certificate is shown in Exhibit 4-7. No matter how expensive, an alarm system without a U.L. certificate may receive no premium reduction, a fact too often discovered only after money has been spent on an alarm.

Deficiencies of Alarm Systems. There are many problems with burglar alarm systems. One of the most difficult problems is false alarms caused by accidental triggering. One survey indicated that more than half of the major police emergency calls in a large city were actually false alarms. As a result, police in some cities assign a low priority to calls that come in from burglar alarm systems.

Another deficiency is that an alarm system does not stop burglaries from occurring—it merely shortens the burglar's operating time. There is always a delay of five to fifteen minutes or more from the time an alarm is given until a guard or police officer can reach the premises. This may be enough time for the burglars to complete their work. The response time is a vital consideration in determining whether the expense of a sophisticated burglary or robbery alarm system is worthwhile.

Central station contracts with merchants ordinarily require that the central station guard remain on the premises for up to two hours after the alarm has been received in order to give the proprietor time to arrive and arrange for securing the premises. There have been cases where the proprietor failed to arrive within the specified two hours, and the alarm company guard left the premises at the end of the two-hour period, after which burglars re-entered the premises at leisure and made off with the property they originally intended to steal.

One alarm that may be used when a central station service is not available is an automatic device that dials the police telephone number and transmits a recorded message to the police department when the alarm is activated. Such a system can be arranged to send a robbery alarm when a button is pushed, or it can be arranged to indicate a burglary when the premises are entered. Unfortunately, there are ways to deactivate such a system by placing other telephone calls from nearby phones or by disconnecting the telephone lines. In fact, a major problem is that telephone circuits generally are used to transmit signals from the premises to the central station or police department. A sophisticated burglar may be familiar enough with telephone lines in general that the security can be breached at some point where the lines are accessible. This may be in the basement of a multiple-occupancy

Exhibit 4-7
Underwriters Laboratories, Inc., Certificate*

CENTRAL STATION BURGLAR ALARM CERTIFICATE   No. **BC** 1031954

(UL) **UNDERWRITERS LABORATORIES INC.**
333 PFINGSTEN ROAD · NORTHBROOK, ILLINOIS 60062 ®
an independent, not-for-profit organization testing for public safety

_____ Property Name and Address _____

File No._____   Service Loc. No._____

System Grade	Type of System	Extent of Protection
☐ A ☐ AA	☐ Premises	☐ Extent 1
☐ B ☐ BB	☐ Stockroom	☐ Extent 2
☐ C ☐ CC		☐ Extent 3
	☐ Safe	☐ Partial
	☐ Vault	☐ Complete
	☐ Night Depository	
	☐ Automated Teller Machine	

THIS CERTIFIES that the Alarm Service Company Whose Name Appears Hereon is included by Underwriters Laboratories Inc. in its Directory as furnishing the burglar alarm system described hereon and is authorized to issue this certificate for the equipment described hereon as its representation that such equipment and all connected wiring and devices is in compliance with requirements established by Underwriters Laboratories Inc. This certificate does not apply in any way to the installation of any additional alerting systems, such as; fire, smoke, holdup, or otherwise, that may be connected to or installed along with the burglar alarm system described hereon.

LIMITATION OF LIABILITY Underwriters Laboratories Inc. makes no representations or warranties, express or implied, that the alarm system will prevent any loss by burglary, hold-up or otherwise, or that the system will in all cases provide the protection for which it is installed or intended. This certificate only evidences that UL conducts countercheck field inspections of representative installations of the alarm service company. UL does not assume or undertake to discharge any liability of the alarm service company or any other party. UL is not an insurer and assumes no liability for any loss which may result from failure of the equipment, incorrect certification, non-conformity with requirements, cancellation of the certificate or withdrawal of the alarm service company from inclusion in UL's Directory prior to the expiration date appearing on this certificate. If an installation is found not in conformity with requirements, it shall be corrected by the alarm service company or the certificate is subject to cancellation.

Alarm Transmission To Central Station
☐ Derived Channel   ☐ Digital Communicator
☐ Direct Wire   ☐ McCulloh
☐ Multiplex   ☐ Radio

Keys	Bell	Response Time Category
☐ Yes	☐ Yes	☐ 15 min.
☐ No	☐ No	☐ 20 min.
		☐ 30 min.

Issued Date_____

Expiration Date_____
(Not to be Issued for a Term of More than 5 Years)

[ ] New Certificate
[ ] Renewal

Alarm Service Company_____

By_____
Authorized Signature

Central Station Location_____
(City, State)

The undersigned, representing the property named in this Certificate acknowledges he has read and understands the terms and conditions of this certificate.

Representative of Property Named Above

_____
Authorized Signature

Dated_____, 19__

© 1986 UL

CERTIFICATE HOLDER COPY

*Reprinted with permission from *The Alarm Handbook for the Security Manager,* Honeywell, Inc.

building, in the overhead lines, or in a telephone line on a pole or box outside the building.

An alarm system may have what is called a shunt switch, which gives the store operator a few seconds to get out of the store when the premises are closed for the night, or get into the store upon entering in the morning, without giving an alarm. This device is particularly common in a local alarm that the proprietor does not wish to activate when leaving or entering the premises. It is a simple matter for the sophisticated burglar to determine in advance exactly what the proprietor does in using the shunt switch. The burglar then does the same thing.

Watchman or Security Patrols Many organizations find it worthwhile to maintain watchman service on the premises. A watchman goes through the building at periodic intervals (typically hourly) to see that everything is in good order. This, of course, protects against fire and, to a degree, against other perils such as burglary. It is considered necessary to use some device to make certain that the watchman does patrol at the required intervals. One common system uses a special clock carried by the watchman that records the visits to stations throughout the building. A key is fastened to each location, and inserting the key into the special clock records the time when the watchman visited that particular station. By checking the records, the employer can be sure the watchman completed all rounds. The weakness of this system is that when a watchman is overpowered during the night, no one knows about it until the premises are reopened the next morning. The presence of the watchman is a deterrent as far as burglars are concerned, but it by no means eliminates loss possibilities.

Central station alarm companies also maintain a *supervised system* under which the watchman signals to the central station upon visiting each station throughout the premises. These systems are arranged so that a guard is sent to the premises by the central station alarm company if the watchman at the premises fails to signal as required. Sometimes burglars or robbers will force a watchman to continue making rounds while a theft is being carried out. Most signaling systems contain an arrangement whereby the watchman can secretly signal for help even while making rounds under the burglar's scrutiny.

Large organizations may contain a complete security system with a central station on the premises for the supervision of one or more watchmen. The expense of such a system to protect against crimes would be justified only if large values were involved or if the supervision of watchmen were needed for other reasons.

Surveillance Cameras Banks and other firms with high robbery exposure frequently install automatic cameras to photograph criminals in the process of committing a crime. Such installations are effective in two ways:

1. They facilitate the identification, conviction, and incarceration of criminals after the offense has been committed.
2. The increased probability of identification and conviction discourages robbery.

Property Protection Procedures A property owner can institute many procedures in addition to the devices just described. One simple procedure used by many merchants is to have the safe or other particularly valuable property located where it can be observed by police patrols from outside the building. A light is installed to keep the inside of the premises illuminated.

Another common procedure is for some businesses to accept only credit cards and/or exact change and to immediately deposit all money into a burglar-resistant safe, making deposits through a one-way slot or chute. Robbers tend to "hit" isolated businesses with large amounts of money or "stealable" property and limited personnel. Steps that reduce isolation, reduce the amount of money or other attractive property on hand, and increase the number of people on duty tend to reduce the likelihood of a robbery.

Controlling the Employee Dishonesty Exposure Other loss control measures described below directly address the employee dishonesty exposure, and should be used by every organization.

- *Loss prevention* measures decrease the probability of employee theft.
- *Loss reduction* measures reduce probable loss severity by increasing the probability that employee thefts will be discovered or by limiting the amount that can be taken without discovery.

The line between loss prevention and loss reduction is not rigid, and some measures serve both to prevent and to reduce losses. For example, an employee who is aware that any theft will probably be discovered quickly is less likely to attempt a theft.

Exhibit 4-8 presents one method of categorizing internal theft prevention systems. The top half of the chart depicts measures that increase the probability of quick discovery. These are labeled "low trust measures" because they are based on the assumption that it is not wise to trust all employees fully. The logical next step is to set up a system that is very hard to beat. Two measures in this type of a system are described below.

- Stringent *accounting controls*, to keep track of cash flows and detect any improprieties, limit loss caused by manipulating a firm's records. Examples of such controls include internal auditing, patrolling, observing, leaving audit trails, and enforcing the use of standardized procedures.
- Stringent *access controls* reduce losses of merchandise and other property (including currency and coins, confidential documents, and trade secrets) by limiting access to target property to a limited number of key employees. For extremely valuable property and information, locked entrances, armed guards, and identification badges may be among the devices used to limit access. Keys and safe combinations are usually given to only a limited number of employees. Authority to sign checks, purchase orders, and contracts is given to only selected employees who cannot operate without this access.

This is the traditional approach to controlling the employee dishonesty exposure, and there is much to recommend it. Yet, it appears that some organizations with tight controls experience high theft rates, while others in an environment with loose controls have few problems. Why this paradox? Jack Bologna suggests that there are practical limits on the effectiveness of conventional accounting and access controls.[4] Cost is a major constraint, especially when one considers the cost of "watchers" and the added cost of people to "watch the watchers." Bologna also suggests that a "police state mentality" among employees may, in fact, invite theft by way of retaliation.

According to a different management theory, a high level of trust between labor and management reduces the need for accounting and access controls. An environment built on trust and ethical behavior is less conducive to dishonesty than an environment that assumes employees will steal if given half a chance.

Unfortunately, a favorable environment does not remove all dishonesty. Therefore, control measures are still needed for those who do not respond to the good attitudes around them. These are the measures previously discussed. Other measures that can be used to handle the employee dishonesty exposure include personnel screening, separation of duties, and employee benefit programs.

Personnel Screening. Personnel screening decreases the probability of employee theft because proper screening filters out dishonest applicants. This is done by gathering information about the applicant's background and checking references before the applicant is hired. In

Exhibit 4-8
An Internal Theft Prevention System*

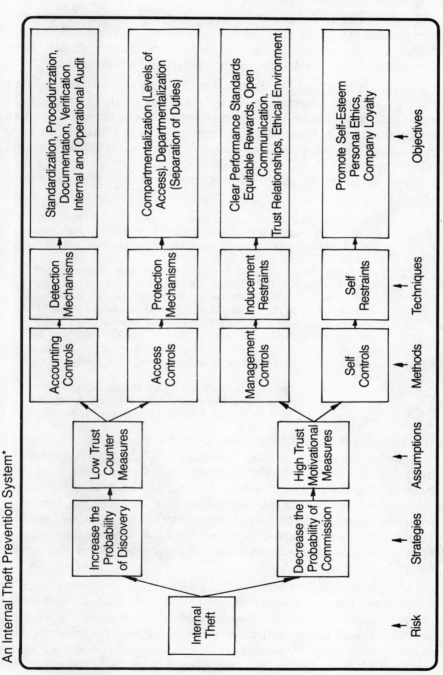

*Adapted, with permission, from Jack Bologna, "A New Look at The Internal Theft Prevention Process," *Assets Protection.* Sept./Oct. 1980, 33.

order to be effective, information regarding a prospective employee's background should be supplied by sources other than the applicant. Although there are many legal restrictions on hiring practices, these restrictions do not prohibit the use of background investigations.[5]

Separation of Duties. Separation of duties is another important strategy in many programs to control employee theft. The majority of employee thefts involve one employee acting alone. Proper separation of duties makes it difficult for any one employee to steal (or to steal a great deal) without the collaboration or cooperation of at least one other employee.

For duties to be effectively separated, the following conditions should exist:

1. No individual should have total control over every phase of any significant transaction or sensitive job. (For example, those who maintain inventory records do not participate in physical counts of inventory.)
2. Work flows should proceed from one person to another so that, without duplication, the work of the second acts as a check upon that of the first. (Merchandise for shipment is picked by one employee, taken to the loading dock by another, and checked onto a truck by a third—all of whose tallies should agree.)
3. Those who authorize the use of assets should not also be responsible for their custody. (The inventory clerk releases materials only upon receipt of an authorization from a department head.)
4. Record keeping and bookkeeping activities should be separated from the handling and custody of assets. (The accounts receivable clerk should not also open mail containing incoming payments.)

If a business is so small that there are not enough employees among whom to divide responsibilities in a manner that would otherwise be desirable, job rotation might be considered. Or assignment of dual responsibility for a given task could achieve the same purpose.

As with any control, the separation of duties could be carried to such lengths that it creates a counterproductive atmosphere of distrust among employees or generates such a labyrinth of procedural red tape that various informal shortcuts are devised over which no controls exist.[6]

Employee Benefit Programs. At first glance, there may seem to be little relationship between employee thefts and employee benefits (except, perhaps, that the undetected thief receives unintended benefits). Recall, however, that one prominent motive for embezzlement is "the astronomical increase in health care costs." Employees sometimes steal in order to pay for essential medical treatment for themselves or their loved ones. When the employer provides a sound group health insurance program for employees and their dependents, this motive is substantially reduced.

Contractual (Noninsurance) Transfers for Risk Control

The third technique that is part of an integrated security risk control program is the use of contractual (noninsurance) transfers for risk control. Organizations that handle large quantities of money or securities may arrange for frequent deposits at a bank in order to keep the amount of money or securities at a minimum. This results in a smaller value on the premises at any one time and also means that messengers carrying property to the bank carry smaller quantities. While these are loss reduction effects, there is also a noninsurance transfer because most exposures are transferred to the bank once the bank obtains custody of the deposited money. For example, by depositing cash in a bank, an organization transfers to the bank responsibility for some losses of that cash. If employees of the bank steal the cash, or if the bank is robbed or burglarized, the bank will generally bear the consequences of the crime without loss to the depositor.

Another procedure followed by many organizations is to transport money and securities by an armored car messenger service. In such situations, when money, securities, or other valuable property is entrusted to another entity who assumes responsibility for its safekeeping, a portion of the crime exposure is transferred along with custody of the property.

The use of an outside security or alarm company may provide some recourse if a guard, watchman, or alarm system fails to perform properly. The extent of the transfer depends in part on provisions in the contract with the service company. Generally, alarm companies use noninsurance transfers to protect themselves by requiring their customers to waive any claim against the alarm company.

However, there are limitations on the use of noninsurance transfers as a method of controlling employee dishonesty. If some operations are transferred to another entity, the other entity's employees may steal (as explained with reference to the bank). However, such a transfer might still be desirable if the transferee is in the better position to exercise control.

SUMMARY

Although "security" in its broadest sense refers to protecting an organization's assets from all types of harm, this chapter focuses on safeguarding assets from loss due to violent or surreptitious criminal activities. The chapter sets forth appropriate procedures for evaluating an organization's exposures to crime, describes the necessary elements of a security program, and explains how an organization can best protect itself against embezzlement, other fraud, robbery, burglary, riot, vandalism, and arson. These protective measures are categorized by (1) the particular type of crime they are designed to combat and (2) the generic risk control techniques they apply (loss prevention, loss reduction, and contractual transfers for risk control). The chapter also discusses the special security measures often required for computer centers.

Analyzing an organization's exposures to surreptitious and violent crime requires that its loss history be studied. This will help to estimate both the probability and the potential criticality (or severity) of specific crime losses. Probabilities of loss by crime are best stated in terms of the following categories: virtually certain, highly probable, moderately probable, and improbable. The criticality of crime losses is similarly stated in terms of other categories: potentially fatal to the organization, very serious, moderately serious, and relatively unimportant. Moreover, both these categorizations recognize that degrees of probability and of criticality of crime loss may be unknown. Such risk management seeks to discover and reduce these unknowns.

A proper security program against any type of crime consists of three crucial elements: (1) employee education in the importance of security and each employee's contribution to it, in security exposures and the hazards that intensify these exposures, and in measures an organization may adopt to minimize actual crime losses; (2) specific physical and procedural safeguards against crime (including screening job applicants, physical barriers to criminal entry, and crisis management for dealing with achieving normalcy after a crime has occurred or been discovered); and (3) procedures for detecting weaknesses in the security system. Many organizations rely on some form of system safety analysis, particularly fault tree analysis, to identify ways in which their security programs may fail or, more positively, to confirm that the essential elements of their security programs are operational and are properly structured.

Because most organizations' largest crime losses are from embezzlement and other employee-assisted fraud, these exposures merit special attention in a sound security program. Management must be aware of the possibility that any employee (especially more senior executives) may commit embezzlement, and there should be detailed procedural and physical controls to detect employees' wrongful taking of cash or other valuable property including ideas and information.

Safeguards against more violent crimes should be tailored to the particular crime as follows:

- Robbery—appropriate measures include making this form of theft appear unattractive or impossible, remaining calm and businesslike while any robbery is in progress, and gathering information about any robber that may be useful in later apprehending and prosecuting the culprit.
- Burglary—safeguards should be designed to keep information away from those who might potentially seek to break into the organization, to "harden" points at which they might attempt to enter, and to provide automatic, human, or canine surveillance for the organization's premises when not occupied.
- Riot or vandalism—risk control measures can be applied before and during any disturbance. These measures include maintaining good relations with the general public and with the immediate community, sheltering sensitive operations well within the organization's facilities, and mobilizing public and private security protection.
- Arson—precautions should include remaining sensitive to the concerns of any employees, other individuals, or groups who may wish the organization harm, maintaining an effective automatic fire detection/suppression system (and perhaps a guard force), and undertaking or cooperating in thorough post-loss investigations to gather information helpful in apprehending and prosecuting the arsonists.

Protecting a computer center and the equipment and information it contains requires coordinating most of the security measures described throughout this chapter. Thus, safeguarding a computer facility entails protecting the computer building and equipment against fire, sabotage, industrial accidents, natural disasters, and mechanical/electrical malfunctions in the equipment serving the building and in the computer hardware itself. Protecting the data processed within a computer center calls for special attention to threats of embezzlement, espionage, and other forms of surreptitious theft. Controlling access to a computer center as a whole, to specific areas in a computer facility, and to particular programs or data is essential to safeguarding the facility and its operations.

Chapter Notes

1. Henry Campbell Black, *Black's Law Dictionary*, revised 4th ed. (St. Paul: West Publishing Co., 1968), p. 165.
2. Yung-Ping Chen and Robert C.A. de Vos, *Choices and Constraints: Economic Decisionmaking* (Malvern, PA: American Institute for Property and Liability Underwriters, 1988), p. 8.
3. The material under this heading is drawn from William H. Rodda, James S. Trieschmann, Eric A. Wiening, Vol. 1, and Bob A. Hedges, *Commercial Property Risk Management and Insurance*, 3rd ed. (Malvern, PA: American Institute for Property and Liability Underwriters, 1988), pp. 378-396.
4. Jack Bologna, "New Look at the Internal Theft Prevention Process," *Assets Protection*, Sept./Oct., 1980, pp. 32-33.
5. Carole Swell, "Preventing Pilferage—Screening Potential Employees Thwarts Theft," *Business Insurance*, 11 May 1981, p. 41.
6. *White Collar Crime* (Washington, DC: U.S. Department of Commerce, 1977), p. 60.

CHAPTER 5

Protecting the Health Potential of Personnel

Every organization's risk management professional has a mandate to protect the organization's assets. This mandate usually emphasizes protecting tangible productive and financial assets. However, virtually every organization's most important asset is its "human capital," the work force that energizes and makes productive its inanimate assets. This chapter and the next two focus on how risk management protects the productive capabilities of an organization's personnel—their present and future potential to use their physical and mental abilities to produce value for the organization. It is an organization's human assets, the capability of its personnel, that give value to its other assets.

Risk management professionals have long been involved in one central aspect of protecting the health (and, therefore, productive) potential of their organization's personnel: safeguarding them from occupational injury and disease—in brief, reducing workers compensation exposures. More recently, risk management concepts have been extended beyond the work site to protecting employees and their families from injuries and illnesses. As discussed in Chapter 7, the risk manager's role also has extended in more recent years to restoring, through appropriate rehabilitation, the productive capabilities of employees who are disabled (whether on or off the job) to return them to work. For this reason, Chapter 7 focuses on rehabilitation.

The present chapter begins by exploring the general concept of human health potential. This concept is the ethical and economic rationale for broad risk management responsibilities of protecting and restoring—even enhancing—the health and productivity of an organization's employees in the present and future. The rest of the chapter turns to specific measures through which various risk control techniques can be used to minimize the frequency and severity of work-related injuries and illnesses. Chapter 7 sets forth a risk management professional's responsibilities in working with others to rehabilitate anyone for whose disabilities an organization may be legally responsible. For both prevention of and rehabilitation from such disabilities, these two chapters also demonstrate how effective risk control can increase the expected present value of an organization's net cash flows, thus augmenting its overall operating efficiency.

Specifically, after completing the present chapter, the reader management professional should be able to do the following:

- Explain the nature and importance of human health potential, and describe the contributions that sound risk management makes to preserving and or enhancing this potential.
- Apply, with respect to risk control techniques, the entire risk management decision process to work-related injuries and illnesses.

HUMAN HEALTH POTENTIAL[1]

Most of the aggregate economic value organizations create is generated through human intelligence and activity. With the possible exception of an organization's financial assets that earn interest and dividends with the mere passing of time, inanimate objects and other assets generate no further value until they are energized by human thought and action. Thus, it is human effort, knowledge, and skill that produce essentially all things of value. (This reasoning has led many economists to conclude that virtually everything derives its economic value from the human effort that must be devoted to creating, locating, or gaining and keeping possession of all things of value. This "labor theory of value" is opposed by some other economists who hold that, for example, the economic value of a thing stems from its scarcity or its value in exchange for other goods and services.)

It follows that the productivity of every organization has its origin in the persons it employs or upon whom it may draw on an occasional basis. The greater the productivity of these individuals, the greater the productivity—and, ultimately, the value—of that organization. Consequently, a risk management professional's responsibility for preserving the value of an organization requires joining with other managers in preserving the productivity of that organization's personnel. This productive potential—encompassing both (1) the ability to produce now and (2) the ability to become more productive in the future—constitutes *human health potential*. The discussion under the following three major headings more fully defines the concept of human health potential, describes the factors affecting the human health potential upon which any given organization may draw, and explores risk management professionals' responsibilities that relate to protecting human health potential.

Definition of Human Health Potential

Every person has productive potential—energy that person may use, well or poorly, to produce goods or services for their personal or others' benefit. An individual's biological makeup and early upbringing provide much of the foundation for his or her future productivity; proper nutrition and sanitation remain essential to that person's health and development throughout his or her life. Education and training can increase an individual's future productive potential (although the time devoted to such personal development may reduce that individual's present production). Disabling injuries or illnesses tend to reduce a person's productivity until he or she recovers (so rehabilitation can restore at least some future productivity lost to disability by speeding recovery). Involuntary retirement or unemployment can take away much of an individual's opportunity for present and future production. Similarly, shortening a person's life expectancy almost certainly reduces that individual's lifetime productivity, and lengthening his or her life just as surely increases productivity.

Generalizing this individual-centered perspective of human productivity—applying it to an entire population or to the employees of an organization—students and practitioners of public health management and of human resource development have formulated the concept of human health potential. The *human health potential* of a group of persons is the collective capacity of that group to produce goods or services of economic, artistic, or other recognized value by using either their present skills and knowledge or the skills and knowledge they may develop during their lifetimes. The concept of human health potential usually refers to the productive capabilities of the currently living members of a group, but the concept of *potential* does permit a longer range view that encompasses the aggregate potential that extends over several generations. *Health*, or freedom from disabling injury or disease, is essential to this concept of *potential* because, from a human resource perspective, continued good health is essential to present and future productivity.

The persons an organization employs (or upon whom it may occasionally use as outside resources) are collectively a sample of the general population. If this sample is randomly drawn, then the average human health potential of an organization's employees can be expected to reflect that of the typical member of the general population. To the extent that an organization can identify and attract, employ, and retain above-average individuals as permanent or temporary employees, the human health potential—and productivity—of those employees should exceed that of the average population. Furthermore, when the organization can provide education and training, protect its employees from disabling injury or illness, provide rehabilitation for those who do become disabled on or off the job, and/or extend the productive working lives of its employees beyond some "normal" retirement age, then the organization can enhance the human health potential of its employees and augment its productivity.

As the discussion under the following headings details, an organization's risk management professional has many opportunities to cooperate with its human resources department in enhancing the human health potential of its employees.

Factors Affecting Human Health Potential

For an organization, a number of factors can contribute to the human health potential of its workforce:

- The *health of the general population* influences the average quality, and potential productivity, of the persons from whom an organization may draw its personnel. With the opportunity to select its employees from a population that enjoys good general physical and mental health, tends to be long-lived, and is well-educated, an organization can select, on the average, persons who have greater productive potential than if the population as a whole did not have these positive characteristics. Therefore, over time, an organization has an interest in preserving, even building, the general health, education, and longevity of the community, even the entire nation or world.
- *Proper personnel selection procedures* increase an organization's ability to reliably select qualified persons from the general population. For example, identifying individuals who have the greatest or potential talent or skills that are most important to an organization can enable it to choose the most appropriate employees for the positions the organization has available. Conversely, being able to screen out persons least likely to be able to perform the tasks the organization most needs, who are particularly susceptible to injury or illness, or who may soon resign helps the organization to avoid the cost of hiring and training persons who cannot be expected to have a long, productive career with the organization.

- *Sound procedures for placing, developing, and promoting employees* can help an organization identify the job assignments for which each employee is most suited, or can best be educated or trained to perform. Through these procedures, each employee may achieve his or her maximum potential, and the organization, in turn, can be more productive. Crucial to proper personnel placement and development is a valid and reliable process for identifying those employees whose present career achievements best qualify them for promotion and/or job reassignment. Moreover, the manifest capabilities of a particular employee may occasionally require creating or reshaping a position so that it takes advantage of that employee's abilities at the present or in the future.

- *Maintaining employees' existing productive capabilities* mandates, at the very least, protecting them from disabling injuries and diseases on or off the job. Work safety and health programs clearly contribute to these efforts; health maintenance (or "wellness") programs and employee counseling also can contribute importantly to preserving each employee's present skills and encouraging that employee to focus his or her skills in ways that best serve the organization.

- *Rehabilitating injured or diseased employees* speeds their recovery, restoring—as fully as possible—their physical, intellectual, social, and personal capabilities to what they were before the injury or illness. Although rehabilitation may not always fully succeed (reasons are given in Chapter 7), good rehabilitation programs almost always produce positive financial returns for an organization.

- *Retaining productive employees* entails keeping them on the job as long as they remain productive, and forestalling both their premature retirement and resignation. The resignation or retirement of a highly productive employee means the loss of that person's potential contributions to the organization's success.

By remaining alert to these factors, an organization's management can maintain, and when necessary restore, the human health potential of its personnel and, ultimately, its own productive capabilities. Conversely, by ignoring or by failing to respond to adverse developments affecting any of these factors, an organization is likely to suffer a long-term decline in its productive potential. Therefore, while risk management traditionally has been directly involved with, at most, two of these factors—(1) maintaining the present health and safety of current employees and (2) rehabilitating those who become disabled—

preserving an organization's present and future productive capacity requires risk management to broaden its concern to reach all of these factors.

Risk Management Responsibilities Related to Human Health Potential

Safeguarding the health potential of the personnel within a department is a direct line responsibility of the managers of those departments. "Staffing" often is recognized as a generic managerial function, along with the planning, organizing, leading, and controlling of an organization's assets and activities. Hence, a risk management professional's contribution to proper staffing is to advise and serve as a resource to line management. The risk manager can best help senior and departmental managers to staff their departments in ways that consider the human health potential of the organization's personnel. For example:

- To preserve, and perhaps even enrich, the pool of talent from which an organization may select its personnel, an organization may wish to consider working with public officials to improve the health facilities, sanitation, nutrition, and educational resources available to the overall population. At the very least, the organization should be wary of any action it might take that would be detrimental to the human health potential of the community; any such action could both impose liability on the organization and weaken the general health of its present and potential future employees.
- Any weaknesses in the organization's hiring criteria leave open the possibility that it may not be attracting the best available employees. Furthermore, employee selection criteria that are in some way unfairly discriminatory may bring liability upon the organization. Therefore, an organization's risk management professional should have a voice in the hiring procedures.
- There should be some risk management input into an organization's employee placement and development practices. Risk management insight can reduce the likelihood of (1) assigning an employee responsibilities for which he or she is not fit; (2) failing to recognize and develop an employee's talents to their fullest, thus depriving the organization of at least some of that employee's future productive capabilities; and (3) unfair discrimination against employees that may bring equal employment opportunity lawsuits against the organization.

- As the main portion of this chapter explains, risk management helps prevent and reduce the severity of injuries and illnesses that can disable an organization's present employees.
- Rehabilitating the disabled—restoring temporarily damaged human health potential—is another growing risk management responsibility (discussed in Chapter 7). It rebuilds the human health potential within an organization; and, offered to members of the public for whose disabilities the organization may be legally responsible, rehabilitation can reduce the severity of the organization's liability losses for bodily injury.
- Retaining valuable employees, i.e., motivating them to stay with the organization rather than joining competitors or retiring early, is a traditional responsibility of line management, usually assisted by the human resources department. A risk management professional may make further staff contributions to the staffing effort in two ways first, by reminding line management of the productive capacities the organization would lose if valued employees resigned or retired prematurely, and second, by alerting other managers to any liability exposures that may lie in unfairly discriminatory incentives offered to some employees but denied to others.

APPLYING THE RISK MANAGEMENT PROCESS TO WORK-RELATED INJURIES AND ILLNESSES

The customary model of the risk management decision process includes five steps: (1) identifying and analyzing loss exposures, (2) examining alternative techniques for risk control, (3) selecting the most promising technique(s), (4) implementing the chosen technique(s), and (5) monitoring the results to control and to strengthen the overall risk control program. This section explains how this process is applied to work-related injuries and illnesses.

Exposure Identification and Analysis

Students of workplace disabilities traditionally have distinguished between injuries and illnesses. While the precise boundary between an injury and an illness is not always clear, *injuries* generally result from an external physical force suddenly exerting more stress on the human body than it can withstand, resulting in some externally manifested injury such as a laceration, fracture, contusion, amputation, or the like. In contrast, an *illness* usually develops more slowly as the result of some organic or inorganic agent being absorbed, ingested, inhaled, or injected into the human body and gradually impairing the function of one or more organs of the body. Thus, a fall, a slip, or a wrench is an injury while an infection, radiation poisoning, or dermatitis is an illness.

In workplace settings, the distinction between injuries and illnesses can be significant for at least two reasons. First, workers compensation statutes often provide different levels of benefits for different disabilities, depending on whether the particular statute classifies that disability as an injury or an illness. Second, the types of controls often applied to reducing the frequency or severity of particular disabilities depend on whether those disabilities arise from sudden external events (and therefore are considered injuries) or from prolonged exposure to injurious conditions (and therefore are regarded as illnesses). In this context, students of work-related injuries and illnesses often distinguish between injury hazards and health (or illness) hazards.

Injury Hazards Four major classes of injury hazards, which together cause the great majority of work-related injuries, relate to (1) machinery and equipment, (2) materials handling, (3) the physical condition of premises, and (4) vehicle fleet operations.

Machinery and Equipment. Machinery and equipment encompasses all mechanical devices employees use or come in contact with on the job. Some of the obvious ones are production equipment such as presses, saws, filling machines, packaging equipment, conveyor belts, and material handling equipment. But even simple hand tools like screwdrivers, hammers, and drills are included in this class.

The most common machine hazards are those that require guarding or isolation to correct. They cause injuries by pinching, crushing, cutting, and twisting. Employees get hurt when they are inattentive, untrained, or unaware of the hazard. The most common of these hazards can be classified as involving (1) cutting and shearing mechanisms, (2) in-running nip points, (3) rotating mechanisms, (4) forming and bending mechanisms, (5) screw or worm mechanisms, and (6) impact mechanisms.

1. *Cutting and shearing mechanisms.* As the name implies, these mechanisms slice or cut the material being processed. Typical cutting and shearing machines are paper cutters, metal cutters, saws, grinding wheels, and lathes.
2. *In-running nip points.* An in-running nip point is formed whenever two rotating cylinders, wheels, or gears are in close proximity and can pull parts of the body into the nip point. An in-running nip point also exists wherever a belt goes over a pulley, or where a chain goes over a gear. The chain and the gears on the rear wheel and the pedal gear of a bicycle form in-

running nip points. Clothing can be pulled into them, and most bicycles are equipped with a cover to guard the chain and gears. Nip points exist on belt-driven pulleys, gears, conveyors, and rollers present on many common kinds of machinery.

3. *Rotating mechanisms.* Rotating shafts, rotating parts extending from a machine, even burrs and protruding screws on rotating machinery can cause injury. Whenever there is a machine with spinning parts, shaft, pulleys, belts and gears, hazards may exist. Typical examples include motors, lathes, drills, flywheels, and clutches.

4. *Forming and bending mechanisms.* As the name implies, these bend or shape materials, usually metal. This hazard exists in power presses of all kinds and has resulted in numerous hand and finger injuries.

5. *Screw or worm mechanisms.* These use a shearing action between a moving screw-type part and a fixed housing. Meat grinders, other food mixers, and screw conveyors use these mechanisms.

6. *Impact mechanisms.* These do their work by striking or hammering a part into shape, or stamping a pattern onto it. Certain kinds of machines that add patterns or textures to metals contain this hazard.

Guarding is necessary to protect against injury from all these types of mechanisms, as are standard operating procedures (SOPs) and training necessary for the operators of these machines. Some of these machines are subject to mechanical failures that can injure employees, making preventive maintenance very important. Complex machinery like power presses should be inspected before each shift.

Maintenance operations and set-up operations (installing a new mold or cutting edge, for example) are often hazardous. Guards often have to be removed, and the machines sometimes have to be energized so that mechanics can make adjustments and test them. The best thing that can be done to prevent injuries is to make sure that mechanics are aware of all of the hazards the equipment contains and what the proper procedures are. One very important procedure is to have the controls that start the machinery under the direct control of the mechanic, not other people, to prevent the machine from being started at the wrong time or in the wrong way.

Whenever possible, maintenance should be done with all power turned off and "locked-out," meaning that locks are used to prevent anyone except the mechanic from turning the power back on. A tag or sign is also used to identify the mechanic and the job being done. When numerous mechanics are working, each should place his or her own lock on the power source, so that only one power source can be activated by one mechanic. This, again, prevents injuries due to miscommunication; controls for power sources are often remote from the equipment being serviced , and mechanics sometimes work far apart.

The safe use of hand tools and manual equipment has more to do with following correct procedures than guarding. Common sense like keeping tools sharpened and lubricated, using the correct tools in the first place, and not using worn or broken tools and equipment should prevent injuries.

Materials Handling. Materials handling refers to all activities associated with moving material of all types around the workplace. This includes raw material, components, work-in-process, and finished goods. Since these materials can be heavy, bulky, and awkward to move, there is a great potential for injury.

One of the greatest problems in materials handling, if not the greatest, is back injuries. People hurt their backs while lifting, bending, twisting, and carrying objects. The injury can be a simple strain or a complex problem involving the spine. The injuries are painful and very costly, often resulting in many lost workdays and sometimes surgery.

Within organizations, an effort should be made to teach employees how to lift things properly using their leg muscles rather than their back muscles (which are relatively weak), while keeping the load close to the body. There are many good educational programs and training aids available on the market and through professional organizations.

One particularly frustrating problem is that some people injure their backs simply by bending over to pick up a paper or reaching around to grab something. Clearly, these people have underlying back problems that require very little aggravation before they cause trouble. Teaching these people how to lift might not help to prevent such injuries.

It is believed that weak abdominal muscles invite back trouble, so general physical fitness programs, under appropriate medical supervision, should benefit all employees. There is a trend toward having physical fitness programs in the workplace, and they deserve the risk manager's support.

The nature of materials handling jobs themselves should be studied. Some tasks should be performed by two people working together instead of just one. This will reduce the likelihood of injury in some cases.

Sometimes the lifting hazard can be engineered out. Instead of having a worker lift a large metal drum of powder and dump it into a blender, a motorized hoist can do the work, thus allowing the worker to avoid the exposure. Or, instead of having the operator of a stamping machine twist around to pick up a piece of metal, then turn back around to insert it in the press, and then turn around to put the finished part down, metal blanks and finished parts can be placed on either side of the machine, eliminating much of the twisting and wear on the back.

Mechanical equipment can also present problems related to materials handling. Mechanical equipment, such as hand trucks and forklifts, is often used to move things around the workplace. Overhead hoists or even overhead cranes that travel along tracks may be used. Each piece of equipment carries its own hazards.

A forklift can be dangerous because, as a motorized, moving vehicle, it can cause collisions. Beyond that, the fork portion of the lifting mechanism can pierce or crush anything that it hits. The driver moves a load by sliding the forks under it, lifting it, and moving it, creating the potential for a falling load. In warehouses, the load may be a pallet full of cases removed from a shelf located ten feet above floor level. Obviously, such a load could be extremely dangerous if it fell. The risk control measures for forklifts and similar equipment are SOPs, classroom and hands-on education and training, re-training on a regular basis, and strong supervision. Overhead protection for the driver should also be provided.

Overhead lifting equipment uses ropes, cables, hooks, and slings, all of which must be inspected and used properly. Again, this should be part of the SOPs.

Shipping and receiving of goods can create hazards in loading and unloading trucks. Trucks that are backed up to warehouse doors must have chocks under their wheels to prevent them from rolling. Dock plates, which are bridges between the building and the truck, must be securely fastened so that they do not move, allowing a forklift full of goods to topple.

Physical Condition of Premises. The condition of the general premises—land, buildings, and other physical improvements—can introduce hazards. An amazing number of injuries result from simple and common hazards. If floors, steps, and other walking surfaces are not properly maintained, they can become hazards that cause injuries from slipping or tripping. These can be temporary hazards resulting from spills or water tracked in from the outside, or more permanent problems like carpeting with tears, or changes in elevation. Once identified, these basic problems can usually be fixed rather easily.

Outside the building, steps, sidewalks, and parking lots present hazards such as holes or cracks, or weather-related problems, such as snow and ice that can cause tripping and slipping. Again, once identified, these hazards are easily controlled.

Good housekeeping is necessary to make sure that hazards do not arise from debris or misplaced materials. Also hazardous are storage areas with boxes precariously piled up to the ceiling or production areas with raw materials and supplies in the aisles. Housekeeping problems can also create fire hazards. Accumulations of trash, for example, can be ignited accidentally by a carelessly tossed cigarette or intentionally by vandals.

Maintenance of a facility and good housekeeping are also important for a less tangible, though equally important reason. A neat, well-maintained facility indicates that management cares and is sincere about loss prevention. Employees are not likely to take loss prevention seriously if management makes no effort to properly maintain the workplace. Four specific conditions often found within the overall premises—(1) sudden chemical exposures, (2) electrical hazards, (3) temperature extremes, and (4) hostile fire—deserve particular risk management attention because of the special controls they require.

Sudden Chemical Exposures. Sudden chemical exposures are accidents in which an employee is exposed to a chemical instantaneously, rather than being exposed to small amounts over an extended period of time. Examples include being splashed by a chemical, or accidentally ingesting or inhaling it. (Long-term chemical exposures are included in the individual topics covered under health hazards.)

The first step in dealing with this hazard is identifying the chemicals that are hazardous and informing employees, through training programs and labeling, which chemicals could be harmful to them. This whole program is the subject of federal and state "right-to-know" laws.

Once the hazardous chemicals have been identified, research will indicate what kinds of precautions should be taken to avoid injuries, such as wearing gloves, aprons, and face shields. First aid needs should also be determined, such as eye wash stations and emergency showers. These measures and the use of personal protective equipment should also be included in employee training programs. It should be stressed that anyone splashed with an acid or alkali, or who has had another kind of acute exposure, will need immediate attention and help from fellow workers to wipe off the affected parts of the body, remove clothing, and drench the affected areas (with water, unless the harmful chemical reacts adversely with water). The injured worker may be unable to help himself or herself and may even resist help. Supervisors should regularly review such first aid procedures with employees.

Entry into confined spaces presents hazards that can be classified as acute chemical exposures. If an employee enters an empty chemical tank to clean or repair it, there is a danger that chemical vapors may be present, or that there might be inadequate oxygen. The worker can be harmed by inhaling the vapors or by the can collapsing, dying from asphyxiation in either case. It should be a standard practice for workers who must enter confined spaces to work with a buddy who remains outside the confined space, ready to assist if necessary. Equipment to detect the presence of harmful or explosive vapors and gases, and for sufficient oxygen should be used to check the space before entry. If necessary, the tank should be ventilated, and a self-contained or air-line supplied breathing apparatus should be worn.

Electrical Exposures. Electrical exposures fall into two basic categories: shock and fire hazards. When a human being comes in contact with an electrical source of significant voltage, and electricity travels through the body to ground, the person has been shocked. An electrical shock can cause varying degrees of injury. It can result in little more than a tingling sensation (and a good scare), or it can result in death. Electrical burns at the point of contact can also occur.

The key to preventing electric shock is a combination of common sense, proper procedures, and training. Obviously, only those trained in electrical maintenance and repair should touch electrical devices or wiring. Most employees have a healthy respect for electricity, so this is not usually a problem. However, when employees are exposed to electrical devices or wiring, some training should be provided in, for example, the handling of downed power lines and switches in the presence of water.

Most of the injuries to experienced electricians and maintenance personnel result from carelessness and other forms of human error. If an otherwise knowledgeable electrician attempts to repair something without de-energizing, injury can result. If the electrician fails to "lock-out" the circuit in addition to de-energizing it, somebody else can unknowingly re-energize it, thus causing injury.

There are times, however, when it is necessary to work with "live" circuitry. In those cases, proper procedures must be precisely followed. This includes having a buddy so that an electrician is not working alone in a dangerous situation. Special tools and insulated clothing may also be necessary.

Fire hazards that result from electrical sources are usually connected with equipment in need of repair—loose connections that overheat or defective insulation that allows a short circuit, for instance. These hazards are most easily overcome through preventive maintenance programs and by responding promptly when repairs are needed.

The use of ordinary electrical equipment in the presence of flammable liquids and combustible dusts is a definite hazard. The National Electrical Code, as well as state and local codes, require that explosion-proof electrical equipment be used in the presence of these materials and in any other areas that are similarly hazardous. Common examples of such hazardous areas are spray booths, dip tanks, flammable liquids dispensing areas, grain storage silos, and other dusty operations. The term "explosion-proof" can be misleading. It does not mean that the device is not capable of igniting vapors. It simply means that if vapors find their way into the equipment and ignition takes place, the explosion will be contained inside the equipment, and the vapors outside will not ignite. Virtually everything can be purchased in an explosion-proof version: conduit, connectors, plugs, outlets, monitoring equipment, motors, lighting, refrigerators, telephones, and so on.

Static electricity can be considered an exposure. Static electricity is generated when two dissimilar materials are rubbed together as when one walks across a carpet and gets a shock from touching a doorknob. A charge builds up on the person walking on the carpet and discharges through the doorknob.

Static electricity can build up when flammable liquids are poured or mixed. Bonding all equipment and containers together and grounding them prevents static buildup capable of discharging and igniting the liquid. Sometimes conductive floors are installed, and employees wear conductive shoes so that they too are drained of any static charges. Precautions of this type are taken in ammunition work and hospital operating rooms when flammable anesthetics are used.

Exposure to Temperature Extremes. Subjecting the body to temperature extremes can cause injury. Extremes can exist not only in an entire operation such as steel manufacturing or outdoor work, but also in limited operations, such as a small oven or freezer.

Risk control for temperature extremes is dependent on personal protective equipment, including insulation. Obviously, employees handling hot objects need the proper protection: gloves, apron, and face shield. Those who work near blast furnaces or outdoors in winter need insulated clothing to protect against the cold. When an employee is introduced to a job that involves temperature extremes, he or she should be exposed to them for progressively longer periods each day until an entire shift has been worked at that temperature.

Since the effect on employees can be the result of a short-term exposure, such as a burn, or a long-term exposure, such as heat stress or dehydration, this hazard can be either an injury or a health hazard.

Fire Exposures. Fire requires fuel, oxygen, and an ignition source. Fire prevention requires that this abstract formula be translated into concrete terms. What materials are likely fuel sources? What are the likely ignition sources? Where and under what circumstances is ignition likely?

Nearly everything can burn under the right conditions; so, as a practical matter, attention should be focused on those things that are easiest to ignite or that produce the greatest danger when burning.

Flammable liquids require special precautions for proper storage, handling, and processing. Special construction features, electrical equipment, and ventilation systems are required for proper protection because flammable liquids are easily ignited and burn rapidly.

Some kinds of plastic materials produce highly toxic gases when they burn. Their use is widespread, and proper fire protection systems (probably automatic sprinklers) are highly desirable. In the workplace, plastics may be found everywhere—in furniture, products, product containers, packaging, and construction material. If employees can be trapped in places where escape is difficult (office buildings, hotels, hospitals, and restaurants, for instance), the presence of plastics, fire protection, and escape planning should be studied carefully.

Some materials are more easily ignited in certain forms or certain arrangements. Crumpled waste paper, loose packing materials, and trash are more easily ignited than solid lumber or tightly packaged paper. The latter will burn, too, but it is important to understand that some forms are easier to ignite than others.

Ignition sources must also be considered. Any electrical or heat producing device can be an ignition source. Although it is possible to check major electrical devices and connections, it is generally impossible to check all of them. Attention should be focused on obvious, known ignition sources that clearly have the potential to start fires: welding, smoking, static electricity, and any equipment that produces heat, sparks, or electrical arcs.

As noted previously, the most serious fire hazard to employees is the potential for being trapped in a fire. For that reason, a comprehensive fire emergency plan should include such things as sounding an alarm, summoning the fire department, escape routes, and fire extinguishers. Training sessions should be held for all employees. Drills should be conducted periodically to test the plan. The primary objective should be to teach everybody how to escape quickly, without injury. Protection of property is secondary.

Vehicle Fleet Operations. The operation of a fleet of cars, trucks, or buses presents acute physical hazards to drivers and passengers alike. Vehicle accident prevention is especially challenging and difficult for a number of reasons. Most of a driver's time is spent without direct supervision, so that careless or reckless acts are more likely to go uncorrected than comparable conduct in a plant or in an office. In addition, drivers do not work with a group of peers who, in other situations, can develop a team spirit aimed toward accident prevention.

Accident prevention should begin with a thorough investigation of a driver's motor vehicle records, background, and skills. While these checks usually are made by whoever manages the drivers, the risk management professional should anticipate problems. For example, traveling sales people, who may have excellent selling skills, are not always the best drivers. Senior management should set hiring policies so that this problem and others like it is unlikely to arise, and so that any employee who develops poor driving habits must be retrained.

Vehicle maintenance is the second line of defense in accident prevention. Preventive maintenance and immediate repair of any mechanical problems that develop should be mandatory.

Health Hazards   Unlike the sudden nature of injury hazards, health hazards are caused by more slowly operating chemical, biological, ergonomic, and physical forces. A risk management professional needs to recognize the health hazards that can make workplace diseases more frequent and/or more severe. It is helpful to classify these health hazards into those arising from (1) long-term chemical exposures, (2) noise, (3) ergonomic stress, and (4) radiation. While not exhaustive, this classification encompasses most worksite hazards likely to lead to disabling illnesses.

Long-Term Chemical Exposures.   In contrast to sudden chemical exposures like splashes, spills, and acute ingestion, longer term, lower dose exposures are health hazards. Chemicals enter the body through three modes of entry: ingestion, absorption, and inhalation.

Ingestion can take place over time when employees are allowed to eat, drink, and smoke in work areas where toxic chemicals are in use. Prohibiting eating, drinking, and smoking, and encouraging thorough wash-ups before breaks and at the end of each shift should prevent ingestion problems.

Absorption occurs when chemicals enter the bloodstream by penetrating the skin. Most times, healthy skin provides a good barrier, but broken skin can provide an entry path. It should also be noted that occupational dermatitis, the irritation and inflammation of the skin, is often caused by working with chemicals. Dermatitis is a very common industrial disorder that is preventable through the use of gloves and other protective equipment.

Inhalation of contaminants in gases and vapors or in particulates like dust, smoke, or mist can likewise lead to injury or illness.

Whether a particular chemical is an ingestion, absorption, or inhalation health hazard depends on the specifics of the exposure situation. The chemical itself is the largest factor, but the process in which it is used, the environment surrounding the work, and the length of the exposure are also key variables.

The concept of permissible exposure levels is important in evaluating health hazards. For the vast majority of chemicals, *permissible exposure levels* are expressed as a concentration over a specific period of time. The most widely used permissible exposure levels are called *threshold limit values*, or TLVs. These specify the concentration in which it is believed nearly all workers can function day after day without adverse effects. They are expressed as a time-weighted average for an eight-hour day. That basically means that although the concentration varies over the course of a day, a formula can be used to calculate the time-weighted average concentration over the whole day. Exposure concentrations are expressed in parts per million for gases and vapors, and milligrams per cubic meter for particulates. Some materials are so irritating or toxic that a maximum instantaneous exposure value is also given. That concentration should not be exceeded at any time during the day.

The TLV is determined in the following way. A qualified individual takes air samples in the worker's breathing zone using an air pump and a collection filter cartridge, or other devices, depending on the chemical. As air is drawn through the cartridge at a known rate, the contaminant is deposited on the filter. Laboratory analysis and computation then determine the time-weighted average exposure concentration. If the TLV is exceeded, a hazard exists. This procedure can be performed by any properly trained technician, although industrial hygienists generally do at least the initial sampling work and make recommendations. If a process requires periodic or continuous sampling, the organization's own industrial hygiene, or other, personnel may do the sampling. If any TLV is regularly exceeded, some further industrial hygiene study should be made. In special situations, the risk management professional may call upon the expertise of an outside consultant.

If the industrial hygiene evaluation shows that there is a health hazard, control measures should be implemented. Depending on the specific situation, material substitution, ventilation, personal protective equipment, or other control measures may be appropriate.

Noise Exposures. Excessive noise levels can cause premature hearing loss. In addition to the sound level, the length of exposure, the frequency distribution of the sound, and whether the noise is continuous, intermittent, or a series of impacts are the key determinants of whether the exposure is harmful.

Permissible exposure levels expressed as time-weighted averages also exist for occupational noise exposures. Again, sampling is necessary to determine if exposure limits are exceeded. Samples are taken with sound level meters (which give instantaneous readings) and dosimeters (which give time-weighted averages). These instruments give direct readouts, and laboratory analysis is not necessary. A great deal of the screening of work areas can therefore be done by the risk management professional or a technician. It should only be necessary to use an industrial hygienist for problem or borderline areas.

If noise above the permissible level exists, engineering methods should be used to reduce these levels. Some of the methods are sound insulation, isolation, barriers, silencing compressed air exhausts on machinery, and installing equipment on cushioned mountings. If the noise cannot be reduced to satisfactory levels, hearing protection should be worn by all exposed employees, and job rotation may have to be considered.

Baseline audiograms, or hearing tests, should be performed for each new employee exposed to excessive noise levels. After that, hearing tests should be performed annually. If measurable loss of hearing is noted (known as *threshold shift*) a medical opinion should be sought concerning the advisability of a change of duties.

Ergonomic Exposures. Ergonomics is the application of scientific disciplines like biomechanics and engineering to improve the fit between people and their jobs to achieve the best possible physiological and psychological well-being.

Physical and emotional stress reduce efficiency, cause fatigue, and contribute to injuries and illnesses. Ergonomics considers physical stress on joints, bones, muscles, and nerves as well as environmental factors like lighting, glare, noise, color, and temperature.

Ergonomic problems could range from an employee performing a lifting task in an awkward (and thus hazardous) position to glare or uncomfortable chairs in a room where people operate personal computers for long periods of time.

Sometimes the solutions involve adjusting the existing conditions, such as raising the temperature in a room or lowering the shades to cut glare from sunlight. Other cases will require major changes like engineering a new device to eliminate the stress on a worker's wrist due to repetitive motion. The key concept is that whenever it is recognized that the job itself or the work environment is harming the employee, an attempt should be made to reduce the physical or emotional stress on the employee rather than just treating the injury or illness.

Radiation Exposures. There are two types of radiation: ionizing and nonionizing. *Ionizing radiation* includes X-rays and gamma, alpha, and beta radiation from radioactive materials. Controlling these kinds of radiation is highly technical work performed by specialists who are trained and licensed by regulatory authorities. The risk management professional should make sure that the proper permits are in effect, that the people working in the operation are qualified, and that SOPs exist and are followed.

Nonionizing radiation includes microwaves, radio waves, visible light, infra-red light, and ultra-violet (UV) light. Microwaves, infra-red, and radio frequency radiation can cause heating and burns at close distances. Isolation, separation, and shielding are the key controls. Ultra-violet light can cause eye damage and sunburn; protective clothing for outdoor work and guarding of interior UV sources like electric arc welders and germicidal lamps are the key controls. Measurement of nonionizing sources may be important, so an industrial hygienist should be consulted. Again, training and SOPs are important.

Industrial lasers can also cause injury because they emit highly concentrated visible light. Eye damage is of particular concern—no one should ever attempt to look into a laser source, either directly or through a reflector. Furthermore, guarding should be used to prevent contact with the beam since lasers can easily cause burns. The danger of high voltage shock also exists.

Evaluating Injury and Health Hazards   Once specific injury and health hazards have been identified, the risk management professional must be able to evaluate the general significance of the specific hazards. This ability involves several components.

The first component is the ability to recognize injury and health hazards—acute physical hazards—by visual inspection. An experienced risk management professional is able to walk through a facility and pick out hazards: a table saw without a guard, flammable liquids improperly stored, or an open electrical panel with exposed wiring. This ability is learned. With each successive survey, recognition skills improve, and more and more hazards are recognized. People such as insurance company loss control specialists, who have the opportunity to visit different operations all the time, develop their skills quickly. But even those who visit the same facilities repeatedly, as most risk management professionals do, will find that they recognize more and more hazards during each visit. (This suggests that during an initial survey, the operation should be viewed at least twice). Of course, unless an organization is static, hazards will change over time, providing yet another challenge.

Risk management professionals are certainly not the only ones who need to be skilled at spotting hazards. It is, perhaps, even more important for first-line supervisors to know what could be hazardous, in general, and particularly, in their operations. The supervisor should catch hazards like the unguarded machine, slippery floors, or improper acid-handling before anybody else does.

A second component of hazard recognition is the ability to

recognize potential health hazards. This is more difficult because health hazards are not always visible; often only their circumstantial clues are evident. For example, suppose that during a visit to a manufacturing plant a risk management professional notes that employees are sitting at a workbench with small pans of liquid in front of them and using rags soaked with the liquid to clean parts before painting. Questions such as the following should be raised: What is the liquid? Is it irritating to the skin? Are the vapors harmful to the employees? In this way, the risk management professional recognizes potential health hazards; analyzing them will require more work.

In this case, the liquid in use must be identified and its characteristics researched. Most common chemicals are fully discussed in reference texts on industrial hygiene or hazardous materials. Information about them can also be found on material safety data sheets (MSDS) provided by the manufacturers under OSHA requirements. The MSDS outline all kinds of hazards associated with materials and may be the only source available for proprietary formulas. An MSDS should be on file for every substance in use in an operation. If the liquid might be irritating to the skin or other organs, personal protective equipment should be used. If an inhalation hazard is associated with the substance, it must be determined if the exposure level is within the threshold limit value (TLV). This calls for air sampling by an industrial hygienist and laboratory analysis of the sample.

Risk management professionals, supervisors, and everyone else with an interest can learn to recognize *potential* health hazards. To determine whether these represent *actual* health hazards requires further study. Eventually, risk management professionals develop a predictive sense. They know what hazards might exist in a particular operation and have some idea of what to expect, what to look for, and what questions to ask when faced with a new operation.

Taken one step further, the risk management professional should be able to play an effective role in planning new facilities. For instance, upon learning of a proposal to build a new machine shop, the experienced risk management professional should ask about guarding and control systems for the equipment, the flammability of the lubricants, the potential for the fluids used in cutting metals to cause dermatitis, and the compounds used to clean the metal. After getting this information, but before the operation begins, he or she should ask about training programs, SOPs, and personal protective equipment.

The same experience and "sixth sense" can be used to advise senior management about the hazards of potential acquisitions. While acquisition decisions are not made based solely on loss prevention considerations, acquisitions were occasionally not made because major hazards or poor injury and illness records were discovered.

Following the initial inspection of an operation, it is a good idea to create a flowchart showing the physical layout and processes, and the related major hazards. This helps clarify the relationship between the parts of the operation and also between the hazards. A flowchart can reveal conditions such as flammable liquids stored in the center of the facility where a fire or explosion could affect many employees, or a welding operation too close to a paint spraying operation. While the same things can be recognized during an inspection, sometimes relationships between parts of the operations in a process are more clear when committed to paper in a flowchart.

After the risk management professional has recognized and has begun to analyze the hazards, it will become apparent that certain hazards do not require much analysis. If an ice-making machine drips water on the floor, it is obvious that the puddle is hazardous, that it should be mopped, and that the ice-maker should be repaired. On the other hand, some hazards have multiple components and require more thought before solutions can be proposed.

Exposure Identification Through Job Safety Analysis Job safety analysis (JSA) is a technique for examining the steps involved in a particular task, cataloging all the hazards to persons and/or property that may arise during each step, and listing all reasonable procedural and mechanical safeguards against each hazard. As explained in detail in Chapter 11 on system safety, JSA provides an effective approach to outlining most of the risk control options for making a particular task acceptably safe.

To illustrate how JSA can be applied to a particular task, assume that the risk management professional for a laundry products manufacturer inspects the point in the production process where liquid chlorine bleach is bottled before being sent to the packaging and shipping departments. Workers load empty plastic bottles into racks, slide the racks into the filling and capping machine, activate the machine by pushing "start" buttons, and then remove the racks of filled bottles and place them on a conveyor belt which carries them to the packaging department.

To identify the hazards involved here, this process must be broken down into steps, and each step analyzed separately. Beginning with the initial step of loading empty bottles into the racks, questions the risk management professional would ask might include: Are the empty bottles available at an efficient level where workers are not required to bend or to reach? After each rack is loaded, how is it carried, and how far must it be carried to the filling and capping machine? Is the floor free from obstructions?

What is the level of the loading point of the filling and capping machine? Are workers required to bend or reach to insert racks into the machine? How far into the machine do workers reach so that the racks are placed into the proper position for filling and capping? Are there any sharp edges or protrusions where hands or forearms could be cut?

Have safeguards been incorporated into the machine to ensure that the filling/capping process cannot begin unless workers' hands are completely free? Should the machine malfunction, will it shut off automatically, thus protecting workers from injury when trying to remedy the problem? Are spills or overfills possible? Should spills or overfills occur, is there any chance of the bleach flowing onto the floor, thus making slips and falls possible? Has the atmosphere been tested for levels of toxicity? Are workers required to wear protective clothing—goggles, gloves, face masks, for example? If protective clothing is required, do workers indeed wear it?

After the bottles have been filled and capped, what is the weight of each rack? Are workers bending or lifting to reach them? How far must these racks be carried to the conveyor belt? Are workers using the proper bending, lifting, and carrying techniques to prevent back strain or other injury? Is the floor of the work area free from obstruction?

Discussion with employees and perhaps first-line supervisors can highlight the kinds of questions the risk management professional should ask in performing a job safety analysis and can provide a basis for identifying loss exposures inherent in a particular task or job. Once these exposures have been identified, the most cost-effective risk control measures to eliminate completely or greatly reduce the possibility of injury or illness can be put into place.

While a JSA is time consuming, it is an effective, powerful tool for reducing work-related injuries and illnesses. It can be applied effectively to any task or job that has an unacceptable level of loss frequency or severity.

Developing Risk Control Alternatives

From the material on specific hazards and risk control measures, it should be clear that there are usually multiple ways to control a hazard. After identifying and analyzing the hazard, the most appropriate control techniques should be proposed. These techniques fall into two general sets. The first set consists of risk control techniques developed by risk management professionals as part of the risk management decision process. The second set consists of the general methods of industrial hygiene control first developed by safety engineering professionals.

The following illustration is an example of the process of identifying and analyzing hazards, and choosing the most appropriate risk management techniques. Suppose a company manufactures an industrial cleaning product by mixing two chemicals, A and B, in an open vat. Through industrial hygiene sampling, it is discovered that the employee who pours and mixes the components into the vat is exposed to vapor concentrations above the permissible exposure level for Chemical A. The risk management professional identifies a number of possible *control* measures:

1. Change from Chemical A to a less hazardous material.
2. Install a cover on the vat.
3. Install exhaust ventilation at the vat.
4. Have the worker wear a respirator while pouring the chemicals.

While developing these measures, the risk management professional eliminated job rotation because of a union policy against rotation at this particular plant. Containment of the process in a separate room was deemed impractical because the flow of materials would have been impeded. A change to an automated process was considered, but rejected as being financially unsound. Medical monitoring is not an issue in this case because there are no latent effects of Chemical A that would show up in the bloodstream or other organs. Any toxic effects are immediate. Training and good supervision were already in place.

Installing a cover on the vat offered some promise as an effective solution—if the vat is covered, vapors cannot escape. But after consulting an industrial hygienist, the risk management professionals realized that the major exposure existed only when the employee poured the chemicals. At that time the vat had to be open, so covering it would not help. After the vat is filled, the worker moves away from it to a distance where the vapor concentration decreases significantly.

The ideal solution would be to substitute a nonhazardous chemical for Chemical A, but a search of the marketplace determined that none exists. However, Chemical X was identified as one whose vapor concentration would be minimal under the operating conditions in question. Substituting X for A would be a very effective solution.

Likewise, installing an exhaust system at the top of the mixing vat would draw off most of the vapors and protect the worker. Still, pouring the components into the vat could require the employee to bend into the vapor zone, so as a precaution, the risk management professional has recommended that a respirator be worn when the chemicals are poured. (If Chemical X is used, a respirator is not necessary since the vapor concentration will be within the permissible exposure level).

Note that multiple *controls* are often applied simultaneously for reliability or adequacy. For example, fitting the employee with a respirator mask to filter the harmful vapors is not a fully adequate solution. The employee has to adjust the mask to fit properly, change the filters as required, and remember to wear the mask in the first place. So, although the mask can be expected to provide protection if the worker bends into the vapor zone, it is not reliable enough to be the complete solution. In addition, the respirator would only protect the employee who mixes the chemicals. It is not believed that the vapors would be harmful to others because they get diluted in the plant atmosphere, but the exhaust system provides a welcome additional precaution.

Another point is that physical controls, in this case the exhaust system or the substitution of one chemical for another, are generally more reliable then procedural controls. Procedural controls depend on people, and people, unfortunately, are fallible. The preferred approach to *control* is to institute physical controls in tandem with procedural controls. If physical controls are truly impossible, then procedural controls become the only option. In either case, multiple controls are advisable.

Risk Control Techniques From Risk Management Exposure avoidance, loss prevention, loss reduction, segregation of exposure units, and contractual transfer for risk control all have applications in work-related injuries and illnesses.

Exposure Avoidance. Exposure avoidance means never undertaking a loss exposure or completely eliminating an existing exposure. In either case, the probability of loss is reduced to zero.

To illustrate the first type of exposure avoidance—never undertaking a loss exposure—assume that a tool manufacturer has developed a new rustproof coating for its tools. Unfortunately,it is a very explosive material and it gives off toxic vapors during application. The manufacturer initially decides against using the product to avoid exposing its employees to these explosion and health hazards.

Eliminating an existing exposure can be more difficult. If this tool manufacturer had begun to use the coating and then discontinued its use, it would completely eliminate all inventories of the coating material. In doing so, the tool manufacturer might well be avoiding completely its exposure to explosion and its consequences. However, the toxic fumes already inhaled by employees who had used the coating may still, after some latency period, give rise to work-related illnesses. If this does happen, the tool manufacturer cannot avoid this disease exposure and the ultimate obligation to pay for any illness that might materialize.

Loss Prevention. Loss prevention measures reduce the frequency of losses—here, work-related injuries and illnesses. To illustrate, assume that upon further study, senior management of the tool manufacturer decides that the potential profits from this coating are such that they must find a way to apply the coating, taking the necessary steps to protect their employees. They install special exhaust ventilation systems in the areas where the work is done to remove as much of the explosive, toxic vapors as possible. Their objective is to reduce the frequency or likelihood of injuries or illness.

Loss Reduction. The goal of loss reduction is to reduce the severity of losses. To illustrate, assume the management of this tool manufacturer decides to supplement its loss prevention efforts by installing an explosion suppression system to interrupt an explosion by rapidly releasing halogenated hydrocarbon gas. A medical monitoring program for employees who apply the coating is also started, so that any toxic effects can be detected early. These are loss reduction measures because they are designed to limit the severity of any injury or illness that does develop.

Quick response following an accident—application of Strategies 9 and 10 from the energy-release theory introduced in Chapter 1—also can reduce losses. Immediate first-aid, longer term rehabilitation and counseling, and returning injured employees to less demanding or less hazardous duties sooner than they can return to their original work all are examples of loss reduction.

All these post-accident loss reduction measures illustrate that—unlike loss prevention which can be applied only before an accident occurs—loss reduction measures can be designed to be effective both before and after an accident. Effective first-aid can limit the extent of physical injury; appropriate rehabilitation and counseling can speed recovery and enhance the restoration of functional capacity. The accelerated return of the employee to work improves morale, reduces the employee's loss of income, and lowers the employer's cost of workers compensation benefits.

Segregation of Exposure Units. The segregation of exposures involves arranging an organization's activities and resources so that no single event can cause simultaneous losses to all of them. Thus, an organization might occupy several buildings at different locations, send its delivery trucks over several different routes, keep spare parts for machines or duplicate sets of records at an off-premises location, or have several suppliers of key raw materials. As a result, no single foreseeable event will deprive the organization of all its buildings, interrupt all its truck shipments, destroy all its records or spare machinery parts, or leave it without any suppliers of key raw materials.

Exposure units can be segregated by two methods. The first is *separation of exposures,* which involves the dispersal of an activity or asset over several locations. The second is *duplication of exposures,* which involves creating backup facilities or assets, or making spares, to be used only if the primary activity or asset suffers a loss. Separation normally is not appropriate for controlling employee injury or illness losses—increasing the number of employees regularly performing any task typically only increases loss frequency without decreasing loss severity. In contrast, duplication may be appropriate for controlling employee injury and illness losses.

Duplication exists if, instead of having two or more crews each working separately as part of the organization's normal operations, only one crew (or even one person) is normally assigned to a task, but another crew (or person) was kept in reserve as a backup. The personnel kept in reserve would then be the "duplicate," used only under emergency circumstances. The cross-training of employees—so that each has a variety of skills useful throughout the organization and is ready to do the others' tasks as needed in an emergency—is an example of duplication.

With respect to the adverse financial effects that employee injuries and illnesses may cause an employer—but not for the physical injuries and illnesses themselves—duplication of exposure units offers some possibilities. For example, employees may be cross-trained so that each of them has a variety of skills useful throughout the organization. Then, if one employee is disabled by a work-related injury or illness, a cross-trained employee with at least acceptable skills can replace the disabled employee until he or she is able to return.

From the employee's standpoint as well, cross-training can reduce the employee's exposure to financial loss from injury or illness. For instance, assume that an employee suffers a work-related injury or illness that prevents him or her from performing one task. The greater diversity of his or her skills developed through cross-training increases the employee's opportunities to perform other tasks that may not have been hampered by the disability. In this sense, the employee's range of skills become the exposure units that are duplicated. Because of cross-training, the employee's alternative skills become backups to be used when his or her primary skills become unavailable from an injury or an illness. Therefore, for the *financial* losses that can stem from injury or illness, duplication of exposure units can be useful to employers and to employees.

Contractual Transfer for Risk Control. A contractural transfer for risk control shifts from the transferor an exposure to some potential loss by requiring the transferee to perform some activity other than the payment of money that rids the transferor of the exposure. Leases and subcontracts are common examples of contractual transfers for risk control. (Contractual transfers for risk control should not be confused with contractual transfers for risk financing, under which the only obligation shifted to the transferee is the duty to pay specified losses of the transferor, not the duty to assume the exposure generated by particular activities or assets.)

To continue with the example of the tool manufacturer, management could use contractual transfer for risk control to deal with the extreme hazards associated with the coating operation. This operation could be done by a subcontractor, who would agree to deliver specified quantities of coated tools according to a schedule designated in the contract. Because the subcontractor's employees would do this coating work in the subcontractor's facilities, the explosion and toxicity hazards involved—and the exposures to work-related injuries and illnesses, as well as property damage—would then all be shifted to the subcontractor.

General Methods of Control From Safety Engineering Professionals Experts in workplace injuries and illnesses have developed a number of "general methods of control" typically associated with the branch of safety engineering that focuses on industrial hygiene. These experts have identified two basic kinds of hazards: (1) physical hazards resulting from incorrect physical conditions and (2) procedural hazards resulting from improper work procedures. The controls fall into the corresponding categories of physical controls and procedural controls. Physical controls are sometimes called engineering controls because engineering is often needed to implement them. Procedural controls are sometimes called administrative controls because they may involve job rotation, supervision, or other administrative steps.

Physical Controls. These involve a variety of physical workplace features that can eliminate or reduce the impact of a hazard.

Process Changes. When a particular job or process poses a hazard, the best control measure is to change the process completely. For example, assume that a broom manufacturer's employees assemble brooms by twisting the handles into the base of the broom. This repetitive motion causes several cases of carpal tunnel syndrome, an affliction of the wrist. In order to prevent future problems, the job is redesigned so that the workers assemble the broom in a different position. This relieves the strain on the employees' wrists, and no additional cases are reported. Fortunately, this change is not complex and is easy to implement. Many times, process changes are economically or physically impractical because they entail large-scale changes.

Materials Substitution. In some cases, when a particular material used in an operation presents a problem, it is often possible to replace the objectionable material with a safer one. Asbestos, for example, is an excellent insulator, but can cause respiratory diseases; other insulating materials have been substituted for it. Asbestos is a well-publicized example, but there are certainly many more. Nonflammable adhesives have been substituted for flammable ones, and toxic dry cleaning solvents have been replaced by less toxic solvents.

Sometimes the substitution of materials has been overlooked as a possibility because suitable alternate materials were not readily apparent. Extensive research sometimes is necessary to determine what replacements are on the market or available through special orders. It may be easier to use personal protective equipment instead, such as respirators, gloves, or special clothing, until a more complete "cure" can be obtained by replacing the problem material.

Isolation. Some hazardous processes can and should be isolated from the people who are associated with them and others who could be exposed to them. For example, the glove box, often used by laboratory employees, enables a worker to slip hands into gloves permanently attached to a box that contains the hazard in question (often a biological hazard). The employee manipulates the objects in the box through the gloves, but is isolated from the hazard.

More often, though, isolation involves placing a hazard in a contained area so that it cannot cause injury. Excessively noisy machinery that cannot be silenced by other means is sometimes enclosed by walls on all sides, effectively containing the noise inside and protecting workers who operate it from outside the isolation room.

Filling aerosol cans using compressed gases and flammable liquids can be very hazardous. The filling process can be automated and isolated in a room which employees need not enter. The room can also be equipped with other necessary safeguards such as an extinguishing system, an explosion suppression system, and an explosion venting system to allow an explosion to dissipate itself to the outside with minimal damage inside. A conveyor belt carries empty cans into the room, and then carries the filled cans out of the room.

If the hazardous process to be isolated can result in an explosion or fire, the location of the isolated area is probably important. The process should be located along the outside perimeter of buildings and, if at all feasible, should be separate from the building to make fire fighting and explosion venting easier.

Some hazards are not severe enough to require complete isolation, but instead require physical guarding or exhaust ventilation.

Wet Method. Closely related to the physical controls of process changes and isolation is the use of wet methods. Wet methods entail introducing moisture into a production process to keep dusts and other particulate matter out of the atmosphere, particularly away from employees' breathing zones. For example, many plants that process cement, fertilizer, or any powdered products are equipped with spraying mechanisms or humidifiers that inhibit the spread of dust. Using wet methods often is more economical and effective than requiring employees to use personal respiratory protection equipment because controlling particulate material at its source usually is more efficient than trying to protect employees from material that has already become airborne.

Guarding. Guarding is used to physically prevent someone from making contact with something. Guards are used to keep hands out of presses that are stamping out parts or out of gears that are turning. They are also used to prevent people from touching electrically energized circuits or hot surfaces. Many types of guards are available for a wide variety of applications.

Fixed guards are motionless. They are simply barriers that prevent physical contact with a hazard, such as a shield around a pulley. Other guards move with machinery and are properly positioned when the machine is in the hazardous part of its cycle. Some presses have guards that are up when material is being fed in and down when the press begins to close so that the operator's hand cannot be caught inside it. This is also an example of a "point-of-operation" guard, which stops people from having their limbs in machinery at the "action" point—the place where the cutting, bending, squeezing, twisting or any other physical function takes place.

Closely related to guards are control systems that make it difficult for an employee's hands to get caught in equipment. The most popular system uses "two-handed" controls. On a paper cutter, for example, the operator must press two buttons simultaneously, and hold them down, for the blade to move. If either button is released, the blade stops moving. This system keeps both of the employee's hands away from the point of operation. Another system projects a beam of light in front of the point of operation. If the beam is broken by part of the body, or anything else, the operation stops.

Ventilation. Often, a process generates hazardous vapors, dusts, mists, or even heat that must be removed to protect employees. This is accomplished through exhaust ventilation systems, which usually consist of a fan to exhaust the air, a duct to carry it to the fan, and a pick-up point, such as a hood or an opening in the duct. A large volume of air to replace that being exhausted also has to be provided, or the exhaust system will create a partial vacuum inside the building and decrease exhaust fan efficiency. This replacement air, called *make-up air*, may be adequately supplied through air leakage into the buildings. For large systems, it might have to be brought in through ducts.

Sometimes part of the air being exhausted is filtered and recirculated back into the building. It might also be filtered or "scrubbed" before release into the atmosphere for pollution control purposes.

The type of hazards that can be diminished through ventilation are sometimes characteristic of an entire industry. For example, workers in the textile industry are exposed to respiratory disease by inhaling particulate matter from specific fibers. Cotton workers are exposed to byssinosis, sometimes called "brown lung disease."

Many other processes also require ventilation systems. For paint spraying operations, there is usually a spray booth that is open only on one wall. The rear wall of the booth contains filters through which air is drawn and exhausted, while the other walls are solid. The operator sprays into the booth from the open wall, and the excess paint spray plus vapors hit the rear wall to be filtered and exhausted. Electroplating is another example of a process that is normally exhausted. Parts to be plated pass through a series of tanks containing acid and plating solutions, generating hazardous gases requiring exhaust.

Ventilation may also be necessary, not for an entire process, but merely for a specific task within the process. For example, electronic assembly is comprised of many individual tasks. The connection of components and wiring by soldering exposes the assembler to fumes containing lead. Consequently, ventilation is necessary at those work stations. Similarly, when metal parts are polished during grinding, the dust needs to be exhausted from the grinding wheel at that work station.

Maintenance. Maintenance is critical to loss prevention efforts because any device or structure that has defects has the potential to injure people, from a broken ladder or a slippery floor to the steering system on an automobile. Although maintenance is often thought of as repair work, preventive maintenance is used to prevent breakdowns and malfunctions. Boilers should be routinely opened for inspection, testing, and replacement of key components. Production machinery should be inspected, tested, lubricated, and adjusted. Motor vehicles of all kinds, from forklift trucks to tractor-trailers, should also receive preventive maintenance—as should protective devices such as machine guards; sprinkler system piping, hangers, and valves; and fire doors and safety interlocks.

Loss prevention achieved by preventive maintenance does not always involve complex and dangerous machinery. Within hospitals, for instance, patient information is often encoded on laboratory test requisitions by imprinting, with pressure, the patient's identification card. If this device is improperly, or not at all, maintained, the pressure may be insufficient to penetrate the multiple copies of the form.

Consequently, if test results cannot be linked to a specific patient, they may have to be repeated, placing the patient at risk due to delays. It also produces duplication of the cost of the test. If test results are linked with the wrong patient, there is the risk of an incorrect diagnosis. This also could place the patient at serious medical risk, and expose the physician and the hospital to malpractice litigation.

Housekeeping.   Housekeeping refers to basic order and neatness. If a facility is cluttered, if trash is scattered around, or if storage extends into the aisles inside, then slipping, tripping, and probably fire hazards exist. Housekeeping eliminates some very basic hazards and helps prevent some very common accidents and injuries.

Personal Protective Equipment.   Personal protective equipment includes devices or garments worn to protect workers from injury or illness. Each of the physical control methods mentioned so far are loss prevention measures concerned with reducing harm to employees. Using protective equipment, such as a hard hat, does not eliminate health hazards or prevent accidents, but such equipment could very well protect a worker from being injured by a falling box. Since wearing the hard hat can reduce a potentially fatal blow to a bump on the head, it is a loss reduction measure.

The same is true of all personal protective equipment. It does not prevent accidents or eliminate health hazards, but it can reduce the severity of the injury, possibly even down to zero—no injury at all. To illustrate, if a worker is cutting a sheet of plastic and a chip breaks off and flies toward him or her, an accident has taken place. The cutting process has caused an undesired projectile. In the absence of goggles, an eye injury could result, but if the person doing the cutting is wearing goggles, the chip bounces harmlessly off. The serious injury potential has been reduced to zero.

There are many kinds of protective equipment for all parts of the body. Hard hats and bump hats provide head protection. Safety glasses, goggles, and face shields protect the eyes and face. Gloves come in all sizes, shapes, and fabrics to protect hands and forearms. Safety shoes and boots have built-in steel plates for foot protection. Suits are available to protect the whole body against chemicals.

Respirators filter the air either mechanically or chemically. They can range from a simple dust mask to a chemical cartridge respirator, which removes harmful chemicals by making them react with materials inside the cartridge. There are also self-contained breathing systems that use tanks of air and other systems that connect employees by hose to a fresh air supply. Each kind of respirator has specific applications. Respirators that provide protection from a particular material may be useless for another. Suppliers and manufacturers provide valuable assistance in choosing the correct respirator. The same is true for all kinds of personal protective equipment. Because they filter air, respirators must fit properly, or there can be leakage around the edges. Here again, the manufacturer's resources can be helpful for employee training. Proper maintenance of respirators is also essential.

Finally, ear devices are also available to protect against noise exposure. Earmuffs cover the entire ear, while ear plugs are placed into the ear. Both kinds are effective when properly used.

Procedural Controls. Procedural controls include education and training, standard operating procedures, proper supervision, medical controls, and job rotation.

Education and Training. If an employee becomes injured or ill on the job because he or she has done something incorrectly, the question should be asked, "Why did you do it this way?" If the answer is that the employee was never shown how to do the job correctly, the employer should be alerted to the need for proper education and training of employees.

In the context of work safety, "training" refers to the tools and tasks involved in performing a particular job—the when and how of that job. "Education" would focus on the reasons why a particular job should be performed in a given way—the underlying efficiency and safety considerations. For example, in a program to reduce back injuries, training would include instruction on how to lift heavy loads without straining the back; and education would focus on the forces involved in lifting, the structure of the back, and how the forces of lifting may overstress the back.

Education and training should be available to all new employees, who should receive, at the minimum, the following:

1. An overview of the loss prevention philosophy and program, preferably presented by senior management.
2. Full information on general accident and illness prevention programs, such as safety rules, medical facilities, disaster plans, and so on.
3. Details on safety and health aspects on the employee's own job, preferably presented by the employee's supervisor. This should include detailed instruction on standard operating procedures and step-by-step job instructions.

New employees are not the only ones who need education and training. Experienced employees need refresher sessions covering many of the same areas as new employees, especially standard operating procedures. People tend to forget what they learn if it is not used constantly, so periodic refreshers are helpful. These sessions also provide the opportunity for management to reinforce the idea that injury and illness prevention are job responsibilities for everyone.

For experienced employees especially, supervisors should provide ongoing informal training such as discussing job skills and procedures. In some fields, technology is constantly changing, which means there is new equipment to learn about or new materials to use and new hazards to cope with.

Certain groups of people need specialized programs. For example, emergency teams, in addition to their jobs, lead evacuations, fight fires, or respond to medical emergencies. These people certainly need intensive, repetitive training and education if they are to perform well.

Standard Operating Procedures.   Standard operating procedures (SOPs) describe how to perform a task in a step-by-step fashion.

Obviously, the SOP for a chemist will be different from the SOP for an assembly line job. The chemist's SOP will specify protective equipment that must be worn, control procedures for chemicals, waste disposal methods, spill cleanup procedures, and so on. For the assembly line job, the SOP will be more like: Tighten bolt A then bolt B, use a sanding machine to smooth the surface, and then wash with a degreasing compound. These instructions are supplemented by explanations of why each step is done the way it is. If the steps are followed as written, the employee (whether assembly line employee or chemist) will not get injured. If the employee studies the supplemental information, he or she will understand why each step is important and what the hazards are.

The most reliable SOP systems use written procedures for every job and an organized method of training and educating people. If the task of implementing such a system seems too complex, it can be implemented in stages by developing SOPs for jobs with the most obvious (or most insidious) hazards first.

SOPs are standards and should be documented so they cannot be changed without proper authorization. Written SOPs can be passed along to future employees without accidental variation, but unwritten SOPs cannot. Written SOPs can be used as the basis for training programs; unwritten ones can suffer from lack of uniformity.

Supervision.   If correct procedures exist for all jobs and everyone has received the necessary training and education, all employees should be doing their jobs correctly and handling hazards properly to prevent injury or illness. Sometimes, however, employees resist following the SOP. For example, a procedure might require all machine operators to wear ear plugs because of the noise levels in their area. Most will comply, but a few individuals might forget or find the plugs uncomfortable. Or, an SOP for maintenance mechanics might require them to turn off the main power switches to machinery before attempting repair. If the electrical panels are too far away, some mechanics might not bother to walk over to them when they have only minor adjustments to make.

In each of these cases, it is the ongoing responsibility of the supervisor to correct unsafe employee practices. The best approach is for the supervisor to point out the reasons for the particular procedure or practice and to tell the employee that doing the work correctly is the safe and required way to do it. This must be done firmly and consistently in order to be effective.

Employees who do their jobs properly, according to procedure, should be rewarded with some recognition. This, too, should be an ongoing effort by the supervisor. Research by behavioral scientists indicates that employees seem to respond well to a supervisor who communicates with them and gives them feedback about what they are doing.

Supervisors must become keen observers and be alert to the actions of people on the job and to hazards in the workplace. This requires constant attention as opposed to a quarterly inspection tour. Formal inspections are important, but they are not substitutes for frequent observation.

Physical hazards will be discovered by the supervisor or brought to his or her attention by subordinates from time to time. Correcting them or arranging for their correction by others is a supervisory function. The first-line supervisor is the first level of management and, as such, must be responsible for the total loss prevention picture.

Another specific duty of supervisors is accident investigation. When an accident happens, a thorough investigation must be conducted to determine the causes of the accident and the corrective measures that should be taken to prevent a repeat occurrence. Although others may also investigate an accident, the responsibility for the accident and its effects belong to the supervisor who should do the primary investigation.

Medical Controls. Medical examinations and testing can provide assurance that health hazards have not caused injury or illness to employees. If the testing shows everything to be normal, then the employee can continue at his or her job. Although a hazard may be present that will eventually affect the employee, the examination results mean that, at present, medical tests have not revealed a problem.

Medical examinations and testing can detect such problems as hearing loss, reduction of breathing capacity, or excessive blood concentrations of harmful materials. These indicate that health hazards are affecting the employee and that action must be taken to prevent further injury by reducing the hazard through physical or procedural controls. When examinations and testing detect a problem, something in the loss prevention program has failed or was omitted from the outset. A health hazard has not been sufficiently controlled to protect employee health and safety.

It is also possible for medical examinations to detect physical conditions that would limit an employee's ability to work safely with or around acute physical hazards. Discovery of a back problem or abdominal hernia, for example, could cause the examining physician to recommend lifting restrictions for that employee or even a transfer to a less strenuous job. Corrective surgery is also a possibility.

Two more points should be stressed. First, these kinds of medical problems can be discovered during periodic employer-sponsored physicals, or they can be discovered during pre-placement exams. These are often given to new employees as a screening technique to make sure an employee can do the job he or she has been hired for and also to establish a medical baseline. Problems detected during pre-placement physicals should trigger a re-evaluation of that employee for a given job. The possibility of a more suitable position should be considered. The second point, and a very important one, is that occupational health nurses can be invaluable in learning of employee health problems. Most employees see their organization's nurse, if there is one, a lot more often than they see their doctor. Employees will frequently see the nurse with their minor complaints: a small cut, a headache, a cold. This gives the nurse an opportunity to get to know the employees and develop a "sixth sense" about their health.

Job Rotation.   Job rotation is a technique to reduce employee exposure to health hazards by limiting the amount of time in which a worker can do a particular job. It could be on a daily basis, such as limiting the exposure to noise to two hours per day. It could also be in response to a specific trigger, like a medical exam. For example, a blood test that showed a concentration of lead in the bloodstream above a predetermined level could trigger rotating the employee to another job.

Job rotation is most often used in conjunction with other techniques like enclosure, containment, or personal protective equipment. If these are not totally successful, it becomes necessary to control the length of the exposure through rotation. Job rotation is a loss reduction technique because harmful exposure has already occurred or is expected to occur because exposure levels to a hazard are known to be excessive. To avert future problems, rotation or reduction in the exposure time is used. Again, the preferred approach is to control the hazard to reduce the exposure, thus making rotation unnecessary in most cases.

Selecting the Best Risk Management Alternative(s)

To select the best risk management alternative, risk control techniques should be evaluated against two criteria: engineering effectiveness and rate of return on the investment required for implementation. Engineering effectiveness is a measure of the likelihood that a control will work. If a decision is made to install sound absorbing panels around a noisy machine, what is the likelihood that they will reduce the noise to the required level, or would total enclosure be required? In this example, the issue is technical feasibility and effectiveness, but the human element must also be considered. For example, if respirators are under consideration for use in a dusty area, precautions must be taken to make sure they fit properly and that they are changed or cleaned as recommended. If allowance is not made for these procedures, the respirators might not be effective. The objective at this point is to propose alternative effective controls, but not to make the selection yet. This screening process should weed out controls that will probably be ineffective and leave the rest for further consideration. Once this is accomplished, the intent is to choose the best controls out of all the alternatives. As mentioned, effectiveness and rate of return are selection criteria. Effectiveness must be the first consideration because achieving the best *risk control* should be the primary objective. Doing so in the most cost-effective manner is the next consideration.

In the example of the manufacturer of the industrial cleaning product discussed previously, the two most effective control methods are (1) substituting Chemical X or (2) a combination of an exhaust system and a respirator. Once these methods have been identified, a financial analysis should be performed to determine which method has the highest time-adjusted rate of return.

If the first option, substitution, is chosen, there is a $5,000 capital expenditure to modify the vat to accept Chemical X and an additional $500 annual cost for the purchase of the new chemical. There are no additional maintenance costs. There are no training costs. The potential expected value of illness losses, assumed to be paid out-of-pocket as current expenses, drops from $2,000 per year to zero, as shown in Exhibit 5-1.

For the second option, an exhaust system plus a respirator, the capital investment is $7,500 for the exhaust system and $200 for the mask. In addition, there is a $300 average annual maintenance and employee training cost. The reduction in the potential expected value of

Exhibit 5-1
Rate of Return Analysis — Option 1

Factors:
    Initial Investment — $5,000
    Useful Life — 10 years
    Salvage Value — 0
    Income Tax Rate — 50%

Net Cashflow Analysis:

Differential Cash Revenues (reduction in loss costs)		$2,000
Less: Increased Cost of Materials		500
Before Tax NCF		$1,500
Less: Differential Income Taxes:		
Before Tax NCF	$1,500	
Less: Depreciation ($5,000/10 yrs.)	500	
Taxable Income	$1,000	
Income Taxes (50%)		500
After Tax NCF		$1,000

Computation of Time-Adjusted Rate of Return:

$$\frac{\text{Initial Investment}}{\text{Differential NCF}} = \frac{\$5,000}{\$1,000} = 5.0 = \text{present value factor}$$

losses is again $2,000, since the two options are equally effective, as shown in Exhibit 5-2.

Since Option 1, the substitution of Chemical X, carries the higher rate of return, 15.1 percent as compared to 10.1 percent for Option 2, it is the preferable risk control method. Both are effective, but the substitution is a better investment, so it is selected as the best alternative.

Implementing the Chosen Risk Control Technique(s)

When implementing a risk control technique, the risk management professional is not operating in a vacuum. Many different employees in various departments may be involved, even when the change to be made is a relatively simply one.

As an illustration, assume that a risk management professional decides that it is necessary to install guards on woodworking machinery. He or she may initially encounter some resistance from line management and from the workers themselves, who may assume that the guards will slow production. When installation of protective

Exhibit 5-2
Rate of Return Analysis — Option 2

Factors:

  Initial Investment — $7,500

  Useful Life — 10 years

  Salvage Value — 0

  Income Tax Rate — 50%

Net Cashflow Analysis:

Differential Cash Revenues (reduction in loss costs)	$2,000
Less: Maintenance and Training	300
Before Tax NCF	$1,700

Less: Differential Income Taxes:

Before Tax NCF	$1,700	
Less: Depreciation ($7,500/10 yrs.)	750	
Taxable Income	$ 950	
Income Taxes (50%)		475
After Tax NCF		$1,225

Computation of Time-Adjusted Rate of Return:

$$\frac{\text{Initial Investment}}{\text{Differential NCF}} = \frac{\$7,500}{\$1,225} = 6.122 = \text{present value factor}$$

equipment necessarily makes the operation more difficult or slower to perform, the reasons for the installation should be explained carefully to all involved.

If the guards to be installed require a custom design, the engineering department usually must become involved; if ready-made guards can be purchased, the purchasing department also has a vital role. Training to show employees how to work with, or perform maintenance on, the newly guarded machines may have to be provided by, or scheduled through, appropriate managers in the production, training, or personnel departments.

This simple example should be sufficient to demonstrate that sometimes implementing protection can be more difficult than deciding what to do and justifying if financially. It is not hard to imagine how much more complex a large-scale improvement project could be.

In the foregoing example, the risk management professional initiated the loss prevention improvement. At times, however, personnel in other departments may propose a project with risk management implications. Clearly, the procedure should work both ways. There should exist within every organization a system to communicate to each of the functional areas what is being proposed or planned by another. With sufficient advance notice, everyone involved will have a chance to offer input and help ensure that what ultimately gets done is in the best interests of the overall organization.

This communication system should exist on two levels: formal and informal. In the formal system, all capital expenditure proposals above a particular dollar amount should circulate through all departments for review and comment. Any negative comments, complaints, or recommendations should be resolved before a proposal is finally approved. This kind of a system gives the risk manager the opportunity to be certain that all loss prevention features such as specific hazard controls, emergency preparedness, facility design, or fire protection are up to standards.

The informal system develops over time and is the result of good working relationship. In many situations, the simplest way to gain the support of others is informally, such as when a design engineer visits the risk management professional with preliminary plans for a plant expansion before the proposal is formalized. This kind of cooperation and communication is effective, simple, and fast. A strong effort in the beginning will speed the more formal process later.

Monitoring the Effectiveness of Risk Controls

Only by monitoring the risk control measures that are implemented can the risk management professional decide if the objectives have been achieved. Sometimes this is a relatively simple matter. If changes have been instituted because a particular kind of accident occurred with a high frequency, deciding if the problem has been corrected is not difficult. The risk manager can simply study the accident history during an appropriate time span following implementation of the corrective measure. If the problem had been an excessive airborne dust concentration, it could have been remeasured to see if the *control* measure helped.

However, *controls* are often implemented merely because an injury or illness is recognized. If that is the case, and there is no history of injuries or illnesses, who is to say if the improvement that was made was responsible for a continued good record? Maybe there would have been no injuries or illnesses even without the improvement, or so it might seem to the casual observer. With more rigorous analysis, it should be obvious that for every system that includes an employee, a hazard, and the rest of the environment, an injury or illness will take place with some (probably low) frequency. That frequency might be so low that it has to be measured in years rather than days, weeks, or months. Still given enough time, the injury or illness is inevitable. What the *control* measure does is reduce the frequency, perhaps making it once every hundred years instead of once every three years. That kind of improvement is real, but the exact results are difficult to document.

What *can* be determined in all cases is whether the implementation was carried out properly. "Properly" means in accordance with all specifications, including the codes and standards. For an exhaust system, the new level of an airborne contaminant should be measured to confirm that it works. There should also be checks to ensure that the exhaust velocity is correct, that the employees have been trained to call for maintenance when the filters are dirty, and that maintenance keeps new filters in stock.

If deficiencies in the controls are found, they must be corrected. Installation errors are generally the easiest to correct. Errors in the basic design are, understandably, tougher to fix, as well as more expensive. Operating problems like incorrect procedures or maintenance are another type of deficiency. There are no hard and fast rules on how to correct problems—each will be unique and will have a unique solution. The point is that monitoring provides feedback so the risk management professional can find the problem and take corrective action.

Accident Investigations One way to monitor the effectiveness of risk controls is by investigating accidents. Whenever there is an injury or illness, a complete investigation should be carried out to determine what caused it and what can be done to prevent a repeat of the occurrence. This investigation is generally called an accident investigation, although the procedure can be triggered by either injuries or illnesses. Some organizations also investigate when there is an incident that produces no injury. They often call this a "near-miss." Investigating injuries, illnesses, and "near-misses" is very desirable.

Ideally, accident investigations should initially be carried out by the supervisor and should involve witnesses and the affected employee. Everybody should understand that his or her participation and cooperation are needed to do a thorough job. It should be stressed to the employees that finding the underlying causes so that they can be corrected is the objective, not to place blame or find fault. Employees are sometimes reluctant to participate openly for fear that they will get in trouble or get someone else in trouble.

Higher levels of management should participate in nonroutine cases and in cases that are particularly serious. They should review all investigations even if they do not participate directly. The same is true for the risk management professional.

A wealth of information can and should be extracted from these investigations. Using the personal computer, establishing a database for analysis is easy. For every accident, incident, injury, and illness, the following types of information should be compiled: date, time, department, process, cause, and nature of injury or illness. An analysis of each type of information can locate trouble spots. For example, what departments are having accidents and why? Are particular processes causing more than their share of problems? Is a particular kind of injury prevalent? Making this kind of analysis is easy with a computer. Answering the questions that arise is more difficult, but very important.

The investigation can be expanded to collect injury cost data. This too can be included in the computer database. Costs can be divided into two categories—direct and indirect costs. Direct costs are medical costs, workers compensation costs, and any other out-of-pocket costs associated with an injury or illness. Indirect costs are those not-so-obvious costs that result from an occurrence. When an employee is injured or ill, another employee might have to work overtime at a higher rate of pay. Or general productivity might decline because the injured employee's co-workers are upset. These are real costs, but they are sometimes difficult to identify and measure. They are covered in more detail in Chapter 10.

Injury and Illness Statistics These statistics are another means of monitoring the effectiveness of risk control measures. The reason for having a statistical system is to generate information for people in the organization. This information is needed by all levels of management to assess the injury and illness prevention program and set future goals. Individual supervisors need to know about the performance of their employees so that they can take appropriate actions. The managers to whom the supervisors report should also be using the data to assess the supervisors' performance, and so on up the line.

Making statistics known within the organization can help make managers and the general work force more aware of workplace hazards. On the other hand, some managers feel that injury and illness statistics can be used as a labor relations issue and are against giving the work force this information freely, except as required by law. This has to be decided on a case-by-case basis. Positive feedback should be provided wherever possible. An example, as mentioned before, is a sign showing the number of days worked without an accident. Another example is publishing accounts of accidents that did not result in injuries because protective equipment functioned as it was supposed to.

Computation of Statistics. Three ratios are widely used today to assess the level of employee safety: (1) the recordable case rate, (2) the lost workday case rate, and (3) the lost workday rate. The calculation of these three ratios is illustrated on the following page. The recordable case rate and the lost workday case rate measure loss frequency, the number of disabilities that are either recordable or result in a lost workday. The third ratio, the lost workday rate, measures loss severity by comparing the total number of workdays lost because of disability to the number of workdays available to all employees in a given year. These ratios, or rates, have become popular because the federal Bureau of Labor Statistics publishes studies using them, and they are the basis for the reports that employers are required to file with the federal Occupational Safety and Health Administration. These rates or ratios have largely replaced those of the earlier ANSI system, developed by the American National Standards Institute.

As a uniform base of exposure among organizations (or within one organization from year to year), all three of these ratios have denominators that reflect 100 employee-years, or 200,000 hours in the workplace on the assumption that 100 employees work forty hours per week for fifty weeks—a typical year. Thus, for any given organization in any given year, the number of "units" of employee exposure, the denominator of each of these three ratios, is the number of scheduled working hours for all employees divided by 200,000 hours. This is equivalent to the number of "100 employee years" of time the employees of the organization ideally would have been available to work.

The numerator of each of these three ratios differs, depending on the aspect of injury and illness experience being measured: the numerator for (1) the recordable case rate is the number of recordable disabilities among employees during the year, for (2) the lost workday case rate is the number of cases during the year in which an employee who was injured or became ill on the job did not return to work on the day of the disability or the day thereafter, and for (3) the lost workday rate is the number of days lost (excluding the day of injury or illness at work) by all employees during the year. Because the lost workday case rate focuses on injuries or illnesses more severe than those reported for the recordable case rate (the latter including many cases in which the employee returned to work the next day and did not lose a full workday), the lost workday case rate normally will be lower than the recordable case rate.

As illustrative computations of these rates, the denominator for all three ratios for an organization having 270 full-time employees averaging two weeks' annual vacation would be 270 multiplied by 40 multiplied by 50, all divided by 200,000, or 2.70. If the employees of this organization suffered forty-eight recordable cases of workplace injury or illness (requiring the employee to leave work for at least some portion of the day), and of these forty-eight cases, twenty-nine also required the employee to miss at least the next workday, accounting for a total of 396 employee workdays lost during the year, then the recordable case, lost workday case, and lost workday rates would be computed as follows:

$$\text{Recordable Case Rate} = \frac{\text{Recordable Disabling Cases per Year}}{\text{Annual Employee Hours} / 200,000}$$

$$= \frac{48}{(270 \times 40 \times 50) / 200,000}$$

$$= 17.78 \text{ cases per 100 employees per year}$$

$$\text{Lost Workday Case Rate} = \frac{\text{Cases Involving Lost Days per Year}}{\text{Annual Employee Hours} / 200,000}$$

$$= \frac{29}{(270 \times 40 \times 50)/200,000}$$

$$= 10.74 \text{ cases per 100 employees per year}$$

$$\text{Lost Workday Rate} = \frac{\text{Lost Workdays per Year}}{\text{Annual Employee Hours}/200,000}$$

$$= \frac{396}{(270 \times 40 \times 50)/200,000}$$

$$= 146.67 \text{ lost workdays per 100 employees per year}$$

Interpretation of Statistics.   For very small organizations (of no more than 100 employees), all three of these rates will fluctuate significantly from year to year, and a study of the reliability of these rates should be made.

For larger organizations, and even for groups within an organization, these rates should be computed at least annually. The objective should be to reduce all of them to zero, of course, but in the interim a downward trend should be sought.

The lost workday rate, which measures the number of days the work force was away from work, is volatile because a single severe injury or illness can cause a big increase in the numbers in any given year. Except for very large organizations, little practical use can be made of this statistic except to point out the impact of lost workday injuries and illnesses of the organization.

Following their annual study, these rates are published by the Bureau of Labor Statistics for every Standard Industrial Classification (SIC) code. There is a strong temptation to compare the results of one organization to others in the same industry. This must be done with extreme caution, since each organization is different and perhaps not comparable to others. Improvement of an organization's own record is what is most desirable.

SUMMARY

This is the first of three chapters describing how risk control protects the human health potential of an organization's employees— the collective present and future capabilities of producing goods and services valuable to the organization. Given an overall state of health and education for the entire population, an organization's risk control efforts can safeguard this productive potential by providing staff support for proper personnel selection procedures; guidelines for placing, developing, and promoting employees; and safety and health rules for maintaining employees' existing productive capabilities.

This chapter demonstrates how the general risk management process can be applied to reducing the frequency and severity of work-related injuries and illnesses. Here the first step in the risk management process—identifying and analyzing loss exposures—requires an examination of an organization's own facilities, as well as the nature of the jobs themselves, to identify the hazards to which employees are subject and the likely frequency and severity of the injuries and illnesses these hazards may generate. In surveying the organization's own facilities and jobs a risk management professional should further evaluate any hazards by conferring with front-line employees and supervisors, who often are particularly aware of the injury hazards of their daily work.

For the second step in the risk management decision process, examining risk control alternatives, the risk management professional should consider risk control alternatives suggested by the risk management decision process (exposure avoidance, loss prevention, loss reduction, segregation of exposure units, and contractual transfer for risk control). The risk management professional should also consider the physical and procedural controls developed by production, health and safety, and management experts. Physical controls include process changes, substitutions of materials, isolation of particularly hazardous processes, guarding of those processes, ventilation to provide comfort and to minimize hazardous airborne substances, machinery mainte-nance, good general housekeeping, and the use of personal protective equipment to safeguard employees' eyes, face, lungs, or hands from specific work-place hazards. Procedural controls focus on educating and training employees to perform their jobs according to safe standard operating procedures, safety-conscious supervision of their work, medical monitoring of their health, and job rotation so that their exposures to particular hazards do not become excessive.

The risk management process next calls for selecting appropriate risk control measures for work-related injuries and illnesses. Those controls that promise the highest expected present value of net cash flows usually are the first choice (especially for profit-seeking organiza-tions), but every organization also must adopt controls that are mandated by law, and many organizations also choose the work injury and illness controls that serve their humanitarian and public image goals.

The implementation of risk control measures for work-related injuries and illnesses requires a high degree of cooperation among the risk management department and all other departments. Management should participate to educate employees about the hazards of their work and to train them in safe standard operating procedures. Cooperation should also manifest itself in the development of a "team spirit" among employees, supervisors, and departmental managers emphasizing that worksafety is part of everyone's responsibility.

The last step is to monitor the effectiveness of controls. The standards by which controls for injury and illness are monitored focus more on results than on activities designed to increase safety. A variety of frequency and/or severity rates may be used to assess the progress of an organization's worksafety program, either historically against its own past performance or currently by comparison with corresponding rates of comparable organizations. Beyond these statistical evaluations, the proper control of work injury or illness hazards requires that all personnel be aware of the causes of work-related disabilities, as revealed through accident investigations, and that they cooperate to control these causes.

Chapter Note

---

1. Material discussed under this heading draws on several sources, most notably, David D. Rutstein, "The Principle of Sentinel Health Events and Its Application to the Occupation Diseases," *Archives of Environmental Health,* vol. 39, no. 3, 1984; Michael Grossman, "On the Concept of Health Capital and the Demand for Health," *The Journal of Political Economy* 80, March-April, 1974; and Avaedis Donabedian, "Models for Organizing the Delivery of Personal Health Services and Criteria for Evaluating Them," *Milbank Memorial Fund Quarterly* 50, no. 4, part 2, October 1974.

CHAPTER 6

Workplace Design[1]

People work best, most productively and most safely, in a proper physical environment. Throughout history, however, people have learned to adapt most remarkably to the demands of their environment, working under extremely adverse conditions of noise, temperature extremes, poor lighting or ventilation, or other physical stresses. Yet this kind of adversity does not foster long-term or high productivity. High productivity requires not so much human adaptation to demanding work environments, but instead, the adaptation of workplace environments to human needs. Thus, rather than asking people to adapt to and work well in a "fixed" environment, it is better to adapt that environment to the capabilities of those who work within it. Changing a workplace physical environment often is easier, quicker, and less expensive than trying to change people or trying to identify and train those few people who have the special characteristics an adverse environment demands.

Many organizations are now using this approach. Workplace design focuses on all physical aspects of the work environment—the size and arrangement of work spaces, the physical demands of the tasks to be performed, and the design of the tools and other devices with which these people work, among other factors. The fundamental goal of workplace design is to improve people's ability to produce, without error or accident, for extended time periods. Proper workplace design improves both safety and productivity.

Workplace design as a scientific discipline began during World War II, when the design of cockpits in British and American fighter aircraft were the first "workplaces" to be closely scrutinized. These cockpits merited attention because shooting down enemy planes while keeping one's own craft aloft required fighter pilots to operate flawlessly two independent control systems—an aircraft artillery system and a

271

navigation system—after perhaps hours of potentially fatiguing flight time. Attention was focused on the spaces in which they worked; the controls through which they maneuvered the aircraft and artillery; and the conditions of lighting, heat, vibration, noise, and other factors that might cause operating errors.

Workplace design has since been extended to perhaps less dramatic, but no less crucial, settings in which people and machines perform tasks together, and where their mutually efficient and error-free operation demands a suitable working environment. In this context, workplace design has become highly relevant to risk management as a source of important strategies for reducing work injuries and minimizing defective output while enhancing productivity. This chapter surveys the principles of workplace design, primarily in settings where these principles have been most fully articulated. Its purposes are the following:

- Explain how the principles of workplace design that adapt the environment to human needs can create generally safer and more productive workplaces.
- Explain how adverse workplace conditions lead to accidents, defective output, reduced productivity, and lowered employee morale.
- Recommend proper controls for specific adverse conditions arising from the excessive physical demands of work, prolonged exposure to stressful conditions, and poorly designed equipment, thereby enhancing workplace safety and productivity.
- Describe how to implement a workplace design program within an organization.

WORKPLACE DESIGN: DEFINITION AND SIGNIFICANCE

"Workplace design" is a fairly recent American term for any or all of three closely related disciplines that have arisen within the past fifty years: ergonomics, human factors engineering, and biomechanics. Among those who devote their careers to various aspects of these disciplines, "ergonomics" is another widely used generic label. Among other risk control professionals, "ergonomics," "human factors engineering," and "biomechanics" are used interchangeably.

Ergonomics is derived from the two Greek words ergon (work) and nomus (natural law). Literally, it means "the law or science of work." Ergonomics denotes the study of physical forces that affect human beings performing specific tasks in given environments. It emphasizes making these human activities more effective by determining how the environment should be designed so that humans can safely be most productive. Ergonomics owes much of its origin to early studies of the best procedures for employees to manually lift quantities of material without unduly stressing the lower spine, one of the weakest and most abused parts of the human anatomy.

In contrast to the essentially mechanical focus of ergonomics, *human factors engineering* embraces techniques for applying knowledge of human behavior in designing equipment used by people in their daily lives, both on and off the job. Human factors engineering combines the expertise of psychologists, engineers, and sociologists in the study of human behavior as it affects productivity. For example, human factors engineers devote much attention to how controls and gauges on machines should be designed to reduce error and fatigue in those who operate these machines.

Biomechanics views people at work as special kinds of "machines" functioning within environments filled with other machines. Biomechanical analysis considers humans to be systems of skeletal "levers" and muscular "motors" that exert given amounts of force in given settings to achieve given results. These human machines function reliably only within the limits of the knowledge and sensory data their brains provide, and in the boundaries of the strength, agility, and endurance they possess. For example, many biomechanical efforts have focused on the proper design of hand tools that enable workers to apply maximum force to the objects of their efforts without overstressing their shoulders, arms, and fingers.

Benefits of Sound Workplace Design

Workplace design, as used in this text, is an applied science that coordinates the physical features, devices, and working conditions within a given environment with the capabilities of the persons working within that environment. The principles of workplace design can be applied on the job or elsewhere. At different times, workplace design may join with ergonomics in emphasizing the physical forces active in that environment, with human factors engineering in stressing human capabilities, or with biomechanics in focusing on the mechanical limitations of people at work.

Workplace design can produce benefits wherever people work—at their job sites, in product design, or in the structures and other spaces in which they perform their activities of daily living. While this chapter highlights occupational settings, the general benefits of all sound workplace design deserve recognition. In all three of the above settings, attention to workplace design can produce important benefits because it provides, directly or indirectly, improved risk control of situations that, if left unmanaged, can produce losses for any organization.

In Occupational Settings Within organizations, workplace design fits the job to the employee. However, the generalized goal of improved working conditions will rarely convince an organization's senior management to spend money and time on workplace design. There must be evidence that financially significant benefits can be achieved. These benefits are usually manifested as follows:

- Increased output per employee hour as human effort is more efficiently blended with mechanical energy to increase productivity.
- Reduced employee absenteeism because a safe, efficient workplace improves employees' attitudes toward their jobs and lowers both the frequency and severity of job-related disabling injuries and diseases.
- Fewer disruptions in normal operations because employees are less frequently injured or fatigued by the strains imposed by their workplaces.
- Reduced liabilities for job-related disabilities, particularly those stemming from prolonged exposures to excessive exertion, noise, temperature extremes, poor lighting, or vibration.
- Reduced employee turnover as personnel throughout the organization find their jobs less stressful, psychologically more rewarding, and more deserving of long-term career commitments.
- Reduced percentages of defective output attributable to human error or fatigue in assembling, testing, or inspecting finished products and, therefore, greater market acceptance of an organization's products.

In Product Design Many organizations produce appliances, tools, or other devices that are used under a great variety of conditions in other workplaces or in private homes. Just as a poorly designed workplace or tool can injure an organization's own employees and disrupt its operations, so can a poorly designed product injure its users and disrupt their work at home or on the job. It follows that an organization aware of the principles of workplace design on its own premises should follow these same principles in designing its products, thereby achieving the following:

- Reduced products liability claims,
- Enhanced organization reputation for quality output, and in the long run, increased revenues.

In Living Spaces Much as an airplane cockpit should be designed for the physical abilities and limitations of pilots, so each employee's workstation should be laid out to encourage the reliable production of large quantity of quality output in comfort and with speed. Within such a workplace, for example, an employee should not be required to lift excessive weights, to sit in an uncomfortable (and ultimately disabling) chair, or to struggle against inadequate lighting or excessive noise.

The same principles of workplace design that promote efficiency and productivity on the job also can add to the quality and enjoyment of life in other living spaces. For example, a well-designed home is free of unnecessary hazards, properly lit, and provides for an easy flow of activities, making appliances, tools, and other needed materials conveniently available. For those organizations whose "output" is living spaces for others—organizations like hotels, home builders, restaurants, or theaters—the principles of workplace design applied to these environments reduce the likely frequency or severity of liability claims.

Indicators of Potentially Unsound Workplace Design[2]

Certain situations are likely to generate particularly great opportunities for increasing safety and productivity through more careful attention to how employees' abilities and limitations mesh with the requirements of their work environments. Several of these types of situations are described under the following headings.

New Process or Equipment Any change in a production process, especially the introduction of new equipment, is likely to place new physical and psychological demands on employees involved in that process. These demands—such as moving materials, performing hand assembly tasks, reading gauges or using machine controls, or adhering to new machine-paced work schedules—may be greater or lesser than those they supersede. Nevertheless, the changed process will alter for better or worse the working relationship between employees and their working environment.

Whenever a new production process or equipment change is even being considered, and long before it is implemented, important workplace design factors to evaluate include the following:

- The dimensions of the physical work environment, including such factors as the heights of work surfaces and the distances an employee must reach, stoop, or lift while sitting or standing,
- The weights of materials an employee must move horizontally or vertically during a given operation,

- The actual hand and other body motions expected of the employee who performs a given repetitive production process,
- The tools required for each step in this process,
- The physical capabilities of the employees (especially any unusual requirements of a task or special limitations of the employee) for each job activity,
- The path of workflow during the operation, and
- The required speed of the activity and daily number of repetitions of manual activities expected of an employee.

Consideration of these factors should be part of the workplace and its equipment, encouraging efficient and safe job operations and promoting correct body posture for the employee. Building adjustable features into the workplace greatly increases the range of workers able to perform a given task. This eases the physical demands on workers and gives employers a greater range of eligible applicants from which to choose.

Apparent Accident/Injury Trends   Changes in the frequency or severity of work-related disabilities, either in total or for particular types of injuries or illnesses, may signal changes in the demands that a particular work environment is placing on employees or in the abilities of those employees to respond to these demands. For example, more back injuries from manually lifting bags of raw materials may suggest that the weights of these bags, the positions to and from which they must be lifted, or the frequency of lifts may have changed—or the characteristics of the employees performing this work may have deteriorated. Similarly, an increase in hand sprains among employees doing assembly work may indicate an adverse change in the nature or volume of the work. This would call for some compensating change in work procedures or tools to keep injuries within reasonable bounds. Conversely, even a decrease in the frequency or severity of a given injury, if otherwise unexplained, may signal workplace design deficiencies: perhaps injuries are decreasing because employees are simply skipping or incompletely performing a particular step in their work process.

Cumulative Trauma Disorders   Quite apart from changes in the incidence of general workplace injuries and illnesses, any cumulative trauma disorders (CTDs) may signal poor workplace design. As detailed later in this chapter, cumulative trauma disorders are malfunctions of any part of the body due to repetitive overuse or prolonged exposure to physical stress. In nontechnical language, the following are some examples of CTD:

- "Tennis elbow" comes from repetitive flections of the elbow—coupled with sudden rotation of the wrist and elbow—usually in lifting, pushing, or pulling some weight, often at an awkward height or angle, causing the elbow to swell and lose mobility.
- "Vibrating white fingers" is caused by prolonged gripping of a vibrating tool or other object, with eventual damage to blood circulation in the finger and loss of feeling and dexterity.
- "Trigger-finger syndrome," is a form of tendonitis or inflammation of the tendons caused by repetitive flexing of a joint (typically fingers and wrists) against some vibrating resistance. The tendons in the affected body part become inflamed and swollen, tending to curl, so that manually extending these joints generates a "clicking" of tendon and cartilage rubbing against bone.
- Carpal tunnel syndrome, in which, as explained further in Chapter 7, nerves passing through the wrist bones of employees performing highly repetitive hand motions that require considerable strength become irritated by abrasion with these bones, causing pain and loss of strength in the hands.
- Low back pain often comes from sitting for months or years in an inappropriate chair with an awkward posture that strains the spine by forcing it to support the weight of the upper body without an adequate foundation.

CTDs often become manifest only after many months or even years of stress from inappropriate workplace settings, procedures, or tools. Furthermore, the employee whose back, elbow, fingers, or any other overworked body part suddenly "fails" may not recognize the prolonged biomechanical forces that caused his or her injury. Therefore, even the very beginnings of a pattern of such injuries, well before they become an "epidemic," should be a danger sign that alerts the risk management professional or other trained workplace design expert to possible workplace design deficiencies.

High Absenteeism, Turnover The increased absence of or resignation by significant numbers of employees typically signals their job dissatisfaction, which may have a number of causes. Undue stress from poor workplace design may be one such cause, although perhaps a cause that the absent or resigned employees may not have consciously recognized. Nonetheless, whenever substantial changes in work processes or in the time requirements of specific tasks are accompanied by increased absences or resignations, greater attention to workplace design may well reverse these trends.

Employee Complaints About, or Changes in, the Workplace An alert manager listens to employees' complaints, if only to be satisfied that they are groundless. When employees find fault with their job surroundings, or when they initiate unauthorized changes in them, they may be trying—consciously or unconsciously—to improve the design of their workplaces in order to enhance their comfort and, indirectly, their productivity. The following are strong indications that employees are trying to cope with poor workplace design:

- Employees add padding to hand tools or put padding on the edges of equipment or work surfaces.
- Chairs are modified or relocated.
- Makeshift platforms are being used for standing, sitting, or kneeling.
- Employees are asking their colleagues for help to complete jobs that are thought to be single-person tasks.
- Employees design or modify their own personal protective equipment or tools.
- Employees change the workflow patterns or bring in their own portable heaters, lights, fans, or other appliances to make their workplace more comfortable.
- Tools and fixtures at specific workstations are relocated within those stations.

Each of these signs is a warning that something probably is causing undue stress in a particular job or workplace, stress likely to lead to accidents, injuries, and decreased productivity.

Incentive Pay Programs Employees who are paid a "piece rate," compensation that increases with the quantity of output, may face extreme pressures to work with great haste either to meet their own or their peers' expectations. While incentive pay programs can do much to increase efficiency, they also may drive some employees, especially younger ones, to attempt rates of output that are physiologically harmful to them in the long run. Such harm is not a necessary flaw in all incentive pay systems; nonetheless, excessive work speeds often create damaging ergonic stress in such settings. This danger can be eased by increasing the variety of tasks to be performed, employee rotation, enforced rest periods, and other workplace design measures discussed elsewhere in this chapter.

Unacceptably High Defective Output Employees working under extreme time pressure or using improper tools or work methods are both symptoms of poor workplace design. These conditions are likely to generate goods or services that have a rising (or permanently high) percentage of defects because the physical conditions or work schedule may not allow employees to produce goods of acceptable quality. The defective output can further compound the pressures and frustrations of the employees' work. Poor workplace design may strike the quality control department itself, so that the defective output goes undetected until it reaches distributors or consumers and generates complaints or law suits. For example, poor light, excessive noise, or inadequate rest periods may place quality control personnel under such strain that they cannot reliably perform their work.

Manual Materials Handling   Any job that requires employees to lift or carry by hand substantial quantities of material over significant horizontal or vertical distances poses a workplace design challenge: human beings are not biomechanically efficient as "beasts of burden." Humans have been an evolutionary success because of their intelligence and agility, not their strength; yet many job descriptions make lifting and carrying an explicit or implicit part of a day's work. Even when these lifting and carrying tasks are performed with aids such as carts, dollies, counterweights, elevators, or wheelbarrows, the aids may themselves be poorly designed or maintained, thus bringing an additional hazard to the workplace. In general, the presence of any significant manual materials handling in a given job signals the possibility of a workplace design problem.

Employees With Reduced Capabilities   Workplace design standards normally presume an "average" level of strength, proficiency, and intelligence for each employee performing a given task. These standards also recognize some normal statistical dispersion around these typical abilities. The physical dimensions of tools, lifting requirements, and other physical features of a workplace or job description typically assume that 95 percent of the "normal" working population will be able to perform a well-designed job. However, if the members of a given work force have clearly reduced physical or mental capabilities, standards for a normal population may be overly demanding. These special employees may be able to work most efficiently and safely despite their impairments, if only some of the physical features of their workplaces were modified to account for their reduced strength, reach, agility, speed, or other limitations.

Workplace Design Checklists

To summarize the scope and significance of workplace design considerations, Exhibits 6-1 and 6-2 are checklists that pose a number of questions that can help a risk management professional or other manager without special expertise in workplace design determine whether a workspace requires attention. In general, the "No" responses to the checklist questions indicate that workplace design is sound; "Yes" responses highlight concerns that should be further explored to determine whether workplace design could be improved. The remaining portions of this chapter discuss many concerns and questions covered by the checklist.

ERGONOMIC APPLICATIONS

Workplace design can help to reduce work injuries and to maintain product quality and operating efficiency when it is applied to five major areas of ergonomic concern:

- Manual materials handling,
- Cumulative trauma disorders,
- The physical layout of workstations,
- Displays from which employees receive information about machine operation and controls through which employees operate machines, and
- Overly stressful physical surroundings that cause fatigue.

For each of these areas, the following discussion considers exposure factors and then control strategies. Often discussed are both strategies based on workplace design and strategies based on more traditional engineering and human relations approaches. The focus throughout is on reducing losses, enhancing product quality, and improving operating efficiency through attention to workplace design.

Manual Materials Handling[3]

The manual handling of materials is lifting, pulling, dragging, pushing, and transferring objects or materials by human power (with or without some mechanical assistance). It is by far the leading workers compensation problem in the United States, probably accounting for 30 to 40 percent of the total dollar amount of all such compensation claims. The prevalence of materials handling injuries pervades all industries, but it is especially pronounced in manufacturing, construction, and transportation activities. This is not surprising, in view of the fact that most employees in these industries spend the majority of their working day moving materials of one type or another.

In addressing materials handling problems, it is important to realize that strenuous tasks naturally cause more injuries and disablements than do others. While an employee can get a back sprain from merely bending down to pick up a paper clip, it is true that, statistically, more materials handling injuries arise from jobs that require heavy

Exhibit 6-1
Workplace Design Checklist—Overall Facility*

A. Indicators of the Need for Ergonomic Engineering Evaluation

☐ Is a new production line or facility being considered?

☐ Is production efficiency too low?

☐ Is product quality low?

☐ Are absenteeism and accident rates unusually high?

☐ Are back injuries or cumulative trauma disorders of the hand occurring frequently?

☐ Are medical visits occurring too frequently?

☐ Is turnover at the facility too high?

☐ Does it take too long to train workers for certain tasks?

☐ Do workers make frequent mistakes?

☐ Is there too much waste material resulting from production?

☐ Is there too much equipment damage?

☐ Are workers frequently away from their work stations?

☐ Are employees making subtle workplace changes?

☐ Are work stations used during more than one shift each day?

☐ Are your plant engineers familiar with ergonomic principles?

☐ Do you utilize an incentive pay system?

☐ Do the employees seem to exercise their hands, fingers or arms often to relieve muscle strain?

B. Indicators of the Need to Redesign Specific Tasks

☐ Are workers frequently required to lift and carry too much weight?

☐ Do workers have to push or pull objects which require large break-away forces to get started? (Carts, boxes, rolls of materials, etc.)

☐ Do workers push or pull hand trucks or carts up or down inclines or ramps?

Continued on next page

☐ Does a job require a worker to push, pull, lift or lower objects while the body is bent, twisted or stretched out?

☐ Do workers complain they don't get enough breaks?

☐ Is the work pace not under the worker's control? Is the pace rapid?

☐ Does the task require the worker to repeat the same movement pattern at a high rate of speed?

☐ Does the worker's pulse rate exceed 120 beats per minute while doing the job?

☐ Is the job overly monotonous?

☐ Does the job involve the frequent use or manipulation of hand tools?

☐ Does the task require the continuous use of both hands and both feet in order to operate controls or manipulate the work object?

☐ Does the job require the worker to raise arms above shoulder height often or for extended periods of time?

☐ In order to perform the task, must the worker maintain the same posture (either sitting or standing) all the time?

☐ Does the job require the worker to keep track of a changing work situation mentally? Does this work situation require monitoring several machines?

☐ Must the operator process information at a rate which might exceed his or her capacity?

☐ Must the operator sense and respond to information signals occurring simultaneously from different machines without sufficient time to do so?

C. Indicators of the Need to Redesign the Workplace

☐ Do workers sit on the front edge of their chairs, not using back supports?

☐ Do workers frequently add cushions and pads to their work chair?

☐ Is it necessary for the worker to get into an unnatural or stretched position in order to see or reach gauges, controls, dials, materials or part of the work object?

☐ In order to operate foot pedals or knee switches, must the worker assume an unnatural or uncomfortable posture?

☐ Does the operator have to operate foot pedals while standing?

☐ If there are foot pedals, are they too small to allow the operator to alter the position of the foot?

☐ Is a raised footrest necessary?

Continued on next page

☐ In order to perform the task, must workers hold their arms or hands up without armrests?

☐ Is it difficult to operate controls or observe dials?

☐ Are dials or controls poorly labeled?

☐ Is the equipment designed or placed in such a way that cleaning and maintenance activities are difficult?

☐ Does there seem to be too much clutter in the workplace?

☐ Must the worker perform his or her job in a chair which cannot be adjusted?

☐ Is it possible to provide clamps or supports which will relieve the worker of the need to hold the work object while performing the task?

D. Indicators that Special Considerations Need to be Made in the Work Environment

☐ Is there so much process noise that hearing loss could occur?

☐ Is there so much noise that it interferes with speech or audible signals of various kinds?

☐ Is special lighting necessary to perform the job?

☐ Is there sufficient difference between the background color for the task and color codes on knobs, handles, and displays?

☐ Does the job require the worker to look from dark to light areas on a regular basis?

☐ Are there sources of direct or reflected glare in the work area?

☐ Do lights reflect off machinery causing distracting flashes or stroboscopic effects?

☐ Is the air temperature too cold? too hot?

☐ Is it too humid in the workplace?

☐ Are radiant heat sources placed near any work stations?

☐ Are there rapid changes in temperature or light in the work environment?

☐ Is there sufficient vibration in hand tools or process equipment for the worker to feel it in hands, arms or whole body?

☐ Is there so much air contaminant in the process that it settles on displays, making them difficult to see?

☐ Is the job so designed that left-handed people can do it as easily as right-handed people?

---

*Reprinted with permission from *Ergonomics: A Practical Guide* (Chicago: National Safety Council, 1988), pp. A-1 to A-3.

Exhibit 6-2
Workplace Design Checklist—Individual Workplace*

Workplace Characteristics

☐ Can the worker keep horizontal stretches within the range of normal arm reach? (Reach should not exceed 16-18.")

☐ Is there adequate space at the work station to perform the work comfortably?

☐ Is clearance space in the workplace adequate for handling and maintenance tasks?

☐ Is the workplace accessible to material handling equipment?

☐ Does the positioning of equipment, controls and work surface make it possible to maintain a comfortable posture?

☐ Is it possible for the worker to alternate sitting and standing when performing the task?

☐ If a chair is provided, is its design satisfactory? (Adequate back support, vertical adjustability, etc.)

☐ Does the height of the work surface permit satisfactory arm posture? (Correct hand height is 2" to 6" below elbow height for most jobs.)

☐ If the work height is unsatisfactory, is it due to:

    ☐ Machine

    ☐ Work surface

    ☐ Controls

☐ Does the height of the work surface permit a comfortable view of the job being done?

☐ Is the height of the work surface adjustable?

☐ Is the texture of the work surface comfortable, taking into account hardness, elasticity, color and smoothness?

☐ If pedals are used, are they positioned comfortably?

☐ Are pedals a comfortable size?

☐ If pedals are used, are they limited to two?

☐ Is the use of pedals required only on jobs performed while seated?

☐ Are hand controls designed to take into account the amount and types of force required to operate them?

Continued on next page

☐ Are footrests and/or supports for hands, arms and back available if needed?

☐ If containers are used, are they placed conveniently?

☐ Are containers designed for easy maintenance and repair?

☐ Does the design of the equipment allow for easy access for maintenance and repair?

☐ Is the level of vibration low enough to avoid adverse effects on the worker?

☐ Is the workplace floor clear of clutter and obstructions which could create the risk of slips, trips or falls?

Physical Demands

☐ Does the task require strenuous two-hand lifting?

    ☐ Lifting at too great a horizontal distance

    ☐ Lifting more than once per minute

    ☐ Lifting over too great a vertical distance

☐ Does the task require strenuous one-hand lifting and reaching? (such as too long a reach feeding parts into a machine)

☐ Are lifts awkward because they are near the floor, above the shoulders or too far from the body?

☐ Does the job require twisting while lifting?

☐ Must the worker handle difficult-to-grasp items? (Are the items difficult to reach? Is the hand-hold poor?)

☐ Does the job require continual manual handling of materials?

☐ Does the job require handling of oversized objects?

☐ Does the job require two-person lifting?

☐ Must force be exerted in an awkward position (for example, to the side, overhead or at extended reaches)?

☐ Is help for heavy lifting or exerting force unavailable?

☐ Does the job involve peak loads of muscular effort?

    ☐ How often do peak loads occur?

    ☐ How long do they last?

☐ Can the job be designed to alternate periods of exertion and rest?

Continued on next page

☐ Can the job be designed to alternate periods of static effort and movement?

☐ Is the pace of material handling determined by a machine? (feeding machines, conveyors, etc.)

☐ Does the job lack material handling aids such as air hoists or scissor tables?

☐ Does the job involve static muscle loading (such as holding or carrying)?

☐ Does the job involve the use of hand tools that are difficult to grasp?

☐ Is there a high level of hand-tool vibration?

☐ Must the worker stand on a hard surface for 45 percent or more of the work shift?

☐ Is there frequent daily stair or ladder climbing?

Perceptual Load

☐ Is the illumination not satisfactory for the task?

☐ Is contrast poor between the work space and its surroundings?

☐ Is glare present in the work place? (If there is a glare, what is its source?)

☐ Does the task require fine visual judgments? (This includes the need to detect small defects, judging distances accurately, etc.)

☐ Are controls, instruments and equipment placed where they are difficult to see? (At a bad angle, too high, too low?)

☐ Are controls, instruments and equipment poorly lit?

☐ If warning lights are present, are they located out of the center of the field of vision?

☐ If there are auditory signals, are they difficult to distinguish from one another?

☐ Are some auditory signals hard to hear?

☐ Does the noise level prevent verbal communication?

☐ Is there a need to tell the difference between parts by touch?

☐ Is it difficult to recognize controls and tools by touch and/or position?

☐ Where dials, instruments or displays are in use, are they difficult to read?

☐ Are dials and instruments difficult to read quickly and accurately?

Continued on next page

☐ Is the information on the displays difficult to read from the required reading distance?

☐ Is the work place so poorly lit that there are great differences between brightness levels in panels, dials and surroundings?

☐ Is glare from displays a problem?

☐ Are dials grouped inconveniently?

☐ Is it difficult to differentiate among dials in a similar category because of location or lack of color coding?

☐ Are displays or dials not located near the corresponding control?

☐ Are the most important or frequently used instruments not in the best position within the field of vision?

☐ Are the most frequently used instruments not grouped together in the same area of the field of vision?

☐ Are controls difficult to reach and operate?

☐ Are controls not standardized on similar equipment?

☐ Are there more controls than needed to perform the job?

☐ Does reading the instruments require a lot of head or body movement?

☐ Does the design of any instrument increase reading errors?

☐ Is the dial too complex for the level of information required?

☐ Are dials arranged out of the order in which they must be read?

☐ When all readings are correct, do the pointers in a group of dials point in different directions?

☐ Is it difficult to see immediately how a control is set?

☐ Does the worker's hand obstruct the dial when operating controls?

Mental Load

☐ Is the task very complex?

☐ Is the job so complex it takes a long time to train workers?

☐ Does the task require a great deal of accuracy?

Continued on next page

☐ Does the worker have to evaluate data before taking action?

☐ Are standards of comparison lacking?

☐ Is it difficult to recognize controls by shape, size, labeling or color? Is this a problem in normal use? Could it be a problem in an emergency?

☐ Is the information available about performance of the job task ambiguous and irrelevant?

☐ Does the information come in faster than the worker is likely to be able to assimilate it?

☐ Must the worker keep track of several different types of information and signals at the same time?

☐ Does the job make heavy demands on short-term memory?

☐ Is the rate of information heavy enough to overload the worker?

☐ Do signals come in when the worker is concentrating on something else?

☐ Can signals from different sources occur simultaneously?

☐ Does the worker have to make a choice in response to a signal?

☐ If the worker must make a choice, does he/she know immediately if the choice was wrong?

☐ Must the job be performed within a specific time frame? (For instance, when a job is paced by a machine.)

☐ Is insufficient time allowed in machine or process cycles for decisions to be made and actions to be taken?

☐ Is the job monotonous, repetitive or unvarying?

☐ Does the job involve critical tasks with high accountability and little or no tolerance for error?

☐ Must too much information be handled in too short a time?

Work Environment

☐ Are there noise levels that interfere with conversation or performing the job?

☐ Is the noise level high enough to cause hearing loss?

☐ Is the temperature or humidity frequently uncomfortable enough to interfere with the job?

Continued on next page

☐ Is air circulation too low?

☐ Is there too much air movement?

☐ Are workers exposed to rapid environmental changes?

☐ Are suspended dust, mists and other particulates present in the air?

☐ Are there wet locations that may produce shock hazards for work with electrically powered equipment?

☐ Are floors uneven?

☐ Are floors slippery?

☐ Is housekeeping poor?

☐ Is lighting inadequate for the job?

☐ Does glare interfere with reading, inspecting, etc.?

☐ Are there hot surfaces which may cause burns?

☐ Are there conditions which should require personal protective clothing or equipment?

---

*Reprinted with permission from *Ergonomics: A Practical Guide* (Chicago: National Safety Council, 1988), pp. A-4 to A-7.

lifting. Furthermore, the frequency of low back pain increases in proportion to the lifting strength required for a particular job. Consequently, sound risk management in the context of materials handling should focus on tasks that require repeated, sustained lifting of substantial weights.

Exposure Factors The frequency and severity of the injuries employees suffer in moving materials by hand is influenced by a number of exposure factors. These may be personal, environmental, and related to the characteristics of a particular load.

Personal Factors. Both gender and age can affect an employee's ability to manually handle materials. A woman's arm and torso have, on average, about 60 percent of the lifting strength of the average man's. For both adult men and women, strength declines slowly with age until, at age 65, a person's strength is about 75 percent of what is was at its peak between ages 20 and 25. Because this decline is gradual, it may go unnoticed by employees most exposed to injury from lifting, those typically between the ages of 30 and 50. On the other hand, endurance—the ability to work continuously—does not diminish with age until, typically, age 60. While many employees approaching age 60 may remain able to perform manual materials handling tasks, their individual abilities must be more carefully evaluated as they grow older.

Environmental Factors. Temperature, humidity, lighting, stability of footing, and the physical layout of the workplace are key factors in the safety of any lift. Employees exerting substantial physical effort in a hot environment are particularly vulnerable to overexertion and to various heat-related illnesses. In contrast, cold environments do not pose such problems, but they may reduce employees' flexibility and manual dexterity, making them particularly susceptible to muscle strains and pulls. In addition, low relative humidity in cold environments may eliminate the skin moisture that creates the friction necessary for a "good grip" on many materials being moved. Proper illumination is important in all work settings. An employee who lifts materials requires enough light to see the work area, the objects being handled, and to have adequate depth perception. An employee must also identify the center of gravity of each object being lifted, either by seeing its overall configuration or by reading instructions. Good footing, essential in all lifting, can be achieved by making sure that the floor is not too slippery or too rough. The employee should also wear shoes appropriate for the floor, which should be clean, level, and unobstructed.

The layout of the workplace is a crucial environmental factor because it largely defines the lifting or other manual materials handling task to be done: the vertical and horizontal distances of movement, the direction of any lift, and the postural constraints under which employees must work. Therefore, workplaces for manual materials handling tasks should be designed to accomplish the following:

- Lifts from the floor should be avoided.
- The torso should never twist while the employee is handling substantial loads.
- Unbalanced (or asymmetrical) one-handed lifts should be avoided.
- Loads should not be lifted across obstacles.
- Loads should not be lifted at extended reaches.
- No uncomfortable postures should be necessary throughout the work cycle of any frequent lift.

For example, it is very poor design to arrange a task in which an employee repeatedly lifts objects from the floor onto a low platform. This task not only involves lifting from the floor, which is itself generally unsafe, but also does not allow the employee to stand straight at any time during the work cycle.

Characteristics of the Load. The physical stress that any materials handling task places on an employee depends on the frequency of the lift, the weight of each load, the stability of the load, the availability of hand holds, the height from which the lift begins, the vertical distance of the lift, and the horizontal distance the load is moved.

Frequency of Lift. The more lifts an employee must perform in a given time period, the greater the cumulative physical stress on the employee's body, especially on the back. This is true even if each individual lift involves a relatively small load. Because the human body needs time to recuperate between lifts, the likelihood of injury increases as the frequency of lifts increases.

Weight of Load. The greater the weight to be lifted, the greater the stress on the employee. The stress is especially great on the lower back, which often is the fulcrum upon which the lift is leveraged. In addition, the farther a load is from the body, the more weight it exerts on the lifter, particularly on the lower back. Manual lifts should therefore be performed with the arms in front of the body and as close to the body as possible. Extremely heavy loads should be lifted by more than one person or with mechanical assistance.

Stability of Load. If the center of gravity of the load shifts, a lift that begins smoothly can end in injury. If at all possible, items to be lifted should be packed or arranged to ensure internal stability. If this is not possible, an alternative to manual lifting should be found.

Stability is also determined by the size and bulk of an object. Lifting an unwieldy twenty-pound object is often more difficult than lifting a forty-pound load that is compact and has good hand-holds. Like extremely heavy objects, large and bulky objects should be lifted by more than one person or with mechanical assistance.

The stability of a load is also affected by the stability of the lifter. To ensure that the lifter maintains his or her center of gravity, a load should be lifted with *two* hands close to and in front of the body. An employee should be able to perform this task without twisting the torso.

Hand Holds. Any object to be manually moved should be designed to accommodate the employee's need for appropriate hand holds or grips. There are essentially three types of grips: (1) the hook grip, in which the fingers are flexed around the object and the thumb is not used; (2) the power grip, in which the object is clamped between the partly flexed fingers and the palm, with the thumb completing the grip at right angles to the palm; and (3) the precision (or "pinch") grip, in which the object is pinched between the flexed fingers and the thumb.

The size and shape of the hand holds directly affect the amount of strength required to perform a task. Handles or hand holds that permit a power grip offer the greatest mechanical advantage to the employee.

Exhibit 6-3 illustrates how the strength requirements of a task are affected by the size and shapes of the hand holds. (Power and precision grips also are illustrated later in Exhibit 6-5.)

Beginning Height of Lift. The geometry and leverage of a standing human generate the greatest upward arm strength for lifts that begin somewhere above the knees or below the shoulders. Arm lifts that begin below the knees or above the shoulders, in contrast, put the body at a mechanical disadvantage and are likely to require much stooping or stretching. Any task that involves more than very occasional lifts beginning outside the knee-to-shoulder range should be automated to eliminate the need for human effort or to supplement that effort; or, the task should be redesigned to change the range of the lift.

Vertical Distance of Lift. The greater the vertical distance of a manual lift, the greater the stress on the employee. Similarly, the greater the distance over which an employee must lower a given object, the greater the stress. The importance of vertical distance is the same regardless of whether the employee lifts or lowers the load, or whether the vertical movement also has a horizontal component (as when an employee moves an object from a low shelf to a higher one several steps away). The vertical distance of a manual lift becomes an especially important exposure factor when the lift ends above shoulder height or below knee height.

Horizontal Distance of Lift. The greater the over-the-floor distance an employee must carry a given load, the greater the hazard. Increased distance often implies walking with a load, rotating it, or shifting the load while passing through doorways or up and down stairs (creating a vertical component to the lift). Each of these actions increases the likelihood that the lifter will suffer acute or cumulative strain from transporting the load.

Control Strategies[4] In manual materials handling, many persons experience low back pain, often solely because the lower spine is not a strong part of the human skeleton. In some cases, however, such pain signals injury to the spine and the tendons and muscles that support the lower back. While control strategies should seek to reduce pain, the real target is to prevent back injuries. A full program for controlling injuries and other problems related to materials handling combines the more traditional strategies of placing workers in appropriate jobs and training in proper lifting procedures with the more modern ergonomic approach of designing jobs to fit employees' capabilities. Job placement, training and education, and job design are three such strategies.

Exhibit 6-3
Characteristics of Hand Holds for Lifting*

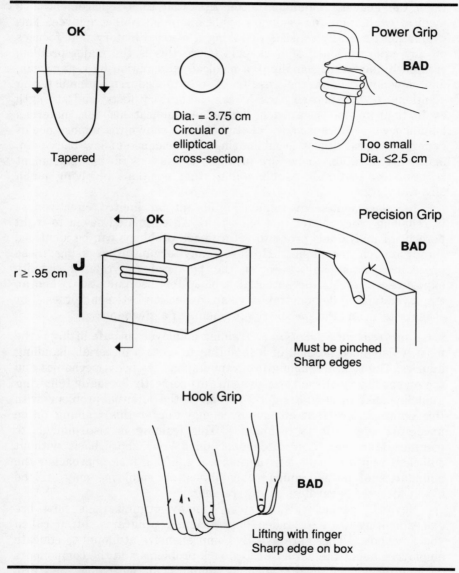

*Adapted with permission from *Ergonomics: A Practical Guide* (Chicago: National Safety Council, 1988), p. 4-6.

Job Placement. Job placement attempts to identify workers who are least susceptible to materials handling injuries and to assign to them the heaviest handling tasks. Essential to job placement is a medical evaluation for each job applicant or current employee. This evaluation generally consists of taking a medical history that focuses on any prior episodes of back pain (since this is the major problem created by materials handling), a medical examination by a physician, and depending upon the results of the procedures, administering additional tests (such as back X-rays, laboratory tests, and strength evaluation) to measure each person's qualifications for materials handling work. Because several studies have shown the importance of general physical fitness in minimizing the incidence of low back pain, many organizations now are using "fitness" as a job placement criterion for materials handling and other positions involving much physical work.

Job placement seems to have significant, but limited, effectiveness in reducing work-related low back pain. An estimated seven to eight percent of individuals prone to future back problems can be identified through such techniques. However, any organization using these procedures must be aware of the potential for related liability exposures—there is the potential liability for discrimination when an employer fails to demonstrate a clear connection between "fitness" or other criteria and the specific requirements of a given job.

Training and Education. Training employees in safe lifting is the most widely-used method of attempting to control materials handling injuries. The typical training program emphasizes body mechanics and the responsibility of each employee to "lift correctly," usually following guidelines like those in Exhibit 6-4. Some of the potential problems with this approach are that an employee may forget this training or be uncomfortable with its techniques. This training is also difficult to monitor. Moreover, it is often done on a "one shot" basis without sufficient reinforcement. Furthermore, if a lifting task approaches the boundaries of normal human capabilities, an employee may still be overly stressed regardless of any training.

Beyond specific "lifting rules," many organizations now are experimenting with expanded back training programs, often called "back schools." These are usually comprehensive attempts to educate employees about the nature of low back problems and the components of long-term back health such as sound body mechanics, posture, nutrition, and relaxation.

Job Design. Designing a materials handling task to fit employees' physical capabilities and to meet the parameters of the lifting procedures in which these employees have been trained is particularly effective in reducing back injury problems. This approach reduces

Exhibit 6-4
Rules of Lifting*

DO	DO NOT
• Be in good physical shape and refrain from any lifting or lowering tasks beyond one's ability.	• Twist the back or bend sideways.
• Think before lifting in order to observe whether or not materials are placed within reach, appropriate materials handling aids are available, and sufficient space has been cleared for the task.	• Lift or lower awkwardly, such as with the arms extended. • Continue lifting when the load is too heavy.
• Get a good grip on a load, test the weight before trying to move it, and secure mechanical lifting aid or another's help before attempting to move a load that is too bulky or too heavy.	
• Keep the load close to the body, placing the feet close to the load, standing in a stable position with the feet pointing in the direction of movement, and lifting mostly with the legs.	

*Adapted with permission from Karl H.E. Kroemer, "Ergonomics," *Fundamentals of Industrial Hygiene*, ed. Barbara A. Plog, 3rd ed. (Chicago: National Safety Council, 1988), p. 396.

employees' exposure to the factors that lead to back pain, and lessens the medical and legal problems associated with selecting employees for this kind of work. Job design also relies less for success on an employee's ability and willingness to follow established lifting procedures.

Four "keys" generally should be followed in redesigning manual materials handling tasks to keep them within employees' capabilities. These keys are eliminating lifting, changing the force required, reducing distances, and increasing the time allowed.

Eliminate Manual Lifting and Lowering Tasks Wherever Possible. Hydraulic and other power-assisted lift tables, lift trucks, elevating conveyers, hoists, and robots should be considered for lifting materials; gravity feeds, chutes, and descending conveyers should be considered for lowering them. Whenever a lift is needed to retrieve material from a storage space, it may be possible to design the storage so that the material is already at the correct work height and location. On other occasions, raising or lowering the employee to the height of the material being processed may minimize lifting and lowering tasks.

Change the Force Required to Move the Load. This "key" generally entails reducing the force to move the load, either by decreasing the weight of the load or by providing some mechanical assistance. However, there are some cases where *increasing* the weight of an object or container may prevent back injuries. That is, a heavier load could make it clear to employees who might otherwise be tempted to lift the load that it is impossible to lift. Ways to reduce the human force needed to move materials include the following:

- Assisting human effort with mechanical devices (pulleys, carts, or ramps, for example).
- Packaging materials in smaller containers or reducing the weight of the container for a given volume of contents.
- Increasing the number of employees performing any given task.

Reduce Reach and Lift Distances. The key to keeping lifting and lowering distances small usually is to redesign the task. This often means that the starting and ending points of a lift should be close together, both vertically and horizontally, as defined by the human body. Lifts should begin as close to the body as possible. Materials to be stacked manually should not exceed shoulder height. Particularly heavy items should not be placed at any height lower than mid-thigh or higher than the shoulders.

The number of steps required of any employee carrying a load should be minimized. This means that materials should be within easy reach. It is also wise to avoid deep shelves that require a long reach and great pulling force to retrieve or to place a load. Spring-lifted bottoms for bins or gravity bins to bring loads into easy reach often are cost-effective in improving materials handling efficiency.

Increase the Time to Perform Lifting Tasks. The strain of any repetitive task on the body increases with the number of times that task must be performed during the work day. Rapid work increases the total amount of energy an employee expends, reduces that employee's opportunities to recover from fatigue, and increases the likelihood of injuries and other accidents. Therefore, increased efficiency in materials handling tasks often calls for lengthening the time available to perform them. This may be done, for example, by changing the standard time for performing a given task, reducing the frequency of lifts, or rotating assignments among employees so that they have a chance to do less stressful tasks in order to recover physically and mentally.

Rest breaks are vital to employees performing tasks that require substantial effort. These periods should be a regular part of the work cycle to allow employees to maintain not only their working strength throughout each day, but also their general health throughout their entire working career. In working environments that present extremes of temperature, noise, or humidity, time should be allowed for each employee to adjust to these environments before each workday. Finally, employees who experience physiological or psychological difficulties making these adjustments should be assigned to other work.

Controlling Cumulative Trauma Disorders

Understanding the nature and scope of cumulative trauma disorders (CTDs) is essential for two reasons. It helps to recognize the exposure factors for these kinds of injuries and to implement the engineering, administrative, and medical controls for this ergonomic concern.

Nature and Scope of Cumulative Trauma Disorders Continuously performing a given task over an extended period of time—typically years or months, but occasionally even for a few weeks or days—often places stresses on the body that it is not designed to endure. These stresses can damage (cause trauma to) the tendons, muscles, and nerves so that, in time, they fail to function properly and begin to generate pain. Cumulative trauma disorders result from the prolonged stress of these tasks rather than from any one particular incident that is disabling. This is true even though some specific event, one more bending or twisting motion like the employee has done many times before, triggers the appearance of the cumulative trauma disorder. The symptoms of cumulative trauma disorders may be viewed not only as the result of physical stress, but also as physiological defense mechanisms against attempts to continue a damaging activity.

Cumulative trauma disorders can be caused by repetitive motions, overexertion, awkward postures, mechanical stresses (such as the pressure of a hand or foot on the sharp edges of tools or equipment) vibration, or exposure to cold. The common element in all these causes is repetitive motion or continuous pressure. CTDs often stem from the simultaneous occurrence of several of these factors, such as performing a repetitive task and overexerting oneself while working in an awkward position at low temperature. The risk factors that lead to cumulative trauma disorders need to be understood as a basis for recommending appropriate administrative, engineering, and medical control measures.

Most cumulative trauma disorders affect employees' upper extremities—their shoulders, elbows, arms, and fingers—because it is these body parts that are most often involved in the repetitive tasks that generate such disorders. However, all parts of the body are, in principle, equally susceptible to cumulative trauma disorders from extended overuse or overstress. Thus, those whose careers require extensive standing or walking activities may suffer the same tendon, muscle, and nerve damage to their legs and feet as others suffer to their arms and hands. Similarly, persons whose jobs require essentially uninterrupted sitting for hours each day (and thus, for years during their careers) are likely to suffer CTD to the spine if the chairs in which they sit are poorly designed or if their posture is poor enough to significantly stress particular vertebrae and the upper body.

Exposure Factors and Controls The six major exposure factors for CTDs—frequency of repetitive motions, the exertion of force during these repetitions, body posture, mechanical stress, vibration, high temperature, and low temperature—can be controlled through various combinations of engineering, administrative, and medical measures.

Frequency of Repetition. Many cumulative trauma disorders represent essentially a "wearing out" of body parts. Therefore, the most critical exposure factor is the number of times in a given day an activity that puts special stress on a particular body part is repeated. Lowering the number of repetitions, usually through administrative measures, is often the most effective way to control this exposure factor. One such administrative measure expands the content of a given highly repetitive job to incorporate additional, varied tasks that do not expose the employee to the same stresses. Another way of varying employees' work, thus reducing its repetitiveness, is to rotate employees among jobs during a given day, from week to week, or from month to month. A third administrative measure removes any "negative incentives" an employee may have for speeding his or her work. These measures may include avoiding "piece-rate" pay systems and being wary of any situations in which the speed of an assembly line or other machine places undue demands on employees to keep pace.

Medical measures offer other control opportunities. The essence of medical controls, for this exposure factor as for others, is two-fold:

first, they may be used to screen out employees who are particularly susceptible to cumulative trauma disorders, perhaps because of their medical history or below-average general physical condition; and, second, they can be used to monitor over several years the general health of those whose work exposes them to particular CTDs. This monitoring requires gathering "baseline" health data on each employee when he or she first joins the organization (or first accepts the position that involves a significant CTD exposure) and then periodically reexamining each employee to detect any deterioration of his or her health. The first sign of any adverse effects often calls for both appropriate medical intervention and for a change in job duties to relieve the stress.

Force of Exertions. Particularly for cumulative trauma disorders of the upper extremities, the force with which an employee must lift, grip, or squeeze an object is a very significant exposure factor. The greater the force required, the more certain and severe is the cumulative trauma. This exposure is particularly great when (1) the weight of the object being held or lifted is substantial, (2) the friction between the hand and the object being held is small, (3) the shape or other features of the object being held makes it awkward to grip firmly, (4) employees are required to wear gloves (which usually reduces grip strength by 20 to 30 percent), and (5) employees are relatively inexperienced at the particular task and thus do not recognize, as do more experienced workers, that many manual tasks require less gripping force than is at first apparent.

The amount of hand strength required for a given task can be effectively controlled through a series of administrative and engineering measures. The key administrative control is training inexperienced workers to overcome their tendency to exert unnecessary force and to instruct them in standard operating procedures that reduce the number of motions they see their work requiring. Perhaps the most important engineering control is to reduce the weight of objects being held. Tools or other objects gripped intermittently should not weigh more than ten to twelve pounds; those that are held continuously should not weigh more than 4.4 pounds. At these weights, ninety percent of the workforce will be able to work efficiently and safely. Other engineering controls include (1) increasing the coefficient of friction through a change in the surface texture of the tools or other objects being held, (2) providing hand tools that permit a "power" rather than a "pinch" grip (as shown in Exhibit 6-5), (3) supplying proper fitting gloves (or even fingerless gloves if protection of an employee's palms is all that is required), (4) using only "balanced" tools so that the employee's hand grasps the tool near its center of gravity (making the tool easier to

Exhibit 6-5
Power Grip Versus Pinch Grip*

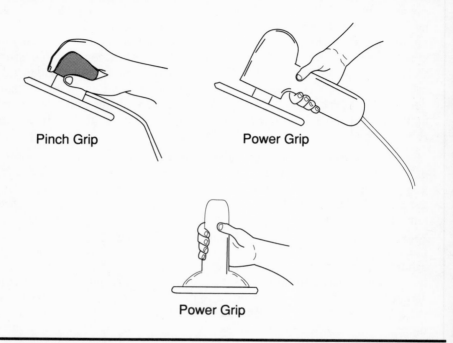

Pinch Grip   Power Grip

Power Grip

*Adapted with permission from *Ergonomics: A Practical Guide* (Chicago: National Safety Council, 1988), p. 4-22.

control), and (5) equipping power and other heavy tools with counterbalancing weights to reduce the effort required for an employee to lift or manipulate them.

Body Posture. Locating work surfaces, tools, and raw materials at positions that make it awkward for an employee to reach often causes that individual to adopt harmful body postures that overstress backs, shoulders, elbows, wrists, hands, and fingers. Cumulative trauma to the back is a special hazard where an employee must stoop, stretch, reach, or twist many times in his or her daily work. Shoulders are especially exposed to harm when an employee is required to raise the elbows above mid-torso, or to reach below the knees or behind the back. Elbows are likely to be harmed when the arm must repeatedly be fully extended or fully bent, especially when the palms are down and wrists are turned to the left or right of the line of the bones in the forearm. The wrist may be stressed when bent sharply above or below the plane of the forearm bones, with the palms facing either up or down. Hands and fingers are especially stressed when the employee uses the pinch grip (which requires four or five times the amount of force that a power grip requires to lift or hold a given weight) or when the fingers must extend to grip an object that is more than 4.5 inches across.

Engineering measures are a key to controlling these stresses that result from poor or awkward posture. The appropriate measure to correct awkward torso motion that leads to back trauma is usually to reengineer the work station and/or to reorder the work flow to reduce these back movements. Reducing shoulder stress requires making both work surfaces and seats adjustable in height so that each employee can work with elbows at the middle of his or her torso. For further shoulder protection, padded arm rests should be provided for tasks that require an employee to work for extended periods with the elbows held out from the body. An alternative to these rests is to redesign the work station or the task so that all materials are close at hand and in front of the employee, letting the arms stay close to the body. Similar redesigning of tasks or work stations may protect elbow joints by eliminating the need to rotate forearms (in tasks like driving screws or flipping papers). In many situations, automating tasks and using power tools may make these repetitive manual activities unnecessary. Wrists retain their strength best in tasks that involve closed-fist or "pistol" grips. Proper engineering of handles, particularly on both manual and power tools, is especially important for protecting fingers and hands. For most employees, handles should be between 1 and 1³⁄₄ inches in diameter to permit a closed-fist, power grip. These handles often come in different sizes to accommodate persons with especially large or small hands.

Mechanical Stress. Many poorly designed tasks can expose employees' hands, arms, and shoulders to forces that, in the long run, they cannot endure. These forces create undue mechanical stress when, for example, employees rest their hands or forearms on narrow edges, press hard with their palms, pound on objects with their hands, or squeeze objects for an extended period. Doing this work, employees often forget a basic law of physics: every action has an equal and opposite reaction. Therefore, every time an employee pushes or strikes an object, that object "pushes or strikes back" on his or her flesh, tendons, muscles, or bones.

Controls for these mechanical stresses are provided through sound engineering and administrative measures. Sharp edges should be eliminated from both hand tools and work surfaces. Wherever possible, tools should have broad handles that distribute forces over large areas of the hand rather than concentrating them on small areas. If hand tools cannot be replaced by power ones, they should be equipped with spring action returns so that the employee need not waste energy pulling apart the handles of tools he or she has just worked to close. For any task that requires even the most occasional pounding, employees should be given appropriate hammers or other mechanical aids so that they are never tempted to pound with the palms or heels of their hands.

An important administrative control for mechanical stresses (as well as postural stresses described above) is education. Employees whose work involves significant postural or mechanical stresses should be informed about these forces. With this awareness, they can then better adhere to proper working procedures to control these stresses. In fact, well informed employees may be an important source of suggestions for better, safer, and more efficient work methods because they often have a practical understanding of their daily tasks not considered by theoretical ergonomic analysis. Moreover, educating employees about the stresses they face may make them more alert to job-induced changes in their own health. They may then be better able to recognize when they need to change their work habits or even their job assignments in the interest of their own long-term well being.

Vibration. Human beings do not work well when exposed to physical vibrations in the range between 10 and 40 cycles per seconds [10 to 40 hertz (hz)] affecting either parts of their bodies or their bodies as a whole. These vibrations cause the physical deterioration of muscles, tendons, and cartilage that, under more normal conditions, act to stabilize the body from external shock. Sensory nerves in specific body parts that experience such vibration lose their responsiveness, becoming "numb" to vibrations that the nervous system eventually comes to recognize as meaningless sensory "noise." This insensitivity, while in a sense a "protective screen," also effectively destroys the normal sense of feeling or awareness that is essential to a person's well-being in other, more stable environments.

Prolonged exposure to vibration produces a number of pathological syndromes. One of the most significant is Reynaud's phenomenon, caused by vibrations in the range of 25 to 150 hz. Symptoms include numbness, pain, and blanching of the fingers; loss of finger strength and control; and increased sensitivity to heat and cold. Typical sources of such vibrations are pneumatic screwdrivers or hammers, chain saws, rotary grinders, and sanding machines.

Employees may experience whole-body vibration when sitting or standing on chains or platforms that vibrate, often because of mechanical activities or electrical operations that pervade their entire working environment. (Electrical workers, especially those employed in power plants, often are essentially surrounded by the "60-cycle hum" that characterizes machinery powered by 120-volt alternating current.) When the entire body vibrates, the tendons and membranes supporting internal organs may be weakened, skeletal desegregation may begin, and blood circulation may be generally impaired.

An important administrative control against vibration exposures is to secure the cooperation of an organization's purchasing department and its equipment suppliers in obtaining power tools and other equipment that generate minimal vibration. The organization's maintenance department also can help identify and repair or replace once acceptable equipment that begins to vibrate excessively. Beyond these administrative measures, important engineering controls include (1) equipping the handles of power tools with devices that absorb vibration before it reaches employees' hands, (2) supplying (and getting employees to use) gloves and shoes designed to absorb vibration before it reaches their bodies, and (3) redesigning (possibly completely automating) operations that involve significant vibration so that employees need no longer be exposed to it.

High Temperatures. Quite apart from personal comfort, prolonged exposure to excessively high or low temperatures is physically harmful and impairs both physical and mental performance by overwhelming the body's ability to regulate its own temperature. The ambient atmospheric temperature may cause the body to either raise or lower its internal temperature beyond the two-or-three-degree range it can tolerate for prolonged periods without harm. Internal temperatures also may rise above tolerable limits because of the heat the body generates during physical or mental work, or because of some deficiency in the body's system for dissipating its own heat. High temperatures generally pose a more widespread threat to people at work than do less frequently encountered low temperatures.

Environmental and physical work factors impose a heat load on every active person. Under proper conditions, a person's body will dissipate excess heat by increasing the blood flow near the skin (thus releasing heat through radiation and conduction) and by perspiration (cooling the body through evaporation). When these automatic physiological regulators fail to control the body's normal temperature, resulting heat stress generates physiological strains that tend to impair a person's central nervous system, internal balance of fluids and their mineral content, skin condition, and behavior. Heatstroke (characterized by confusion and then by convulsions and loss of consciousness) or heat syncope (fainting) are two forms of an impaired central nervous system failure. Loss of internal water and minerals (especially salt) as the body temperature rises leads eventually to exhaustion, nausea, headache, and giddiness as well as clammy skin, heat cramps, and fainting. When internal body temperatures become too high, the skin often erupts in a rash or assumes a grayish "gooseflesh" appearance. An overheated person's behavior is often manifested as transient or chronic fatigue, reduced efficiency, and antisocial conduct. Most of these adverse effects of prolonged increases in body temperature are reversible once the body is returned to a suitable temperature environment and can better regulate its own temperature.

Handling the adverse effects of high internal body temperatures may involve engineering, administrative, and/or medical controls. From an engineering standpoint, it may be possible to redesign a task so that employees performing it generate less heat, to lower the ambient temperature of the work area, to enhance ventilation, or to provide employees with protective clothing that shields them from unavoidable heat sources. Administrative controls may include frequent rest periods and job rotation so that no employee is exposed to excessive temperatures for weeks or months. Closely related to these administrative controls may be such medical measures as screening employees to select those with the greatest tolerance of hot environments, allowing employees to gradually become acclimated to extreme temperatures over a period of time, and encouraging employees to maintain their fluid intake to avoid dehydration and mineral imbalances. (Taking salt tablets, however, is no longer generally appropriate for increasing endurance of hot environments; today's normal dietary intake of salt usually is sufficient.)

Low Temperatures. Working in cold environments adversely affects, first, the extremities of the body and then, if cold conditions persist, the body as a whole. There is a loss of feeling and dexterity in the hands and feet. This is a problem because sensory feedback is reduced. It is this feedback that provides information about extremes of pressure, heat, and cold. Feedback from the feet is also important to proper balance. As a result, exposure to low temperatures can ultimately lead to awkwardness, loss of agility, and injuries and accidents.

If the entire body becomes affected by low temperatures, hypothermia can result as blood vessels near the skin contract to conserve body heat. Sustained shivering is one of the first symptoms of hypothermia, which is followed by loss of manual dexterity, forgetfulness, and speech difficulties as the body's supply of blood retreats from the perimeter of the body in an attempt to maintain warmth.

Discomfort is not a decisive sign of dangerously low temperatures, but loss of dexterity in the extremities and sustained shivering do call for corrective administrative, engineering, or medical action. Administrative measures may focus on (1) helping employees to adjust to new temperature environments through gradually exposing them to these environments or training them to use an exercise routine to stimulate the body's own heat production and (2) changes in work practices, such as rotating employees at approximately hourly intervals into warmer environments or increasing the scope of their work so that they remain more physically active. Engineering controls often involve (1) better controlling the surrounding ("ambient") temperature if the nature of the work permits; (2) supplying employees with and/or encouraging them to use warm clothing; (3) providing tools whose handles have low thermal conductivity (so that employees lose less body heat through them); and (4) carefully designing ventilation systems so that no employee is inadvertently exposed to a draft as, for example, when the exhaust port on an air-powered tool propels air on an employee's hands or feet. Medical controls include taking a history of each employee being considered for cold-environment work in order to screen out those with arthritis, poor circulation, or wrist or feet abnormalities that may reduce the heat output of these parts of the body. Furthermore, employees working in cold environments should be monitored regularly to ensure that they maintain their alertness, sense of touch, agility, and blood circulation. Should any of these deteriorate, a prompt job change often leads to full recovery.

Design of the Workplace[5]

Employees come in "all shapes and sizes." Therefore, designing workplaces for only one segment of the population—such as "average" males—causes problems for those not physically fitting this group. This section emphasizes the human, design, and occupational factors that need to be considered in workplace design.

Anthropometry Anthropometry is derived from Greek and would literally be translated as "the measurement of humans." It has come to mean the gathering and interpretation of data on the "shapes and sizes" of humans, i.e., their average heights, weights, other dimensions, and the statistical deviations from these averages. The science of anthropometry takes account of human differences by measuring various characteristics as a basis for designing tools, equipment, workplaces, and living spaces to accommodate the people who occupy them. Anthropometric information, as illustrated in Exhibit 6-6, can be applied in workplace and equipment design to increase employee comfort, safety, and efficiency. It can be applied to product design to make an organization's output safer and more enjoyable for its customers.

The inappropriate use of "average" (or arithmetic mean) anthropometric data from a population sample has resulted in much misinterpretation of its significance and in a misconception called the "average person." People, in reality, are highly unlikely to be "average." For example, in a series of anthropometric dimensions like those in Exhibit 6-6, less than four percent of a large sample group possessed three average (arithmetic mean) dimensions, and less than one percent of the group was average in five or more dimensions. Therefore, workplace design tailored for the "average" does not fit much of the population.

Rather than using a single-valued arithmetic mean, a better design approach uses percentiles, or hundredths. A percentile is a point at or below which a given percentage of the population can be expected to fall. To illustrate from Exhibit 6-6, the 5th percentile for males with respect to height is 63.6 inches (5 feet, 3.6 inches), meaning that five percent of the male population will be equal to or less than 5 feet, 3.6 inches tall. Similarly, a height of 72.8 inches (or 6 feet, 0.8 inch), shown as the 95th percentile height for males, means that 95 percent of the male population can be expected to be no more than 6 feet, 0.8 inch tall. Consequently, a work station designed to accommodate a male at least 5 feet, 3.6 inches in height but no more than 6 feet, 0.8 inch in height should "fit" all males except those below the 5th percentile or above the 95th percentile—meaning that this space would accommodate, with respect to height, ninety percent of the male population.

This range may be adequate for the design of most workstations, but not for the design of a consumer product. For example, an automobile that would safely accommodate a driver who was at least 5 feet, 3.6 inches in height, but no more than 6 feet, 0.8 tall would be unsafe for 10 percent of the male population—those below the 5th percentile and those above the 95th percentile. Few automobile manufacturers would wish to exclude ten percent of the population from their potential market. Therefore, the anthropometric range for the design of consumer products may need to be significantly wider than the range for workplaces. Nevertheless, employers who want access to the largest possible pool of employees may seek to widen the anthropometric range of the workplace. Therefore, the key to accommodating the various sizes, reaches, and other physical characteristics of a workforce is the adjustability of workplaces. Adjustable-height workbenches, chairs, stock platforms, workplace fixtures, and other furnishings can be used to accommodate almost all individuals.

Design Considerations and Principles The design of a particular workplace depends upon the answers to several basic questions:

Exhibit 6-6

Selected Structural Body Dimensions and Weights of Adults (Ages 18 to 79)*

Body feature (See accompanying diagrams)	Male percentile			Female, percentile		
	5th	50th	95th	5th	50th	95th
1. Height	63.6	68.3	72.8	59.0	62.9	67.1
2. Sitting height, erect	33.2	35.7	38.0	30.9	33.4	35.7
3. Sitting height, normal	31.6	34.1	36.6	29.6	32.3	34.7
4. Knee height	19.3	21.4	23.4	17.9	19.6	21.5
5. Popliteal height	15.5	17.3	19.3	14.0	15.7	17.5
6. Elbow-rest height	7.4	9.5	11.6	7.1	9.2	11.0
7. Thigh-clearance height	4.3	5.7	6.9	4.1	5.4	6.9
8. Buttock-knee length	21.3	23.3	25.2	20.4	22.4	24.6
9. Buttock-popliteal length	17.3	19.5	21.6	17.0	18.9	21.0
10. Elbow-to-elbow breadth	13.7	16.5	19.9	12.3	15.1	19.3
11. Seat breadth	12.2	14.0	15.9	12.3	14.3	17.1
12. Weight (in pounds)	120	166	217	104	137	199

Dimensions (inches)

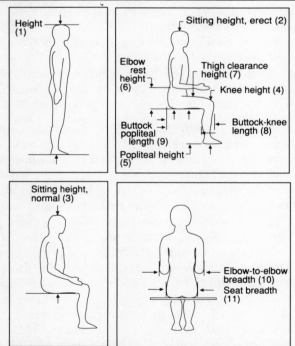

*Reprinted with permission from "Ergonomics—Human Factors Engineering,"
Accident Prevention Manual for Industrial Operations: Administration and Programs,
9th ed. (Chicago: National Safety Council, 1988), pp. 210-211.

- Should the workplace be designed for the employees to function while standing, sitting, or both?
- How much space should be provided for each of the tasks employees will perform?
- If the employee is to operate machine controls, where should they be located?
- What arrangements of materials, equipment, and tools in the workplace will enable the employee to produce most efficiently?
- At what heights should tools, equipment, and inventory items be positioned within the workplace?

Ergonomists who have sought answers to these questions in a variety of work settings have developed a number of general workplace design principles, including the following:

- Design the workplace for maximum adjustability.
- Allow, even encourage, employees to frequently change position or posture to reduce fatigue and cumulative trauma disorders.
- Minimize the need for bending, reaching, or twisting.
- Eliminate employees' need to sustain positions in which the arms or hands are raised.
- Position loads and create tasks so that employees' elbows may remain close to the body.
- Keep visual displays (such as for machine controls or typewriter or computer work) slightly below the employee's normal line of sight (typically 15° of arc below the horizontal).

Sitting Versus Standing Work Different sets of workplace design principles apply to work done while standing and that done while seated. Whether an employee should stand or sit while performing a particular task at a particular work station depends on several factors, such as the mobility required for the task, the muscular force the employee must exert, the size of any materials being worked on, and the required precision of any manual work. Standing rather than sitting allows for greater mobility, more arm strength, less front-to-back operating room, eliminating space that might otherwise be needed for a chair, and greater latitude in workplace design. In contrast, an employee seated while performing a given task may operate foot pedals with greater strength and more precision, is less likely to experience fatigue, and typically is able to better perform tasks that require precise hand movements or great visual acuity. Unless the specific tasks to be performed in a workplace strictly demand either a seated or standing position, the workplace should allow the employee to sit or stand as he or she wishes.

For tasks best performed in a standing position, the following are some tested design principles:

- Structure tasks to eliminate prolonged, uninterrupted standing.
- Eliminate the use of foot controls, or if such controls are absolutely necessary, design them for use by either foot.
- Avoid hard floors, and always provide floor mats.
- Provide a foot rest on which the employee can rest either foot in order to adopt a variety of personally comfortable postures.

Where an employee is to be seated, sound workplace design usually indicates the following:

- Provide an appropriate chair, i.e., one that
  - is cushioned, but not shaped or contoured,
  - has a backrest that is easily adjusted by the employee to move both up/down and forward/backward,
  - has a seat that is fully and easily adjustable by the employee,
  - swivels to allow freedom of movement,
  - has a stable, five-point base, and
  - lacks castors (unless the task requires the employee to move about the workplace while seated).
- Allow sufficient leg clearance, both horizontally within the workplace and vertically beneath any work surface or other potential obstacles.
- Allow the feet to rest flat on the floor or on an angled footrest.
- Use arm supports to relieve upper body fatigue.
- Avoid sharp edges on work surfaces by, for example, providing padding.
- Leave unoccupied the first three inches of any work surface nearest an employee to allow resting—rather than awkward positioning—of wrists and forearms.

The National Safety Council has integrated many of these principles for standing and seated work into a single statement, "Ergonomic Guidelines for Workplace Design." This statement, appearing as Exhibit 6-7, also highlights many of the potential benefits of such sound design.

Computer and Other Office Workstations Although office work appears to involve more mental than physical effort, it biomechanically stresses the employees who perform it. This happens largely because their tasks often require them to adopt awkward postures for extended periods. Moreover, because many of the ergonomic forces related to office work are not immediately apparent, the office work-

Exhibit 6-7
Ergonomic Guidelines for Workplace Design*

1. In the design of the facility, assure a proper match between the facility and the operator to avoid static efforts, such as holding a work piece or hand tool. Static (isometric) muscle tension is inefficient and leads to rapid fatigue.

2. The design of the task and the design of the workplace are interrelated. The work system should be designed to prevent overloading the muscular system. Forces necessary for dynamic activities should be kept to less than 30% of the maximal forces the muscles are capable of generating. Occasionally, forces of up to 50% are acceptable when maintained for only short durations (approximately 5 minutes or less). If static effort is unavoidable, the muscular load should be kept quite low—less than 15% of the maximal muscle force.

3. Aim for the best mechanical advantage in the design of the task. Use postures for the limbs and body that provide the best lever arms for the muscles used. This avoids muscle overload.

4. Foot controls can be used by the seated operator. They are not recommended for continuous use by a standing operator because of the imbalanced posture imposed on the operator. If a pedal must be used by the standing operator, it should be operable with either foot. Avoid hard floors for the standing operator; a soft floor mat is recommended, if feasible.

5. Maintain a proper sitting height, which is usually achieved when the thighs are about horizontal, the lower legs vertical, and the feet flat on the floor. Use adjustable chairs and, if needed, footrests. When adjusting the chair, make sure that:

   a. elbows are at proper height in relation to work surface height;

   b. the footrest is adjusted to prevent pressure at undersides of the thighs;

   c. the back rest is large enough to be leaned against, at least for a break; and

   d. special seating devices are used if the task warrants them.

6. Permit change of posture—static posture causes problems in tissue compression, nerve irritation, and circulation. The operator should be able to change his or her posture frequently to avoid fatigue. Ideally, the operator should be able to alternate between sitting and standing; therefore, a workplace that can be used by either a sitting or standing operator is recommended.

Continued on next page

7. In designing the facility, accommodate the large operator first and give that operator enough space. Then provide adjustments and support so that the smaller operator fits into the work space. For standing work, the work surface should be designed to accommodate the taller operator; use platforms to elevate shorter operators. (But watch out for stumbles and falls!) For reach, design to accommodate the shorter operator.

8. Instruct and train the operator to use good working postures whether sitting or standing, working with machines and tools, lifting or loading, or pushing or pulling loads.

---

*Reprinted with permission from Karl H.E. Kroemer, "Ergonomics," *Fundamentals of Industrial Hygiene*, ed. Barbara A. Plog, 3rd ed. (Chicago: National Safety Council, 1988), p. 306.

place frequently does not receive the design attention more commonly given to heavily "physical" work. Nonetheless, complaints related to posture and vision are, by far, the most frequent health problems mentioned by office workers. They may be typists, computer operators, file clerks, or others who do close work in creating, organizing, or reading written or other visual information.

Muscular-skeletal discomfort, eye strain, and fatigue constitute at least half (and in some surveys 80 percent) of the reported complaints from office workers. These problems are ergonomically related: difficulties in seeing (such as focusing distance and the angle of the gaze) strained positions for the spine (particularly in the neck and lower back), and fatiguing postures of the shoulders and arms can combine to create stresses that build cumulatively on each other.

In all office (especially typing and computer) workstations, the employee is the most important determinant of workstation design. Hence, accommodating the employee is the first priority. The workstation should accommodate all employees assigned to it, while allowing many individual variations in working postures. The traditional notion of "one healthy upright posture, good for everybody, anytime" is a myth.

One of the first steps in designing appropriate office furniture is establishing the main clearance and external dimensions, derived from anthropometric data, for the workstation. Thus, operators' body dimensions determine the proper specification for their workstations as follows:

- Eye height is the primary determinant of the proper location (distance from the eye and height) of visual targets: papers or monitors to be read, keyboards and keypads, and input and output documents.

- Elbow and forearm length are related to the proper location of typewriters, desks, and machine controls.
- Knee height and thigh size largely determine the leg room required beneath tables or other work surfaces; knee height also determines the appropriate height of the seat.
- The forward protrusion of the knees determines the necessary depth of the seat and the appropriate depth of leg room under each work surface.
- Thigh and buttocks size determine the minimum required width of the seat and open leg room.
- The functional reach of each employee determines the proper depth and width of the work surface as well as the vertical range within which necessary materials and implements should be located.

Given these considerations, there are three main strategies to follow in designing computer or other office workplaces. The first is to make adjustable the height of the seat, the keyboard or other input device, and the computer monitor or other visual output display. The adjustability of these objects is portrayed in the lower portion of Exhibit 6-8. The second strategy assumes that the height of the input device is fixed (as are tables or desks in most traditional office settings), but that the heights of the seat and of the visual display are adjustable. The third strategy assumes that the seat height is fixed, but that the heights of the input device and the visual output are adjustable.

Whatever objects may be adjustable, the common workplace design standard is to provide a range of positions that will accommodate 90 percent of the population—that is, only persons smaller than the 5th female percentile and larger than the 95th male percentile are beyond the range of the feasible adjustments. The upper portion of Exhibit 6-8 shows the maximum and minimum heights in inches to which the seat, keyboard work surface, and the center of the visual display (here, computer screen) should be adjustable to accommodate the heights of most employees (excluding only the shortest five percent of the female population and the tallest five percent of the male population).

These design features do not seek to impose any "ideal" upright posture. In fact, good workplace design allows the employee to sit (or stand, if that option is realistic) almost any way he or she likes—from bending forward to leaning backward, holding the legs in any posture within the leg room provided, and changing positions frequently during the workday. These options allow an employee to avoid or relieve any

Exhibit 6-8
Range of Height Dimensions and Range of Adjustability for
a Computer Workstation (in Centimeters)*

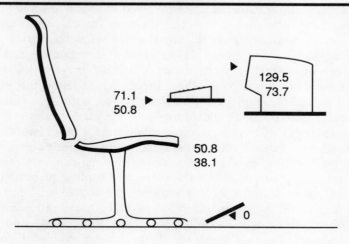

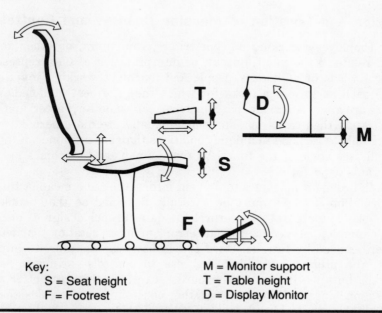

Key:
  S = Seat height
  F = Footrest

M = Monitor support
T = Table height
D = Display Monitor

*Adapted with permission from Karl H.E. Kroemer, "Ergonomics," *Fundamentals of Industrial Hygiene*, ed. Barbara A. Plog, 3rd ed. (Chicago: National Safety Council, 1988), pp. 315, 317.

strains on the legs, back, arms, or neck as soon as discomfort or fatigue signal the need to do so.

At a workplace in which an employee must focus on a document as well as a keyboard, all visual targets involved in this work should be located close to each other—at the same distance from the eyes and in about the same direction of gaze (ideally slightly below the horizontal). If these visual targets are spaced widely apart in direction or distance, the employee's eyes must be continuously redirected or refocused while sweeping from one target to another. Proximity of these targets is particularly critical for employees who wear glasses with lenses shaped for a particular focal distance and/or assumed direction of sight. When an employee is required to view a screen or document at an improperly high or low height, the neck often must be tilted unnaturally forward or backward. This position causes muscle tension, generating a strain on the neck and the upper portion of the spine and leading to headaches and pains in the neck and shoulder regions. Employees who have to hold their arms and hands in stressful (usually too high) positions complain about similar pains. Most of these symptoms, and the biomechanical stresses that generate them, can be avoided through proper workplace design, especially in making workplaces adjustable at each employee's option.

Design and Location of Machine Displays and Controls[6]

Employees working at typewriters, computers, or other devices that relate to the input, output, or interpretation of data represent a special class of activities—people and machines working together to help each perform the tasks for which they are best qualified. While there are many functions that a machine can do better, faster, and more accurately than can a human, people usually are more perceptive and more able to respond to unique conditions than are machines. Exhibit 6-9 indicates some of the functions that humans and machines are each best able to perform.

In order for machines to present information in a meaningful way, information displays must be carefully designed so that people can promptly and accurately interpret the data. Proper design of displays, for example, can reduce human errors of interpretation, particularly errors caused by fatigue. Once people have the appropriate information, the prompt and reliable access to controls—switches, levers, pedals, buttons, knobs, or keyboards—can help them to better direct these machines and the processes they control. A properly designed set of machine displays and controls thus enables people and machines, together, to most efficiently perform the tasks for which each is best qualified.

Exhibit 6-9
Comparison of Human Versus Mechanical Abilities

Superior Abilities of Humans	Superior Abilities of Machines
• Detecting a wide range of external stimuli, including some with low energy levels	• Checking the performance of people and other machines
• Generalizing from patterns	• Doing repetitive tasks for long periods of time with great accuracy
• Absorbing a great deal of information over a long period of time, and recalling all or parts of it at will	• Computing various mathematical operations with a high degree of accuracy and great speed
• Improvising procedures in an emergency or when instructions are not complete	• Reacting rapidly to input signals
• Responding to unexpected occurrences	• Storing a great deal of information over a short period of time; recalling it on demand
• Creative problem-solving	• Using force, when required, easily and accurately
• Making better decisions by learning from the past	• Picking up signals beyond the range of human perception
• Finishing a job despite a sense of fatigue	• Performing numerous operations simultaneously
• Reasoning from the particular to the general	• Reasoning from the general to the specific
	• Operating consistently, despite "distractions"

Exhibit 6-10
Visual Versus Auditory Displays of Machine Performance*

Use Auditory Display If:	Use Visual Display If:
• Message is simple	• Message is complex
• Message is short	• Message is long
• Message will not be referred to later	• Message will be referred to later
• Message deals with events in time	• Message deals with location in space
• Message calls for immediate action	• Message does not call for immediate action
• Receiving location is too bright	• Receiving location is too noisy
• Person's job requires him or her to move continually	• Person's job allows him or her to remain in one position
• Visual system of person is over-burdened	• Auditory system of person is overburdened

*Adapted with permission from "Ergonomics—Human Factors Engineering," *Accident Prevention Manual for Industrial Operations, Administration and Programs*, 9th ed. (Chicago: National Safety Council, 1988), p. 218.

Machine Displays There are two major ways of displaying information on how a machine is performing: visual displays and auditory displays. Exhibit 6-10 indicates where each of these displays is best used. As mentioned above, the appropriate information must be displayed in a clear format.

Visual Displays. Visual displays best present three types of information:

- Quantitative data—the exact quantity of a force or material involved in a process, which may be shown by a scale,
- Qualitative data—the state or condition of the machine, such as speed or temperature, which is shown to be above, within, or below acceptable levels, and
- "Either/or" conditions—one of two alternative conditions, such as ON/OFF or HIGH/LOW, that may exist at a given time.

The purpose for which a display is to be read dictates its best design. In general, however, the simplest design is the best. The direction of movement of a display indicator should correspond with, or reflect, the state or level of the machine's performance. That is, a pointer moving to the right, upward, or clockwise should show an

Exhibit 6-11
Visual Display Limited to Essential Information *

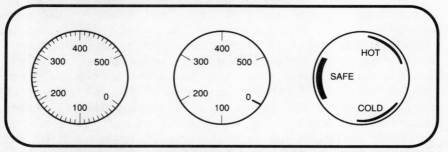

*Adapted with permission from Karl H.E. Kroemer, "Ergonomics," *Fundamentals of Industrial Hygiene*, ed. Barbara A. Plog, 3rd ed. (Chicago: National Safety Council, 1988), p. 330.

increase in some machine variable; a corresponding control mechanism should be designed so that a right, upward, or clockwise movement of the control increases the machine variable, such as speed, temperature, pressure, or some other force.

Multiple displays should be grouped according to their function or sequence of use. If several dials to be read at the same time are arranged in groups on a large control panel, indicators on the dials should be pointing in the same direction when the machine is operating within the desired range. Such an arrangement reduces employees' reading time and increases the accuracy of their response to changes in signals.

All visual displays should be clearly labeled so that the employee can immediately tell to what machine or variable the display refers, what units are being measured, and what the critical range of these measurements is. If the equipment is in a dimly lighted area, the display should be properly illuminated. Visual displays should never give more information than is necessary. For example, it is possible that the divisions in the left dial in Exhibit 6-11 give excess information. Perhaps only the major divisions in the center dial of the exhibit would suffice. Moreover, if the information the machine operator needs is only qualitative, then the dial shown at the right of this exhibit probably would be most appropriate.

Lights, either constant or flashing, should be used sparingly, whether for conveying information or for giving emergency warnings. Although flashing lights generally are more effective in attracting attention than are constant ones, only the most critical information or warnings should be conveyed by lights. A panel of blinking, multicolored lights may only distract an employee and may not convey the nature of the situation or the employee's appropriate response.

Auditory Displays. In workplaces where employees use their eyes extensively in normal operations, the use of visual displays to convey machine control information may result in "information overload." Here, clearly audible bells, buzzers, or horns may be the best way to attract employees' attention to the need to control a machine or process. The choice of auditory signals depends first on the degree of emergency (sirens warning of an impending explosion should be louder than bells or buzzers signaling the end of a work shift), and second on the characteristics of the ambient workplace environment (crucial signals must stand out from background noise).

An advantage of an auditory signal over a visual one is also the "continuous" nature of humans' sense of hearing. Although visual displays require an employee to look in the proper direction, auditory signals are typically all-pervasive. This allows the employee to direct his or her attention to another task, such as reading a dial or throwing a lever, while interpreting the auditory signal.

Machine Controls A machine control is any device through which a machine operator inputs information into a system that affects the operation of that system. Like visual displays, controls typically work most effectively when they are located and designed to facilitate the interaction between the operator and the machine. To this end, this section covers the arrangement (or location) of controls, control design principles, and the hazards of poorly designed controls.

Arrangement of Controls. Machine controls should be arranged to foster swift, efficient, and reliable interaction between the machine operator and the machine. For this purpose, the components of the controls system should be located according to the following guidelines:

- Locate controls, in general, to encourage a convenient, accurate, and quick response by the operator to information about machine operation as conveyed by visual displays.
- Place controls so that they can be easily reached, but far enough apart from *each other* so that the operator does not confuse one control with another.
- Group control components and visual displays according to the logic of that relationship.
- Position controls and their associated displays according to their importance to machine operation so that the most important are most conveniently located.
- When controls are used in a particular sequence or pattern, arrange them to take advantage of this sequence, allowing the

operator's hands and eyes to move from left to right or from top to bottom of a control panel.

● Place less frequently used controls in relatively "distant" locations, and vice versa.

If these guidelines conflict, thus requiring compromises, first priority generally should be given to frequency and sequence of use. Second priority should be given to the grouping of related controls and displays so that the operator does not have to shift his or her eyes too often from one section of a control panel to another.

Control Design Principles. The three fundamental principles of designing control devices by which humans operate machines emphasize (1) the compatibility of the control movement with the level or state of machine performance; (2) the coding of the controls; and (3) the ability of humans to manipulate the control devices rapidly and reliably.

As in the movement of display indicators, control movements should be compatible with the level or state of the machine's operation. For example, the forklift controls that move the forks up and down should themselves move up and down, and those that move the forks to the left or right should themselves move left or right. Such design reduces operator error and relieves the operator of having to consciously "think through" his or her response when immediate action is required.

This principle of compatibility also takes advantage of people's expectations about how controls work. Whether on or off the job, people expect switches, levers, buttons, and other control devices to operate in certain ways. Most Americans, for example, expect a light to be turned on by flipping its switch up; most Europeans and some Asians, on the other hand, expect the opposite. People throughout the world, however, expect the clockwise turning of a knob to increase some machine function, and an opposite turn to reduce or halt that function. Such "directional stereotypes," some of which are illustrated in Exhibit 6-12, should be used in designing controls on the basis that most operators will naturally understand these "stereotypes," thus reducing training time and the chance for error.

In addition to control movement, coding is an important principle of control design. Whenever possible, all machine controls should be coded in some way, as with distinguishing shapes, textures, locations, or colors. This can reduce confusion about control devices that perform different functions, as in the following example:

● Shape and texture are particularly good for coding controls that need to be operated through touch alone because the coding is functional even with inadequate illumination or if the employee

Exhibit 6-12
Illustrative American "Directional Stereotypes" for Machine Controls*

CONTROL MOVEMENT	SYSTEM (OR EQUIPMENT COMPONENT) RESPONSE				
	DIRECTIONAL				NON-DIRECTIONAL
	UP	RIGHT	FORWARD	CLOCKWISE	INCREASE
UP	RECOMMENDED	NOT RECOMMENDED	RECOMMENDED	NOT RECOMMENDED	RECOMMENDED
RIGHT	NOT RECOMMENDED	RECOMMENDED	NOT RECOMMENDED	RECOMMENDED	RECOMMENDED
FORWARD	RECOMMENDED	NOT RECOMMENDED	RECOMMENDED	NOT RECOMMENDED	RECOMMENDED
CLOCKWISE	NOT RECOMMENDED	RECOMMENDED	NOT RECOMMENDED	RECOMMENDED	RECOMMENDED

*Adapted with permission from "Ergonomics—Human Factors Engineering," *Accident Prevention Manual for Industrial Operations: Administration and Programs*, 9th ed. (Chicago: National Safety Council, 1988), p. 220.

has to operate the controls while focusing his or her eyes elsewhere.

- Location as a coding factor can be illustrated by the control panel of an overhead crane. Controls for raising or lowering the boom often are located at the top of the panel, those for grasping or releasing a load are set at the bottom of the panel, and those for moving the crane to the left or right are placed in the middle of the panel.
- Color codes can help the operator to quickly and visually identify particular buttons or levers. The same color can also be used to group together controls for a particular operation.

A third essential principle in control design is that the control knobs, switches, levers, wheels, and other devices are easily and accurately operated by a wide range of employees. No machine control should require strength, reach, dexterity, precision, speed, endurance, or other ability exceeding the capacities of at least 90 percent of the population (or all of the workforce assigned to operate such controls). Controls should be designed so that all employees operating a designated machine can promptly and accurately activate the controls at all times, even during an emergency or when these employees are extremely fatigued. At the same time, however, these controls should not operate so easily that gravity, vibration, or some inadvertent operator movement can accidentally activate a control device.

In addition to arrangement, compatability, coding, and size, all machine controls should be clearly labeled so that—in an emergency or an unusual situation—an employee who is reasonably familiar with the machinery can read and meaningfully interpret these labels and take any appropriate action.

Hazards of Poorly Designed Controls. Any departure from the proper location and design of machine controls creates a hazard—the increased chance an employee will make an error, cause or sustain an injury, create defective output, force a slowdown or shutdown of operating to correct the error, or damage equipment or goods in process. Exhibit 6-13 illustrates some "wrong" and "right" control designs.

In the upper left portion of the exhibit, the top drawing shows that the incorrect placement of controls makes it possible for an employee to inadvertently activate them with his or her legs. The drawing below this shows that the absence of a safety "stop" button on one side of a machine could make it impossible for an employee to reach the existing button. The drawings on the right show the correct arrangement of controls.

In the lower left portion of the exhibit, the top drawing shows an

Exhibit 6-13
Placement and Arrangement of Machine Controls—
Some Good and Bad Examples*

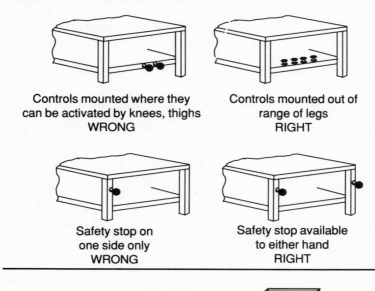

Controls mounted where they
can be activated by knees, thighs
WRONG

Controls mounted out of
range of legs
RIGHT

Safety stop on
one side only
WRONG

Safety stop available
to either hand
RIGHT

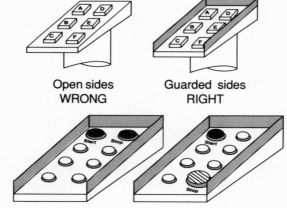

Open sides
WRONG

Guarded sides
RIGHT

Start-up and stop buttons
same color and together
WRONG

Start-up and stop buttons
separated and different color;
also stop button is larger
RIGHT

*The lower half of this exhibit is adapted with permission from Karl H.E. Kroemer,
"Ergonomics," *Fundamentals of Industrial Hygiene,* ed. Barbara A. Plog, 3rd ed.
(Chicago: National Safety Council, 1988), p. 328.

open-sided button panel, which could allow some object besides the operator's finger to touch a button and inadvertently activate (or inactivate) the machine or some part of it. This arrangement could also allow an operator to press the wrong button if he or she were unable to locate, by touch, the correct button based on the existence of sides. The bottom drawing on the left shows that "start" and "stop" buttons are not only the same color, but also that they are close together. This increases the possibility for operator error. The right side of the exhibit shows correct designs for both button panels.

Reducing Fatigue[7]

An important benefit of the proper design of machine controls, is reducing human fatigue and errors in operating machines. Employees' unintentional mistakes cause many losses including, for example, workplace accidents, defective output, and reduced productivity. The major cause of such errors is fatigue. Inadequate workplace design leads to fatigue and resulting errors wherever poor illumination, excess noise, the energy demands of work, or a generally uncomfortable, ill-fitted workplace lead to employee performance that is in any sense "degraded."

Importance of Fatigue Reducing such fatigue through good workplace design can both cut accidental losses and enhance the quality of an organization's output. How fatigue causes accidents and other losses is suggested by Exhibit 6-14, which presents a conceptual model of the variations in the demands of an employee's job and that employee's capabilities during a given workday. As long as the employee's abilities exceed the job demands, his or her performance remains acceptable, and no accidents or other discernible losses occur. When, however, as at Point B during the workday, the job demands exceed the employee's ability, the employee's "fatigue" may be said to lead to an accident, defective output, or other loss. Notice that, had the employee been more fatigued at Point A earlier in the workday, another accident or other loss might well have occurred. For risk management professionals and other managers responsible for safety, one of the essential missions of ergonomics is to keep employees' abilities well above their job demands, both by maintaining these abilities and by keeping job demands within reasonable limits.

Causes of Fatigue Fatigue is caused by sustained exertion—physical, intellectual, or emotional—over a prolonged period. It leads to a temporary decrease in an individual's physical or mental perfor-mance. Fatigue often manifests itself physiologically through the accumulation of lactic acid in the tissues of the body. This acid can be

Exhibit 6-14

Conceptual Model of Accidents: Demands Sometimes Exceed Abilities*

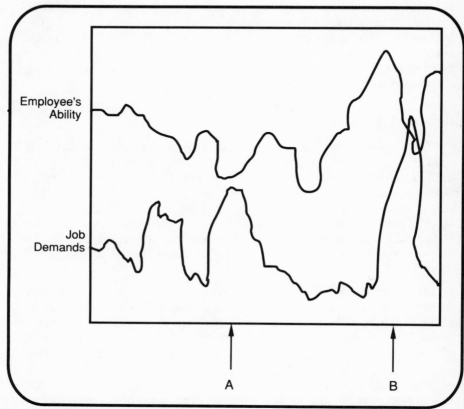

*Adapted with permission from P.O. Astrand and K. Rodohl, *Textbook of Work Physiology*, 3rd ed. (New York: McGraw-Hill Book Company, 1986), p. 248.

metabolized into harmless carbon dioxide and water when the body is able to rest. If periods of rest are inadequate, lactic acid builds up, causing fatigue. Fatigue can ultimately cause general impairment of performance, general weakness, reduced motivation for work, increased irritability, and a tendency toward depression, headaches, loss of appetite, or insomnia. Fatigue that persists over several weeks or months is a pathological condition known as "clinical fatigue." This may result in general depression, failing health, and overall disinterest in life's normal activities. Short of this extreme condition, any employee who suffers prolonged fatigue (whether or not it is job-related) is likely to lose interest in doing his or her job well, will seek opportunities to be absent from work, and may generally fall short of acceptable job performance.

Controls for Fatigue In its broadest sense, all workplace design seeks to control fatigue by keeping stresses on employees within manageable bounds so that their energy can be directed toward productive work rather than being consumed by overcoming physical or mental barriers to working efficiently. More specific measures to control fatigue may be engineering, administrative, or medical. Engineering approaches look to the proper layout of the workplace; suitable equipment and tools; control of light, noise, and temperature; and make provisions for some physical and mental variety during the workday. Administrative controls aim to (1) broaden the content of each employee's work so that it remains interesting, challenging, and varied; (2) provide adequate rest periods during the day, and job rotation cycles over weeks or months; and (3) afford employees opportunities to modify their own jobs or surroundings so that each employee maintains a sense of control over his or her job situation. Medical controls focus on identifying, during periodic physical examinations or employee interviews, physiological or psychological evidence of chronic fatigue or other dissatisfaction.

ESTABLISHING A WORKPLACE DESIGN PROGRAM[8]

Successful workplace design programs demonstrate that sound ergonomics can make the following achievements:

- Enable each employee to perform his or her job better, safer, with less effort, and with more high quality output,
- Reduce injuries, accidents, workers compensation costs, and other accidental losses, and
- Increase profits or reduce operating costs.

To establish a successful workplace design program, it is essential that those in an organization who have some expertise in (or at least appreciation for) workplace design do the following:

- Obtain senior management commitment to the workplace design program,
- Initiate training programs for supervisors and employees involved in the program, and
- Encourage these supervisors' and employees' participation in the program.

In many organizations, achieving these objectives will require some use of outside expertise and other external resources to supplement the talents of the organization's risk management, human relations, safety, or other related personnel. These resources often may be obtained through insurers, risk management consultants, or other specialized providers of risk management, ergonomic, and safety services.

Obtaining Management Commitment

If the highest level of management is actively supportive of a workplace design program, the program becomes a priority for the entire organization; otherwise, the program will be largely ignored. Senior management's support for the program may be motivated by any of several benefits that the program might provide. These can include (1) reduced cost and increased productivity, (2) prevention of employee injuries as a humanitarian objective in itself, (3) reduced downtime, (4) higher quality output, (5) improved employee and public relations, or (6) compliance with legal requirements and fewer public liability claims for injuries stemming from deficient workplace design. The risk management professional or others responsible for implementing the workplace design program should recognize which of these benefits appeals to senior management so that they can use such benefits as rationale for requesting financial or other support for a workplace design program.

Initiating Training Programs

The first step in a training program must make employees aware of what workplace design is, how it can improve their job performance, physical well being, and what financial and psychological rewards employees may expect from their work. Additional training will be needed for those who are expected to recognize workplace design problems or to be involved in creating solutions to these problems. This further training should typically encompass a general understanding of human physiology; the physical, mental, and emotional stresses that work may create; and the basic engineering, administrative, and medical controls applicable to these stresses.

Beyond this general knowledge, particular groups within the organization should benefit from further education in workplace design:

- Senior and middle management should be made aware of the organization's overall ergonomic problems, especially how these problems may lead to property, net income, liability, and personnel losses.

- In a manufacturing organization, plant engineers and their subordinates who supervise activities that generate special ergonomic hazards should receive training in the causes of, and controls for, these problems.
- All supervisors should be trained to recognize workplace design problems.
- Employees whose jobs may generate known ergonomic exposures should be trained in the nature of, and appropriate controls for, these hazards.

Exhibit 6-15 summarizes the knowledge and skills that types of groups of employees throughout the organization should have with respect to workplace design. The exhibit demonstrates that all employees should be able to at least identify potential workplace design problems, but only workplace design specialists need to be able to design solutions to these problems or to teach others the technical aspects of such design.

Successful workplace design programs almost always proceed through two distinct growth stages: a reactive stage and a proactive stage. In the reactive stage, changes are made in response to individual ergonomic problems as they occur. While these responses certainly should be productive, they are relatively inefficient and fragmented because much time and other resources are used to "put out fires" instead of preventing them.

In the proactive stage, which typically occurs as a sound program matures, the organization's entire management works to recognize and manage ergonomic stresses before they produce significant losses. This preventive approach involves developing permanent procedures for designing jobs and equipment that are ergonomically sound—that at least 95 percent of the general workforce (and 100 percent of the employees actually assigned to specific tasks) can perform safely and efficiently without accident or other error.

Encouraging Employee Participation in the Program

Employees exposed to ergonomic hazards need to actively participate in reaching and implementing decisions about controlling these hazards. This participation can be achieved through establishing a workplace design committee composed of representatives from management, the risk management and personnel staff, and front-line employees. This committee typically is chaired by a manager from within the organization or by an outside expert specializing in safety

Exhibit 6-15
Appropriate Level of Workplace Design Knowledge
Among an Organization's Personnel

Level of Workplace Design Knowledge	Operators	First Line Supervisors	Managers	Designers & Engineers	Ergonomic Specialists
Problem Identification	X	X	X	X	X
Recognize Recommen-dations		X	X	X	X
Comprehend Trends of Problems			X	X	X
Design Solutions				X	X
Ability to Teach Workplace Design					X

and health, industrial engineering, and physiology. This chairperson acts as the administrator/coordinator for the efforts of the committee, each member of which should receive enough intensive training in workplace design to understand its objectives and basic principles. The committee should meet periodically to discuss ergonomic problems within the organization and to develop plans for managing them. An important function of the committee is to facilitate communication vertically and laterally throughout the organization on the practical benefits of, and specific measures for implementing, the principles of sound workplace design.

SUMMARY

Because human beings have limited physical and mental capacities and endurance limits, they function best—most efficiently and most safely—when their workplace and living environments are suited to their capabilities. In employment settings, workplace design combines elements of ergonomics, human factors engineering, and biomechanics to create workplaces and products that "fit" the abilities of employees and product users. Workplace design is especially important to risk management because it can help reduce the accidents, errors, defective output, and interruptions in operations that create losses.

An organization's risk management professional or other managers can look to a series of ergonomic indicators to determine the organization's need for, and potential benefits from, implementing a workplace design program. Should such a program be needed, it should be implemented through securing senior management support, providing a variety of training and education opportunities for personnel throughout the organization, and encouraging wide-spread participation in the program.

The processes for measuring each person's (and, collectively, the general population's or workforce's) physical and mental abilities provide a statistical basis for designing suitable workplaces and products. Anthropometry can be applied to designing tasks, tools, and workplaces that minimize the ergonomic hazards associated with manual materials handling, cumulative trauma, machine displays and controls, computer and other office tasks, and human errors stemming from fatigue. Combinations of engineering, administrative, and medical safeguards and controls can be used to correct poor workplace design and to monitor the success of new designs.

Chapter Notes

1. Major portions of this chapter have been adapted from training materials developed by the Liberty Mutual Insurance Group, Boston, MA. That material, copyright Liberty Mutual Insurance Group, is used here with permission. Sections of this chapter that have been drawn from other sources are footnoted accordingly.
2. *Ergonomics: A Practical Guide* (Chicago: National Safety Council, 1988), pp. 2-1 to 2-5.
3. The discussion under this heading is consistent with the recommendations presented in *National Institute for Occupational Safety and Health: Work Practices Guide for Manual Lifting* (DHHA-NIOSH) Pub. No. 81-122 (Washington, DC: Government Printing Office, 1981). The continuing validity of these 1981 recommendations is supported by Stover H. Snook in the paper, "The Control of Low Back Disability: The Role of Management," presented May 17, 1988, at the San Francisco annual meeting of the American Industrial Hygiene Association.
4. Much of the material under this heading is adapted from Stover H. Snook, "Approaches to the Control of Back Pain in Industry: Job Design, Job Placement and Education/Training," *SPINE*, vol. 2, no. 1 (September 1987), pp. 45–59.
5. The material under this heading draws substantially from three sources. The first is Karl H.E. Kroemer, "Ergonomics," *Fundamentals of Industrial Hygiene*, ed. Barbara A. Plog, 3rd ed. (Chicago: National Safety Council, 1988), pp. 283–334. The second is "Human Behavior and Safety," *Accident Prevention Manual for Industrial Operations, Administration and Programs*, 9th ed. (Chicago: National Safety Council, 1988), pp. 223–238. The third is Bruce A. Hertig, "Ergonomics," *Fundamentals of Industrial Hygiene*, ed. Julian B. Olishifski, 2nd ed. (Chicago: National Safety Council, 1979), pp. 401–437.
6. The material under this heading draws on two sources. The first is "Ergonomics—Human Factors Engineering," *Accidents Prevention Manual for Industrial Operations: Administration and Programs*, 9th ed. (Chicago: National Safety Council, 1988), pp. 218–222. The second is Bruce A. Hertig, "Ergonomics," *Fundamentals of Industrial Hygiene*, ed. Julian B. Olishifski, 2nd ed. (Chicago: National Safety Council, 1979), pp. 424–432.
7. The material under this heading is adapted from E.P. Grandjean, "Fatigue," *American Industrial Hygiene Association Journal*, vol. 31, no. 4 (July–August, 1970).
8. The material under this heading is drawn largely from *Accident and Prevention Manual for Industrial Operations, Administration and Programs*, 9th ed. (Chicago: National Safety Council, 1988), pp. 209–222.

CHAPTER 7

Rehabilitation Management

The first objective of preserving human health potential is to *prevent* injury and illness from diminishing the productivity of an organization's employees. When prevention fails, however, preserving human health potential requires *restoring* the health and productivity of those whom injury or illness has temporarily disabled. Returning disabled persons to the best possible state of health increases their value to the organization while improving the quality of their lives. Whenever the benefits of restored health exceed the costs of restoring that health, the employers, the individuals or families, and society as a whole benefit.

Restoring the health and productivity of injured or ill persons involves a process most commonly called rehabilitation. The rehabilitation process encompasses all events that involve the injury or recovery process. This process may or may not completely restore the person's original capabilities. Nonetheless, rehabilitation strives to return as much of a person's pre-injury or pre-illness capacity as is medically and psychologically feasible for the disabled person and economically feasible for the organization financing the rehabilitation. Restoring these capabilities reduces losses—returning employees to work and reducing liability claims for long-term medical treatment and loss of income for the disabled. For this reason, risk management professionals have a great interest in the rehabilitative process, particularly in rehabilitation management decisions about when and how this process is best employed.

Rehabilitation management involves an active planning, directing, and controlling of the rehabilitation process to ensure recovery in a timely, cost-effective manner. Risk control through rehabilitation management is a means for the risk management professional to control the direct and indirect costs of lost productivity when employees are disabled. It is also the means to control the costs of medical treatment and income replacement for others who suffer some injury connected with the organization's premises, products, or activities.

The early identification of and response to such work-related injuries and illnesses directly affect management's ability to control these costs. If controlled promptly, costs can be held down by helping the person recover and return to work faster—especially if he or she is treated at an appropriate facility at a reasonable fee. Although an organization's ability to influence the selection of treatment facilities is usually greater for work-related injuries than for other injuries, any ability to influence the treatment process is a valuable tool for controlling rehabilitative and legal liability costs. The cost/benefit advantages of rehabilitation decrease proportionately to the amount of time that elapses between the onset of the injury or illness and rehabilitation.

This chapter describes how an organization can provide, encourage, and/or facilitate rehabilitative treatment for injured employees and other bodily injury claimants. It also describes the key role the organization's risk management professional should have in rehabilitation activities. Specifically, the ideas in this chapter should enable one to do the following:

- Describe, and give examples of, the nature and benefits of rehabilitation, both for injured persons and for those financially responsible for such injuries.
- Explain and perform the functions of a risk management professional as a catalyst for rehabilitation of the injured.
- Explain the need for, and promote cooperative efforts throughout, the various departments of an organization in making rehabilitation cost-effective for the injured and for the organization.
- Identify and describe how to overcome conditions and forces that can interfere with effective rehabilitation.
- Describe the elements of effective medical management of cases calling for rehabilitation.
- Identify and evaluate the cash flow effects that rehabilitation programs for injured claimants are likely to have on an organization's profitability.

DEFINITION OF REHABILITATION MANAGEMENT

Rehabilitation is the process of restoring an injured and disabled person to his or her highest attainable levels of function and independence in self-care, vocational, and recreational activities. Rehabilitation offers any organization many opportunities to control its costs of bodily injury claims, both employees injuries and illnesses (as discussed in Chapter 5), and other injured claimants (as discussed in Chapter 8).

Rehabilitation may be physical, psychological, or vocational. Physical rehabilitation restores, as far as possible, motor skills impaired by injury or illness. Psychological rehabilitation returns a person, as far as possible, to the presumably healthy mental condition he or she enjoyed before becoming disabled, freeing that person from any loss of confidence or fears that may have stemmed from the disability. Vocational rehabilitation enables a person to return, as fully as possible, to his or her work tasks, and to other productive activities.

These three kinds of rehabilitation are related. Rehabilitation entails not only the physical ability to perform tasks, but also a psychological willingness and ability to do so. It also means that the injured person will have the vocational opportunity to benefit economically from restored capabilities.

Rehabilitation training is the instruction and counseling a disabled person receives on how best to restore or compensate for lost physical abilities, the psychological consequences of disability, and economical productivity in a vocation. Rehabilitation training is the primary function of medical, psychological, vocational, and other rehabilitation professionals. Because rehabilitation management is the main focus of risk management professionals, this facet of the rehabilitation process is discussed more fully in the next section.

Rehabilitation Management

Rehabilitation management is the development and implementation of a plan for rehabilitating an injured person through communication with, negotiation with, and control over all parties likely to influence a disabled person's rehabilitation program. For a disabled employee, rehabilitation management coordinates the efforts of the following people to return that employee to the highest possible level of activity in the least amount of time:

- Risk management and safety personnel,
- Personnel department,
- Disabled person's supervisor,
- Medical personnel from outside and perhaps within the organization,
- Possibly a union representative,
- Possibly legal counsel for the injured,
- Insurance claims person, and
- Injured person and his or her family.

If the disabled person is not an employee, but the organization is responsible for this person's disability, rehabilitation management still involves communication, negotiation, and control, but with more outside people, particularly legal counsel and insurers. In either case, the organization is legally responsible for providing treatment for the injury or disability.

For the organization, rehabilitation management provides an opportunity and a procedure for directing the rehabilitation process and for controlling its costs. When used effectively, it becomes a tool for risk control because it reduces the severity of disability or employee income losses. For instance, it helps to limit the financial costs of incurred claims by (1) avoiding litigation, (2) providing quality medical care, (3) ensuring a prompt return to work, and (4) providing vocational rehabilitation. Rehabilitation management generally has proven to be cost-effective because, as a planned strategic, rather than a reactive response, it reduces surgeries, hospital and treatment costs, legal fees, settlements, lost work time, and disability benefits. In short, when an organization takes control of a rehabilitation case, it is in a better position to direct funds in general, and to demand more quality control from the medical profession.

Rehabilitation management, then, is a strategic process that can be applied to any injury or illness, regardless of its duration. The greatest savings are realized when the process is begun at the onset of the injury or illness. The chances for success decrease proportionately to the amount of time which elapses between the onset of the injury or illness and the time that active rehabilitation management is implemented.

Development of Rehabilitation Management

Rehabilitation management has resulted from advances in rehabilitative medicine and from insurers' and employers' interests in containing medical care costs for work-related and other disabling injuries and illnesses.

Medical Influences Rehabilitation originally addressed the highly specialized medical needs of the catastrophically disabled (spinal cord injury, burns, cerebral trauma, amputation, stroke, polio, and other similar conditions). Research centered on the development of adaptive equipment or devices to make the individual independent in the activities of daily living (dressing, feeding, and other personal care). A main objective was to minimize nursing and attendant care.

As research and medicine progressed, disabled individuals were surviving at increasing rates. A new area within medicine emerged to provide the specialized rehabilitation training and treatment centers needed to address this new patient population. Allied health personnel now are licensed and receive specialized education in the area of rehabilitation. Physicians, nurses, psychologists, occupational and physical therapists, speech therapists, vocational rehabilitation counselors, and activity therapists prepare the disabled individual to return to the workplace. Specialized hospitals and treatment facilities specialize in different disabilities. The treatment techniques developed for a catastrophic population are now applied to an expanding range of disabilities, from orthopedic injuries to psychological trauma and even inborn learning disabilities.

Insurance Influences During recent decades, insurers have recognized rehabilitation as a means to control claims costs. Insurers have added rehabilitation specialists to their staffs, or have contracted with rehabilitation consulting firms, to monitor reasonableness and quality of medical care provided by physicians, hospitals, and other healthcare providers. Insurers paying for workers compensation and other bodily injury claims have developed, independently or by relying on consultants, expertise in evaluation of claimants' conditions, developing job modification, job retraining, and specialized job placement programs. Several insurers have developed in-house rehabilitation programs as part of their claims departments, believing that the insurer's own claim control activities and direction of medical and vocational rehabilitation management reduce claims costs.

Business Influences Employers, both in private industry and government, are the largest single ultimate source of funds to pay for medical care, primarily through employee benefits plans and workers compensation and other bodily injury liability insurance. As "prime consumers," these employees can significantly influence the nature and costs of medical care provided to the disabled through the plans these employers finance.

Business organizations, both public and private, have come to stress rehabilitation in response to legislative and economic concerns. State and federal compensation statutes for both injured employees and automobile accident victims often mandate rehabilitation. In addition, employers have realized that rehabilitation reduces the ultimate total costs of disabilities.

Opportunities for Rehabilitation Management

The variety of injuries a person can suffer provides numerous opportunities for rehabilitation management. Exhibit 7-1 shows just some of these injuries, their related conditions, and appropriate

Exhibit 7-1
Representative Opportunities for Rehabilitation

Type of Injury or Illness	Resulting Condition	Typically Indicated Rehabilitation
Amputation	If the claimant suffers an amputation and is not able to return to his regular job, rehabilitation intervention should be requested. Extended stay in a general care hospital can be avoided by immediate entry into a specialized facility.	Surgical revision for specialized fitting of prosthesis may be necessary; expertise in preparation of the area for prosthetic devices is generally found in hospitals with large prosthetic departments. It may be necessary to modify a job or provide special devices for the claimant to return to employment.
Arthritis	Osteoarthritis: a slowly progressive, degenerative joint disease causing pain, swelling, stiffness, etc. Osteoarthritis is not generally seen in claimants under 40. Long-term pain and physical restrictions frequently make job modifications necessary. Deformities and nonfunctioning joints may sometimes be restored surgically.

Rheumatoid Arthritis: a chronic disease whose cause is unknown, characterized by inflammation, pain, and swelling of the joints accompanied by spasms in adjacent muscles and often leading to deformity of the joints. Rheumatoid arthritis is usually more disabling then osteoarthritis; it causes depression and general fatigue, and requires medication and passive exercise to prevent contractures. Rheumatoid arthritics may have remissions lasting months or years. | Rehabilitation evaluation can determine if medical specialists, therapists, and job modifications are necessary. In advanced stages of the illness, "self-help" devices may allow the arthritic to care for herself or himself independently, rather than using long-term nursing services. Appropriate training and positioning will reduce or prevent future deformities that can limit functional abilities. |

Burns	The claimant's age, burn location, and the possibility of disfigurement determine the seriousness of a burn. For example, a half-dollar sized, third degree acid burn on the arm is not as serious as the same burn on the elbow or face.	Immediately refer burn cases to rehabilitation if it is anticipated that there will be disfiguration or loss of limb motion.
Cancer	The severity of cancer is often determined by the type of tumor and how early it is detected. Remission is often possible through chemotherapy or other treatment methods.	Rehabilitation can assist with coordinating information on treatments and prognosis, and can assist with data gathering for claims to set proper reserves. Because 100% recovery is possible, each case must be evaluated and monitored on its own merits.
Coronary Condition	Myocardial infarction (Heart attack)	Utilization of rehabilitation programs within the hospital setting has been found to significantly increase activity levels and reduce lost work/activity time. A rehabilitation program can be developed to increase activity toward part-time employment. If necessary, job modification or retraining may be recommended to enable the individual to return to full-time employment.
Dermatitis	Irritations to skin, especially hands, face, and lower extremities.	Rehabilitation should be instituted to assess medical treatment and vocational implications.
Eye Injury	Cataracts and detached retina	Appropriate medical care must be obtained, and the claimant's job may have to be restructured or changed. Rehabilitation professionals specializing in visual orientation and related patient mobility can evaluate the claimant and the claimant's job. Special transportation may have to be arranged on a long-term basis.

Fractures	Nonunions may be caused by medical problems warranting rehabilitation. In addition, frequent surgery can cause excessive healing times, inactivity, and emotional problems.	Refer fractures of major, weight-bearing bones as soon as possible. The many medical uncertainties and variables necessitate prompt medical management and rehabilitation.
Herniated Disc	Injury to, or gradual deterioration of, cushioning cartilage between spinal vertebrae, so that these bones run together and pinch nerves that run down legs or arms (depending on whether lower or upper vertebrae are affected).	Immediately refer herniated disc cases confirmed by myelogram, particularly if the claimant declines surgery. Rehabilitation can assist claimant understanding of the injury, pain adjustment, return to work, and can work with the employer. In some cases, alternate forms of surgery may warrant investigation so that the claimant will have a faster recovery and an earlier return to work.
Mental Disorders	These may range from mild emotional fluctuations to more severe depression or other disturbances.	Immediately refer mental or personality disorder cases. Psychotherapists use many types of therapies, some of which are greatly protracted, and few of which have any bearing on the claimant's ability to return to work. Rehabilitation will develop cost-effective treatment goals that emphasize employee return to work.
Spinal Cord and Neurological Disorders	Severe neurological injuries often result in subjective complaints, such as vertigo, loss of sensation, blurred vision, and behavior changes.	Immediately refer spinal cord and neurological disorder cases. General-care hospitals typically are not adequately equipped or staffed to handle these injuries. The claimant should be transferred to an accredited facility where special medical expertise and innovative procedures are available. Specialized physical restoration facilities are necessary for these injuries to avoid long-term complications and costs.

Sprain and Strain (Back and Neck)

Frequent physician visits, large pain medication or muscle relaxant dosages, or indications of surgical intervention are signals to refer back and neck strains or sprains to rehabilitation. Such injuries involve both objective and subjective musculoskeletal symptoms.

The claimant's activities will have to be evaluated and perhaps part time, lighter or sedentary work will be necessary.

Stroke (Cerebral Vascular Accidents — CVA)

Stroke can result from disease or trauma, and can produce residual functional disabilities.

Because of the complexity of CVA cases, quickly obtain as much medical information as possible and request rehabilitation.

Referrals: generally, CVA cases can be helped by rehabilitation only if the evaluation reveals obvious functional disabilities. Many CVA cases produce disabilities of a minor order when compared to other types of injuries and disorders. If there are only minor disabilities that neither affect high cognitive and sensory functions nor produce significant limb weakness, the claimant generally will recover without rehabilitation.

However, if functional disabilities are obvious, medical and vocational rehabilitation are vital. These services and an appropriate return-to-work plan all work to control costs.

rehabilitative procedures. In any rehabilitation case, early involvement by the organization ensures that management will establish and maintain control of the case—the administrative procedures, the persons involved, and the costs. Early involvement also encourages a good rapport among the involved persons and prevents the injured or disabled persons from developing equally disabling psychological reactions associated with the injury or disability. The failure to become involved at the outset of a case also can result in a prolonged recovery for the injured person, a loss in production for the organization, and related financial losses for both parties.

Exhibit 7-2 more specifically describes an opportunity for rehabilitation management and how that opportunity can be seized. The exhibit presents the case of a federal liability insurer who provides rehabilitation management for an injured youth. The case is typical of many opportunities for returning disabled persons to productive lives while controlling the costs of their treatment. Also illustrated are the key elements for success in physical and vocational rehabilitation, as listed below:

1. Early intervention: immediate and appropriate medical care was initiated.
2. Prompt hospital transfer: the boy was immediately transferred to a hospital that specialized in microsurgery.
3. Supervised functional treatment program: a comprehensive treatment program, including attention to skills like those involved in the boy's job, was initiated to prepare him to return to work.
4. Employment options: modifications of equipment and tools, reassignment to a less physically demanding job, trial return to work, and part-time work were explored so that if full function were not regained, the return-to-work process could still proceed. This would reduce lost work time and disability benefits for an individual who was originally anticipated to have a permanent and total disability.
5. Communication: regular, ongoing communication and clarification of information enabled all parties involved in the case to participate in a strategic planning process. A rehabilitation consultant submitted monthly reports that identified potential problems that could be resolved through negotiation.

RISK MANAGEMENT'S RESPONSIBILITY IN REHABILITATION

In most organizations, the risk management professional is in the

Exhibit 7-2
Successful Rehabilitation of an Injured Hand

An eighteen-year-old friend of the owner of a service station volunteered to help the owner repair a customer's automobile in the service garage of the station. Due to a faulty switch on a powered cutting tool they were using for this repair work, the volunteer had the index, middle, and ring fingers of his right hand severed just beyond the metacarpal joints (where the finger joins the hand). After calling the ambulance, the service station owner telephoned his general liability insurer, whose claims representative initiated rehabilitation management from the outset. The rehabilitation management firm, which regularly worked as a consultant to this insurer, received a "hot line" referral which guaranteed immediate monitoring by medical personnel. An air ambulance was arranged, and the boy was flown from the rural area to a university medical center. Following several hours of microsurgery, the fingers were reunited.

To rehabilitate the hand through extensive occupational and physical therapy, the rehabilitation consultant began communication among the boy's employer (a supermarket chain, for which he performed delivery truck maintenance), his physician, the insurer's claims staff. Their objective, even while the boy was still in the hospital, was to develop and to initiate a plan to return the boy to work as soon as he was physically able.

For this purpose, as well as to develop contingency plans if the hand did not regain full strength or range of motion, the equipment with which the boy worked, his workplace, and possible tool modifications and alternative jobs were explored. Part-time and trial return to work options also were investigated so that the boy could be returned to the mainstream of employment at the earliest opportunity.

To counter the frequent financial disincentive to return to regular employment after a disabling injury, the boy's treatment program incorporated simulated job tasks so that all the movements required to operate the machinery with which he regularly worked could be practiced in a supervised environment. Nondirective psychological counseling also enabled the boy to more fully understand his own responses to his injury and to focus his plans on continuing his career rather than letting him focus on the potentially devastating effects his injury could have produced.

Because the boy had been practicing actual job tasks, he was not afraid to return to using machinery similar to that which had mangled his hand. Following four months' intensive treatment, the boy received a medical release to return to his job which his employer, immediately following the injury, had assured him would be awaiting his recovery.

best position to understand the complexity of rehabilitation, and therefore, to coordinate a rehabilitation program. Rehabilitation is complex for many reasons, but one of great concern to risk management professionals is the interdisciplinary problem that arises when so many people—family members, insurance claims personnel, attorneys, and medical personnel—have legitimate, but often conflicting, interests in the recovery of the injured or disabled person. Because a risk management professional deals with these and numerous other people in many loss-related situations, he or she is best suited to organizing the diverse interests and efforts in a rehabilitation case.

Within the organization, rehabilitation management must be seen as an interdepartmental activity because losses and expenses associated with disabled claimants impact the entire organization. The responsibility of the risk management professional is to coordinate the activities of the various departments that may become directly or indirectly involved with the treatment of disabled employees or other claimants. These departments include personnel, claims, legal, and medical departments. In many cases, labor unions are also involved in the process. The following sections describe the roles of each department and of the risk management professional in rehabilitation management.

Personnel Department

The personnel department can be an invaluable resource in rehabilitation management. As an early and effective employee disability loss prevention measure, an organization's personnel selection process should be evaluated by the personnel department. Each job should be functionally analyzed, and applicant risk factors carefully evaluated so that applicants can be, in part, selected on the basis of their physical ability. The purpose of this selection procedure is to decrease the likelihood of employee disability losses due to physical "un-fitness." For example, an applicant with previous back or hand injuries should be evaluated for his or her appropriateness for a materials handling position. Other risk factors that should be considered include obesity, emphysema, cardiac conditions, or diabetes.

Job evaluation while a rehabilitation case is in progress is also an important function of the personnel department. Each job description should be reviewed to ensure that it includes specifications for the range of motion, strength, and dexterity needed to perform a given task or tasks. These specifications can then be used to determine if a formerly disabled employee has the skills needed to return to work. Employees, too, can be encouraged to participate in prevention and wellness programs.

Finally, because employee injury and illness records are often best maintained in the personnel department, the risk management professional has a reliable, complete source of information with which to analyze and track the organization's disability loss experience. This analysis helps the risk management professional to identify the needs and opportunities for rehabilitation as a means of controlling the disability loss exposure. To this end, the risk management professional should develop information with respect to the following areas:

- Major types of disabling injuries and illnesses for which the organization has been legally responsible and the incidence and severity of these injuries,
- Average amount of time lost and expenses incurred for each such injury,
- Types of cases that have gone to litigation, and
- Procedures the organization has followed in securing and monitoring rehabilitation for those who have been disabled.

Claims Department

To benefit the organization and the disabled claimant through effective rehabilitation, the organization's claims department should develop procedures that (1) provide or encourage rehabilitation wherever medically warranted and (2) monitor the progress of rehabilitation to make sure that it is both appropriate and not abused. To this end, the risk management professional should work with the organization's (or its insurer's) claims personnel to achieve the following objectives:

- The choice of medical/rehabilitative facilities and personnel is appropriate for treatment of the disability as diagnosed.
- Wherever consistent with the quality of care, the most cost-effective treatment facilities and personnel are chosen.
- Diagnosis and treatment plans targeted toward the patient's discharge and return to daily activity are developed on a timely basis.
- Appropriate medical/rehabilitative documentation is developed to justify the diagnosis and treatment plan as well as any temporary/permanent restrictions on the patient's daily activities.
- Unnecessarily extended stays in hospitals or other costly facilities are minimized.
- Cooperative, positive communication among the patient, medical/rehabilitative personnel, claims personnel, the employer, and the patient's family are begun promptly and continue.

- Any controversies among such persons are resolved as promptly and as amicably as possible, both to speed rehabilitation and to minimize litigation.
- The patient's options for return to daily activity—in his or her previous position, a modified job assignment with the same employer, or in a new job assignment with a different employer—are actively and concretely explored at the earliest feasible date.
- The organization, all interested insurers and legal counsel, and all medical/rehabilitative personnel treating the patient are kept informed of the patient's medical condition, progress, and treatment plans.
- Specific rehabilitation guidelines should be developed for specific injuries or disabilities.
- Criteria should be developed as to when the risk management professional and other senior management should be made aware of potentially severe claims.

Legal Department

Rehabilitation of injured claimants can be very effective in reducing the amounts an organization must pay ("mitigating legal damages," in legal terminology) to those for whose disability the organization is responsible. Yet, the organization's or its insurer's legal counsel may not remain mindful of the rehabilitation possibilities in many injury or illness cases. Therefore, the organization's risk management professional should make a point of requesting rehabilitation evaluations to provide measurable and objective data on the functional capabilities, rather than the disabilities, of claimants. Expert witnesses, treatment results, and vocational testing provide objective data as to transferrable job skills and job aptitudes. Rehabilitation programs also should be suggested during settlement negotiations for bodily injury claims, particularly those that call for periodic payments for medical expenses the claimant may incur in the future.

Medical Personnel in the Organization

Medical directors, plant and occupational health nurses, and allied health personnel should be utilized to develop medical resource information for the organization in preparation for when this information may be needed for dealing with particular disabilities. Such wellness activities as cancer screening, stop-smoking clinics, stress management programs, blood pressure screening, and nutritional counseling help identify the earliest symptoms of disabling conditions, signaling the need for preventive or rehabilitative care. In addition, an organization's own medical personnel, once adequately oriented toward rehabilitation, may well be the best qualified experts in modifying particular jobs within the organization so that they are less likely to cause injury or can be performed with less effort.

Labor Unions

Labor union officials or other employee representatives should be made aware of the full cost of disabilities to both the organization and its employees so that they will understand that it is mutually beneficial to return the disabled to some form of productive employment as soon as possible. Labor and management should be allies in these efforts.

Reductions in lost work time, disability benefits, insurance premiums, experience ratings, litigation, and settlement fees can be realized if employers work with unions to develop aggressive, early return-to-work programs. Options such as trial/return to work, part-time/return to work, and job modification can promote an early return to work for disabled employees. These options can also assist in obtaining medical release-to-work statements.

CASE MANAGEMENT STRATEGY

A general strategy for managing rehabilitation cases requires careful planning of the organization's response to disabling accidents. The plan should anticipate and overcome the administrative barriers that sometimes block otherwise sound rehabilitation plans.

Planning the Initial Response

Rehabilitation management actually begins before an injury or an illness develops or is reported. That is, there should be policies and procedures in place to address the needs of an injured or disabled employee. By following these procedures, the risk management professional can better control the case, monitoring medical care and other services that might otherwise raise the costs of rehabilitation. The following three subsections describe the philosophy and methods that guide an organization's response to a rehabilitation case toward a humane and cost-effective recovery.

Initial Reaction to an Injury/Disability A misguided initial reaction by the injured person or the organization to an injury or disability can worsen that injury and increase the severity of the disability loss. For instance, there is often a tendency to ignore the fact that an injury has occurred—a response that can lead to increased costs, greater physical damage, and litigation. However, if guidelines for initial reactions to injury are established as part of the rehabilitation process, it is more likely that an organization will respond correctly, using appropriate funds and resources to return the injured person to work as soon as possible. The following are three mandatory initial steps in an organized and appropriate response to an injury or disability:

1. The injured person should be given immediate medical attention and urged to remain still. An initial injury may be aggravated if the injured person remains active.
2. Medical personnel on the premises should examine the individual and document the following:
    * location and quality of the pain,
    * positions (bending, sitting, and so on) that the injured person can and cannot assume,
    * appearance of skeletal alignment in the affected area, and
    * muscle tone around the affected area by observation and palpation (touching) or feeling.
3. If a first aid-trained person is responsible for the initial examination, a referral to a physician or emergency room should be made.

Initial Disposition The second phase in an organized initial response to an injury is making the disposition. It is imperative that the initial observations discussed above be documented. This should be done by a properly credentialed person as soon as possible after the injury. This is the employer's first line of defense in controlling the recovery process. If the organization does not document its immediate actions and observations with regard to the injured person, there is the chance that other physical problems not related to that injury will be associated with that injury, thus increasing the employer's liability for compensation.

After examining the injured person, a decision must be made concerning his or her disposition. Under no circumstances should the individual be allowed to continue his or her daily activities while still in pain. Serious injury can occur if the person continues to work at this time. The individual should be encouraged to see a physician who is qualified to provide a balanced program of medication, rest, and activity. Should the individual refuse to see a physician at this time, the industrial nurse or designee must ensure that the person assumes a position that rests the affected area until the pain resolves. Before allowing the individual to return to the job or to leave the treatment area, a repeat examination should be done. The person should not be sent back to the job site until he or she has performed all of the motions necessary for the job (i.e., bending, stooping, and so on) without observable signs or complaints of pain.

Referral to a Physician When a referral to a physician is necessary, or when the disabled person has seen a physician on his or her own, the industrial nurse or designees should request the following information:

- Results of X-ray,
- Diagnosis,
- Medications prescribed,
- Recommended rest and activity,
- Anticipated return to work date, and
- Physician's specialty.

This information is essential in evaluating the potential success of the treatment program and will allow the employer to plan the future course of action. It is at this point that control of the information and the treatment program must be established, either by the employer or the claimsperson. For certain diagnoses, a rehabilitation consultant may be requested to become involved. Furthermore, this information should be collected within the first two to five days after the injury.

After the initial response, the next step in rehabilitation case management is to anticipate any administrative barriers to the disabled person's recovery. In doing so, those involved in the rehabilitation process can plan ways to handle these barriers.

Administrative Barriers to Rehabilitation

An essential part of rehabilitation management is anticipating and overcoming administrative barriers to effective rehabilitation. The risk management professional coordinating an organization's rehabilitation program needs to be aware of these barriers in order to recognize when one or more of them is blocking progress on a given case. There are two kinds of barriers: (1) general barriers that may arise in any case and (2) disability-specific barriers.

General Barriers to Rehabilitation Once rehabilitative treatment has begun, it is important that it progresses well. Otherwise, the disabled person will not achieve the expected recovery, and the organization will not achieve the financial objectives of reducing its overall long-term cost of the disability claim. There are a number of general barriers that can impede the progress of a rehabilitation program. The risk management professional and other managers involved in the case need to be aware of these barriers or "danger signs." While no one of these signs necessarily signals the failure or mismanagement of the program, their presence calls for corrective action, i.e., intervention by anyone having responsibility for rehabilitation management. These barriers are described below.

Extended Hospitalization. Seven days or more is considered extended hospitalization. This may be the result of a lack in the coordination of medical care and/or poor discharge planning. Is the hospital stay extended because of a scheduling problem? Could the disabled person receive comparable care by a home health care nurse or be seen on an outpatient basis? Discharge planning is also essential for the patient's continued recovery following hospitalization. Readmission to a hospital often is the result of medical complications and a lack of family education about good home care.

Uncoordinated Medical Treatment. Medical care involves not only physician's services, but also services provided by nurses, occupational and physical therapists, psychologists, and social workers. Coordinating medical treatment means (1) scheduling each service or treatment so that it will work most effectively and (2) establishing joint treatment goals among the health care personnel. If this does not happen, it is likely that the recovery will be longer and the costs greater. The following are some examples of uncoordinated medical treatment:

- Duplicate diagnostic tests because results have not been properly recorded or made available to all involved health care personnel,
- Conflicting treatment programs and medications because there is no primary physician who coordinates the many specialists who often contribute to a case,
- "Doctor shopping" by the patient because he or she may not be properly guided in seeking appropriate care,
- The use of inpatient care when outpatient care would be appropriate, and
- Potentially harmful results if treatment is not carefully monitored.

In addition to ensuring that medical treatment is coordinated, the risk management professional should also ensure that the organization's (or insurer's) claims department requests copies of the treatment records. The organization, too, can provide valuable information to the treatment team on the physical requirements of a job. Job-simulated tasks can be included within the treatment program and will be beneficial both psychologically and physically to the disabled person.

Extensive Medication. The extensive use of medication should always be evaluated. Patients may make faster recoveries as the drug regime is upgraded or combined with other treatment modalities, such as exercise. It is also possible that medication can be changed or reduced.

Lack of Clear Diagnosis. All medical providers should be required to establish and document a diagnosis. A documented diagnosis is essential in justifying treatment planning, as well as the time and cost parameters for medical care and consequent claim reserves. A generalized diagnosis, or the lack of a clear diagnosis, may be a red flag. This can result in poor treatment planning and the need to revise the plan—which ultimately increases the costs of rehabilitation.

Lack of Clear Prognosis. A prognosis is the prospect of recovery expected for a patient. The diagnosis and prognosis are equally important and should be consistent, for they are the bases of all further treatment planning. If a medical provider is unable to give a prognosis, the type and quality of care provided should be questioned. If a prognosis is not reached on schedule, the treatment regimen, the treatment goals, or the diagnosis may have been inappropriate.

Round-the-Clock Nursing Care. Nursing care may not be appropriate or necessary. The patient or a family member may be trained in any necessary medical procedures. Adaptive or "self-help" devices may be designed to assist with all activities of daily living. A home health nurse may only need to monitor a program rather than to supervise a patient directly. Inappropriate attendant care also often promotes patient dependency and lengthens the recovery period.

Nongoal-Oriented Physical Therapy. Rehabilitation is an active process. Any treatment program requires ongoing evaluation and upgrading in response to treatment results. If a therapy program is not upgraded at least every six weeks, this may be a red flag signaling medical mismanagement or inappropriate treatment planning.

Lack of Discharge Planning. Discharge planning should be initiated when the injured person is admitted to a medical facility. The treatment team should establish the steps that will be taken to lead to discharging the patient. The time of discharge should also be specified. The treatment team must be made aware of the factors to consider at discharge: local medical resources, attendant/family care, transportation, and employment. Patients often are discharged from the hospital without coordination between the hospital and family in following through on treatment procedures. The family may require training as well as counseling.

Lack of Specific Date for Return to Work. For anyone who was employed before a disabling accident, definite plans for return to some form of employment should be made as soon as the disabled person's prognosis becomes clear. Such plans are crucial to the patient's outlook, expectation of recovery, and optimism in cooperating in his or her rehabilitation training. Regardless of whether the patient was an employee of the financially responsible organization or some other organization, his or her employer should become actively involved in planning the return to work; anticipating, and sharing with the patient, the job duties he or she will have upon discharge and any need to redefine the patient's job duties or to redesign the physical features of the workplace or the equipment the patient will use upon return to work. An employer's reluctance to accept the return of a formerly disabled employee, if not corrected, can "sour" that employee's entire rehabilitation efforts.

Disability-Specific Barriers to Rehabilitation If an organization's risk management professional was not already aware of the common types of injuries or illnesses that strike employees on the job, this professional will become familiar with them as he or she becomes more involved in rehabilitation management. The disabilities to which the organization's employees are particularly prone will become well known to this professional so that, in time, he or she should become almost as expert in their treatment and rehabilitation as are many members of the medical/rehabilitative community. To illustrate how such expertise in particular disabilities can facilitate rehabilitation management, the following sections describe the medical nature of, and the potential administrative barriers to, rehabilitation for two of the most common work-related disabilities: carpal tunnel syndrome and back injury.

Carpal Tunnel Syndrome. Persons performing repetitive tasks that require fine hand and wrist movements—for example, garment, automotive, and other assembly-line employees; postal workers; assemblers of electronic components; and musicians—quite often suffer a gradual compression of a particular nerve that serves the wrist and hand muscles. This nerve passes down the arm and through a narrow opening among the bones of the wrist known as the "carpal tunnel." A person whose nerve is thus compressed experiences numbness, clumsiness, tingling, and burning in the wrist, hand, and fingers, and dry, shiny skin on the palm of the afflicted hand.

The incidence of carpal tunnel syndrome increases for employees exposed to cold environments and vibrations, is two to ten times more frequent in women than in men, and is more common among those experiencing personal or job-related psychological stress. An early sign of carpal tunnel syndrome is an employee's attempt to alleviate numbness and tingling by rapid shaking of the hands; advanced carpal tunnel syndrome makes fine hand work impossible.

Carpal tunnel syndrome is best diagnosed by examination by an orthopedic surgeon, who normally will prescribe splinting or other immobilization of the afflicted wrist for six to eight weeks. This will allow the irritated, inflamed nerve to rest and recuperate, with little or no medication needed during this period. If rest does not alleviate the numbness and tingling, surgery may be indicated to widen the carpal tunnel. This would be followed by light physical and occupational therapy to restore normal hand movement.

Some administrative "danger signals" that *may* indicate poor rehabilitation management of a person suffering from carpal tunnel syndrome include the following:

- Extensive use of diagnostic X-rays or a diagnosis of tendonitis.
- The selection as the primary treating physician of a chiropractor, osteopath, or other practitioner specializing in treatment that emphasizes physical manipulation.
- Immediate surgery.
- A recommendation for immediate therapy that emphasizes exercising the afflicted wrist, hand, or fingers.
- Any prescription of drugs beyond what is needed to counter any pain following surgery.
- Return to work arrangements that involve:
  - return to the same job without physical modification of the job or restriction on the employee's physical activities,
  - return to any job that involves repetitive twisting or pounding activities, and
  - return to any job without full vocational evaluation of the employee.

Back Injury. Pain in the lower back can often extend into the legs and may be accompanied by cold or warm sensations localized in the back or legs, back stiffness or tightness, and popping or cracking sensations in the back. Back injury is the most common work-related disabling injury in the United States and probably in the world. The spinal column typically is the weakest portion of the human skeleton. The lower portion of the back most frequently is injured through improper body mechanics while lifting, pushing, pulling, turning, stooping, or squatting, especially if the object is heavy; falling or attempting to avoid falling; being hit by a moving object while standing still; and prolonged sitting or standing in any fixed position that strains a particular portion of the back and, over a period of years, causes that portion to deteriorate. Many back injuries occur gradually and do not stem from a single traumatic event; a person suffering genuine back pain may not be able to identify the accident or other incident that brought on the pain.

Other than pain, a variety of symptoms may characterize back injury: the reduced ability to cough, sneeze, or eliminate bodily wastes; reduced range of motion in the back, pelvis, and legs; a pronounced change in gait; and numbness in some portion of the back or in one or both legs.

There is no single proper regimen for treating all forms of back pain. Successful forms of treatment include doing nothing except encouraging the employee to return to work, appropriate drugs (for relaxation, reduced inflammation, or reduced anxiety), bed rest for up to three weeks, restricted activity and modified job duties, inpatient or outpatient physical therapy, and surgery (when orthopedically indicated or as a last resort).

Despite this diversity of treatment, there are a number of fairly universal indicators of poor medical/rehabilitative management of a back injury. The following are just some examples:

- Diagnosis based only on the observations of a medically unqualified practitioner.
- The absence of a physical examination that does not include at least:
  - appropriate diagnostic X-rays,
  - tests that eliminate organic diseases, congenital or pre-existing deformities, or traumatic injury to internal organs as the cause(s) of the pain,
  - a complete medical and family history of the patient, and
  - full range of motion testing of all the patient's extremities.
- Excessive initial medical tests without clear clinical evidence of back injury.
- Recommendations for surgery before more conservative treatments have been tried.
- Excessive medications.
- Physical or occupational therapy that does not:
  - have defined goals,
  - show a pattern of graded, progressive activity, or
  - include active, as well as passive, treatment for periods longer than two weeks.
- Absence of a detailed evaluation of the patient's ability to perform typical daily activities and job-related physical activities.

FINANCIAL EVALUATION OF REHABILITATION PROGRAMS

The rehabilitation of disabled employees and other claimants, in addition to fulfilling humanitarian objectives and demonstrating good citizenship, also usually can be justified as a sound financial investment—generating an acceptable rate of return—for the organization financing that rehabilitation. By investing funds now in the rehabilitation of a disabled claimant, the organization typically can expect to receive future benefits in the forms of reduced future outflows for medical treatment and income replacement benefits as the disabled person recovers more promptly and/or more fully than without rehabilitation. If the disabled person is an employee of the organization, an additional benefit is the value of the output the employee can be expected to produce in the interval between the time he or she actually returns to work and the time he or she would have returned without rehabilitation.

These two types of financial benefits are analytically comparable to the benefits the organization would derive from investing in, say, a fire detection/suppression system that could be expected to reduce its future outflows to repair fire damage. For fire damage that otherwise would have been sufficiently severe to cause a temporary shutdown, the system would hasten the day of reopening by lessening that fire damage.

As detailed in the closing chapters of the ARM 54 text, *Essentials of the Risk Management Process,* a sprinkler system can be evaluated financially by comparing (1) the present value of the reduced fire losses (or other cash savings that are, in effect, cash inflows) attributable to the sprinkler with (2) the initial cost of the sprinkler (a cash outflow). If the present value of the reduction in fire losses (or the present value of other cash savings, such as lowered insurance premiums) is greater than the present value of the required investment (the cost of the sprinkler) when both are discounted at the lowest acceptable internal rate of return, then the sprinkler can be expected to raise the organization's profitability or operating efficiency. On the other hand, if the present value of the required cash outflow is greater than the present value of the cash inflows when both are discounted at the minimum acceptable internal rate of return, then investing in the sprinkler would not be financially advantageous to the organization.

Logic of Evaluation

The investment analysis that is true for sprinklers is also true for the rehabilitation of a disabled person (or for any other investment under consideration) when evaluated strictly from the organization's financial perspective. In the absence of legal requirements (such as the demands of a workers compensation statute) or other constraints, financial considerations dictate investing rehabilitation only if the expected present value of cash inflows exceeds the expected present value of cash outflows from that rehabilitation.

The cash inflows from rehabilitating a disabled person equal the sum of (1) reductions in future outflows for medical treatment and income replacement benefits for the disabled person and (2) if the disabled person is an employee of the organization, the value of the added output the employee can be expected to produce in the interval between the time he or she actually returns to work and the time he or she would have returned to work without rehabilitation. For proper decision making, these cash inflows and outflows both need to be expressed as present values, discounted at the organization's minimum acceptable internal rate of return.

The pattern of cash inflows and outflows attributable to investing in rehabilitation differs in three significant ways from the pattern of cashflows from investing in a sprinkler system. First, the outflows for rehabilitation normally are periodic payments to providers of rehabilitation services, not single, one-time-only payments for equipment like a sprinkler system. (However, rehabilitation programs can also call for one-time major outflows—for example, to equip a disabled person's home or to modify the person's job site.) Thus, the cash outflows for rehabilitation usually need to be expressed as the present value of a *stream of payments*. With rehabilitation, there probably is some immediate outflow, but it is almost certainly only the first of a series of payments.

The second difference is that cash inflows from rehabilitation will not begin immediately. Unlike a sprinkler system that begins to reduce the expected value of fire losses from the day it is installed, rehabilitation of a disabled person cannot be expected to generate benefits for the organization until the rehabilitation training has had time to take effect—that is, until (1) the disabled person's medical expenses or income replacement benefits are reduced below what they would have been without rehabilitation and/or (2) the disabled person returns to productive employment sooner than if there had been no rehabilitation. Hence, unlike sprinklers, rehabilitation produces deferred, rather than immediate, cash inflows for the organization.

Third, the cash inflows from a sprinkler system usually can be expected to continue for the life of the system, but the cash inflows to an organization financing rehabilitation will cease when the disabled person normally would have reached, without rehabilitation, the same level of function that rehabilitation can achieve. To illustrate, suppose rehabilitation will return a once-disabled person to full productivity and eliminate his or her need for medical care after two years' treatment, and that full recovery would take nine years without rehabilitation. The cash inflows from rehabilitation then consist of what the organization (1) would have paid in income replacement and medical expense benefits and (2) would have lost in the employee's unrealized output during the third through ninth years of disability that, without rehabilitation, would have been necessary. Thus, for this organization, the cash inflows attributable to this rehabilitation are the sum of the present values of (1) the benefits it will not have to pay and (2) the productive output of the once-disabled employee it will receive for seven years—both beginning not immediately, but two years hence.

Illustrative Evaluation

To illustrate how rehabilitating a disabled person can raise the present value of an organization's net cash flows (and thus its profitability or operating efficiency), assume that an outside rehabilitation consultant has recommended that the organization invest $25,000 now, $20,000 one year from now, and $20,000 two years hence to rehabilitate one of its employees who has been injured in a boating accident not related to employment. The consultant estimates that this rehabilitation will enable the employee to recover fully and return to work after two years. Without rehabilitation, the consultant estimates, the employee will recover much more slowly and would not be able to return to any kind of work for nine years. For each year this employee is disabled, the organization currently employing him is obligated to pay him $15,000 a year in income replacement benefits plus, the organization's personnel department estimates, $3,000 a year in medical expenses—a total of $18,000 annually. (Note that these amounts and the following computations ignore, for simplicity, such factors as the subjective value of this employee's output during the seven years' additional productive employment the rehabilitation will provide, income tax considerations for both the organization and the employee, indirect financial and psychological benefits to the employee, and the internal administrative costs of rehabilitation management for the organization.)

Should the organization agree to pay for this rehabilitation—that is, should it pay $25,000 now and $20,000 at the end of each of the next two years in order to save the $18,000 a year in income replacement and medical expense benefits in each year of the third through ninth years if the employee were not rehabilitated? Exhibit 7-3 demonstrates that this question can be answered by determining and evaluating the cash

Exhibit 7-3
Illustrative Present Values of Cashflows from Rehabilitation Program

	Time	Undiscounted Payments	PV Factor (12% assumed)	Present Value
Outflows	Now	$25,000	1.000	$25,000
	1 year hence	20,000	0.893	17,860
	2 years hence	20,000	0.797	15,940
	Totals:	$65,000		$58,800
Inflows	3 years hence	$18,000	0.712	$12,816
	4 years hence	18,000	0.636	11,448
	5 years hence	18,000	0.567	10,206
	6 years hence	18,000	0.507	9,126
	7 years hence	18,000	0.452	8,136
	8 years hence	18,000	0.404	7,272
	9 years hence	18,000	0.361	6,498
	Totals:	$126,000		$65,502

Net Present Value at 12%
$65,502 — $58,800 = $6,702

flows for the organization that this rehabilitation program is expected to generate. (To demonstrate the principles involved without overly complicating the computations, this example assumes that (1) payments are made or received at the end of each year rather than in monthly or other periodic installments throughout the year and (2) the estimates of the rehabilitation consultant and the personnel department prove to be accurate.)

The left side of the exhibit and the first column of amounts summarize the presumed timing and actual, undiscounted amounts of the cash inflows and outflows the organization will have from the present until the disabled employee presumably would recover without any rehabilitation, if it agrees to finance this rehabilitation now. (If, without rehabilitation, this employee had no prognosis for recovery, these computations would be continued for all the years until the earlier of his death or planned retirement, when the employer's obligation to provide income replacement and medical expense benefits would terminate.)

The next column of present value factors shows the present value of $1 to be paid or received at the end of each of the respective years, when discounted at the 12 percent minimum internal rate of return the organization is assumed to be willing to accept. (For example, the 0.797 shown for two years hence in the "Present Value Factor" column means that, discounted at 12 percent, $1 to be received at the end of two years has a present value of 79.7 cents. This is because 79.7 cents invested now at 12 percent will grow to 89.3 cents at the end of the first year and, if left invested, to $1 in two years.)

The organization's cash outflows and inflows are computed separately for each year. This procedure prevents confusion and allows for situations in which the outflows or inflows are more varied from year to year, so that each year's flow must be separately discounted. These computations require tables of present values of single payments and of streams of equal annual payments discounted at various rates, which are presented as Exhibits 1A-1 and 1A-2 in the Appendix to Chapter 1. The *factors* in the "Present Value Factor" column in Exhibit 7-3 are excerpted from Exhibit 1A-1.

Weighting the actual cash outflows and inflows by their respective present value factors permits accurate comparisons among, and calculations with, payments and receipts occurring at different times. (Note that $1 received or paid in the present has a present value of 1.000—no discounting is required here.) Thus, the present value of the three cash outflows for this rehabilitation program is a total of $58,800. The cash inflows (from savings in the form of $18,000 yearly income replacement and medical expense benefits made unnecessary at the end of the third through ninth years) have a present value of $65,502, giving this particular rehabilitation program a net present value of $6,702. Therefore, this particular investment in rehabilitation can be expected to generate more than the 12 percent the organization requires of its other investments and, consequently, will add to the organization's profitability or operating efficiency.

This analysis is not intended to demonstrate that rehabilitation is always financially advantageous. If, for example, the initial outflows for rehabilitating the disabled employee had been $50,000 instead of $25,000, and if all other assumptions had remained the same, the net present value of this rehabilitation program, discounted at 12 percent, would have been negative.

The financial evaluation technique illustrated here, cost-benefit analysis, is subject to two potential weaknesses in measuring benefits:

1. Differences in medical results between any two patients may be difficult to express accurately as different monetary "amounts of benefit" from rehabilitation.
2. Discounting to "present values" medical results that require different periods to achieve may make a more complete eventual

medical recovery appear less attractive than shorter-term, but medically less successful, treatments.

To illustrate the first difficulty, a given rehabilitation regimen may well achieve different degrees of success for different patients—one patient may reach a higher level of performance simply because he or she was less seriously injured or was more diligent or cooperative than another patient during rehabilitation. Is there a sense in which the first patient's rehabilitation generated greater "benefits" than that of the second patient? If so, what dollar amount properly reflects this difference in "benefits" achieved?

The second difficulty stems from differences in the timing of "benefits"—different periods over which different levels of medical recovery can be achieved. Cost-benefit analysis requires that all future benefits be discounted to present values, regardless of whether these benefits can be achieved in, say, three months or five years. Because of this discounting, those medical results that rehabilitation generates only after several years have a lower present value than do shorter-term results, even though the more delayed results may represent a more complete recovery and, therefore, be medically preferable.

Both of these potential difficulties can be reduced through an evaluation procedure that looks at "benefits" only in medical terms, without seeking to place dollar values on them. This approach, called "cost-effectiveness analysis" rather than "cost-benefit analysis," assumes that the goal of all rehabilitation is to restore a disabled person to his or her fullest potential of self-care, mobility, communication, and cognitive activities. At the completion of a patient's rehabilitation program (when the patient's maximum achievable performance has been attained), the patient's performance before and after rehabilitation are measured, and the difference becomes the collective "gain" as a result of rehabilitation. Each medical "gain" can then be compared with the dollar cost of achieving that gain—either for one patient over separate periods of time or for several patients during the same time period. Those rehabilitation measures which generate the highest cost-effectiveness ratio of "gains" divided by cost of rehabilitation can then be deemed the most beneficial.

SUMMARY

Rehabilitation means restoring an injured or disabled person to his or her highest attainable level of functioning and independence in self care, vocational, and recreational activities. It offers any organization many opportunities to control the costs of bodily injury claims, employee injuries and illnesses (discussed in Chapter 4), and other injured claimants (discussed in Chapter 8). Because of its wide applicability, humanitarian appeal, and financial value in claims control, rehabilitation is becoming an increasingly significant loss reduction tool. Its continued development is made possible both through advances in rehabilitative medicine and the support of liability insurers and business executives.

Rehabilitation management is the development and implementation of a plan to return an injured or disabled person to work. It depends not only on medical treatment, but also on communication and coordination between all persons who are likely to influence the injured person's recovery, including claims, legal, health care personnel, and often union representatives. The objective is to create the best environment for a speedy, cost-effective, and psychologically beneficial recovery.

Rehabilitation management also establishes guidelines for the nature and timing of health care and other services. These guidelines provide a basis for monitoring and evaluating the progress of any specific rehabilitation program. Sound rehabilitation management also recognizes and attempts to overcome the general and disability-specific barriers to an efficient, effective recovery.

Rehabilitation management usually can be supported on financial, as well as medical and humanitarian grounds. In many cases, an organization that would otherwise have to pay income replacement benefits and medical expenses to, or on behalf of, a disabled person will find that investing in rehabilitative services for that person will speed his or her recovery and return to work, thus ending the disability and medical expense payments. For the organization, therefore, the investment in rehabilitation adds to the present value of its net cash flows, enhancing its profitability or operating efficiency.

Index

A

Absorption, *240*
Access, building/facility, *194*
Access to computer software and output, *195*
Access controls, *218*
Access controls for computer facilities, *194*
Accident, *5, 9*
  industrial, *186*
Accident causation and control, theories of, *9*
Accident control points, *15*
Accident factors, *10*
Accident investigation, *258, 264*
Accidental losses, forecasting, *35*
Accounting controls, *218*
Administrative barriers to rehabilitation, *347*
Aftershocks, *145*
Alarm systems, *102, 207*
  approved, *213*
  deficiencies of, *214*
  selection of, *213*
Alarms, auxiliary, *101*
  central station, *101, 213*
  local, *101, 207*
  proprietary, *101*
  remote, *101*
Ambient temperature, *305*
Analyzing options, in risk control decisions, *161*

Analyzing sequential risk control decisions, *158*
And gate, *178*
Annual after-tax net cash flow, *57*
Anthropometry, *305*
Apparent accident/injury trends, *276*
Applicant screening, *181*
Applications of risk control techniques, *22*
Applying the risk management process to work-related injuries and illnesses, *231*
Approved alarm systems, *213*
Area access within buildings, *195*
Arithmetic mean, median, and mode, *43*
Arrangement of controls, *318*
Arson, *204*
Auditory displays, *318*
Automatic fire detection/suppression system, *95*
Auxiliary alarms, *101*
Avalanche, *150*

B

Back injury, *351*
"Back schools," *294*
Barriers to rehabilitation, disability-specific, *350*
  general, *347*

Beginning height of lift, *292*
Benefits of sound workplace design, *273*
Biomechanics, *273*
Blasting, *146*
Body posture, *200*
Box action design, *145*
Brown lung disease, *254*
Building construction, *78, 89*
Building construction and design, *78*
Building/facility access, *194*
Buildings, area access within, *195*
  exposed, *90*
  exposing, *89*
  types of, firesafety and, *71*
Burglary, *201*
Business influences, on rehabilitation management, *335*
Byssinosis, *254*

C

Calculations, probability, *47*
Carbon dioxide systems, *98*
Carpal tunnel syndrome, *277, 350*
Case management strategy, for rehabilitation, *345*
Cash flow analysis, summary of, *66*
Cash inflows from rehabilitation, *354*
Cash outflows for rehabilitation, *354*
Causes of fatigue, *323*
Central station alarms, *101, 213*
Central tendency, *43*
Ceteris paribus, *36*
Change in a predictable way pattern, *41*
Characteristics of the load, *291*
Characteristics of persons, for firesafety considerations, *71*
Characteristics of probability distributions, *42*
Chemical exposures, long-term, *236, 240*

sudden, *236*
Claims department, role in rehabilitation, *343*
Classification of ignition sources, *92*
Classification of security exposures, *166*
Clinical fatigue, *324*
Coding of controls, *319*
Cold snaps, *137*
Cold weather, *136*
Collapse, *154*
Computation of statistics, *265*
Computer center-related exposures, *184*
Computer facilities, access controls for, *194*
Computer operations, firesafety and, *115*
Computer and other office workstations, *309*
Computer security, *184*
Computer software and output, access to *195*
Computer time, theft of, *193*
Concept of present value of expected annual after-tax net cash flow, *55*
Conditions leading to embezzlement and fraud, *198*
Consequential costs, *173*
Constructing decision trees, *159*
Construction, fire resistive, *86*
  frame, *78*
  joisted masonry, *82*
  masonry noncombustible, *85*
  mill, *82*
  mixed, *86*
  modified fire resistive, *85*
  noncombustible, *85*
  ordinary, *82*
Contractual (noninsurance) transfers for risk control, *221*
  application of, *28*
  definition of, *27*
  in work-related injuries and illnesses, *250*
Control design principles, *319*

Control of fuel and ignition sources, *91*

Control strategies, in manual materials handling, *292*

Controlling cumulative trauma disorders, *297*

Controlling the employee dishonesty exposure, *217*

Controlling exposures (fire), *90*

Controlling fire losses, *69*

Controlling losses from natural perils, *121*

Controls, access, *218*
   accounting, *218*
   arrangement of, *318*
   coding of, *319*
   for fatigue, *325*
   hazards of poorly designed, *320*
   lack of, *199*
   machine, *318*
   medical, *258*
   two-handed, *253*

Coordination of emergency response, *157*

Corrosion, high humidity and, *140*

Cost of risk, *9*

Costs, types of, *173*

Costs and criticality of security losses, *172*

Covert removal of tapes, *193*

Criticality, *166*, *174*

Criticality of security losses, costs and, *172*

Cross-training of employees, *250*

Cumulative trauma disorders (CTDs), *276*
   controlling, *297*
   exposure factors and controls in, *298*
   nature and scope of, *297*

Cutting and shearing mechanisms, *232*

D

Data, theft of through surreptitious listening gear or covert removal of tapes, *191*

Data-related exposures, *189*

Decision trees, constructing, *159*

Defective output, unacceptably high, *278*

Deficiencies of alarm systems, *214*

Definition and importance of risk control, *6*

Definition of rehabilitation management, *332*

Definition of risk control, *6*

Degraded performance, *323*

Deluge system, *97*

Design considerations and principles, *306*

Design and location of machine displays and controls, *314*

Design principles, control *319*

Design of the workplace, *305*

Detection devices, *99*

Detection of losses, *183*

Detection and signaling systems, *99*

Developing risk control alternatives, for work-related injuries and illnesses, *246*

Development of rehabilitation management, *334*

Diagnosis, clear, lack of, *349*

Differential net cash flows, *62*

Direct costs, *265*

Disability-specific barriers to rehabilitation, *350*

Discharge planning, lack of, *349*

Discounted, *57*

Dispersion (variability), *43*, *44*

Displays, auditory, *318*
   machine, *316*
   visual, *316*

Domino, *10*

Domino theory, *5*, *10*

Drought and heat wave, *139*

Dry chemical systems, *97*

Dry system, *96*

Dry-pipe system, *96*
Duplication of exposure units, *25*
  opportunities for, *27*
Duplication of exposures, in work-related injuries and illnesses, *249*
Dust bowl, *139*, *151*
Duties, separation of, *220*

E

Earthquake, *142*
Economic perils, *121*
Education, in security program, *179*
Education and training, in worksafety, *256*
Electrical exposures, *237*
Embezzlement, *189*
Embezzlement and fraud, conditions leading to, *198*
  prevention of, *197*
Emergency planning/crisis management, *182*
Emergency response, coordination of, *157*
Emergency response plan (ERP), *155*
  major areas addressed by, *156*
  for natural perils, *155*
  procedure for establishing, *157*
  reasons for developing, *156*
Employee benefit programs, *220*
Employee complaints about or changes in the workplace, *278*
Employee dishonesty exposure, controlling the, *217*
Employees with reduced capabilities, *279*
Encoding, *192*
Encouraging employee participation in the program, *327*
Energy-release theory, *5*, *13*
  the fire triangle and, *91*
Engineering, human factors, *273*
Engineering effectiveness, *260*

Environmental factors, manual materials handling and, *290*
Epicenter, *143*
Ergonomic applications, *280*
Ergonomic exposures, *242*
Ergonomics, *242*, *272*
"Ergonomics Guidelines for Workplace Design," *309*
Erosion, *151*
ERP (emergency response plan), *155*
Espionage, *193*
Essentials of a security program, *179*
Establishing a workplace design program, *325*
Evaluating exposures (fire), *89*
Evaluating injury and health hazards, *243*
Evaluating investment alternatives, *55*
Evaluation of net cash flows, *62*
Exertions, force of, *299*
Expected net cash flows, *56*
Explosion-proof, *238*
Exposed buildings, *90*
Exposing buildings, *89*
Exposure avoidance, *204*
  definition and applications of, *22*
  for work-related injuries and illnesses, *248*
Exposure factors, in manual materials handling, *280*
Exposure factors and controls, in cumulative trauma disorders, *298*
Exposure identification and analysis, *231*
Exposure identification through job safety analysis (JSA), *245*
Exposure to temperature extremes, *238*
Exposure units, duplication of, *25*
  segregation of, *25*
  separation of, *25*
Exposures, computer center-related, *184*
  controlling (fire), *90*

data-related, *189*
duplication of, *249*
electrical, *237*
ergonomic, *242*
exterior, *89*
facilities and equipment
    (computer center), *185*
fire, *238*
noise, *241*
radiation, *242*
separation of, *249*
Extended hospitalization, *348*
Extensive medication, *349*
Exterior exposures, *89*
External fire protection, *106*

F

Facilities and equipment exposures
    (computer center), *185*
Factors affecting human health
    potential, *228*
Fainting, *303*
Fatigue, *323*
Fault tree analysis, *176*
Faults, *176*
Fender walls, *88*
Financial effects of rehabilitation,
    illustrative evaluation of, *355*
Financial evaluation of
    rehabilitation programs, *353*
Fire, *185*
    hostile, *69*
Fire brigades, *105*
Fire department, *106*
Fire divisions, *78, 87*
Fire doors, *87*
Fire exposures, *238*
Fire extinguishers, *101*
Fire legal liability, *69*
Fire losses, controlling, *69*
Fire protection, external, *106*
    internal, *95*
    private, *93*
    public, *93*
Fire resistive construction, *86*

Fire resistive safes, *206*
Fire triangle, *24*
    energy-release theory and, *91*
Fire-resistance rating, *87*
Firesafety, principles of, *73*
Firesafety and life safety, *70*
Firesafety for typical occupancies,
    108
Fire-stop device, *78*
Firewall, *87*
Fixed guards, *253*
Flammable liquids, handling, *113*
Flash floods, *132*
Flood, *131*
Food preparation activity, *114*
Force of exertions, *299*
Forecasting, need for, *35*
Forecasting accidental losses, *35*
Forecasting techniques, *40*
Forming and bending mechanisms,
    233
Frame action design, *145*
Frame construction, *78*
Framework for risk control, *5*
Fraud, embezzlement, and sabotage,
    189
Frequency of lift, *291*
Frequency of repetition, *298*
Fuel, *238*
Fuel and ignition sources, control
    of, *91*
Fusible link, *88*

G

General barriers to rehabilitation,
    347
General methods of control
    approach, *12*
General methods of control from
    safety engineering
    professionals, in work-related
    injuries and illnesses, *251*
General methods of industrial
    hygiene control, *6*
General windstorm, *124*

Geological perils, risk control for, *141*
Glowing cloud, *154*
Gooseflesh, *304*
Grip, pistol, *301*
Grips, types of, *291*
Ground floor area and building height, *89*
Guard, point of operation, *253*
Guard services, *105*
Guarding, *233*, *253*
Guards, fixed, *253*

H

Haddon, Jr., Dr. William, *13*
Hailstorm, *127*
Halon systems, *98*
Hand holds, *291*
Handling flammable liquids, *113*
Hazard recognition, *243*
Hazards, health, *240*
  injury, *232*
Hazards of poorly designed controls, *320*
Health, *227*
Health hazards, *240*
Heat load, *303*
Heat syncope, *303*
Heat wave, drought and, *139*
Heatstroke, *303*
Heinrich, H.W., *10*
High absenteeism, turnover, *277*
High humidity and corrosion, *140*
High temperatures, *303*
Highly protected risk (HPR), status as a, *105*
Hook grip, *291*
Horizontal distance of lift, *292*
Hospitalization, extended, *348*
Hostile fire, *69*
Housekeeping, *255*
HPR (highly protected risk), *105*
Human factors engineering, *273*
Human health potential, *226*
  factors affecting, *228*

risk management responsibilities related to, *230*
Humidity, high, and corrosion, *140*
Hurricane/typhoon, *128*

I

Ice storm, *135*
Ignition source, *239*
Ignition sources, classification of, *92*
Illness, *231*
Illustrative evaluation of financial effects of rehabilitation, *355*
Impact mechanisms, *233*
Implementing the chosen risk control techniques, for work-related injuries and illnesses, *261*
Importance of fatigue, *323*
Importance of risk control, *8*
Incentive pay programs, *278*
Income, taxable, *62*
Indicators of potentially unsound workplace design, *275*
Indirect costs, *265*
Industrial accident, *186*
Ingestion, *240*
Inhalation, *240*
Initial disposition, *346*
Initial reaction to injury/disability, *345*
Initiating training programs, *326*
Injury, *231*
Injury/disability, initial reaction to, *345*
Injury hazards, *232*
Injury and health hazards, evaluating, *243*
Injury and illness statistics, *265*
Inland flooding, *132*
In-rack sprinklers, *110*
In-running nip points, *232*
Inspections and spot checks, *184*
Insurance influences, on rehabilitation management, *335*

Integrated security risk control program, *204*

Internal and external fire protection, *93*

Interpretation of statistics, *267*

Investment alternatives, evaluating, *55*

Ionizing radiation, *242*

Isolation, *252*

J

Job design, *294*

Job placement, *294*

Job rotation, *259*

Job safety analysis (JSA), exposure identification through, *245*

Joisted masonry construction, *82*

K

Keys to redesigning manual materials handling tasks, *296*

L

Labor unions, role of in rehabilitation, *345*

Lack of clear diagnosis, *349*

Lack of clear prognosis, *349*

Lack of controls, *199*

Lack of discharge planning, *349*

Lack of specific date for return to work, *349*

Land subsidence, *146*

Landslide/mudslide, *149*

Legal department, role of in rehabilitation, *344*

Life safety, firesafety and, *71*
  fundamental considerations in, *71*

Life Safety Code, *73*

Lift, beginning height of, *292*
  frequency of, *291*

horizontal distance of, *292*
  vertical distance of, *292*

Lifting rules, *294*

Linear regression, *52*

Load, characteristics of, *291*
  stability of, *291*
  weight of, *291*

Local alarms, *101*, *207*

Locked-out, *233*

Long-term chemical exposure, *236*, *240*

Loss control (prevention and reduction), *205*

Loss prevention, applications of, *24*
  definition of, *23*
  in employee dishonesty exposures, *217*
  for work-related injuries and illnesses, *248*

Loss prevention measures, emergency response plans and, *156*

Loss reduction, *22*
  definition and applications of, *24*
  in employee dishonesty exposures, *217*
  for work-related injuries and illnesses, *249*

Loss reduction measures, emergency response plans and, *156*

Lost workday case rate, *265*

Lost workday rate, *265*

Low back pain, *277*

Low temperatures, *304*

M

Machine controls, *318*

Machine displays, *316*

Machine displays and controls, design and location of, *314*

Machinery and equipment hazards, *232*

Magma, *153*

Maintaining security, *165*

Maintenance, *254*
Major areas addressed by an
    emergency response plan, *156*
Make-up air, *253*
Management, rehabilitation, *331,
    333*
Management commitment,
    obtaining, *326*
Managerial naivete, *198*
Manual materials handling, *278, 280*
    control strategies in, *292*
    environmental factors in, *290*
    personal factors in, *289*
Manual materials handling tasks,
    keys to redesigning, *296*
Masonry noncombustible
    construction, *85*
Material safety data sheets (MSDS),
    244
Materials handling, *234*
Materials substitution, *251*
Matrix technique for recognizing
    exposures, *169*
Mean, *43*
Mechanical/electrical incompatibility
    or malfunction, *187*
Mechanical stress, *297, 301*
Median, *43*
Medical controls, *258*
Medical influences, on rehabilitation
    management, *334*
Medical personnel in the
    organization, role of in
    rehabilitation, *344*
Medical treatment, uncoordinated,
    348
Medication, extensive, *349*
Meteorological perils, risk control
    for, *124*
Mill construction, *82*
Mining, *147*
Mixed construction, *86*
Mode, *43*
Modified fire resistive construction,
    85
Modified Mercalli Intensity Scale,
    142
Money safes, *206*

Monitoring the effectiveness of risk
    controls, for work-related
    injuries and illnesses, *263*
MSDS (material safety data sheets),
    244

N

Natural disasters, *187*
Natural perils, controlling losses
    from, *121*
    emergency response plan for, *155*
Nature and scope of cumulative
    trauma disorders, *297*
Nature of security exposures, *166*
Near-miss, *264*
Negligence, *198*
Net cash flows, evaluation of, *62*
    tax considerations and, *65*
Net present value method, *64*
New process or equipment, *275*
No change pattern, *41*
Noise exposures, *241*
Noncombustible construction, *85*
Nongoal-oriented physical therapy,
    349
Normal distribution—a special case,
    45
Nursing care, round-the-clock, *349*

O

Obtaining management commitment,
    326
Occupancies, firesafety for typical,
    108
Occupancy, *89*
Opportunities for rehabilitation
    management, *335*
Opportunity costs, *173*
Or gate, *176*
Ordinary construction, *82*
Oxidation, *92*

P

Pallet construction, *108*
Palletized storage, *108*
Parapet, *87*
Payments, stream of, *354*
Payoff, *159*
Percentile, *306*
Performance, degraded, *323*
Permanent replacement costs, *173*
Permissible exposure levels, *241*
Personal factors, in manual
    materials handling, *289*
Personal protective equipment, *255*
Personnel, protecting the health
    potential of, *225*
    transfer of, *182*
Personnel department, role in
    rehabilitation, *342*
Personnel screening, *218*
Physical condition of premises, *235*
Physical controls, for work-related
    injuries and illnesses, *251*
Physical protection, *205*
Physical rehabilitation, *333*
Physical security controls, *181*
Physical therapy, nongoal-oriented,
    349
Physician, referral to, *347*
Piece rate, *278*
Pinch grip, *291*
Pistol grip, *301*
Planning the initial response, in
    rehabilitation case management,
    345
Point of operation guard, *253*
Post-emergency recovery actions,
    157
Post-loss measures, *24*
Posture, body, *300*
Power grip, *291*
Preaction system, *97*
Precision grip, *291*
Pre-loss measures, *24*
Present payment, *57*
Present value of expected annual
    after-tax net cash flows, *55*

Present value of net cash flows, *56*
Present value table, *57*
Prevention, in security program,
    181
Prevention of embezzlement and
    fraud, *197*
Prevention of violent crime, *199*
Principles of firesafety, *73*
Private fire protection, *93*
Probabilities of security losses, *169*
Probability analysis, *41*
    summary of, *51*
Probability calculations, *47*
Probability distributions,
    characteristics of, *42*
Procedural controls, for work-
    related injuries and illnesses,
    256
Procedure for establishing an
    emergency response plan, *157*
Process changes, *251*
Profit, *36*
Prognosis, lack of clear, *349*
Property protection procedures, *217*
Proprietary alarms, *101*
Protecting the health potential of
    personnel, *225*
Protection, physical, *205*
    property, *217*
Protective equipment, personal, *255*
Psychological rehabilitation, *333*
Public fire protection, *93*
Pure risks, *39*

Q

Quantitative techniques for risk
    control, review of, *35*

R

Rack storage, *110*
Radiation, ionizing, *242*
    nonionizing, *243*
Radiation exposures, *242*

Rate of return (selection criteria), *260*

Reasons for developing an emergency response plan, *156*

Recognition of security exposures, *168*

Record safes, *206*

Recordable case rate, *265*

Reducing fatigue, *323*

Referral to a physician, *347*

Regression analysis *41, 51*

Rehabilitation, *332*
  administrative barriers to, *347*
  cash inflows from, *354*
  cash outflows for, *354*
  disability-specific barriers to, *350*
  general barriers to, *347*
  physical, *333*
  psychological, *333*
  risk management's responsibility in, *340*
  vocational, *333*

Rehabilitation case management strategy, *345*

Rehabilitation management, *331, 333*
  business influences on, *335*
  definition of, *332*
  development of, *334*
  financial evaluation of, *353*
  insurance influences on, *335*
  medical influences on, *334*
  opportunities for, *335*

Rehabilitation training, *333*

Remote alarms, *101*

Repetition, frequency of, *298*

Return to work, lack of specific date for, *349*

Review of some quantitative techniques for risk control, *35*

Reynaud's phenomenon, *302*

Richter Scale, *142*

Ring of Fire, *153*

Riot, *202*

Risk, cost of, *9*

Risk control, contractual transfer for, *27, 221*
  definition of, *6*

framework for, *5*
  for geological perils, *141*
  importance of, *8*
  for meteorological perils, *124*
  review of some quantitative techniques for, *35*
  security, *178*

Risk control decisions, analyzing options in, *161*
  analyzing sequential, *158*

Risk control techniques, applications of, *22*
  from risk management, *248*

Risk management responsibilities related to human health potential, *230*

Risk management's responsibility in rehabilitation, *340*

Risks, pure, *39*
  speculative, *39*

Robbery, *199*

Rotating mechanisms, *233*

Round-the-clock nursing care, *349*

S

Sabotage, *185*

Safety cans, *112*

Safes, fire resistive, *206*
  money, *206*
  record, *206*

Screening, personnel, *218*

Screw or worm mechanisms, *233*

Security, *165*
  computer, *184*
  maintaining, *165*

Security controls, physical, *181*

Security exposures, classification of, *166*
  matrix technique for recognizing, *169*
  nature of, *166*
  recognition of, *168*
  system approach to recognizing and analyzing, *175*

Security losses, costs and criticality of, *172*
  detection of, *183*
  probabilities of, *169*
Security patrols, watchman or, *216*
Security program, essentials of, *179*
Security risk control, *178*
Security risk control program, integrated, *204*
Security system, testing the, *184*
Segregation of exposure units, *25*
  applications of, *27*
  for work-related injuries and illnesses, *249*
Seismic risk map, *143*
Selecting the best risk management alternatives, for work-related injuries and illnesses, *260*
Selection of alarm systems, *213*
Separation of duties, *220*
Separation of exposure units, *25*
  opportunities for, *27*
Separation of exposures, work-related injuries and illnesses, *249*
Series of unequal future payments, *57*
Severely cold weather, *136*
SIC (Standard Industrial Classification) code, *268*
Signaling systems, *101*
  detection and, *99*
Simultaneous transmission, *192*
Single future payment, *57*
Sinkholes, *148*
Sitting versus standing work, *308*
60-cycle hum, *303*
Slow-burning floor or roof, *85*
Snowstorm, *134*
Soil expansion, *152*
SOPs (standard operating procedures), *256*
Speculative risks, *39*
Spray painting activity, *111*
Sprinkler protection, *90*
Sprinklers, in-rack, *110*
Stability of load, *291*
Staffing, *230*

Standard deviation, *44*
Standard Industrial Classification (SIC) code, *268*
Standard operating procedures (SOPs), *257*
Standing work, sitting versus, *308*
Standpipe systems, *103*
State of nature, *159*
Static electricity, *238*
Statistics, computation of, *265*
  injury and illness, *265*
  interpretation of, *267*
Storage, *108*
  palletized, *108*
  rack, *110*
Stream of payments, *354*
Stress, mechanical, *297, 301*
Strike, *202*
Sudden chemical exposures, *236*
Supervised system, *216*
Supervision, *257*
Supervisory signals, *101*
Surreptitious listening gear, *191*
Surveillance cameras, *217*
System approach to recognizing and analyzing security exposures, *175*
System safety approach, *6, 19*

T

Tax considerations and net cash flows, *65*
Taxable income, *62*
Technique of Operations Review (TOR) system, *6, 16*
Temperature extremes, exposure to, *238*
Temperatures, high, *303*
  low, *304*
Temporary replacement costs, *173*
Tennis elbow, *277*
Testing the (security) system, *184*
Theft of computer time, *193*

Theft of data through surreptitious listening gear or covert removal of tapes, *191*

Theories of accident causation and control, *9*

Threshold limit values (TLVs), *241*

Threshold shift, *242*

Thunderstorm, *125*

Tidal wave, *132*

Time value of money, *56*

Time-adjusted rate of return method, *65*

Time-sharing arrangements that result in unauthorized but overt access to data, *190*

TLVs (threshold limit values), *241*

TOR (Technique of Operations Review), *6, 16*

Tornado, *130*

Training, education and, in worksafety, *256*
rehabilitation, *333*

Training and education, in manual materials handling, *294*

Training programs, initiating, for workplace design, *326*

Transfer of personnel, *182*

Trend analysis, *41, 51*

Trigger-finger syndrome, *277*

Tsunami, *132*

Turnover, high absenteeism, *277*

Two-handed controls, *253*

U

Unacceptably high defective output, *278*

Uncoordinated medical treatment, *348*

Unequal future payments, *57*

V

Vandalism, *203*

Vehicle fleet operations, *239*

Ventilation, *253*

Vertical distance of lift, *292*

Vibrating white fingers, *277*

Vibration, *302*

Violent crime, prevention of, *199*

Violent winds, *124*

Visual displays, *316*

Vocational rehabilitation, *333*

Volcanic action, *153*

W

Wall openings, *90*

Watchman or security patrols, *216*

Water spray system, *97*

Water systems, *95*

Weaver, D.A., *18*

Weight of load, *291*

Wet method, *252*

Wet system, *96*

Wet-pipe system, *96*

Windchill index, *137*

Windstorm, general, *124*

Winter weather, *133*

Workplace, design of the, *305*
employee complaints about or changes in, *278*

Workplace design, *271*
benefits of, in living spaces, *275*
in occupational settings, *274*
in product design, *274*
definition and significance, *272*
sound, benefits of, *273*
unsound, indicators of, *275*

Workplace design checklists, *279*

Workplace design program, encouraging employee participation in the, *327*
establishing, *325*

Work-related injuries and illnesses, applying the risk management process to, *231*
contractual transfer for risk control and, *250*
developing risk control alternatives for, *246*

exposure avoidance in, *248*
implementing the chosen risk
    control techniques, *261*
loss prevention for, *248*
monitoring the effectiveness of
    risk controls, *263*
physical controls for, *251*

procedural controls for, *256*
segregation of exposure units in,
    249
selecting the best risk
    management alternative, *260*
Workstations, computer and other
    office, *309*